REVEL enables students to read and interact with course material on the devices they use, **anywhere** and **anytime**. Responsive design allows students to access REVEL on their tablet devices, with content displayed clearly in both portrait and landscape view.

Highlighting, **note taking**, and a **glossary** personalize the learning experience. Educators can add **notes** for students, too, including reminders or study tips

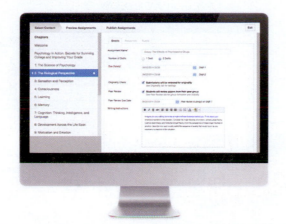

REVEL's variety of **writing** activities and assignments develop and assess concept **mastery** and **critical thinking**.

Superior assignability and tracking

REVEL's assignability and tracking tools help educators make sure students are completing their reading and understanding core concepts.

REVEL allows educators to indicate precisely which readings must be completed on which dates. This clear, detailed schedule helps students stay on task and keeps them motivated throughout the course.

REVEL lets educators monitor and individual student ach information that helps educa in meaningful ways, such as time on task.

Predominant forms of religions in the world today

Legend:
- Indigenous religions
- Hinduism and Islam
- Buddhism
- China: Remnants of Confucianism, Buddhism, Daoism
- Japan: Shinto, Buddhism, Sects
- Christianity (Roman Catholicism, Protestantism, Eastern Orthodox)
- Islam
- Judaism
- Sikhism
- Varied religions
- Parsism (Zoroastrianism)

RUSSIAN FEDERATION

ESTONIA
LATVIA
LITHUANIA
BELARUS

UKRAINE
MOLDOVA

GEORGIA

ARMENIA
AZER.

TURKEY

SYRIA
LEB.
ISRAEL
IRAQ
JORDAN
KUWAIT

EGYPT

SAUDI
ARABIA

ERITREA

OMAN

YEMEN

SUDAN

ETHIOPIA

SOMALIA

KENYA

TANZANIA

MBIA
MALAWI
ZIMBABWE
BANA

MOZAMBIQUE
SWAZILAND

LESOTHO

SOUTH
FRICA

KAZAKHSTAN

UZBEKISTAN

TURKMENISTAN

KYRGYZSTAN

TAJIKISTAN

AFGHANISTAN

IRAN

PAKISTAN

NEPAL

BANGLADESH

INDIA

SRI LANKA

MADAGASCAR

MONGOLIA

CHINA

NORTH
KOREA

SOUTH
KOREA

JAPAN

TAIWAN

MYANMAR
(BURMA)

THAILAND

LAOS

VIETNAM

CAMBODIA

MALAYSIA

PHILIPPINES

INDONESIA

PAPUA
NEW
GUINEA

NORTH PACIFIC OCEAN

SOUTH PACIFIC OCEAN

INDIAN OCEAN

AUSTRALIA

NEW ZEALAND

Religions of the World

Thirteenth Edition

Lewis M. Hopfe

Revised by

Mark R. Woodward
Department of Religious Studies
Arizona State University

and

Brett Hendrickson
Department of Religious Studies
Lafayette College

PEARSON

Boston   Columbus   Indianapolis   New York   San Francisco   Amsterdam
Cape Town   Dubai   London   Madrid   Milan   Munich   Paris   Montreal   Toronto
Delhi   Mexico City   São Paulo   Sydney   Hong Kong   Seoul   Singapore   Taipei   Tokyo

Editor-in-Chief: Sarah Touborg
Sponsoring Editor: Helen Ronan
Editorial Assistant: Victoria Engros
VP, Product Marketing: Maggie Moylan
Director of Field Marketing: Jonathan Cottrell
Project Management Team Lead: Melissa Feimer
Production Project Manager: Joe Scordato
Program Manager: Barbara Marttine Cappuccio
Senior Operations Supervisor: Mary Fischer
Senior Operations Specialist: Mary Ann Gloriande
Cover Designer: Kathryn Foot
Cover Photo: Thinley Namgyel
Senior Digital Media Director: Amanda Smith
Digital Media Project Manager: Rich Barnes
Full-Service Project Management: S4Carlisle Publishing Services
Composition: S4Carlisle Publishing Services
Printer/Binder: Courier/Kendallville
Cover Printer: Courier/Kendallville

Library of Congress Cataloging-in-Publication Data

Hopfe, Lewis M.,
  Religions of the world / Lewis M Hopfe, Mark R Woodward, Department of Religious Studies Arizona
State University, Brett Hendrickson, Department of Religious Studies, Lafayette College.—Edition 13.
    pages cm
  Includes bibliographical references and index.
  ISBN 978-0-13-379382-6 (alk. paper)—ISBN 0-13-379382-6 (alk. paper) 1. Religions—Textbooks.
I. Woodward, Mark R., II. Title.
  BL80.3.H66 2014
  200—dc23

                                                                                            2014035172

10 9 8 7 6 5 4 3 2 1

ISBN-10:   0-13-379400-8
ISBN-13: 978-013-379400-7

Brief Contents

Contents

Preface

A few years ago, I was teaching an introductory class on world religions to a group of students that included several young veterans from war zones in Iraq and Afghanistan. On one occasion, one of these students stayed to talk to me after a class session on Islam. He explained that he had recently completed a long tour in Afghanistan, and he lamented that he had not had the opportunity to take the class before his time abroad. "We would have understood the people there so much better if we had known this stuff," he said.

Thankfully, not all education about the religions of the world is a matter of war and peace. However, this brief example helps illuminate why it is essential that we learn about other people in our world. The histories, deep-seated beliefs, ritual practices, and ethical systems that make up the world's religions are some of the most important forces at play today on our incredibly diverse planet. A careful study of world religions, therefore, is both a key to responsible global citizenship and an excellent exercise in helping one understand one's own assumptions, beliefs, and moral codes.

In addition to these weighty concerns, learning about people and their religions is fascinating and enjoyable. Many students come to an introductory course on world religions with little or no exposure to most of the religions covered in this textbook. When they learn how exciting, complex, and even beautiful the world's religions can be, they return over and over to the study of religions, in their college careers and throughout their lives. This book invites you to what I hope will be a lifelong engagement with the religions of the world.

New to This Edition:

- The revised first section of the book has been refocused on living religions in the Americas and Africa.

- "Religion and Public Life" boxes throughout the text invite reflection on religion's role in contemporary political and social issues.

- The revised account of the origins of Hinduism in Chapter 4 reflects more recent scholarship.

- Expanded "key terms" lists are included at the beginning of all chapters.

- Chapter 13 on Baha'i, previously available online only, is now included in the main text.

- The reconceived and expanded learning architecture throughout the text coordinates the main headings in the running text with both the Learning Objectives listed at the beginning of each chapter and the Think About It questions listed at the end of each chapter.

- One of the most exciting developments that took place during this revision was the development and design of REVEL, a new digital format that makes *Religions of the World* excitingly interactive. We believe that REVEL presents the same material found in the printed version in a dynamic design that actually functions more like a classroom than a textbook. We are sure that this will make the study of religion more engaging to the current generation of college students.

REVEL™

Educational technology designed for the way today's students read, think, and learn

When students are engaged deeply, they learn more effectively and perform better in their courses. This simple fact inspired the creation of REVEL: an immersive learning experience designed for the way today's students read, think, and learn. Built in collaboration with educators and students nationwide, REVEL is the newest, fully digital way to deliver respected Pearson content.

REVEL enlivens course content with media interactives and assessments—integrated directly within the authors' narrative—that provide opportunities for students to read about and practice course material in tandem. This immersive educational technology boosts student engagement, which leads to better understanding of concepts and improved performance throughout the course.

Learn more about REVEL
www.pearsonhighered.com/REVEL

Additional Resources

Build Your Own Pearson Custom Course Material: For enrollments of at least 25, the Pearson Custom Library allows you to create your own textbook by

- combining chapters from best-selling Pearson textbooks in the sequence you want

- adding your own content, such as your syllabus or a study guide you've created

A Pearson Custom Library book is priced according to the number of chapters and may even save your students money. *To begin building your custom text, visit* **www.pearsoncustomlibrary.com** *or contact your Pearson representative.*

Instructor's Manual (0134027469): For each chapter in the text, this valuable resource provides a detailed outline, list of objectives, discussion questions, and suggested readings and videos. This manual is available at www.pearsonhighered.com.

Test Item File (0134027485): Test questions in multiple-choice and essay formats are available for each chapter. This manual is available at www.pearsonhighered.com.

MyTest (013379492X): This computerized software allows instructors to create their own personalized exams, edit any or all of the existing test questions, and add new questions.

PowerPoint Presentation Slides (0134027477): These PowerPoint slides summarize the content for each chapter to help instructors convey religious concepts and principles in a clear and engaging way. The slides are available at www.pearsonhighered.com.

Acknowledgments

I am grateful to the many, many people that make a textbook become a reality, especially the editors and staff people at Pearson. I would also like to thank Rabbi Dan Stein of B'nai Abraham Synagogue in Easton, Pennsylvania, and Professor Jeff Halverson of Coastal Carolina University in Conway, South Carolina, for their valuable advice. My gratitude goes to the reviewers who contributed comments that helped shape this edition of *Religions of the World*:

Charles Comer, *Harrisburg Area Community College*
James Doan, *Nova Southeastern University*
Jonathan Gainor, *Harrisburg Area Community College*
Olive Hemmings, *Washington Adventist University*
Lisa Kemmerer, *Montana State University*
Tony Roberts, *Tarrant County College–Northwest*
Jerome Soneson, *University of Northern Iowa*

Brett Hendrickson
Lafayette College
Easton, Pennsylvania

About the Authors

Lewis Moore Hopfe

Lewis Moore Hopfe (1935-1992) graduated from Baylor University in 1956 with a B.A. in history and religious studies, an M. Div. degree from Southwestern Baptist Theological Seminary in 1960, and his Ph.D. in Old Testament studies from Boston University in 1965.

Dr. Hopfe began his teaching career in 1965 as an instructor in religious studies at Kendall College, Evanston, Illinois. During his early years of teaching it became apparent that there was a need for an introductory textbook for the study of world religions. He said, "Religion is never a simple subject, and can become complex and intricate to the complete dismay of the beginning student." His goal was to provide the student with a reasonably brief and readable text that did not shortcut or simplify religions, but did not delve too deeply into the technicalities. Responding to this need the first edition of *Religions of the World became* a reality and was published in 1979.

Dr. Hopfe was "an author, teacher, pastor, archaeologist, college dean, weight lifter, and spiritual guide to students, colleagues, and parishioners" whose lives he touched via the written and spoken word. *Religions of the World* is his legacy to academia.

Mark R. Woodward

Mark R. Woodward is Associate Professor of Religious Studies at Arizona State University and Visiting Professor of Comparative Religions at the Center for Religious and Cross-cultural Studies at Gadjah Mada University in Indonesia. He received his Ph.D. in Cultural Anthropology from the University of Illinois and also studied at the Divinity School at the University of Chicago.

His research has focused on Islam, Buddhism, Christianity, and indigenous religions in Southeast Asia, especially Indonesia, Burma, and Singapore. For most of the past decade his research has centered on issues of religion, conflict, and violence in Southeast Asia and globally. He is the author, co-author, or editor of five books and many scholarly articles. He has taught the introductory level university course World Religions more than fifty times in the last twenty-five years.

Brett Hendrickson

Brett Hendrickson is an Assistant Professor of Religious Studies at Lafayette College in Easton, Pennsylvania, where he teaches courses on the religious history of the Americas, religion and healing, religion and public life, and the introductory course on world religions. He received his Ph.D. in Religious Studies from Arizona State University, a Master of Divinity (M.Div.) from Austin Presbyterian Theological Seminary, and an A.B. in Latin American Studies from Columbia University.

Hendrickson's research examines lived religious practices in Latin America and among Latinos and Latinas in the United States, with a special interest in religious and folk healing. His work attempts to explain religious interactions and exchanges among various ethnic and cultural groups in complex political and social contexts. He is the author of *Border Medicine: A Transcultural History of Mexican American Curanderismo* and several scholarly articles.

Religions
of the World

Introduction and Overview

*S*tudying religion is deeply rewarding. Religions have been and continue to be some of the most important aspects of people's lives all over the planet. As we will see over the course of this book, world history has been profoundly influenced by religious leaders, religious ideas about society, and religious ethical codes. The way people have thought about nature, the human person, the cosmos, and questions of ultimate meaning and concern are intrinsic parts of religion. In modern times, religion continues to affect individuals, families, and whole societies, and it has entered into new and exciting conversations with science. The academic study of religion has many tools at its disposal and draws on insights from philosophy, psychology, history, comparative literature, anthropology, sociology, and other disciplines. Students of religion can expect to hone their critical thinking skills as well as their cross-cultural understanding.[1]

Perhaps the greatest contribution that knowledge of world religions can make to a citizen of the twenty-first century is in the area of world politics. Religion has always played an important role in political conflict at home and abroad. Religious differences are fundamental to debates concerning civil rights, abortion, and gender relations in the contemporary United States. Catholic Christians fight with Protestant Christians, Hindus conflict with Muslims, Buddhists battle Hindus, Muslims debate with Christians, Jews struggle with Muslims, and secularists do not always see eye to eye with religious people on issues of public policy. Certainly, these conflicts have other dimensions, but the religious differences are imposing. If we are to fully understand these conflicts, we must know that Muslims, Christians, Jews, Hindus, and Buddhists have basic philosophical differences and that religion can be a source of conflict as well as of understanding. Given the severity of these conflicts, it is essential that government and private-sector leaders and the general public be aware of the ways in which religion can exacerbate and ameliorate regional and global conflict.

The twenty-first century pushes us out of our insulated worlds into closer and closer contact with what were formerly considered exotic and distant religions. Television brings instant coverage of events in formerly remote parts of the Earth. Industrialization brings us together in urban centers. The most rapidly growing religion in Europe and North America is Islam, due to the influx of Turks, Arabs, Iranians, and Pakistanis, as well as internal conversion. The largest concentration of Hindus outside of India is found in Leicester, England. Hollywood figures proclaim their conversion to Buddhism and pop stars to Islam. Dance clubs play music recorded by Sufi devotional singers. One simply cannot be a well-informed citizen of this era without knowledge of the religions of the world.

If there is to be peace among the nations, cultures, and religions of the world, religious differences must be known and respected. In the early 1960s, a young professor (Lewis Hopfe) and his wife gave a dinner party on a Friday evening. The guest list included Jews, Catholics, and Muslims. The entrée was ham! Jews and Muslims are forbidden by their religion to eat pork, and Roman Catholics of that period abstained from all meat on Fridays. Needless to say, it was not a happy party. Whether the choice of food was made due to ignorance or arrogance does not matter. The guests, because of their religions, were offended. That dinner party was a microcosm of what happens all too frequently because of ignorance of the religions of the world. More sensitive and better-informed hosts would have asked if their guests had any "dietary restrictions," or they would have served a religiously "safe" entrée such as trout. Many of us are familiar with the concept of "kosher" foods that can be eaten by conservative religious Jews. Increasingly one encounters "halal," the Muslim equivalent, in the supermarkets and restaurants of American cities. In August 2002, a street food vendor near the American Museum of Natural History in New York posted a sign stating that his food was kosher and halal—one small indication of the growing religious diversity in our world.

Although in North America and Western Europe religion is sometimes imagined to be a private, personal matter, religion almost always has an important influence on public life. Throughout the world, collective social and political identities are defined on the basis of religious criteria. The end of the Cold War and the collapse of Communist states have vastly increased the importance of religion in world affairs. It is now essential for those who seek to understand regional and global politics, economics, and conflict to be thoroughly grounded in the study of religion.

A Definition of Religion

If we assume an interest in religions and a willingness to study them, what constitutes the subject matter of a course in world religions? Humankind has been on Earth for a long time. Our cultures, historic and prehistoric, are too numerous to even begin to detail. Which cultures and religions shall we study? Whole texts have been written solely on prehistoric religions, not to mention the great families of religion, such as those found within Hinduism. Therefore, any text or course on religions must be selective about its subject, and a definition of the subject is necessary.

In Western cultures, we tend to define religion in terms of a set of beliefs having to do with the gods, through which one is taught a moral system. Although this definition contains elements that are found within many of the religions of the world, it cannot do justice to them all. For example, some religions recognize the existence of gods but actually have very little to do with them. Jainism and, to some extent, some forms of Buddhism may be called nontheistic religions because their emphasis is on people's delivering themselves from their plight without the help of gods. Some religions do not emphasize moral systems. Some religions that have existed on Earth have been more concerned with humanity's proper relationship to gods, demons, and spirits, worldly prosperity, and well-being than with ethical relationships among people. One distinctive characteristic of the religion of the early Hebrews was the ethical dimension their God required of them. This emphasis was in turn passed on to Christianity and Islam. Similar concerns can be found in Buddhism, Hinduism, and other religions that have a broad, universal appeal. Modern adherents to these religions associate the word *religion* with the word *moral*, but among many religions, these terms are not synonymous.

The contents of this text have been chosen from the hundreds of world religions because they share many overlapping characteristics: (1) They usually, but not always, deal in some way with people's relationship with spirits, ancestors, gods, and demons; (2) they usually have developed a system of myths about these beings and rituals designed for communing with or propitiating them; (3) they usually have developed a system of organized rituals, temples, priests, and narrative or scriptural traditions at some point in their history; (4) they usually have some understanding of life beyond death, either as survival in some shadowy existence, in some version of heaven and hell, or through rebirth; (5) they usually have developed a code of conduct or moral order; and (6) they generally have attracted large followings, either currently or at some time in the past. The religions included here have also been traditionally important to the discipline of religious studies.[2]

As there are many religions from which we must choose, so there are many methods by which we might organize them. We might present the religions of the world in terms of their effects on the societies that support them; in terms of their forms or styles of worship; in a comparative manner (in which each religion is compared with the others in terms of its outlook toward its God or gods, the nature of humankind, sin, and so on); or in terms of their histories and impact on the histories of the nations in which they were found. This text combines some of these methods and presents the major religions of the world as simply yet as thoroughly as possible. For each religion, five major points are considered: (1) What culture produced this religion? (2) If there was a founder, and if anything can be known of the founder's life, what factors caused this person to found this religion? (3) If there are scriptures or sacred texts, what do they tell us about this religion? (4) What have been the major historical developments of this religion? (5) How do participants practice their religion? What are the religious rituals, behaviors, and events that shape how they live their lives?

Theories of Religions

What is the nature of religion itself? Why are people religious? Scholars have conceptualized these questions in a variety of ways. Some of theories of religion focus on religion's origins. In the nineteenth century, when the social sciences were being developed and anthropologists were first beginning to investigate so-called "primitive" cultures, early anthropologists based their theories on observations. These nineteenth- and early-twentieth-century scholars, enamored of the belief that the biological theories of evolution taught by Charles Darwin could be applied to the social sciences, investigated contemporary "primitive" religions, reread ancient reporters (such as Herodotus), and hypothesized *ad infinitum* about the origin and development of the phenomenon of religion. Over time, these theories divided into two basic and overlapping groups: those that focused on the seemingly unique aspect of human cultures to relate to supernatural beings, deities, or forces and those that focused on how religion functioned in its surrounding society.

Relating to Gods, Deities, and Spirits

One of the first exponents of this type of theory of religion was the English ethnologist Edward Burnett Tylor (1832–1917). Although Tylor held no formal degree, he was a leading figure in anthropology for many years. Near the end of his career, he was named Britain's first professor of anthropology (1896–1909). Tylor's greatest contribution to the study of the origin of religions was his book *Primitive Culture* (2 vols., 1871). In the 1850s, Herbert Spencer had theorized that the gods of "primitive" people were based on dreams about the recent dead. According to Spencer, when "primitive" people dreamed of the dead, they came to believe that the former chiefs and heroes were actually alive in another world or another form. Tylor was aware of Spencer's theory, which was called "Manism," but he did not totally accept it.[3] Tylor maintained that "primitive" people developed a sense of other or soul from experiences with death and dreams. According to Tylor, "primitive" people also believed that these souls were to be found not only in people but in all of nature. There were souls in stones, trees, animals, rivers, springs, volcanoes, and mountains. The entire world, the very air itself, was seen as being alive with spirits of all kinds. These spirits could be helpful or harmful to humans and had personalities that could be offended or flattered. Therefore, it became a part of the life of "primitive" societies to pray to these spirits, offer sacrifices to them, seek to appease them, and avoid offending them.

From this understanding of the world developed the practice of ancestor worship or veneration, in which one attended to the spirits of the dead. An awareness of the existence of spirits in nature led to the worship of various aspects of nature, such as water, trees, stones, and so on. Ultimately, this spirit-infused view of nature produced religions that worshiped sky, earth, and water deities. Finally, monotheistic religions developed, which is to say, religions that recognized only one god. Tylor's theories were widely accepted and regarded as classic for many years. An alternative theory of religion was developed by an Oxford professor, Max Müller (1823–1900). Müller's interests were mythology and the religions of India, but he entered the debate over the nature of religion with Tylor and others. From his studies, he became convinced that human beings first developed their religions from their observations of the forces of nature. According to this theory, "primitive" people became aware of the regularity of the seasons, the tides, and the phases of the moon. Their response to these forces in nature was to personalize them. Thus they gave a name to the sun, the moon, and so on, and began to describe the activities of these forces with tales that eventually became mythology. An example of this process is found in the Greek myth of Apollo and Daphne. Apollo was in love with Daphne, but she fled from him and was changed into a laurel tree. By searching out the etymology of these names, Müller found that Apollo was the name given the sun and that Daphne was the name given the dawn. Thus, the original myth simply described how the sun chases away the dawn. Müller further believed that all of the stories of the gods and heroes in Indo-European cultures were originally solar myths. Müller became convinced that he had found the key to the origin of all religions: "Primitive" people identified the forces in nature, personified them, created myths to describe their activities, and eventually developed pantheons and religions around them.

Between 1890 and 1915, Sir James George Frazer (1854–1941), a fellow of Trinity College, Cambridge, produced his encyclopedic work on religion, *The Golden Bough*. Frazer constructed his theories by reading the reports of anthropologists, colonial officials, missionaries, and ancient writers. On the basis of his studies, Frazer came to agree with Tylor that the human mind had developed in a linear fashion in the same way as the process of physical evolution. He taught that humankind had gone through three phases of development regarding the spirit world. First, people had attempted to control the world of nature through what Frazer called "magic." In Frazer's evolutionary framework for human development, when humanity realized nature could not be coerced through magic, it turned to a second stage of development—religion—whose premise was that nature can be implored to cooperate. When religion was also seen to fail, humankind, in a third phase, turned to science, in which a more rational understanding of nature is operative. Therefore, the modern farmer who needs rain turns to neither the magician nor the priest. He turns to the scientist, who will seed the clouds and cause it to rain, although a skeptic might note that there is little proof that seeding the clouds produces rain any more frequently than rain dances or prayers.

Modern proponents of theories of religion that focus on people's relationship to the supernatural have done away with Tylor's and Frazer's evolutionary thinking about "primitive" and "advanced" societies. In other words, scholars no longer maintain that there are stages of human and cultural development that move naturally from nature worship, to multiple deities, to one god, to science. Even a cursory look at the modern world demonstrates that peoples with a wide variety of religious beliefs and practices embrace science; moreover, religions are not more or less "advanced" than other religions. However, these kinds of theories focus on what they perceive to be a unique feature of all religions. Namely, religion is the one aspect of human experience that (almost) always dedicates itself to interactions with gods, spirits, and other supernatural forces.

Functional Theories of Religion

Other theorists have focused on what religion does, that is, how religion functions. A well-known example of this kind of thinker is Karl Marx (1818–1883). Marx saw the origin and development of religion in terms of his personal view of history and the economic and social struggle between classes. Marx said:

> Man makes religion, religion does not make man. In other words, religion is the self-consciousness and self-feeling of man who has either not yet found himself or has already lost himself again. . . . Religion is the sigh of the oppressed creature, the heart of a heartless world, just as it is the spirit of a spiritless situation. It is the opium of the people.[4]

Marx also believed that religion was used by the ruling classes to suppress the underclass. According to Marx, the social principles of Christianity preach the necessity of a ruling and an oppressed class, and for the latter all they have to offer is the pious wish that the former may be charitable. The social principles of Christianity declare all the vile acts of oppressors against the oppressed to be either just punishment for original sin and for other sins, or trials that the Lord, in his infinite wisdom, ordains for the redeemed. Sigmund Freud (1856–1939), the founder of psychoanalysis, theorized about religion from a psychological perspective. Freud saw religion as having originated as guilt that men supposedly feel in hating their fathers. Freud saw in the ancient Greek myth of Oedipus a pattern of human experience. Oedipus was a man who, through a long and tragic series of events, killed his father and married his mother. Freud saw that in all males there was a similar tendency to desire their mothers and therefore hate their fathers.[5]

Freud further referred to practices of "primitive" people he believed to be representative of the total human experience. The dominant male/father kept the women of the group for himself and drove the younger males away from his territory. Finally, the younger males joined together in killing the father and eating his flesh. Freud proposed that guilt from this desire for the mother and this great act of patricide was at the heart of every religion. He believed that totemic religion arose to allay the filial sense of guilt and appease the father through deferred obedience to him and that all later religions are attempts at solving the same problem.[6]

Because of this subconscious hatred and ensuing guilt, Freud believed humans project in the sky a great father image called God. He also thought that religious ideas are "illusions, fulfillments of the oldest, strongest, and most urgent wishes of mankind."[7] The truly healthy and mature person, according to Freud, is content to stand alone and face the problems of life without gods or religions.

Religions of the World

In the long period of human life on Earth, there have been thousands of religions. Because recorded history covers only the last 5,000 years of our existence, there are undoubtedly more unknown than known religions. In addition, many religious systems have lived and died within the relatively short span of recorded history. This text does not pretend to address all religions, historical or prehistorical. It deals only with religious systems that are active and viable today.

Religions Originating in Africa and the Americas

The hundreds (perhaps thousands) of religions that originate in the continents of Africa and North and South America have often been neglected in world religions textbooks. One reason for this neglect has to do with the colonial realities of European expansion and the massive missionary efforts that have occurred around the world that converted many in these areas to Christianity and Islam. Colonial attitudes in academia likewise sidelined these traditions; the evolutionary notions of Tylor, Frazer, and many others often supposed that these important religions were superstitious vestiges of "primitive" peoples. Another reason these religions have not enjoyed the same scholarly attention as other religions is because of their vast diversity. The many different tribes, nations, and peoples in Africa and the Americas each practiced their own unique religious traditions, rituals, and customs. In this text, we have endeavored to discuss some of the common themes that tie together these diverse religions across large geographic areas. Today, many religions that originated in Africa and the Americas work alongside, and sometimes in tension, with the missionary religions of Christianity and Islam.

Religions Originating in India

Four of the great religions of the world originated in India: Hinduism, Jainism, Buddhism, and Sikhism. India remains the home of Hinduism, Jainism, and Sikhism. Buddhism is now found in other Asian nations, such as China, Japan, Korea, Vietnam, Burma, Cambodia, and Thailand. The basic beliefs of these religions are that there are many gods (Sikhism is the exception, taking its belief in one god from Islam) and that one person may lead many lives through a system of reincarnation. A common objective of these religions is release from the cycle of life, death, and rebirth. Sometimes this goal is achieved through the aid of the gods, but often believers are expected by their actions, or lack thereof, to work out their own release.

Religions Originating in China and Japan

Religions that originated in China and Japan include Daoism, Confucianism, and Shinto. Daoism and Confucianism expand our notion of what constitutes religion because both of these traditions, and especially Confucianism, focus on philosophical concepts, nature, and social relationships rather than on worship of a supernatural deity, which is not to say that they deny the existence of gods. Indeed, these religions have in common the belief in many gods and include the worship of nature, the worship or veneration of ancestors, and, in the case of Shinto, a reverence for the nation itself.

Religions Originating in the Middle East

Religions originating in the Middle East include Judaism, Christianity, Islam, and Baha'i. All believe in one Supreme Creator God; they believe each person lives only one earthly life; they regard the material universe positively, hold a linear view of time, and believe in divine judgment of the world. Christianity and Islam have been two of the great missionary religions of the world. Today, their adherents are found all over the globe and number in the billions.

Religion and Public Life

A common notion is that religion is strictly a private matter. However, the histories of the various religions covered in this text immediately demonstrate that religion has always had a tremendous impact on public life. Although sometimes practiced individually, religions are normally expressed in a community of others. Rituals and worship services bring people together to perform meaningful activities, which remind the group of their common stories and heritage. Religions are well known for their ethical content; here again, religion—as a force for ethical and moral guidance—is intrinsically relational. Even personal beliefs, which often contribute to one's sense of self, are forged in communities. Therefore, one of the express objectives of this text is to highlight how important religion is in political, social, and economic spheres. To that end, special sidebars occur throughout the text to accentuate religion's role in public life.

Of course, an unavoidable feature of religion's public role is that it often plays a part in conflicts. These conflicts can range from minor disagreements between two like-minded co-religionists all the way to brutal warfare between nations. We know that religion can be the inspiration—or at least the justification—for horrific acts of violence. But, religions can also be a force for reconciliation between peoples. Many acts of service toward the poor and the disenfranchised are carried out by religious people. James Calvin Davis, a professor of religious studies, challenges us to consider what religion can accomplish in public life, both for weal and for woe:

> To the extent that religion has contributed to the *disintegration* of political discourse, it has been because religious communities have too zealously incorporated the worst strategies and values from our current political environment, not because of some fundamental incompatibility between religion and public life. To the contrary, religious perspectives at their best provide necessary correction to our downward slide. Critics of religion in politics may be unconvinced, given the media's apparent preference to cover religion only when it is polarizing, so it remains for us to demonstrate the substantial contributions religious perspectives can and do make.[8]

All of this brings us back to the point with which we began this introduction: religion demands our attention and study because it is one of the most vital forces on the planet. To understand the religions of the world is intrinsic to responsible global citizenship.

THINK ABOUT IT

1. List several advantages of a knowledge of the differing religious viewpoints of the world.
2. Define *religion*.
3. What was the focus of Tylor's theory of religion?
4. According to Müller, what role did nature play in the formation of religion?
5. Contrast the Marxist view of religion with the Freudian view.
6. Why is religion not merely a private matter?

Part I
Religions Originating in the Americas and Africa

In this first section, we turn our attention to the great diversity of Native American religions and African religions. Many of the religions in these regions are oral traditions. Their systems of knowledge and behavior are inscribed upon human memory, not in some form of writing. Another characteristic of these religions is that they are usually intrinsically tied to a specific tribe, people, or nation. Because of this, we can say that there have been as many religions on these continents as there are unique groups of people. Nevertheless, in both Africa and the Americas, we can talk about some general features of religions that are common across these respective regions. By studying the characteristics of these religions, the student will be able to compare their unique features with other world religions, such as Hinduism, Christianity, and Islam. To help us approach these subjects, this part of the book begins with a chapter on the study of religion itself.

Native American Religions—Basic Teachings

Native American Religions Are Very Diverse

There are hundreds of Native American religions. It is difficult, if not impossible, to generalize about them. Native American cultures are equally diverse, ranging historically from small bands of hunter-gatherers to large-scale states and empires. Today most Native Americans are Christians, although in many cases they retain elements of traditional beliefs and practices.

Many Native American Religions Emphasize Geographic Space and the Natural Environment

Plants, animals, and some geographic and geological features are understood as living beings with whom humans can establish relationships. This has often brought native people into conflict with Euro-American communities.

A Great Importance Is Placed upon the Dead

In some cases—including the Navajo of Arizona and New Mexico—the dead are greatly feared. Even their clothing and other possessions are avoided. Many Native Americans are greatly concerned by the fact that the skeletal remains of their ancestors have been disinterred and are stored in museums.

Native Americans Suffered Greatly at the Hands of White Settlers

There have been many wars and massacres, some of which rose to the level of genocide. Native peoples were often driven off their lands and forced to relocate in less productive areas. In many instances, children were taken from their families and placed in boarding schools, where they were forbidden to conduct traditional ceremonies or even to speak native languages.

Today There Are Religious Movements That Cross Traditional Tribal Boundaries

One of the first of these was the Ghost Dance. It began among the Pauite of Nevada and spread rapidly across the Great Plains. It foretold the end of white settlers and the return of the buffalo, which were almost extinct at the time. Some believed that wearing "ghost shirts" would protect them from the U.S. Army's weapons. A more recent movement is the Native American Church, which combines elements of Native American religion with Christianity. It also uses the hallucinogenic peyote cactus in ceremonial ways.

African Religions—Basic Teachings

Like Those of Native Americans, African Religions Are Extremely Diverse

African cultures are also extremely diverse, with groups including small bands of hunter-gatherers all the way to states and empires. Today, most Africans are either Christians or Muslims, although in many cases they retain elements of traditional beliefs and practices.

The High God Is a Typical Figure in Many Traditional African Religions

The belief in a High God who created the world but is no longer actively involved in it is very common. In these religions, lesser spirits who were part of his creation are more important than the High God in daily life. The Earth is often understood to be a goddess and is associated with fertility.

Ancestor Veneration Is an Important Element of Many Traditional African Religions

Ancestors often communicate with the living through dreams. They can be either helpful or harmful, depending on how they are treated. They are offered sacrifices to promote human health, well-being, and prosperity. They are also believed to enforce moral codes by punishing those who violate them.

Dance, Music, and Ritual Movement Are Essential Parts of Many African Religions

Dance and singing are common elements in traditional African worship. Sometimes, drumming and dancing serve as conduits for communication with gods and spirits. Physical movement is often part of religious celebrations.

In Some African Religions, It Is Believed That Illness Is Often Caused by Witchcraft

Spiritual healers are employed to counter the effects of witchcraft. A specific person is often identified as the witch. These accusations present difficulties for African governments because people often demand that officials take action against those accused of witchcraft, and modern legal systems make that impossible. There are also cases of revenge killings, especially in countries like South Africa that have witnessed political turmoil.

Chapter 1
The Study of Religions

 Learning Objectives

After reading this chapter, you should be able to:

1.1 Name the two primary sources of information about religions.

1.2 Discuss some of the features that are common in many world religions.

Religion is notoriously difficult to define. As we saw in the Introduction, there have been considerable efforts to theorize about the nature of religion by an ever-growing contingent of scholars. Some focused on the supernatural beings and deities that are so essential to many religions. Others turned their attention to what religion does. Of this latter group, some highlighted religion's ability to make meaning and undergird social structures, others focused on its psychological effects, while yet others considered its ethical admonitions. For our purposes, it is not required that we produce a precise definition or theory of religion. We can content ourselves with thinking about religions as phenomena that share many—if not all—basic characteristics. This means that not all religions will feature all of these characteristics in the same measure, but that they all do share what the philosopher Ludwig Wittgenstein called a "family resemblance."[1] In this chapter, we will explore these characteristics and also examine what sorts of materials are available to the scholar of religion as he or she delves into the many religious traditions around the world.

Sources of Information about Religion

1.1.   Name the two primary sources of information about religions.

Humans have been active on planet Earth for thousands of years, but we know only a tiny fraction of human history. Only within the past 5,000 to 6,000 years has *Homo sapiens* used writing. Although non-written sources (such as cave paintings, burial sites, religious statuary, and archaeological remains) indicate human culture and religious experiences, our strongest source of knowledge is the written record. Of the total period of time during which people have been on Earth, we have written records chronicling perhaps less than one-half of 1 percent. From these records, we know a great deal about different cultures and religious experiences, but there is an enormous amount we do not and cannot know.

There are two primary sources of information about religions. The first is contemporary religious people themselves. In this approach, the anthropologist or other scholar of religion visits a group and studies its religious beliefs and practices. Study of living religions can yield much information about how religions are practiced, how religious narratives are conveyed, and what sorts of moral behavior is both expected and performed by contemporary people. The scholar can observe people in their religious gatherings, can listen to them perform religious or sacred music, and can ask them questions about their beliefs and assumptions. This kind of study can also reveal much about how a religious group remembers its own past, and how people understand the development of their own religious tradition from its inception to today.

As interesting as the study of contemporary religions may be, it is helpful for scholars to explore the historical record. All contemporary societies, even the most technologically simple, have long and complex histories. They have developed and evolved over thousands of years in response to ecological and social environments and have built upon the wisdom of many generations. The history of religions can be uncovered in the written scriptures of some religions. In addition to sacred writing, other written records, artwork, and other historical artifacts can also tell us a great deal about the history of a religion. Likewise, archaeology is a helpful source. Archaeologists meticulously attempt to uncover the physical remains of past civilizations and to reconstruct the life and history of their cultures. In an archaeological examination of relatively recent cultures, such as the Roman or Classic Mayan, the task is simplified because of the wealth of buildings, burial sites, coinage, and other elaborate artifacts these civilizations left. Archaeologists gain considerable information from scrolls, clay tablets, and inscriptional materials from literate cultures.

Common Features of Religions

1.2. **Discuss some of the features that are common in many world religions.**

The following features are common to many religions. They have appeared in the historical religions of which we are aware, and many of them are evident in one form or another in living religions. Sacrifice, for example, appears in the earliest form of nearly every extant religion. Finally, some of the features not currently part of living religions may be found subliminally in modern cultures. For instance, although few followers of the world's religions would admit that magic is part of their theology, belief in the lucky coin, the unlucky day, the avoidance of the number thirteen, spiritual or magical healing, and so on is widely found, even in the most technologically advanced societies of the twenty-first century.

Gods, Spirits, and Forces

Sir Edward Tylor theorized that people originally envisioned the world as being alive with souls or spirits and, on the basis of this understanding of nature, developed religions.[2] Indeed, the belief that nature is alive with spirits that have feelings and can be communicated with is one of the most common to human religious experience. In many religions, people believe that they are not the only spirits—that animals, trees, stones, rivers, mountains, the heavenly bodies, the seas, and the Earth itself have *anima* (spirit). It is also believed that these spirits communicate, can be flattered or offended, and can either help or hurt humans. These spirits are therefore believed to be personal. Other religions do not associate spirits, or gods, with a specific feature of the natural environment but instead consider them to be either personal deities or impersonal forces. Some of the world's largest religions likewise embrace belief in gods and other supernatural persons. For instance, many Christians, Muslims, and Buddhists believe that spirits have the ability to bless or curse human beings.

On the basis of this supernaturalist understanding of the cosmos, many religions have revered or openly worshiped nearly everything in nature. Almost any animal one can think of has at some time or another been worshiped; stones have been worshiped or have been the sites where gods have spoken to people or received the blood of their sacrifices; mountains have frequently been the objects of worship or the places of revelation; the seas and the creatures in them have been objects of veneration; trees have frequently been the objects of religious cults; the heavenly bodies—the sun, moon, and stars—play a part in nearly every religion; and fire, water, and the Earth itself have

Hindu pilgrims bathe in the Ganges
River at Varansi.

become objects of worship or important elements in worship. The list of nature-based
spiritual expressions is almost endless.

This relationship to the divine, or supremely meaningful, in nature persists in contemporary society. People place historic stones at the corners of their new buildings;
they build expensive, elaborate, useless fireplaces. Christians bring evergreen trees
into their homes to celebrate Christmas; Muslims walk around the sacred black stone
and kiss it during their pilgrimage to Mecca; Hindus bathe in the sacred river Ganges;
Christian and even secular Americans go on pilgrimages to the graves of presidents
and rock stars; and on and on.

Another characteristic of religions having to do with supernatural or other-worldly
beings is the veneration or worship of deceased members of the family. Those who believe in the continued life of the ancestors often greatly fear the evil the dead might do
and frequently take great pains to prevent the dead from returning from their graves
to harm the living. Bodies are buried beneath large stones or with stakes implanted
in their chests, apparently to prevent them from roaming. Among some societies, the
names of the dead are dropped from common usage for a time, and the houses in
which they died are burned to discourage their return.

At the same time, those who venerate ancestors also seem to feel the dead can
benefit the living. Therefore, steps are taken to please the dead. Possessions such as
tools, weapons, favorite foods, and ornaments are sent to the grave with the dead.
Graves and tombs (such as the vast tombs of the Egyptian rulers) are decorated and
elaborately tended so the dead might be comfortable. Among the ancient Chinese,
grave mounds were rebuilt each year and offerings of food, drink, flowers, and even
blankets were left for the comfort of the deceased. Perhaps no people made such a
great effort to placate the deceased as the ancient Chinese. Their special concern was to
keep alive the memory of their ancestors by memorizing their names and biographies
and passing this information on to future generations. Ancestor veneration remains a
very important part of traditional Chinese religion, especially among Chinese in places
like Taiwan and Singapore where traditional beliefs were not affected by Communist
rule. Even some Chinese Christians engage in ancestor veneration to some degree.
Saint Andrew's Anglican Cathedral in Singapore, with a congregation that is largely
Chinese, holds prayer services in cemeteries on the Saturday before Easter to prepare
the ancestors for resurrection.

Stories and Scriptures

One of the most common characteristics of all religions is mythology. In modern parlance, the word *myth* connotes a lie or false belief. We speak of the myth of Aryan supremacy or the myth of historical objectivity, and we mean that these concepts are out-and-out fabrications with little or no basis in truth. In the study of religions, the word *myth* is used in another sense. Almost every religion has its stories about the dealings of the gods with humans. We call these stories myths, or poetic ways of telling great truths. Myths are a way of thinking in pictures and stories rather than abstract concepts. Very few people today might believe that the story of Prometheus is a factual account of a great hero of the past; perhaps no one ever did. But the story of Prometheus reveals the truth of the sacrificial love of one divine figure for humanity. Especially in societies that do not rely on the written word, religion is sustained and explained by the transmission of its myths from one generation to the next.

Religious myths often are used to explain the whys and hows of the world; they may explain the origin of a people by tracing it back to the beginning of creation. In the Greek myth of Prometheus, for example, there is an explanation for the creation of the world and the origin of fire and civilization. Myths also may explain the power of certain religious functionaries. The Japanese myth of the sun goddess Amaterasu gives background to the belief that the emperor is a divine figure. Often, myths are attached to and explain why the worshiping community keeps certain religious holy days.

In many religions, myths, histories, ritual instructions, songs, and other religious information is recorded in writing. Judaism, Christianity, and Islam, religions that all originate in the Middle East, have a pronounced commitment to their written texts, and generally consider them to be revealed to humankind by their God. These scriptures, not surprisingly, play an important role in the day-to-day religious practice and in the regular community gatherings of these traditions. Many other religions also feature central texts. For example, the Daodejing is central to Daoism, the Lotus Sutra has tremendous importance for many Buddhists, and the Adi Granth is deeply revered by

Statue of Confucius in the Great Hall of Ceremonies in a Taoist temple (photo).. /Hanoi, Vietnam/ Photo © Luca Tettoni/The Bridgeman Art Library

Statue of Confucius in the Great Hall of Ceremonies in a Daoist temple in Hanoi, Vietnam. Here we see the mutual influence that Confucianism and Daoism have had on one another.

Sikhs. In other religions, holy writ maintains importance for religious specialists and religious philosophers but is not part of the daily religious practice of most people. The great Hindu Vedas fall into this category.

Rituals and Behaviors

Rituals, in religious contexts, are the set behaviors that people carry out for religious purposes. Rituals can rehearse ancient myths, they can attempt to know the otherwise unknowable, they can offer sacrifices to supernatural beings, and they can be expressions of worship and veneration. Some rituals happen in communities and are overseen by religious specialists such as priests, imams, or rabbis. Other rituals occur more informally or in private. Some rituals require paraphernalia like water, food, statues, and fire. Others may require only a time of prayer and quiet.

One family of ritual is called divination and has to do with the prediction of the future. Usually, this is the work of priests or people who have been specially prepared for the task, and it is accomplished by various means. Frequently, divination is accomplished through the examination of the entrails of a sacrificed animal. Sometimes, it is achieved by observing the flights of birds or by casting sacred dice. In ancient China, a tortoise shell was heated until it cracked, and the pattern of the cracks was interpreted as a prediction of the future. This approach was later refined into the practice of casting yarrow stalks, and these patterns were interpreted in a book called the *Yi Jing*. Among the ancient Greeks, the future was predicted when a priestess sat on a tripod and breathed in fumes that escaped from the ground at Delphi. What she said after breathing in the fumes was interpreted by a priest as being the message from the gods regarding the future.

Some societies seek knowledge of the future from a member of the group believed to have been possessed by the spirits. Among the peoples of Siberia, this person is called a *shaman*. Although the word *shaman* often connotes an image of a priest or magician, the original meaning related to one who was possessed by the spirits and spoke their messages to the group.

Often, religious societies are served by those who are designated "prophets." In the Hebrew Bible, the prophet revealed the message of God. Sometimes this message dealt with present events; other times the prophet's words concerned the future. Thus, the word *prophet* in modern English carries the connotation of being a "predictor" or "diviner."

Another ritual practice in some religions is totemism. The word *totem* itself is a corruption of the Ojibwa word *ototeman*, and indeed, totemism is common among some Native American groups. It is based on the feeling of kinship that humans have for other creatures or objects in nature, and it generally involves some form of identification between a tribe or clan and an animal, although totems in some parts of the world have been identified as plants or even as the sun, moon, or stars. For example, a clan may believe it is basically related to the bear. The bear may be the ancestor of the clan; the clan may possess the characteristics of the bear (strength, ferocity, or size); or clan members may believe that when they die they will take the form of the bear. If the bear is the totem of the clan, members may not eat or kill this animal except in self-defense or on sacred occasions, when they may eat its flesh in a ceremonial meal that binds the clan closer together. Members of another neighboring clan, whose totem is the deer, may hunt and eat the bear, whereas members of the first clan may hunt and eat the deer.

Many cultural and religious groups do not clearly and religiously adhere to totemism but still observe some forms of this practice. For instance, nations are symbolized by animals, such as the eagle, bear, or lion, and schools choose mascots to symbolize the spirit of their athletic teams.

One of the most common ritual practices in all of the religions of the world is sacrifice. Throughout history, people have offered sacrifices of nearly every imaginable material to the gods, spirits, and demons, or for ancestor veneration. Often, the sacrifices are animals, which are slaughtered and then burned or cooked and eaten before the gods. However, the sacrifice of nearly every other item of value can be found. People have sacrificed grain, wine, milk, water, wood, tools, weapons, and jewelry to the gods. Occasionally, religions call for the sacrifice of a human, but in most religions this is a relatively rare practice. Usually the human who is sacrificed is an enemy taken prisoner in battle; infrequently, it is a beloved child or young person chosen especially for the altar. When human sacrifice is mentioned in religious literature, it usually is considered an extreme but effective method of persuading the gods.[3]

Religion and Public Life

A 1993 United States Supreme Court case highlights how important an understanding of various religious practices can be in the public sphere. Santería is a religion with West African and Christian roots that is popular in Cuba and in many places in the United States. One important element of Santería is the sacrifice of various items to the deities, known as "orishas." Occasionally, these sacrifices include live animals, oftentimes chickens. When the Florida city of Hialeah made religiously motivated animal sacrifice illegal, members of a Santería-based organization called the Church of Lukumi Babalu Aye sued for the protection of their right of religious freedom. In 1993, the Supreme Court decided in their favor.[4]

Among the Oche of ancient Peru and the Aztec of pre-Columbian Mexico, human sacrifice was both routine and extremely important. Headhunting, which was thought to ensure the fertility of the land, was practiced by many of the tribal peoples of Southeast Asia well into the twentieth century. There are unconfirmed reports that the practice continues in remote areas.

The act of sacrifice has various meanings. Sometimes it is considered a means of feeding the residents of the spirit world. How does one feed the spirits? One may pour water, wine, and milk on the ground and believe that as the fluid is soaked up, the spirits are drinking it. One may leave food in a sacred place and assume that when the food has disappeared, the gods have been fed. One may burn meat or grain, and the gods may inhale the smoke of the offerings. Thus, the spirit world is sustained by the human world and acts favorably toward it.

At other times, the sacrifice is understood simply as being a gift of some sort to the spirit world. Gifts of tools, weapons, ornaments, money, incense, or even tobacco may be left in sacred places for the spirits by a person who wishes the favor of the spirits or simply wants to avoid offending them.

Sacrifice in some religions also implies the establishment of a communal bond between spirits and human beings. The worshiper brings food to the sacred place, burns a portion of it for the gods, and then eats a portion of it or shares it with the community. Thus, the spirits and the living share a meal together, and their bond is renewed and strengthened. In other contexts, the sharing of a ritual sacrifice is recognized as a gift from God or the gods to the gathered religious community.

Another category of religious ritual behavior has to do with marking and celebrating the passage of time and the cycle of the seasons. All religions observe special days in which to remember special segments of their myths, to celebrate harvests, to commemorate important events, and to observe special behaviors such as fasting or purification. The New Year is an important holiday for many people in East and Southeast Asia. Springtime religious observances include the Jewish Passover and Christian Easter. Other religious holidays honor a religion's founder; for example, many Buddhists celebrate the Buddha's birthday. Religious holiday festivals and observances serve to remind people that their religious beliefs and practices extend throughout the time of their lives.

Manipulating the World

One of the principal functions of religious ritual is to make something happen. This can be as simple as a prayer for the healing of a sick relative or as complex as an international pilgrimage to seek God's favor. Sometimes people ask deities and other supernatural beings to grant them favors. In other cases, the ritual has a contractual power that can extract the desired results from gods or powerful forces.

In the latter case, when ritual behavior leads almost inevitably to given results, this is sometimes referred to as "magic." When modern people speak of magic, they often think in terms of sleight-of-hand tricks or illusions performed by a professional whose job is to deceive and amuse them. In the study of religion, the term "magic" takes on a far more serious meaning.

Practitioners of so-called magic perceive the world as being controlled by forces that can be manipulated. They know that if they perform their formulas, dances, or incantations correctly, they will in fact be able to control nature; they can make rain, cause crops to be bountiful, create conditions for a successful hunt, or kill their enemies. Probably the most common form of magic is sympathetic or imitative magic. In this form of magic, one attempts to coerce nature into some act by performing that act oneself, but on a smaller scale. Another aspect of magic frequently found in religions is the fetish. A fetish is any object used to control nature in a magical fashion. For the possessor, the fetish is used to bring good fortune and ward off evil. The fetish may be almost anything: a wooden stick, a stone or a collection of stones, a bone, an amulet, or an image. Fetishes may be held singly or collectively, or they may be used as an ornamentation of some kind. In any group of people, one is likely to encounter a large collection of lucky coins, rabbits' feet, religious medallions, and so on. The existence of fetishes and other elements of magical manipulation in all societies speaks of their enduring appeal to the human race.

In addition to the manipulation of the world and cosmos known as magic and the use of fetishes, prayer is another form of ritual that religious people use to get results or make something happen. Many religions feature rituals and prayers for the healing of

A minister in Tanzania "lays on hands," an ancient component of Christian prayers for healing.

Jake Lyell/Alamy

the sick or for the eternal status of the deceased. For example, in Pure Land Buddhism, bereft loved ones pray that their deceased family members and friends will be reborn in the Pure Land overseen by Amitabha Buddha. This is an especially auspicious place in which to be reborn.

Other religions maintain that the universe and the human person are imbued with and surrounded by energy. Religious rituals can manipulate that energy to bring peace, wellness, and even environmental restoration. In North America and Western Europe, an example of this kind of world review is the "New Age" movement and the related Deep Ecology movement, which straddles the border between environmentalism and religion. For many supporters of Deep Ecology, the Earth is a spiritual consciousness as well as a planet. The environment is seen as a self-regulating system, all elements of which are to be valued equally. Change or evolution is directed by a spiritual force. Other New Age faiths maintain that particular places are vortexes at which a variety of types of spiritual power may be acquired.

Social Structures and Moral Systems

All religions, to some extent, give moral guidance to their followers. Myths about gods and supernatural beings may contain ethical lessons for contemporary devotees. They may also suggest social structures regarding leadership positions and the proper way for human beings to relate to one another. In some cases, religious texts incorporate legal material and specific rules and laws to guide human society. These texts may encourage or demand specific behavior even as they forbid other actions. Likewise, they may also give instruction as to what is right and wrong in general.

In the scheme of life in many religions, certain actions must be avoided, lest the spirit world release harmful effects on the person or group. In some societies, holy persons, places, and objects are generally considered off-limits to the ordinary person. Chieftains, priests, sacred places, fetishes, and so on are to be avoided by the unordained, except on special occasions or when there is special preparation. For example, in the Hebrew Bible, we find occasions when people either knowingly or accidentally step over the limits. Second Kings 2:23–25 speaks of an occasion when boys mocked and taunted the prophet Elisha. As a result, the children were mauled by two bears. Second Samuel 6:1–7 tells of a man who merely touched the Ark of the Covenant to prevent its falling off a cart and as a result was struck dead by God. In many other cultures, the person of the king is so sacred that it is considered taboo to come into his presence without special invitation. Until fairly recent times, the Japanese thought it forbidden to look upon the face of the emperor, even when he toured the city streets.

Other examples of these kinds of taboos are numerous. In many cultures, those who handle the dead for burial are considered ritually unclean, at least for a certain period of time after the handling. One of the most universal taboos regards women during their menses. In some cultures, menstruating women are required to live in houses that are separate from the rest of the group. Some religions prohibit women from prayer during their periods.[5] Many cultures have developed ritual stipulations regarding certain foods. Certain kinds of food, such as pork, beef, or shellfish, are thought of by particular groups as being ritually unclean, and thus off-limits. For example, Muslims and Jews consider pork unclean. Most Hindus do not eat beef, not because the cow is unclean, but rather because it is viewed as being sacred. Until recently, Roman Catholics abstained from eating all forms of meat on Fridays.

Another practice among most societies is the establishment of certain rituals at key transitional points in the life of the individual. These rituals are called rites of passage. The key points of life usually recognized are birth, puberty, marriage, and death. Rituals carried out at these critical periods recall the myths of the culture and symbolize separation from the former status, transition to the new, and incorporation.

Often, these rituals involve a dramatic reenactment of a sacred story; they also help to re-create and cement social structures.

Ceremonies at birth are important. The rites surrounding birth identify the child as a member of the community. In Judaism, male children are circumcised. In many branches of Christianity, there is the ritual of baptism, a ceremony that names the infant and makes him or her a member of the Christian religion.

Some cultures give greatest attention to rituals regarding the passage from childhood into adulthood. The rites of passage at puberty are preceded by a period of instruction in the basic knowledge of the society, as well as in such arts as survival, hunting, agriculture, and fire making. At puberty, the child may undergo an ordeal of some kind. Among some Native Americans, children are expected to live apart from their families for a certain period of time, to fast and to seek a vision from the spirits. In other societies, children may be set apart for a specific task or time outside their families. After completion of these experiences, the individual may also be circumcised or given some other mark of identity. During these ceremonies, young people are more fully instructed in the religious traditions, secrets, and lore of the society and thereafter may take their place as fully matured members of the group.[6] Other puberty rites of passage are confirmation for some Christian youths and the Bar Mitzvah or Bat Mitzvah for young Jews.

Other key points at which religious rituals and symbols are important are marriage and death. Marriage is frequently celebrated with fertility rituals and the full attention of religious functionaries. The passage at death is likewise given the attention of religious rituals, both at the time of death and at the burial.

Think About It

1. What are two primary sources of information about religions? How trustworthy are these sources?

2. Name some common features of all religions. What are some of the rituals that religious people use to manipulate the world? What are some ways that people express their relationship to the divine?

Suggested Reading

Eliade, Mircea. *The Sacred and the Profane.* Translated by Willard Trask. New York: Harper Torchbooks, 1961.

Evans-Pritchard, E. E. *Theories of Primitive Religion.* New York: Clarendon Press, 1965.

Frazer, Sir James. *The New Golden Bough.* Abridged by Theodore H. Gaster. New York: Criterion Books, 1959.

Gill, Sam D. *Beyond "The Primitive": The Religions of Nonliterate People.* Englewood Cliffs, N.J.: Prentice Hall, 1982.

Harvey, Graham. *Indigenous Religion, A Companion.* London: Casell, 2000.

Masuzawa, Tomoko. *The Invention of World Religions, Or, How European Universalism Was Preserved in the Language of Pluralism.* Chicago: University of Chicago Press, 2005.

Pals, Daniel L. *Eight Theories of Religion,* 2nd ed. New York: Oxford University Press, 2006.

Sharpe, Eric J. *Comparative Religion: A History,* 2nd ed. La Salle, Ill.: Open Court, 1986.

Chapter 2
Native American Religions

 ## Learning Objectives

After reading this chapter, you should be able to:

2.1 Describe the spirit world and the relationship that different Native American groups have with gods, deities, or spirits.

2.2 Explain the Native Americans' connection to nature.

2.3 Discuss Native American religious practices and the purpose of ritual in day-to-day life and practice.

2.4 Describe death and life after death in Native American religious practice.

2.5 Discuss Native American religions and religious practice in today's world.

A Timeline of Native American Religions

+/− 20,000 B.C.E.	First people arrive in North America; thousands of years of oral tradition
3500 B.C.E.	Urban centers in Peru created
1492 C.E.	European "discovery" of the Americas, beginning of Spanish conquest, and conversion of indigenous peoples to Christianity
1540	Spanish arrive in what is now the Southwest United States and establish Roman Catholic missions; beginning of 150 years of conflict
1607	First successful English settlement in North America; beginning of conflict with indigenous people and Christian missionary activity
1848	United States acquires southwestern territories at the conclusion of the Mexican-American War; beginning of large-scale Euro-American settlement and "Indian Wars"
1862	Homestead Act prompts displacement of many Native American communities
1863–1864	Thousands of Navajo killed by U.S. forces
1878–1933	Period of Indian Boarding Schools and involuntary conversion to Christianity

1890	Battle of Wounded Knee and the end of "Indian Wars"
1890	Ghost Dance religion
1918	Incorporation of Native American Church
1941–1945	Navajo serve as code talkers during World War II
1968	Dennis Banks founds the American Indian Movement to fight for civil rights
1994	Amendments to the United States American Indian Religious Freedom Act of 1978 legalize the use of peyote in religious ceremonies
2004	Dedication of the National Museum of the American Indian in Washington, D.C.

Key Terms

Earth Mother	**peyote**
Ghost Dance	**Sun Dance**
Great Spirit	**vision quest**
Native American Church	

One of the oldest and most enduring forms of religion is that which is practiced by the various Native American peoples. Because of the role played by Native Americans in North American history over the past 400 years, their religious practices have been of interest not only to scholars but also to the general public. In recent years, more and more attention has been focused on the subject. Native Americans have experienced something of a religious revival and have become increasingly concerned with the preservation of their cultural and religious heritage. Many non–Native Americans have turned greater attention to the religions of native peoples because of their emphasis on nature and personal religious experience, and the absence of a formal organizational structure.

When speaking of the religion of Native Americans, we must be aware that we are not speaking of a monolithic structure. The people identified as Native Americans migrated to the North American continent 15,000 to 20,000 years ago.[1] Since then, they have lived in nearly every section of the Americas.[2] They have resided in many different climates, with differing lifestyles. Some Native American tribes have been hunting and gathering societies, whereas others lived in settled agricultural communities. Some lived in small nomadic bands, while others built towns, cities, states, and empires. Many now live in towns and cities and are integrated into non-native social and economic systems to a high degree. Many more live on reservations established by treaties with the U.S. government.

Many people tend to identify Native Americans with the nomadic hunting peoples who roamed the western plains of North America in the nineteenth century. The lives of these people centered on the pursuit of the bison. However, many of these tribes were at one time primarily agricultural. All of these hunting societies were influenced by aspects of European culture, particularly the horses and guns that made life on the open plains possible. Because of the long time span involved and the many differing lifestyles, it is impossible to talk about one set "Native American religion."

In studying these religions, one must also be aware of the relative dearth of sources. Although Native American life covers perhaps 20,000 years, in most cases literary sources exist from only the last 400 years. Most of the early sources are reports of Christian missionaries and explorers, who may or may not have been sympathetic or objective witnesses. Furthermore, the great bulk of information on Native American religions has been written during the past 100 years—after there had been contact with European civilization, its religions, and its technology. Scholars often debate whether some aspect of these religions truly reflects "pure" Native American religion or whether it developed in response to some aspect of Christianity. Although none of the Native American religions has survived unchanged, many have incorporated elements of European culture and religion into native belief systems rather than giving up traditional ways entirely. Like all living religions, Native American religions have grown and changed in response to changing times and contexts. One source of knowledge about Native American religions prior to the arrival of the Europeans is archaeology. Although archaeology can show much about the total culture of a people, it does not tell us much about religion, particularly of those people who did not construct stone monuments or other lasting religious images and structures. Because most pre-Columbian American people were not literate and left few religious artifacts, our knowledge of their religious beliefs is very limited. Another source of knowledge about Native American religions both before and after European contact is the many oral traditions, indigenous histories, and memories that have been passed along from one generation to the next.

Because there are as many Native American religions as there are Native American tribes and peoples, it would be impossible to cover all of them here. We are left with two options: We can either describe the specific religions of a few tribes, or we can draw out general features that are shared across many Native American religions. In this text, we take the second option. Following are some general features that run through many of the better-known Native American religions.

The Spirit World

2.1. **Describe the spirit world and the relationship that different Native American groups have with gods, deities, or spirits.**

To investigate the religions of Native Americans, one might begin by asking what kind of relationship different groups have with gods, deities, or spirits. Do they recognize one Supreme God or multiple deities, or do they find the divine present in a variety of forms? In one sense, many Native American religions recognize a multiplicity of gods. All nature is alive with spirits. Close at hand are the spirits of animals or plants, which appear in visions. There are also the guardian spirits of various animals, and there are the spirits of the dead, who live in the land of the dead. Nature is personified in many spirits. At the heart of nature is **Earth Mother**, who provides the bounty of the Earth. Thunder and lightning are believed to be individual beings. Therefore, in the broadest sense of the word, Native American religions are polytheistic. Native Americans believe that many levels of gods and spirits exist in the universe.

However, many forms of Native American religion hold that, in addition to the multiple spirits of nature, there is a single Supreme Being. They believe in the Supreme Being in a manner found in many basic religions. These religions take the position that, above and beyond all the lesser deities, there is a High God. However, this High God is separate from the concerns of Earth. Matters of daily life are the business of the nature spirits and sometimes the ancestors. It is to these spirits that one prays and gives attention. The High God is appealed to rarely, perhaps only in an extreme emergency, and is seldom mentioned in religious conversation. Many of the Native American religions take this attitude toward the Supreme Being.

Some Native Americans think of the High God or **Great Spirit** as a personal God. Others understand the High God in a more abstract way. For them, the High God is not a personality, but rather a divine or sacred power that is revealed in humans, nature, and the spirit world. The Lakota (Sioux) belief in Wakan Tanka is an example of this abstract understanding of the High God. Wakan Tanka, or the "Great Mysterious," is a creative force found in all beings and spirits. Any object or being that has influence over the course of life is seen as a manifestation of this divine power.

Connection to Nature

2.2.   Explain the Native Americans' connection to nature.

Much is made of the contrast between the Native American attitude toward nature and that of the Europeans who came to the Americas. Generally, Native American cultures maintain a reverent attitude toward the land, trees, rivers, and mountains. On the other hand, the European cultures have tended to look upon nature as something to be exploited. Thus, they were willing to sacrifice the beauty and even the life of the land to build technologies that would make life less dependent on the cycles and unknowns of nature. Whether this is an accurate characterization of either Native Americans or Europeans is a matter of debate. There are examples of native people who unintentionally abused their environment. In the American Southwest, for example, there are many cases in which overpopulation and the resulting pressure on fragile desert environments led to the decline of large-scale civilizations and long-term environmental change. There are also Europeans who love and respect nature. In general, however, Native Americans have a more reverent attitude toward nature than do most European Americans. This reverence for the land and for nature in general is at least in part the result of the fact that survival within traditional Native American cultures depended on living close to and in balance with nature, rather than on changing the environment to suit human needs.

For some Native American groups, this connection to nature is expressed religiously in that trees, rocks, rivers, plants, and animals are often believed to be spiritually alive. The spirits that exist in nature have the power to help or harm. Therefore, the believer offers some form of worship to these spirits. Moreover, these religions teach that the Supreme Being lives in all creation. If the Supreme Being lives and manifests itself in nature, nature should be respected and cared for. Therefore, nature is not seen as an object to be tamed by humankind. Rather, one must seek to live in harmony with nature.

Hunting has been an important part of life in many Native American cultures. Because Native Americans did not keep large domestic animals prior to the arrival of the Europeans, wild game played an essential role in the diets of native people. Animal hides and bones were important raw materials for making clothing, tools, ornaments, and religious objects, and for constructing dwellings. Hunting was also a religious pursuit in which the hunter saw the animal as a fellow creature with a similar spirit. Therefore, a hunter prayed to the spirit of the animal before the hunt. Only those animals that were absolutely needed were killed. After the hunt, one asked the animal for forgiveness. Care was taken to use every part of the slaughtered animal. Nothing was wasted. Sometimes animal bones were buried in such a way that they might be exhumed and used later. These practices were in marked contrast to the actions of Euro-American hunters, who slaughtered great herds of bison for their hides or tongues and left the bulk of the animal to rot. The Euro-American type of hunting led to the destruction of the herds on which many Native Americans depended.

Native Americans who practice agriculture revere the soil, plants, and trees. Planting and harvesting are surrounded with rituals and taboos. Plants, like animals, are thought to have spirits and are treated as persons by many Native Americans. For many Native American people, farming is a religious activity. Many of the Hopi of the Southwest continue to grow corn because of its religious meaning, even when the great bulk of their food comes from "modern" sources. Even the gathering of clay for the production of pottery is done with an understanding of the life in the soil. The Tohono O'odham women of southern Arizona speak of the clay that they dig for pots: "I take only what I need. It is to cook for my children."[3] Even the cutting of wood has religious overtones. One makes an offering to the tree before cutting it. No wood is wasted because trees are sacred and, like humans, have feelings that must be respected.

The reverent attitude of the Native American toward nature and its contrast to that of many whites is best summarized in the words of a Wintu:

From the Source

The White people never cared for land or deer or bear. When we Indians kill meat, we eat it all up. When we dig roots we make little holes. When we build houses, we make little holes. When we burn grass for grasshoppers, we don't ruin things. We shake down acorns and pine nuts. We don't chop down the trees. We only use dead wood. But the White people plow up the ground, pull down the trees, kill everything. The tree says, "Don't. I am sore. Don't hurt me." But they chop it down and cut it up. The spirit of the land hates them. They blast out trees and stir it up to its depths. They saw up the trees. That hurts them. The Indians never hurt anything, but the White people destroy all. They blast rocks and scatter them on the ground. The rock says, "Don't. You are hurting me." But the White people pay no attention. When the Indians use rocks, they take little round ones for their cooking . . . . How can the spirit of the earth like the White man? . . . Everywhere the White man has touched it, it is sore.[4]

This Wintu tale is as much about the coming of the Europeans as it is about the role of nature in Native American religious thought. It is also an example of the way in which many Native Americans understand their relationships with the beings of the natural environment. Rocks, for example, are more than minerals. They are intelligent beings that can communicate with humans. Reverence for nature was part of Native American religion prior to contact with Europeans. Most likely, the encounter with European farmers and ranchers led Native Americans to emphasize this aspect of their religion as they saw environmental change lead to the destruction of their ways of life. Differing understandings of nature and its role in human culture became one of the ways in which Native American peoples distinguished themselves from white settlers. As non–Native Americans have become increasingly concerned about the preservation of the natural environment, they have found Native American spirituality increasingly attractive.

Native American Religious Practices

2.3. Discuss Native American religious practices and the purpose of ritual in day-to-day life and practice.

Although some Native American people understand the universe to be under the control of one Supreme God, it is more common in Native American religion to concern oneself with the day-to-day life among the multiple kinds of beings found in the world. The bulk of religious attention is directed toward achieving good relations with the spirits of the Earth, the forests, the streams, and the animals on which their peoples have traditionally depended. For Native Americans, the purpose of ritual is not so much to control nature but to communicate and establish good relationships with the spiritual beings that share the world with humans.

Sacrifice

Most of the religions of the world have practiced some form of sacrifice as a way of pleasing the deities. Throughout history, animals, grain, wine, beer, and sometimes humans have been sacrificed to the gods. Such sacrifices are rare in the religions of the native peoples of what are now the United States and Canada, although human sacrifices were an important element of the religions of the Aztec and some other native peoples of Central and South America.[5] When it occurs, sacrifice is understood as being a gift to the spirits in exchange for assistance to human beings. Some rituals, such as the **Sun Dance** of the native peoples of the Great Plains, require self-torment or sacrifice. This is seen as a way of acquiring the spiritual power necessary for human survival. Medicine bundles, which are made from animal hides and bones, plants, and minerals, are also sources of spiritual power and are greatly valued both by the people who make them and by those of subsequent generations who treat them as living beings. Many native people are concerned that the medicine bundles found in museums may be in danger of death. While power and gifts are important concepts in native religions, the great blood sacrifices found in many religions are generally not a part of their worship.

Taboos

One of the ways Native Americans protect themselves from possible danger from the spirit world is through taboos. The concept of taboo, as it applies to Native American religions, refers to cultural and religious rules of avoidance. In this sense, a taboo is a kind of religious action that demands people avoid doing things that would offend the spirits of nature and the ancestors. A collection of widely held taboos relates to menstruating women. Such taboos were particularly strong in societies that depended largely on hunting for survival. In many cultures, women are believed to have special powers for either good or evil, but the menstruating woman is thought to be particularly powerful. During this time, she is obviously set apart by the spirit world as one who can participate in the miracle of child production. Many Native American peoples believed in the unusual power of a woman at these times in her life. Therefore, during menstruation, a woman was kept away from ordinary society. In some communities she was required to leave her family and live in a special location because her power could make her especially damaging to the magic necessary for a hunt. It was believed by some that even a glance from a menstruating woman could destroy the hunting ability of a man for the rest of his life. Her gaze could also destroy the magic of hunting weapons, and her presence in the forests might drive away the game forever.

Another widely observed taboo is the avoidance of the dead. No matter how beloved a person may have been in life, the fear is that after death the spirit will continue to stay around its former home and perhaps attempt to take friends and family. At best, the spirits of the dead might haunt their families, causing them bad dreams. This taboo is still widely observed. Among the Navajo and other tribes of Arizona and New Mexico, dead bodies, and even the clothing, belongings, and houses of the dead, are greatly feared, to the extent that many are reluctant to touch the bodies of the victims of automobile and other accidents. Except in extreme emergencies, their care is left to non-native people. Taboos concerning the dead led Native Americans to be greatly concerned about their final resting places. Often, steps are taken to keep the bodies in the grave and away from contact with the human world. Sometimes, the names of the dead are not spoken for years after their death. In some Native American societies, the dead were buried by special members of the tribe, and not their immediate families. These corpse handlers were considered to be ritually unclean for a period of time after they had touched the body. They were separated from the community for a period of several days and forbidden to eat the regular food of the tribe. Burial grounds and human remains continue to be both sacred and feared and should not be disturbed for any reason. Concern with the dead and their resting places has been the cause of many controversies between Native Americans and the scientific community. Archaeologists and other scientists often study human remains to learn about the diets and health of prehistoric peoples. Native Americans are often greatly troubled by what they view as dangerous disrespect for the dead, and they have fought for the return and reburial of the remains discovered and studied by archaeologists.

Ceremonies and Rituals

Along with the observance of taboos, Native Americans often seek to control the forces of the spirit world with ceremonies. As is the case with many other religions, ceremonies are extremely important to the Native Americans. The purpose of their ceremonies, rituals, songs, and dances is not necessarily worship. They are a means of renewing the partnership between humans and the spirit world. Frequently, they involve dancing, singing, fasting, ordeals, bathing, and the observance of certain taboos.

One of the most common elements in Native American religions is the use of dance as a means of contacting the spirit world in preparation for some special event in life. Dance is an event in which the entire community participates. It is used to prepare the tribe for the hunt, for the agricultural season, or for the celebration of tribal gatherings and, previously, the preparation of war. It is also used in the rites of passage. Whatever the occasion, dance is accompanied by song, the beating of drums, the shaking of rattles, and the playing of sacred flutes. The song may be made up of only a few lines repeated over and over again, or it may tell the story of creation or of the great heroes of the past. Some songs speak of the spirits of animals such as deer or bison. The drumbeat might be nothing more than several people beating on a log with sticks, or it might involve complicated rhythms played on animal skin drums, but the hours of song and steady rhythm are hypnotic. Long hours of dancing in this atmosphere prepare the participants for contact with the spirit world.

Among those tribes whose livelihood depended on hunting, rituals prepared the hunters for their work. Hunting, like agriculture, tended to develop highly religious societies because of its capricious nature. During one season, the hunters would go forth and find an abundance of game, their weapons extremely accurate and effective. In the next season, the same hunters could find game scarce or their weapons virtually useless. Therefore, the spirits of the animals and the hunters themselves, along with their weapons, had to be properly prepared to ensure success. The following is a description of a Pueblo ritual before a hunt:

> One of my most dramatic memories is that of standing in the plaza of a Pueblo, in the dark of a January morning, to watch the Mother of Game bring in the deer. It was almost dawn when we heard the hunter's call from the hillside. Then shadowy forms came bounding down through the pinon trees. At first we could barely see the shaking horns and dappled hides. Then the sun's rays picked out

Oglala Sioux Sun Dance, Pine Ridge Reservation, South Dakota, United States.

(Michael Matthews/Alamy)

men on all fours, with deerskins over their backs and painted staves in their hands to simulate forelegs. They leaped and gamboled before the people while around them pranced little boys who seemed actually to have the spirit of fawns.

In their midst was a beautiful Pueblo woman with long black hair, in all the regalia of white boots and embroidered manta. She was their Owner, the Mother of Game, but she was also Earth Mother, the source of all live things including man. She led the animals where they would be good targets for the hunters, and one by one, they were symbolically killed.[6]

Those persons imitating the game animals in the ceremony were called forth and symbolically killed in the belief that during the actual hunt the real animals would be similarly killed. Because of the identification of a kindred spirit between Native Americans and their game, the ritual of the hunt also included a merciful killing of the animal and festive treatment of its body. For example, there are reports in which hunters apologized to the animal before they killed it. Afterward, the body of the animal was brought back to the tribe and was treated as an honored guest.

The Vision Quest

To gain special power at some point in life, some Native Americans seek visions that put them in contact with the spirit world. Visions are especially sought for young people at the time of puberty. Early in life, children are taught that one day they must go alone into the wilderness and seek a vision of the spirit world. When the time for a **vision quest** arrives, the young person may be sent away from the family and required to live alone until a vision is received. The vision quest is often accompanied by several days of fasting. Usually, the young person on a vision quest lives without food, perhaps without water, and with only the barest of possessions and clothing. This is done to make the individual appear poor and humble before the spirits. Sometimes, the young person's face and body are painted to resemble some special member of the tribe. When the vision comes, the spirits often appear in the guise of animals in a dreamlike or trancelike state. When this happens, the animal becomes the special guardian of the young person, whose name may be changed to include this animal. The animal that appears in the vision is believed to have a close spiritual bond with the young person throughout life. In some Native American societies, there are also spirit animals or beings for clans or other family groups. The vision may also be of a man or a woman. When the vision finally comes, the young person returns to the community as a full member of the group, having moved through this rite of passage.

Visions are sought by Native Americans at other times in life. In the past they were particularly important on the eve of great battles, when extraordinary strength was needed to achieve honors. Visions were also connected with hunting, particularly during the days of the great buffalo hunts in the nineteenth century. Today, they are sought at times of political, economic, or spiritual crisis, and when a person is contemplating a life-changing decision such as marriage, running for a political office, or moving from a rural reservation to an urban area for employment or education.

An example of a communal effort toward achieving visions is the Sun Dance, mentioned earlier, practiced by the people of the Plains. This dance takes place in summer, often at the solstice, when the heat of the sun is near its peak. Participants in the dance seek a vision and an identification with the divine. They gather in a lodge especially built for this purpose. The center of this lodge is a sacred pole, cut from a tree chosen for the dance. The dance usually lasts three days and nights. During this time, the dancers fast and dance continually. On some occasions and among some tribes, the Sun Dance once involved putting thongs through the flesh of the pectoral muscles of the dancers and hanging them from the center pole of the lodge to attach the dancer to the source of the divine. Because it is dangerous to stay too long in the spirit world, the dancers had to free themselves quickly. At times, the thongs tore through the flesh. As painful as this sounds, it apparently inflicted no permanent injury.[7]

Religious Leadership

Native American religions are remarkably free of a priesthood. Although there are those in every tribe who have special connections with the spirit world, basic religious functions are performed by every member of the group. Prayers, dances, songs, and visions are all performed by every member of the tribe, according to each person's need—not by the specialist in religion. Because there is very limited use of sacrifice, there is little need for the trained professional to perform a ritual on behalf of the untrained layperson—a procedure so common in many other religions. Nevertheless, among Native Americans, several categories of religious specialists are used occasionally in encounters with the spirit world.

The specialist most often connected with Native American religions is the so-called medicine man or woman. The designation "medicine man" was given to the functionary by early white settlers because they recognized this person as one who specialized in healing. To the traditional Native American, sickness is caused by the invasion of the body by a foreign object and healing comes about when the foreign body is removed. It is the job of the healer to remove such objects. The medicine man receives power through visions from the spirit world, which give him power over the forces that cause sickness. The spirits may appear after a period of fasting and prayer, or sometimes without any preparation. They usually take the form of a special animal, such as the bear or badger, because these two animals are connected with healing in some Native American religious narrative. The spirits do not take possession of the healer; they only appear and instruct on a frequent basis, perhaps giving a song or instructing in taboos.

Because of this special contact with the spirit world, medicine men and women are empowered to heal, but they can also curse and bring sickness and even death to those who incur their wrath. This power brings a great responsibility to those who are recognized as healers. If medicine men or women encounter a sickness too serious to be healed, they can claim that it is the work of a more powerful person or spirit. But if a number of patients are dying, the healer can be held responsible for the deaths and can even be executed. These beliefs often lead to accusations of sorcery and witchcraft.

The healing process sometimes consists of a sucking ritual. If sickness is caused by the intrusion of a foreign object into the body, it is the healer's job to remove the object. Thus, the healer attempts to literally suck the offensive object or spirit from the body of the sick person. This ritual is often accompanied by songs, dancing, or incantations. At other times, the patient is given various herbs and teas to alleviate pain and induce healing.[8]

A Navajo man constructs a ritual sand painting. These ceremonial artworks often depict scenes from Navajo mythology and are used in various ritual contexts.

Denver Post/Getty Images

A Navajo wedding ceremony.

(Mike Greenlar/The Image Works)

Other Means of Contact with the Spirit World

One of the most common elements of Native American religions is the use of tobacco and the sacred pipe in religious ceremonies. Tobacco smoke, a form of incense, is a link with the spirit world. In the past, tobacco was a part of many ceremonies; it was smoked when people gathered to talk of peace, war, or the hunt, and it was smoked by the medicine man during healing ceremonies.

Tobacco was originally grown and used only for religious purposes by Native Americans. One of the reasons tobacco was reserved for special religious occasions was that it was far too strong to be used more frequently. The tobacco used in religious ceremonies is *Nicotiana rustica*, which is far stronger than the tobacco used in cigarettes. The fumes of this tobacco are so strong they can be intoxicating. Smokers who have tried Indian tobacco marvel that anyone is ever able to smoke the six or more puffs required in Native American ceremonies.

The ritual tobacco is occasionally smoked in cigarettes rolled from corn husks, but it is more frequently smoked in pipes. The bowls of these pipes are made from either clay or stone and the stems from reeds. Sometimes, the most ceremonial of the pipes have stems up to four feet long. They are often decorated with paints and feathers and, in the past, were carried into battle or the hunt as tribal talismans.

The use of **peyote** in Native American religions has received a great deal of attention in recent years. Peyote has been used in religious ceremonies for centuries by the people of Mexico. The practice has spread to North American tribes over the past 100 years.

Peyote is a small, spineless cactus growing in the Rio Grande Valley and southward. It contains nine narcotic alkaloids. In pre-Columbian times, the Aztec, Huichol, and other Mexican Indians ate the plant ceremonially, either in the dried or green state.

Mission Church in Guadalupe, Arizona, a Yaqui community in the Phoenix metropolitan area.

(Mark R. Woodward)

Peyote produces profound sensory and psychic experiences lasting twenty-four hours, a property that led the natives to value and use it religiously.[9] One of the alkaloids found in peyote is mescaline. After a certain quantity of peyote is eaten or ingested in a tea, mescaline produces hallucinations and visions. It is because of these colorful visions that peyote has been made a part of some religious ceremonies. Peyote and related substances are used by healers and others seeking knowledge and experience of the spirit world in many of the native cultures of South and Central America.

Religion and Public Life

With the military defeats and humiliation Native Americans suffered at the hands of the U.S. government at the end of the nineteenth century, some began to turn to peyote ceremonies. Previously, the vision was sought only occasionally—at the rite of passage at puberty, prior to a great hunt or battle, or by the medicine man at crucial points in his life. However, when so little was left to the Native Americans, and when they had been defeated and crowded into reservations, many felt the need for more frequent visions. Therefore, the peyote cult grew and developed rituals. Today, it plays an important role in the religious lives of many Native Americans, particularly in the southwestern United States.[10] In the early part of the twentieth century, there developed an amalgamation of the peyote cult and a form of Christianity. Many Native Americans had been taught the principles of the Christian religion but also appreciated the values of their own religion and peyote. Some reasoned that Christians used wine and a wafer in celebrating communion and Native Americans used the peyote button and tea in communing with the spirit world. In 1918, the **Native American Church**, a group that blended Christianity and the peyote cult, was legally organized in Oklahoma. In 1944, the movement became nationwide and was called the Native American Church of the United States. In 1950, it expanded to include Canadian Indians and was called the Native American Church of North America. Currently, it is estimated that this religious movement has about 225,000 members. Members of the Native American Church differ considerably about the importance of Jesus and the Bible. Extreme traditionalists are concerned almost exclusively with traditional beliefs and practices. On the other end of the continuum are church members for whom Christianity is of central importance. The entire range of viewpoints may be found in a single community. There is an unspoken rule that one does not criticize the views of other church members. Many members of the Native American Church refer to peyote as medicine and are convinced that it helps them to cope with and heal from the psychological wounds brought on by war, domestic violence, and alcohol and drug abuse. The use of peyote in Native American religions has had a running battle with the various courts of the United States. In the early part of the twentieth century, peyote was outlawed by many states because it was considered a narcotic. In 1990, the U.S. Supreme Court upheld state laws that banned the use of peyote in Native American Church rituals. Many Native Americans felt that restrictions on their use of peyote in religious ceremonies violated constitutional guaranties of freedom of religion.[11] An amendment to the Native American Religious Freedom Act passed by Congress in 1994 now permits the use of the substance in Native American ceremonies. The government of Mexico has placed the cactus on an endangered species list and has prohibited its export.

Death and Life after Death

2.4. **Describe death and life after death in Native American religious practice.**

In discussing the beliefs of the Native Americans about death and life after death, we must be reminded again that we are discussing a great variety of people who lived in various climates and had diverse cultural systems. Therefore, attitudes toward death and practices regarding death vary widely. Furthermore, Native Americans have been exposed to Christian eschatology for more than 400 years. It is difficult to distinguish the original Native American view of the dead from the view that has evolved in response to Christianity. Therefore, one can no more speak of the Native American concept of life after death than one can speak of the Native American religion; one can only generalize.

As we have noted, some groups of Native Americans tend to fear the dead and handle them with great care lest they return and somehow trouble the living. Many of the most serious taboos of Native American life are built around the treatment of the dead. Yet despite the fear of the dead, there is apparently little fear of death itself. Missionaries, anthropologists, and other observers have noted again and again the remarkable lack of fear demonstrated by Native American people when facing death.

Generally, many Native Americans have believed in two souls, neither of which could be considered immortal. One soul is the life, or breath, that accompanies the body. When the body dies, or at least when it decays, this soul also dies. The second soul is what might be called a free soul. This soul wanders about during dreams or leaves the body during sickness. After death, this free soul goes to the land of the dead. Little is said about this land of the dead; sometimes it is considered a happy place, and sometimes it is a place of sadness. Often, the land of the dead seems to be a continuation of this current life but on another plane of existence. Most descriptions of the land of the dead seem to indicate that all go to this land. There is no heaven for those who have been righteous and no hell for those who have been wicked.

Some attempt to aid the deceased in the journey to the land of the dead by burying food and drink with the body. In the past this was sometimes carried further when an important person died. An attempt was made to send along a guide to aid the deceased in finding the land of the dead. Sometimes an animal was killed to act as guide, and on other occasions, an enemy was killed for the same purpose. Among the Natchez people of Mississippi, when a great chieftain died, large numbers of wives, children, friends, and animals were sacrificed to accompany the dead.[12]

When the free soul reaches the land of the dead, it does not necessarily live forever. Perhaps, like the Hebrews' concept of Sheol or the Greeks' idea of Hades, traditional Native Americans believe that the soul exists in the land of the dead only as long as the person is remembered by the living. When the person begins to be forgotten, the free soul begins to fade and eventually disappears.

Occasionally, among Native Americans, references are made to a belief in reincarnation. Sometimes an infant resembles a deceased relative in some fashion, and it is believed that the ancestor might have returned to live again. However, this feature is missing from most Native American religions. There seems to be no widespread belief in reincarnation. Neither is there an emphasis on ancestors in the manner of the Chinese.

Native American Religions Today

2.5. **Discuss Native American religions and religious practice in today's world.**

With the arrival of European settlers and their religions, Native American cultures have undergone severe stress. In what is now the United States, there were many wars as European settlers moved east from the Atlantic coast and north from Mexico. The last of these, and one of the most tragic, was the consequence of white Americans' fear of the **Ghost Dance** religion. By 1890, when the movement began, many Native American peoples had been forced onto reservations. The buffalo on which Plains tribes had formerly depended had nearly vanished. Many faced starvation because the U.S. government had failed to deliver the supplies it had promised. The Ghost Dance movement began among the Paiute of Nevada and rapidly spread across the Great Plains. The Ghost Dance religion combined elements of Native American religions, including visions, song, and dance, and Christianity. Wovoka, the founder of the movement, believed that he had been visited by Christ, who had taught him songs and dances and foretold the destruction of the white people and the return of the ancestors and the buffalo.

In what is now South Dakota, many of the Lakota people believed that the "ghost shirts" worn by the dancers would protect them from army bullets. On December 29, 1890, units of the U.S. Army 7th Calvary attempted to disarm a band of Lakota at Wounded Knee. A single shot rang out, after which the soldiers used machine guns in a massacre of men, women, and children. As many as 350 Native Americans died. To this day, the Lakota and other Native American peoples have not forgotten what transpired at Wounded Knee.

One of the first acts of European American settlers was to seek to convert Native Americans to Christianity. This movement has continued, with varying degrees of success, for more than five centuries. Governments often supported missionaries, thinking that the conversion to Christianity would help to pacify groups opposed to European encroachment on their territory. Some forms of Christianity insist on an all-or-nothing conversion. For native people, this meant that to become Christian they had to turn their backs on their former religion and culture. Other forms of Christianity are more open to native customs and, at least to some extent, religious ideas. The influence of Christianity has been so strong that today most Native Americans are Christians. But Native American Christianity is as complex and variable as the cultures in which it is found. Some Native Americans have almost completely adopted the European style of Christianity. Others have added Christian symbols and myths to native religions. Most Native Americans would probably place themselves between these two extremes.

Many traditional practices and beliefs are continued even by those Native Americans who consider themselves devout Christians. A belief in the power of spirits to cause illness, and of medicine men and women to cure it, is found even in the most urbanized Native American communities. On many reservations, curing combines Native American and biomedical treatment. In hospitals on the Apache reservation in the White Mountains of Arizona, two types of medical practitioners exist. Medical doctors and nurses work by day; by night medicine men and women, many of whom outwardly function as custodians and support staff, perform traditional healing rituals. In many cases, this combination of healing practices is seen as cooperation rather than competition. Increasingly, medical specialists from both traditions have come to respect the healing powers of one another.

Many Native American Christians celebrate Christian holy days in very traditional ways. This is particularly true of Good Friday and Easter, which celebrate the death and resurrection of Jesus Christ. Throughout South and Central America and the western United States, Holy Week is celebrated with Native American song and dance. Among the Yaqui of Arizona and northern Mexico, Jesus Christ is often associated with the deer because both represent a sacrifice so humans may live and prosper. Many modern Native American songs speak of characters from Bible stories as well as native spirits. Visions of Jesus Christ and his mother, the Virgin Mary, are common in many Native American communities.

Some Native Americans have incorporated elements of Christianity and even missionaries into their own traditions. This practice helps to explain the appeal of the Church of Jesus Christ of Latter-day Saints (Mormons) to Native Americans. Mormons believe that Native Americans are the children of the lost tribes of Israel and that Jesus Christ preached in the Americas during the period between his crucifixion and resurrection. This enables some Native Americans to understand Jesus and Christianity as being less foreign. Other Native Americans understand the God of Christianity as being similar to the traditional High God. Christian ritual also can be understood in native terms. In the 1930s, missionaries on the Lakota (Sioux) reservations often observed that hymns were the most effective means of drawing Native Americans to the church. Perhaps it was the Native American belief in the power of song and dance that attracted them to mission churches. Missionaries and their children were often given native names, carrying them into both the community and the spirit world.

In recent decades, traditional Native American religions have experienced both revival and change. Numerous groups have reasserted the values of native culture, including religion. These groups teach that traditional ways are better for Native Americans than those of other cultures. Therefore, there is a resurgence of interest in the study and practice of traditional religion. There are also new developments, including intertribal dances and ceremonies based on aspects of Native American tradition shared by more than a single tribe. These ceremonies reflect and help build a growing sense of Native American cultural identity that transcends tribal boundaries.

There also is a growing interest in Native American arts and religion among non-native peoples, particularly those attracted to "New Age" philosophies and religious movements. Native Americans have mixed reactions to this. Many welcome the growing recognition of the universal value of their traditions. Others are concerned that traditional knowledge, objects, and rituals will fall into the hands of non-native people who do not fully understand or appreciate them. This concern has led some Native American artists to make minor changes in traditional music performed or recorded for non-native audiences and to produce works of art that reflect Native American values and symbols that are, from the perspective of Native American religious traditions, secular in nature.[13]

Think About It

1. Describe the various ways different Native American groups understand the spirit world.

2. Give several examples of Native American reverence for the natural world.

3. Briefly describe Native American religious practices.

4. What are some of the attitudes toward death and practices regarding death among the diverse Native American cultural systems?

5. How have Christianity and contact with non-native cultures influenced the development of Native American religions?

Suggested Reading

Craven, Margaret. *I Heard the Owl Call My Name.* New York: Dell, 1973.

Deloria, Vine. *God Is Red.* New York: Grosset & Dunlap, 1973.

DeMallie, Raymond J., and Douglas R. Parks, eds. *Sioux Indian Religion.* Norman: University of Oklahoma Press, 1987.

Hultkrantz, Ake. *Belief and Worship in Native North America.* Syracuse, N.Y.: Syracuse University Press, 1981.

La Barre, Weston. *The Peyote Cult.* New York: Schocken Books, 1969.

Martin, Joel W. *The Land Looks after Us: A History of Native American Religion.* New York: Oxford University Press, 2000.

McLuhan, T. C. *Touch the Earth.* New York: Outerbridge & Dienstfrey, 1971.

Silko, Leslie. *Ceremony.* New York: Penguin, 2006. This is a novel about the struggle of a Native American veteran returning to reservation life.

Underhill, Ruth M. *Red Men's Religion.* Chicago: University of Chicago Press, 1965.

Wenger, Tisa. *We Have a Religion: The 1920s Pueblo Indian Dance Controversy and American Religious Freedom.* Chapel Hill: University of North Carolina Press, 2009.

Source Material

Native American Myths

The following materials demonstrate the perspective on nature held by some Native American religions. The first is the story of a divine visitor to a Sioux tribe and shows the reverence for nature that is an integral part of these religions.[14]

Sioux Legend of the Buffalo Maiden

Braided sweet grass was dipped into a buffalo horn containing rain water and was offered to the Maiden. The chief said, "Sister, we are now ready to hear the good message you have brought." The pipe, which was in the hands of the Maiden, was lowered and placed on the rack. Then the Maiden sipped the water from the sweet grass.

Then, taking up the pipe again, she arose and said: "My relatives, brothers, and sisters: Wakan Tanka has looked down, and smiles upon us this day because we have met as belonging to one family. The best thing in a family is good feeling towards every member of the family. I am proud to become a member of your family—a sister to you all. The sun is your grandfather, and he is the same to me. Your tribe has the distinction of being always very faithful to promises, and of possessing great respect and reverence towards sacred things. It is known also that nothing but good feeling prevails in the tribe, and that whenever any member has been found guilty of committing any wrong, that member has been cast out and not allowed to mingle with the other members of the tribe. For all these good qualities in the tribe you have been chosen as worthy and deserving of all good gifts. I represent the Buffalo tribe, who have sent you this pipe. You are to receive this pipe in the name of all the common people (Indians). Take it, and use it according to my directions.

The bowl of the pipe is red stone—a stone not very common and found only at a certain place. This pipe shall be used as a peacemaker. The time will come when you shall cease hostilities against other nations. Whenever peace is agreed upon between two tribes or parties this pipe shall be a binding instrument. By this pipe the medicine men shall be called to administer help to the sick."

Turning to the women, she said:

"My dear sisters, the women: You have a hard life to live in this world, yet without you this life would not be what it is. Wakan Tanka intends that you shall bear much sorrow—comfort others in time of sorrow. By your hands the family moves. You have been given the knowledge of making clothes and feeding the family. Wakan Tanka is with you in your sorrows and joins you in your griefs. He has given you the great gift of kindness towards every living creature on earth. You he has chosen to have a feeling for the dead who are gone. He knows that you remember the dead longer than do the men. He knows that you love your children dearly."

Then turning to the children:

"My little brothers and sisters. Your parents were once little children like you, but in the course of time they became men and women. All living creatures were once small, but if no one took care of them they would never grow up. Your parents love you and have made many sacrifices for your sake in order that Wakan Tanka may listen to them, and that nothing but good may come to you as you grow up. I have brought this pipe for them, and you shall reap some benefit from it. Learn to respect and reverence this pipe, and above all, lead pure lives. Wakan Tanka is your great-grandfather."

Turning to the men:

"Now, my dear brothers: In giving you this pipe you are expected to use it for nothing but good purposes. The tribe as a whole shall depend upon it for their necessary needs. You realize that all your necessities of life come from the earth below, the sky above, and the four winds. Whenever you do anything wrong against these elements they will always take some revenge upon you. You should reverence them. Offer sacrifices through this pipe. When you are in need of buffalo meat, smoke this pipe and ask for what you need and it shall be granted you. On you it depends to be a strong help to the women in the raising of children. Share the women's sorrow. Wakan Tanka smiles on the man who has a kind feeling for a woman because the woman is weak. Take this pipe, and offer it to Wakan Tanka daily. Be good and kind to the little children."

Turning to the chief:

"My older brother: You have been chosen by these people to receive this pipe in the name of the whole Sioux tribe. Wakan Tanka is pleased and glad this day because you have done what is required and expected that every good leader should do. By this pipe the tribe shall live. It is your duty to see that this pipe is respected and reverenced. I am proud to be called a sister. May Wakan Tanka look down on us and take pity on us and provide us with what we need. Now we shall smoke the pipe."

Then she took the buffalo chip which lay on the ground, lighted the pipe, and pointing to the sky with the stem of the pipe, she said, "I offer this to Wakan Tanka for all the good that comes from above." (Pointing to the earth:) "I offer this to the earth, whence come all good gifts." (Pointing to the cardinal points:) "I offer this to the four winds, whence come all good things." Then she took a puff of the pipe, passed it to the chief, and said, "Now my dear brothers and sisters, I have done the work for which I was sent here and now I will go, but I do not wish any escort. I only ask that the way be cleared before me."

Then, rising, she started, leaving the pipe with the chief, who ordered that the people be quiet until their sister was out of sight. She came out of the tent on the left side, walking very slowly; as soon as she was outside the entrance she turned into a white buffalo calf.

Wooing Wohpe

One of the best-loved myths of the American Plains people is the story of Wooing Wohpe. Wohpe is the beautiful woman who mediates between the worlds of the human and the divine. The story of her relationship to the Four Winds describes the founding of the four directions.[15]

Before the world, the South Wind, and the North Wind, and the West Wind, and the East Wind, dwelt together in the far north in the land of the ghosts.

They were brothers. The North Wind was the oldest. He was always cold and stern. The West Wind was the next to oldest. He was always strong and noisy. The East Wind was the middle in age and he was always cross and disagreeable. The South Wind was the next to the youngest and he was always pleasant. With them dwelt a little brother, the Whirlwind. He was always full of fun and frolic.

The North Wind was a great hunter and he delighted in killing things. The South Wind delighted in making things. The West Wind was helper of his brother the South Wind and sometimes he helped his brother the North Wind.

The East Wind was lazy and good for nothing.

The little Whirlwind never had to do anything so he played all the time and danced and made sport for his brothers.

After a long time a beautiful being fell from the stars. Her hair was like the light and her dress was red and green and white and blue, and all the colors; and she had decorations and ornaments of all colors.

As she was falling, she met the five brothers and begged them to give her some place to rest.

They took pity on her and invited her into their tipi.

When she came into the tipi, everything was bright and pleasant and all were happy, so all the four brothers wanted her, each for his woman.

So each asked her to be his woman.

She told them that she was pleased with their tipi and would be the woman of the one who did that which pleased her the most.

So the North Wind went hunting and brought to her his game.

But everything he brought turned to ice as soon as he laid it before her.

So that when he laid his presents before her, the tipi was dark and cold and everything was dreary.

Then the West Wind brought his drum and sang and danced before her, but he made so much noise and disturbed things so much that the tipi fell down and she had hard work to put it up again.

Then the East Wind sat down by her and talked to her so much foolishness that she felt like crying.

Then the South Wind made things for her and they were all beautiful so that she was happy and the tipi was warm and bright.

So she said she would be the South Wind's woman.

This made the North Wind very angry, for he claimed that he was the oldest and should have the being by a right.

But the South Wind would not give her up.

So the North and South Winds quarreled all the time about her and finally the South Wind said to his woman that they would go away so that they might live in peace. They started to go away but the North Wind tried to steal her. When she found what the North Wind was trying to do, she took off her dress and spread it out and got under it to hide. So when the North Wind came to the dress, he thought that he had found the beautiful being and he embraced it but everything on it grew hard and cold and icy. He heard the South Wind coming and he fled back to his tipi. . . .

Then the South Wind followed on the trail of the North Wind until he came to the tipi where he found him boasting to the other brothers of what he had done.

The South Wind went in and reproached his brother and they quarreled and finally fought and the North Wind was about to conquer when the West Wind helped the South Wind and they conquered the North Wind. He could not be killed so they bound his feet and hands and left him in the tipi.

The other brothers all sided with the South Wind and determined to live no longer with the North Wind.

So the West Wind went to live where the sun sets and the East Wind went to live where the sun rises and the South Wind went to the opposite of where the North Wind's tipi is, as far as he could go.

The little Whirlwind was too small to have a tipi by himself so he went to live with the South Wind the most of the time, but he was to live with the West Wind sometimes. But the East Wind was so lazy and disagreeable that he would not even visit him. . . .

Thus began the warfare between the brothers which has lasted ever since, to the present time.

Chapter 3
African Religions

Learning Objectives

After reading this chapter, you should be able to:

3.1 Identify the religions originating in Africa.

3.2 Name the non-native African religions.

3.3 Talk about African religions today.

A Timeline of African Religions

TENS OF THOUSANDS OF YEARS OF ORAL TRADITION

1st and 2nd centuries C.E.	Christianity arrives in North Africa
7th century	Islam comes to North Africa
1501–1807	Atlantic slave trade brings tradition of African religions to the Americas
1886	Africa divided among European colonial powers
19th century–present	Large-scale conversion to Christianity and Islam in sub-Saharan Africa
20th century–present	Development of indigenous African Christianities
1960s–1980s	African countries gain independence
1971	Many in Rhodesia believe ancestral spirits aid in independence struggle
1984	Archbishop Desmond Tutu of South Africa awarded the Nobel Peace Prize

Key Terms

African-initiated churches	**lesser spirits**
ajwaka	**Nuer**
High God	*orishas*
Kwoth Nhial	**Yoruba**

Africa is the second-largest continent. It is home to nearly 3,000 ethnic and linguistic groups and a total of over 700 million people. Traditional African societies range from small nomadic bands living deep in the tropical forest and the deserts of North and South Africa to large-scale kingdoms and empires. Because so many Africans were brought to the Americas as slaves and struggled for many centuries to regain freedom and dignity, African religions have had an influence that extends far beyond the continent's borders. In the nineteenth and early twentieth centuries, most of Africa came under European colonial rule. During the last fifty years, colonial regimes have given way to independent nations, but colonialism's effects remain. The new nations of Africa have become a vocal and active segment of the developing world. Many of them control raw materials vital to the industrialized world. At the same time, poverty and disease are widespread, and many African nations are torn by civil war. Understanding African religions is an essential factor in understanding the multifaceted history and modern challenges of Africa. It is also important for understanding the history and cultures of people around the world—but especially in the Americas and the Caribbean—who are descended from African slaves. Therefore, a basic understanding of African religions will provide knowledge of customs and attitudes toward the family, society at large, the environment, and death and the life beyond.

Perhaps no religions have been more confused in the minds of Western people as those of Africa. Western perceptions and understandings of African religions and cultures have been limited by two quite different stereotypes that have more to do with Western ethnic and racial politics than with the realities of African civilizations. The first presents Africa as a land of savagery and superstition, and has been used all too often to justify white racism and the mistreatment of African and African American people. The other stereotype is more positive but unfortunately no less inaccurate. It values African symbols, literature, and art but treats this vast continent as a unified whole. Although this positive stereotype has helped to combat older, negative images of Africa, it contributes very little to the understanding of Africa, its peoples, and its cultures. Both of these images are based on a combination of half-truths and fertile imaginations. To arrive at a genuine understanding of the richness of African civilizations and their contributions to the world, it is necessary to overcome both of these stereotypes.

A feature of religion in African countries today is that the vast majority of people on the continent practice some form of Christianity or Islam. Christians have lived in Africa since the years shortly after the life of Jesus in the first century C.E. Likewise, Muslims have been active in many African countries since the late seventh century. Both religions are flourishing in Africa, and Christianity especially has experienced exponential growth in many regions of the continent since the demise of European colonial oversight. Religions that originated among African peoples are today often practiced alongside Christianity and Islam. Sometimes this creates tension; in other instances, people find ways to integrate their complex religious identities.

Religions Originating in Africa

3.1. **Identify the religions originating in Africa.**

When discussing African religions, we cannot speak with authority about a single religion, theology, worldview, or ritual system. Africa is a huge continent with many varied and ancient cultures. For many years, most of what was known about traditional African religions had been collected by European and American anthropologists and missionaries. Today African scholars and writers as well as African religious practitioners are more and more active in the study and documentation of their own traditions. These African voices help to provide a more balanced and accurate picture of the religious lives of African peoples. As we have come to understand the richness and diversity of African cultures, it has become increasingly clear that the religious beliefs and customs of one group of Africans are not necessarily shared by others. Even when we speak of the basic concepts of these religions, we must keep in mind that these ideas are not universally shared or evenly distributed throughout the continent. There is a great variety of beliefs and practices in African tradition. As in the previous chapter about Native American religions, we have chosen to discuss features of African religions that are generally shared across many different religious traditions in Africa rather than focus on one or two specific African-origin religions.

The High God

The belief that there is a supreme **High God** who created the world and then withdrew from active participation in it is common in several religions around the world. This belief is shared by many African people. Although most African religions recognize multiple gods in day-to-day practice, there is a common belief that beyond all of the minor gods, goddesses, spirits, and ancestors there is one High God who created and in some sense still governs the universe.

In many African religions the High God appears as a creator who did his work and retired to a distant place. It is often believed that he has little contact with the world and its daily operation, although he may be appealed to at times of great crisis. The **Yoruba** story of Olorun is typical of African understandings of this High God. The Yoruba live in the West African nation of Nigeria.[1] In Yoruba mythology, the High God, Olorun, gave the job of creating the world to his eldest son, Obatala. This son failed to complete the task, so Olorun passed it on to the younger son, Odudua—but he too failed. Therefore Olorun had to complete the work of creation himself. He assigned tasks of creation to various *orishas*, the name for deities under Olurun's direction in the Yoruba pantheon. After the work of creation was done, Olorun seems to have retired to the heavens with little interest in, or control of, his universe. Although various Yoruba villages have special *orishas* who have saved them or helped them in times of trouble, there is no record that Olorun ever has been of direct assistance. He remains detached from the problems of the world and allows the *orishas* to intervene when necessary.

The **Nuer** of the Sudan and South Sudan provide a striking exception to the retiring nature of the High God. The Nuer believe that the High God, known as **Kwoth Nhial**, or the spirit of the sky, continues to play an active role in the lives of human beings. He is the guardian of moral law, punishing those who do evil and rewarding those who uphold the moral virtues of Nuer society. He is believed to love and care for

Santería is a religion practiced in Cuba and other parts of the Americas that can trace its roots to the Yoruba religion. Here, worshipers in Havana dance in a ceremony to the orishas Obatala and Oshun.

his creation and is asked for blessings and assistance during troubled times and prior to dangerous undertakings such as battles.

Few African people focus as much attention on the High God as the Nuer do. Most Africans regard the High God as too distant and too great to pay much attention to the prayers and petitions of human beings. It is the **lesser spirits** and the ancestors who receive the greatest attention in African religions. Even among the Nuer there is a host of lesser deities known to them as the "children of God."

The Lesser Spirits

When we move beyond tales of the High God that are found in many African religions, we encounter spirit-based faiths. Like many other peoples, most Africans believe that the universe is populated by spirits as well as humans and animals. The Earth, the sky, and the waters are believed to contain spiritual or life forces similar to that of humankind. These forces can be beneficial or harmful. In either case they are subject to prayer, flattery, and sacrifice. Because they have a direct influence on human life, African people try to understand the spirits and seek their favor.

Spirits or life forces are present in the mountains, forest, pools, streams, and many plants and animals. They are also found in storms, thunder, lightning, tides, and other forces of nature. They can be female or male. In some African cultures there are temples and priests dedicated to the worship of storm gods. The Earth is also worshiped. As in ancient Europe and many other traditional cultures, the Earth is often pictured as a goddess and associated with fertility. Among the Ashanti people, for example, there are regular ceremonies for the Earth Mother in which the following prayer is recited:

From the Source

Earth, while I am yet alive,
It is upon you that I put my trust
Earth who receives my body,

We are addressing you,
And you will understand.[3]

Water is often seen as a sacred element. Water is used in religious ritual the world over and is particularly sacred and important in many basic religions, including those of Africa. When the life of a people depends on water in the form of rainfall, rivers, streams, and lakes, it often appears to have a life of its own. When Africans use water for religious rituals such as the washing of the newborn and the dead, the water must come from a source of *sacred, living water*, such as a river or a spring. It must not be heated or boiled, or in modern times treated with chemicals, because that would kill the spirit or power in it. Because snakes are often connected with bodies of water, they too are regarded with awe and are sometimes worshiped as powerful spiritual forces.

Even though nature gods, goddesses, and lesser spirits are not always major elements of African religions, they are recognized and worshiped in most traditional African religions. Their worship varies from elaborate systems of temples, priests, and rituals to less formal worship conducted by individuals and family groups. Perhaps the most common form of worship of these lesser spirits is an offering of food or drink. An African who wishes to acknowledge the spirits or ask them for

Yoruba Epa mask as worn by a dancing figure. The Yoruba are a tribal people living in West Africa (Nigeria, Dahomey).

(Marsha van der Heyden/Pearson Education/PH College)

help will often pour water, wine, beer, or milk on the ground. When more elaborate offerings are required the spirits may be presented with elaborate meals accompanied by singing and dancing. In general they are treated with signs of honor and respect similar to those with which important and powerful people are treated.

The worship of the Yoruba goddess Osun provides an illustration of the ways in which these elements are combined in a major African religion. Osun is one of the most important female *orishas* and is described as a powerful, beautiful, and graceful goddess. She is a strong mother and the guardian of the life force responsible for the fertility of the land and the birth of children. She is worshiped by women and men at an annual ceremony that includes music, dance, and offerings of food and drink. The worshipers celebrate the power of the goddess and her ability to bestow health and fertility on her devotees.[4]

Ancestors

The most commonly recognized spiritual forces in African religions are ancestors. Many Africans believe that departed family members continue to live in the spirit world and that the ancestors, unlike the High God, take an active interest in the well-being of those who live in this world. The ancestors are thought of as being part of a "Cloud of Witnesses." They are believed to watch the spectacle of life and actively participate in the affairs of the living. They can help a person, a family, and even a nation if they wish. Ancestors are often consulted before the birth of a child, at the beginning of the agricultural season, and even prior to battles or political conflicts. In some areas no one may eat the first fruit of the harvest before a portion of it has been offered to the ancestors.

It is the ancestors' ability to harm as well as to help that makes them such a potent force in many African religions. Although it is common in many Asian nations to revere and respect ancestors, many Africans are also often afraid of them because they are often capricious and unpredictable. In this way they are much like other powerful people. Despite all of the offerings and respect that they are given, ancestors may turn on a person or even a community. They are often believed to be the causes of famines, droughts, earthquakes, and other natural disasters. They are thought to cause sickness and even death. One of the worst misfortunes that can befall a couple among some African groups is childlessness; it is often thought to be caused by the anger of the ancestors. Because respect for and fear of the dead is a basic part of African consciousness, it is the ancestors, rather than the gods, who are believed to enforce social and moral codes.

Because many people believe that the ancestors are the actual owners of the land and its products, it is not uncommon for Africans to offer gifts and sacrifices to them. At harvest time, rural people make large offerings to them. When new animals are born, some must be slaughtered and offered to the ancestors to ensure continued blessings. Urban Africans continue these traditions, often returning to their native villages to make offerings to their ancestors or finding homes for them in urban places.

Ancestors communicate with the living in a variety of ways, most often in dreams. At times the message of the dream is clear and direct, but at other times the dreamer must seek the help of a diviner or other religious specialist to understand it. The ancestors might send signs that can be seen in nature or in the organs of sacrificial animals. Diviners who can recognize and explain these signs play important roles in many African religions.

Sometimes, ancestors use more direct means to communicate with the living. Among the Tallensi of northern Ghana, there is a story of a young man named Pu-eng-yii who left his own family and settled with a rival group to earn more wealth. By doing this he cut himself off from his ancestors as well as his family, offending them both. In his search for wealth, Pu-eng-yii suffered a serious leg injury in an automobile accident. When he asked a diviner about the cause of the accident he was told that his ancestors were angry. Actually, they had intended to kill him but had failed to follow through with their plan. The diviner told Pu-eng-yii that he must make restitution to his family and his ancestors and cut his ties with his adopted family. The unfortunate man gave in to these demands, returned to his own family, and offered the proper sacrifices because he feared death.[5]

Diviners who have the ability to contact the ancestors are often asked to inquire about the future. Not only do the ancestors know about what is happening among the living in the present, they also know what the future will bring and are believed to have the power to influence it. Therefore, Africans often consult the ancestors before special events ranging from building a house to fighting a war.

Sacrifice

African religions usually include rituals and sacrifices that seek to honor or appease gods, goddesses, and ancestors, and provide safe and proper transition through the various stages of life. Sacrifice and ritual smooth these transitions and provide a point of communion between humans and the spirit world. Perhaps the most common rituals in African religions are daily offerings to the gods, goddesses, and ancestors. As a display of recognition to the deities and ancestors, those who live in this world pour out a bit of their drink or toss away bits of their food. These simple ritual acts are believed to maintain good relationships with the spirits and ancestors who play such important roles in the daily lives of many African people.

Some African religions practice animal sacrifice for particular occasions or for specific needs. The blood of animals such as dogs, birds, sheep, goats, and cattle is poured on the ground to placate deities when they are angry or to ensure their support in some difficult period. Blood sacrifices may be offered when a community is preparing for a battle or, in modern African nations, for an election campaign; when there has been a long drought; or in times of illness. In modern times, the Yoruba god Ogun, who was for centuries described as the god of iron, has become known as the god of automobiles and trucks. Drivers engaged in the all-too-often deadly business of operating motor vehicles on unsafe roads and streets offer dogs to him and decorate cars and trucks with his symbols. His protection is sought for other iron objects as well, as this sacrificial song illustrates:

From the Source

Ogun, here are Ehun's kola nuts;
He rides a bicycle,
He cultivates with a matchet,
He fells trees with an axe,

Do not let Ehun meet your anger this year,
Take care of him,
He comes this year,
Enable him to come next season.[6]

Often, on the occasion of animal sacrifice, the worshiper shares the flesh of the animal with the deity or ancestor to whom it is offered. After the blood of the animal has been poured on the ground or an altar, the meat is roasted or boiled. A portion is given to the deity by placing it on the altar, and another portion is eaten by the person who brought the sacrifice and his or her family. This establishes a communion between the living and the spirits and is an expression of the almost universal human belief that eating together establishes a social or spiritual bond.

Religion and Public Life

One question facing many Africans is to what extent traditional practices, customs, and beliefs can or should interact with the religions of Christianity and Islam. In many regions in Africa that are now predominantly Christian or Muslim, there remain strong traditions of ancestor veneration, sacrificial rituals, and other aspects of religious devotion that originate in one or more African religions. Problems can sometimes arise due to the fact that both Christianity and Islam are doctrinally exclusive, which is to say that converts to these religions are often expected to leave behind practices from other religions. Nevertheless, in a recent survey carried out in nineteen sub-Saharan African nations, people in twelve of those nations reported that between one-fifth and one-third of the population owns traditional African sacred objects like amulets, skeletons, feathers, or carved figures. Likewise, up to one-half of the population in many of the countries under study holds traditional African religious beliefs and participates in traditional rituals or visits traditional healers.[7]

Rites of Passage

In almost all societies, important points on the pathway of life are marked and celebrated with ritual. These passage points are most often birth, puberty, marriage, and death. In societies where religion is a major force in social life, there is often no clear distinction between the secular and the religious. In Africa, and in many other religious societies, rites of passage are usually regulated by religious practices and functionaries.

Of course, the first rite of passage involves the birth of children. In many African societies, including the Ashanti, children are not named or given much consideration for the first week of life. Because of the high infant mortality rate, it is considered unwise for a family to become too attached to what might be a ghost child who has come to trick them into loving it. These concerns unfortunately persist because colonial powers did little to establish adequate health care systems. If the baby lives through the first week or so of life, it is considered to be a real human baby, and attention and joy are lavished on it. At this point, the baby is named. In some cases a lengthy process of divination may be used to choose a proper name for the child. Other African people recite the names of ancestors until the child makes a motion or gesture of recognition. In this manner, the names of the ancestors are kept alive.

The ceremony of naming is often followed by showing the child to the moon. The Gu people of Benin throw their children gently into the air several times, instructing them to look at the moon. The Basuto of South Africa lift their children toward the moon and say, "There is your father's sister."[8] Some African people practice male circumcision at birth, but most wait until puberty.

A Fulani wedding in northern Burkina Faso. Friends and family of the bride carry her gifts and possessions to her new home.

(Irene Abdou/Alamy)

During childhood, young Africans receive instruction in their roles in society as well as training in agriculture, crafts, and increasingly modern education. As they approach puberty, instruction in the norms of social behavior becomes more intensive. Special classes are established separately for boys and girls in which they are taught how to behave as proper young men and women. They are also prepared for the initiation rituals that mark the passage from childhood to adult life. For boys, these rites may involve harsh physical trials including whipping and fasting designed to test their courage and resourcefulness. During these rituals they learn about the religion, myths, and morality of their people. Among some African groups, girls are secluded in special houses and encouraged to eat a great deal and grow plump to make them more attractive as brides. Both boys and girls receive special training in what is considered to be proper sexual behavior and conduct. These puberty rites and initiations may take a few days or several years. In recent years their length and severity have declined because of the opposition of modern governments, the decline in the power of traditional village elders, and the desire of many parents that their children receive as much modern education as possible.

Puberty rites for boys often include ritual circumcision. No one seems to know where or when this practice began, but it is widely practiced in Africa and many other parts of the world. Because circumcision is performed at puberty without any form of anesthetic, it is often regarded as a test of courage. The initiate is expected to endure the operation without crying out, flinching, or showing other signs of pain. Among some African people, the operation is performed by a man wearing a mask who represents the ancestors. This indicates that circumcision may provide a bodily sign of religious and cultural identity as it does for Jews and Muslims throughout the world.

Female circumcision is practiced by some African people, but there is growing opposition to it both among Africans with modern education and the international human rights and feminist communities. As with male circumcision, there seems to be no clear reason for the practice, although it is sometimes described as a means of controlling erotic desire.[9] The severity of both male and female circumcision varies greatly. It ranges from very small cuts that pose no serious health threat to the initiate to extreme forms of genital mutilation that can be life-threatening, particularly when performed in unsanitary conditions.

After puberty rites and initiation, young people are considered to be adults and are expected to assume both the responsibilities and privileges of adult life. One of the first of these adult roles is marriage. In many African societies, marriage is more of a secular contract between the families involved than an explicitly religious arrangement. Polygamy is practiced by the elites of many traditional African societies. Frequently, a husband is forbidden sexual contact with his wife during pregnancy and for as long as she is nursing a child. Because this can often be for as long as two years, it is considered wise for a man who can afford it to have several wives living in separate houses. There are also occasional instances of polyandry, in which one woman is the wife of several brothers.

As in most societies, death is surrounded with a great deal of ritual. The purpose of death rituals is to make the newly dead as comfortable as possible in their new existence so that they will not return to haunt the living. Many steps are taken during and after burial to prevent the dead from returning to their villages, homes, and families. Women fear that their husbands will return as ghosts and cause their wombs to die, making them infertile.

Because of the warm climate of much of Africa, the dead are buried as quickly as possible. On rare occasions, there are attempts to embalm or mummify the bodies of great leaders, such as kings. Money, trinkets, tools, and weapons are buried with the body to make life in the next world as comfortable as possible.

In this Mami Wata healing ceremony, a priestess sacrifices a chicken to the *orisha* Ogun in Cotonou, Benin, West Africa.

In some African societies it is believed that illness, misfortune, and death never "just happen" but are caused by witchcraft or foul play of some kind. In the past, the dead were allowed to identify the person or persons who caused their deaths. Often, corpses would seem to point out the house of the killer or fall from the backs of bearers as they passed the guilty party. Persons accused in this way had to find some means of proving their innocence.

African religions generally do not have a system of eschatology or concepts of judgment and retribution after death. The dead simply move into the world of the spirits and continue to be interested in and effective among the living. Death rituals transform living humans into sacred ancestors. An exception to this is the belief of the LoDagaa people of Ghana. According to their religion, the departed person takes a long journey toward the land of the ancestors. Just before this land is reached, there is a river. A waiting ferryman must be paid to take the deceased across the river. If the deceased has led a good life, the crossing will be easy. If the deceased has been wicked, she or he must swim across the river. This takes three years. People who have debts must wait on the bank until their creditors arrive to be paid. Once the deceased is in the land of the dead, there are further tests and ordeals in which the person's lifetime deeds play a great part. Those who suffer because they are judged to have been evil ask the great god: "Why do you make us suffer?" God replies, "Because you sinned on Earth." And they ask: "Who created us?" To which god replies, "I did." And they ask, "If you created us, did we know evil when we came or did you give it to us?" God replies, "I gave it to you." Then the people ask, "Why was it that you knew it was evil and gave it to us?" God replies, "Stop, let me think and find the answer."[10] Here the LoDagaa are asking a very basic religious question shared by many faiths: Why should it be that an all-powerful god would allow evil a place in creation?

Religious Leaders

Because a great deal of traditional African religion is based on rituals performed regularly by individuals without the aid of priests, such as offerings of food and drink to the ancestors, the need for religious functionaries is not as great as in religions that rely on specialists, priests, or other religious professionals. Nevertheless, African religions do have leaders and specialists who are essential at critical times or places.

African religions generally do not require a priesthood. In western Africa, however, some communities maintain temples and altars to the gods. The existence of a temple almost requires a priesthood to maintain and control it. In these areas there are priests and sometimes priestesses who undergo lengthy periods of training in the ritual, mythology, and laws connected with religion before they are allowed to serve.

One of the most common religious specialists in Africa is the spiritual curer. In almost all societies illness is believed to have religious as well as natural causes. As previously mentioned, many African worldviews do not include the idea of what modern science would call "natural" causes of death and disease. There is generally a spiritual cause for these misfortunes: Someone has cast a spell or placed a curse on the one who has fallen ill, or the sick person has in some way offended one of the lesser spirits or ancestors. It is the spiritual curer's job to find the cause of the illness and prescribe a cure. The curer uses some form of divination to determine the nature of the curse and the one responsible for it. Then the curer, who can be either male or female, uses a combination of spiritual powers, offerings, and herbal remedies to drive away the witchcraft and dispel the curse. Some of these herbal remedies have proven to be effective medicines in the modern sense. It is also common for African people to call on a spiritual curer to clear a house or other building of witches, spirits, and curses before the owners occupy it. People suspected of sorcery or witchcraft are sometimes killed. Some African communities have been angered when local governments fail to prosecute suspected witches. Among the Acholi of Uganda, the evil spirits that cause a person to become ill are called jok.[11] The healer is called **ajwaka**. When the ajwaka enters the presence of the sick person, he attempts to draw the jok up into the head of the patient through music and song. When this is accomplished, the ajwaka enters into conversation with the jok. "Why have you come? What do you want? What is your name?" Finally, the evil spirit is driven out of the sick person by the ajwaka, captured in a gourd, and buried in the ground. The spiritual curer is part religious specialist, part herbalist, and part psychologist. The curer's skills are highly valued and are sometimes imported into modern hospitals and clinics by Africans who don't want to leave anything to chance. For many, modern medicine is understood to be a developed form of herbalism and divination that can treat some, but not all, of the causes of disease and misfortune. Becoming a spiritual curer is a long and involved process. When a young person decides to join or is called to this profession, he or she must apprentice with an established curer for several years to learn the many skills and secrets involved. In many African communities the role of diviner is closely allied to that of healer. The diviner's task is to use spiritual powers and knowledge to find the causes of present misfortune, past secrets, and things to come. This individual can also ferret out witches and sorcerers. In some African communities, the diviner is primarily one who investigates the causes of trouble. In other communities, the action of prediction is more important. Among the Ndembu of northwestern Zambia, individuals are chosen as diviners by being inhabited by a spirit. The spirit Kayong'u seeks out those whom he wants to become diviners, and it is believed that he first makes them ill. The deity thus shows people what he wants. A person so selected then goes through an elaborate initiation ritual and a long period of training.

Dogon masked dancers from Mali, West Africa. Most Dogon rituals reenact creation narratives.

The tools that African diviners use vary widely. Most commonly, they cast the shells of nuts to form a pattern and then read the pattern to find the answer they seek. Among the Yoruba, a diviner shakes sixteen palm nuts out into one of 256 possible patterns. Each pattern is associated with several poems, each of which contains a message. Even the beginning diviner is supposed to know from memory a minimum of four poems for each pattern. This means that a person must memorize at least 1,024 poems to be a diviner; an experienced diviner will know many more. When the pattern has been cast and the poems recited, the person who has sought divination selects the poem that he or she believes to be the most meaningful.[12] Other methods of divination include casting dice and gazing into a bowl of water. At one time, among many African people, trials by ordeal determined the guilt or innocence of a person accused of a crime. The person being tried was given a poisonous substance to drink. If the person did not die, innocence was proven. In more recent times, a fowl has been substituted. When the fowl dies from the poison, guilt or innocence is determined by the way in which it falls.

Another religious functionary found from time to time in many parts of Africa is the prophet, a person who speaks for the gods. Usually, African prophetic figures gain their authority by the power of their personalities and their message. They have great influence during their lifetimes, but they seldom leave successors.

Religion and Public Life

When there is a political upheaval or religious revival, charismatic leaders appear and proclaim the words of the gods to their people. In the nineteenth century, several prophets led African people in resistance to the slave trade and colonialism. One of these was Ngundeng, who arose among the Nuer of the southern Sudan and who spoke in the name of the sky god, Dengkur. One of the most enduring of the religious figures in Africa is the chief-king. Although some African societies have no monarchs, those that have kings and queens look upon them with great awe and reverence. These rulers are regarded as the tribal connection to the ancestors and are revered as the living symbol of the tribe. Because of this, they are the objects of many traditional restrictions. In some societies, they are considered so sacred that commoners may not look upon their faces. In others, it is regarded as certain death to eat food that has been prepared for the monarch. Some peoples, such as Bantus, traditionally looked upon their rulers as gods incarnate. Because the rulers represent the community, they must always be in good health. A sick monarch means a sick land.

When the monarch dies, the death often is kept secret until a successor can be chosen and enthroned. It is believed that the former king or queen fully becomes a god as he or she enters the land of the ancestors. African monarchies are sometimes hereditary and the child of the monarch automatically comes to the throne. In others the person who is believed to be the wisest or who has been chosen by the gods is selected. Enthroning a monarch often includes very complicated initiation rituals. In many societies the new king or queen is belittled and even physically abused for a period of hours or days to teach lessons in humility before being allowed to assume the position of monarch.

Non-Native African Religions

3.2. Name the non-native African religions.

In addition to religions native to Africa, many others have found a home on the continent. Egypt was among the world's first centers of civilization. Later, the urban centers of North Africa were strongly influenced by Greek culture and religion, producing some of the most important scientific and religious innovations of the classical period. Christianity has played an important role in northern Africa since the first century. Judaism has flourished in the region at least since the time of the destruction of the second temple in Jerusalem in 70 C.E. In Ethiopia there is a distinct branch of Judaism among the Falasha people. The Falashas trace their ancestry to the queen of Sheba in the tenth century B.C.E. and practice a form of Judaism influenced by the Pentateuch, but they do not recognize the Talmud and other later Jewish religious texts. Islam first came to Africa during the lifetime of the Prophet Muhammad, when a party of Muslims fled to Ethiopia to avoid persecution. It became a major force in Africa early in the seventh century and displaced Christianity in many regions. Muslim missionaries have been active in sub-Saharan Africa since at least the seventeenth century. They were followed by Christian missionaries in the early nineteenth century. The greatest growth in Christianity came after the 1950s when the Bible became widely available in African languages and Christianity became less and less connected to European colonial regimes. Hinduism, Buddhism, and the Baha'i faith came to Africa with immigrants from the Middle East and southern Asia in the nineteenth century.

African Religions Today

3.3. Talk about African religions today.

The past hundred years have been extremely difficult for African religions. The European colonial empires on the continent worked to break up traditional tribal units and to enforce other forms of authority. With the end of colonialism following World War II, Africa was divided into greater than forty nations. The drawing of first colonial and then national boundaries tended to break up tribal life. The pressures of modernization, urbanization, and a rapidly increasing population have further changed African life.

If current trends continue, it is likely that conversion to Christianity and Islam will increase. There, are, however, still millions of Africans who practice traditional religions and millions more who combine traditional African beliefs and customs with those of non-native faiths.[13] However, many of the values of these religions will continue; the Christianities and Islams emerging in Africa have distinctive African qualities.

Traditional African religions are closely linked to specific places and to tribal or ethnic groups. Modernization and urbanization have decreased the importance of place in the lives of many Africans. Moreover, **African-initiated churches**—Christian churches that have their origins among Africans rather than European or North American missionaries—have grown and proliferated in recent decades. This has encouraged conversion to non-African-origin religions, which tend to have a broader, universal message. However, African beliefs concerning the High God have both encouraged conversion and shaped African understandings of these religions. In many places belief in lesser spirits continues in the form of Christian saints and Muslim *jinn* (spirits). Beliefs in divination continue in both Christianity and Islam. Among the Woloff of West Africa, for example, it is believed that there are a large number of non-Muslim spirits who can be understood and controlled only by traditional diviners. In recent years local religious movements that combine African, Christian, and/or Islamic beliefs and rituals have emerged in many parts of the continent. Similar religious movements can be found among the African American peoples of the Caribbean and South and Central America. Afro-Caribbean religions like Vodun and Santería, which trace their roots to both African religions and Christianity, are also found in many urban areas in the United States. At the same time, Africans are playing an increasingly important role in more orthodox forms of Christianity and Islam. Struggles for national independence, equality, and human rights have produced strong African and African American voices, including such internationally recognized figures as Dr. Martin Luther King Jr. and Malcolm X in the United States and Archbishop Desmond Tutu in South Africa.

Think About It

1. Discuss those religions originating in Africa and why we cannot speak with any authority to a single religion, theology, worldview, or ritual system in any discussion centering on African religions. With that in mind, discuss some of the beliefs common to religions originating in Africa.

2. Why are some religions that originated in different parts of the world, such as Christianity and Islam, now considered non-native African religions?

3. Briefly summarize the state of African religions today around the world.

Suggested Reading

Badejo, Diedre Osun Seegesi. *The Elegant Deity of Wealth, Power and Femininity.* Trenton, N.J.: Africa World Press, 1996.

Bongmba, Elias Kifon, ed. *The Wiley-Blackwell Companion to African Religions.* Malden, M.A.: Wiley-Blackwell, 2012.

Evans-Pritchard, E. E. *Nuer Religion.* New York: Oxford University Press, 1956.

Idowu, E. Bolaji. *African Traditional Religion.* Maryknoll, N.Y.: Orbis Books, 1973.

Magesa, L. *African Religion: The Moral Traditions of Abundant Life.* Maryknoll, N.Y.: Orbis Books, 1997.

Olupona, Jacob K., and Terry Rey, eds. *Orisha Devotion as World Religion: The Globalization of Yoruba Religious Culture.* Madison: University of Wisconsin Press, 2008.

Parrinder, Geoffrey. *African Traditional Religion*, 3rd ed. New York: Harper & Row, 1976.

Ray, Benjamin C. *African Religions: Symbol, Ritual and Community.* Englewood Cliffs, NJ: Prentice Hall, 1976.

Soyinka, Wole. *You Must Set Forth at Dawn: A Memoir.* New York: Random House, 2007. This is an autobiographical account of life and struggle in post-colonial Africa by the Nobel Prize–winning Nigerian author.

Turner, Victor. *The Forest of Symbols: Aspects of Ndembu Ritual.* Ithaca, N.Y.: Cornell University Press, 1966.

Source Material

An African Divine King

There are divine kings in many cultures. A careful look into this office and the religious concept that surrounds it often gives the reader an understanding of the supporting culture. The following is a brief description of the life (and death) of the divine king of the people of Malawi.[14]

Mbande is a hill on the plain of north Nyasaland with a commanding view of the surrounding country and well suited to defense. The west side is precipitous and below the scarp edge there used to be a marsh; to the north the hill is protected by a wide reach of the Lukulu River. It is a sacred place and for many generations was the home of the "divine king," the Kyungu. Like the Lwembe he was the living representative of a hero, and was selected by a group of hereditary nobles from one of two related lineages, the office alternating (if suitable candidates were available) between the two. They sought a big man, one who had begotten children and whose sons were already married, not a young man, for, the nobles said, "young men always want war, and destroy the country." He must be a man of wisdom (*gwa mahala*) and generous in feeding his people.

The Kyungu's life was governed by taboos even more rigorous than those surrounding the Lwembe. He must not fall ill, or suffer a wound, or even scratch himself and bleed a little, for his ill health, or his blood falling on the Earth would bring sickness to the whole country. "Men feared when Kyungu's blood fell on the ground, they said, 'It is his life.' If he had a headache his wives (if they loved him) told him not to mention it, they hid his illness; but if the nobles entered and found him ill they dug the grave and put him in it, saying, 'He is the ruler (*ntemi*), it's taboo for him to be ill.' Then he thought: 'Perhaps it is so' (with a gesture of resignation)."

Great precautions were taken to preserve his health. He lived in a separate house with his powerful medicines. His food was prepared by boys below the age of puberty lest a menstruating woman, or a youth who had lain with a woman, should touch it and so bring sickness upon him; and his numerous wives were immured in the royal enclosure—a great stockade—and jealously guarded, for any infidelity on their part was thought to make their husband ill, and with him the whole country.

When the Kyungu did fall ill he was smothered by the nobles who lived around him at Mbande, and buried in great secrecy, and with a score or more of living persons—slaves—in the grave beneath him, and one or two wives and the sons of commoners above. And in the midst of all this slaughter the nobles brought a sheep to look into the grave that the dead Kyungu might be gentle (*milolo*) like the sheep!

The living Kyungu was thought to create food and rain, and his breath and the growing parts of his body—his hair and nails and the constantly replaced mucus of his nose—were believed to be magically connected with the fertility of the Ngonde plain. When he was killed his nostrils were stopped so that he was buried "with the breath in his body"; while portions of his hair and nails and of his nasal mucus were taken from him beforehand and buried by the nobles of Ngonde in the black mud near the river. This was "to defend the country against hunger, to close up the land, to keep it rich and heavy and fertile as it was when he himself lived in it."

His death was kept secret—a relatively easy matter since he lived in seclusion—and one of the nobles (*Ngosi*) impersonated him wearing his clothes. After a month or two when the nobles had decided whom to choose as the new Kyungu, the luckless man was summoned to Mbande: "Your father calls you." Then he came with his companions and entered the house to make obeisance; they seized him and put the sacred cloth on him and set him on the stool, *Kisumbe*, saying "Thou Kyungu, thou art he," and he became the Kyungu. Then they struck the drum, *Mwenkelwa*, and everyone knew that the Kyungu had died and another had been installed. Men feared greatly to be seized as the Kyungu, just as they feared to be seized as the Lwembe, because the life of a divine king was short. Ngonde historians quote a number of cases of sons of the Kyungu who fled to escape being set on the stool; once they had sat on it they dared not flee lest they die.

In time of drought the nobles of Ngonde would go to a diviner to inquire who it was who was angry; they would mention all the names of the sacred groves of the Kyungus in turn and he would tell them it was so-and-so. They would inform the living Kyungu and he would give them a bull or a sheep, together with some beer—they would take one of the pots of beer from his own house, brought by his people as tribute. And he would give them some flour and cloths also. Then he would go with them into the grove and build a miniature hut. Next they would kill the beast and hang some of the meat up on a tree—the rest they would eat later outside the grove. Then they would tear up the cloths and fasten some of the pieces on to the hut in the grove—an action they would explain as "giving him cloths." And finally, they would pour out some of the beer and the flour. Nearly always, in time of drought, they would thus build a hut and make an offering in the grove of the Kyungu whom the diviner had mentioned.

But occasionally, if one of the chiefs had recently insulted the Kyungu, they concluded that it was the living Kyungu himself who was angry. They would go to a diviner and mention all the names of the dead Kyungus, but he would refuse to accept any of them: "No . . . no." And at length he would tell them that it was the living Kyungu who was angry because so-and-so had insulted him. Then there would be no sacrifice at the grove at all, but the nobles of Ngonde would go to the one who had insulted the Kyungu and charge him with it, asking him what he meant by thus killing them all, would not the whole land starve? And so the wrongdoer would take a cow to the Kyungu who, thereupon, would address the nobles of Ngonde saying: "If it was my anger which brought the drought then it will rain (for I am no longer angry). But if the rain does not come then it cannot have been my anger, it must have been someone (of the dead Kyungus) whom you forgot to ask about." And if, after that, the rain came soon, then it was not likely that anyone would insult the Kyungu again.

Thus to insult Kyungu was not only treasonable, it was blasphemous, and the whole plain was believed to be cursed with drought or disease in reply. An "insult" might mean any neglect of the obligations of the chiefs and nobles and commoners of the plain to their lord.

The majesty (*ubusisya*) of the Kyungu was cultivated in a variety of ways. He smeared himself with ointment made from lion fat, and his bed was built up with elephant tusks and lion pelts. He was enthroned on the sacred iron stool called Kisumbe, he had a spear, and Mulima, a porous piece of iron "like a mouth organ" used to make rain, all handed down from the first Kyungu. His zebra tails, set with medicines in horn handles, were waved in war and during prayer to the shades, and he also had the famous drum on which the blood of a child was poured.

But the majority of their subjects worshiped only from afar in fear and trembling. At Mbande no ordinary commoner was ever conducted into the sacred enclosure, but only the territorial nobles and the elder chiefs, and they only occasionally; while when the Kyungu traveled through his country all men save the very oldest fled from his approach. Even in speech fearful circumlocutions were used to refer to his journeyings—"The country is on the move"—"the great hill is moving"—"the mystery is coming." It was taboo both for the old men who stayed to see him, and for those who entered the sacred enclosure, ever to greet him in the usual way. Falling down and clapping the hands was the only greeting for the Kyungu.

From the wives of the Kyungu also men fled in terror, fearing lest they be compromised and thrown over the cliff of Mbande, and this both added to the atmosphere of terror that surrounded him and was an expression of it.

An African Creation Story

The following is the creation story of the Boshongo, a Bantu people.[15]

In the beginning, in the dark, there was nothing but water, and Bumba was alone.

One day Bumba was in terrible pain. He retched and strained and vomited up the sun. After that light spread over everything. The heat of the sun dried up the water until the black edges of the world began to show. Black sandbanks and reefs could be seen. But there were no living things.

Bumba vomited up the moon and then the stars, and after that the night had its light also.

Still Bumba was in pain. He strained again and nine living creatures came forth; the leopard named Koy Bumba, and Pongo Bumba the crested eagle, the crocodile, Ganda Bumba, and one little fish named Yo; next, old Kono Bumba, the tortoise, and Tsetse, the lightning, swift, deadly, beautiful like the leopard, then the white heron, Nyanyi Bumba, also one beetle, and the goat named Budi.

Last of all came forth men. There were many men, but only one was white like Bumba. His name was Loko Yima.

The creatures themselves then created all the creatures. The heron created all the birds of the air except the kite. He did not make the kite. The crocodile made serpents and the iguana. The goat produced every beast with horns. Yo, the small fish, brought forth all the fish of all the seas and waters. The beetle created insects.

Then the serpents in their turn made grasshoppers, and the iguana made the creatures without horns.

Then the three sons of Bumba said they would finish the world. The first, Nyonye Ngana, made the white ants; but he was not equal to the task, and died of it. The ants, however, thankful for life and being, went searching for black earth in the depths of the world and covered the barren sands to bury and honor their creator. . . .

When at last the work of creation was finished, Bumba walked through the peaceful villages and said to the people, "Behold these wonders. They belong to you." Thus from Bumba, the Creator, the First Ancestor, came forth all the wonders that we see and hold and use, and all the brotherhood of beasts and man.

Part II
Religions Originating in India

Several of the world's religions began in India, and they have spread around the globe, affecting billions of people. The great depth and variety of religious teaching and experience one finds in Hinduism, Jainism, Buddhism, and Sikhism are indeed awesome. Today, the beauty of the great poem of Hinduism (the *Bhagavad Gita*), the complexity and variety of Hindu ritual life, the many expressions of Buddhism, and the concept of **ahimsa** (non-injury of living beings) taught by the Jains are appreciated not only by practitioners but by students all over the world. An understanding of the basic literature, history, and doctrine of these religions is essential for understanding modern Asia and the cultural heritage of Asian peoples living in Europe, Africa, and the Americas.

Hinduism—Basic Teachings
The Vedas Are the Oldest Hindu Religious Texts

Composition of the Vedas probably began between 2000 and 1500 B.C.E. The Vedas are a collection of hymns, many of which were recited during sacrifices to the many gods. Indra is the god of thunderbolts, clouds, and rain, and is the ruler of heaven. Agni is the god of fire. He brings offerings to the other gods. Rudra is the god of death and destruction.

In Modern Hinduism There Are Thousands of Gods and Goddesses

Some gods and goddesses are worshiped by hundreds of millions; others are known only in particular villages. Hindu divinities often come in male and female pairs. Brahma is the creator but is rarely worshiped. His spouse Sarasvati is the goddess of wisdom. Shiva is the god of death, destruction, and dance. His spouse is alternatively Parvati, the female half of the perfect couple, or Kali, who wears a necklace of skulls and is the goddess of time and destruction. Vishnu is the preserver of the universe and the god of love. His spouse is Lakshmi, the goddess of wealth and fertility.

Karma Is Moral Action

The karma one accumulates determines the nature of future lives. Hinduism assumes that there is a constant cycle of birth, life, death, and rebirth. Karma drives this process. One may be reborn as a human or animal and in one of the many heavens or hells. Buddhism and Jainism share this belief with Hinduism.

The *Law of Manu* Is the "Blueprint" for Hindu Society

It provides the outline for the caste system. Castes are hereditary occupational groups. The four major caste groups are Brahmins (priests), Kshatriyas (rulers and soldiers), Vaishyas (artisans, merchants, and farmers), and Shudras (manual workers). There are also Dalits, or untouchables, who perform the most menial and ritually defiling tasks.

The *Bhagavad Gita* Is among the Great Epic Poems of Hinduism

The *Bhagavad Gita* describes the life and teachings of Krishna, a human incarnation of Vishnu. It was probably composed in the second or third century B.C.E. It is a conversation between Krishna and the young warrior Arjuna as he ponders the folly, human consequences, and karmic consequences of war. Krishna explains that because Arjuna is a Kshatriya, and obligated to fight, he will not suffer the consequences that members of other castes would for joining in the battle.

Jainism—Basic Teachings

Jainism Was Founded in the Sixth Century B.C.E.

Mahavira, the founder of Jainism, is thought of as a Tirthankara, or "crossing builder," who discovered the path leading out of the cycle of karma and rebirth. He renounced a life of wealth and power and practiced an extreme form of asceticism. He did not wear clothing and sought out the most uncomfortable environments. One of Mahavira's core teachings is that humans must find their own ways to salvation and that gods cannot aid in the process.

The Jain Worldview Is Dualistic

Jainism teaches that the universe consists of spirit (*jiva*) and matter (*ajiva*). Because both are eternal, there are no Jain creation mythologies. As long as the soul is bound to matter, it is destined to remain caught in the cycle of birth, death, and rebirth.

Non-Injury of Life (Ahimsa) Is Among the Most Important Teachings of Jainism

Jainism, Hinduism, and Buddhism all teach that injuring other beings—especially killing them—produces karma that leads to rebirth in abodes of suffering. Jainism places the greatest emphasis on ahimsa. Unlike Hindus and Buddhists, all Jains are vegetarians. They avoid occupations that could lead to the injury of animals. Jain monks sweep the road in front of them as they walk to avoid harming insects. For the most part, Jains have avoided participating in the religious conflicts that have plagued India for much of the last century.

Jain Monks Follow a Strict Moral Code

Jain monks vow to always tell the truth and never to take things that are not given to them. Lay Jains also seek to keep these vows. This ethical code has contributed to their reputation as honest and reliable business partners.

There Are Very Few Jains

Jainism places serious restrictions on one's choice of occupation. It is almost exclusively an urban religion. In India, Jain birthrates are lower than those of Hindus and Muslims, so the proportion of Jains in the total population is declining.

Buddhism—Basic Teachings

Buddhism Was Founded by Siddhartha Gautama in North India in the Sixth Century B.C.E.

Like Jainism, Buddhism rejects the authority of the Vedas and the caste system. The only Buddhist society that retains the caste system is Sri Lanka, where there are different monastic orders for different caste groups. Buddhism was the world's first missionary religion. By the third century B.C.E., it had spread throughout much of Asia.

Buddhism Is an Extremely Diverse Religion

The Buddhist schools that have developed over the centuries are very distinct with respect to both their worldview and religious practices. The early Theravada school teaches that there have been many Buddhas, but only one exists at any given time. It also teaches that monks must be celibate and follow a complex set of rules. The later Mahayana schools teach that there are many Buddhas simultaneously. Some allow monks to marry and own property.

Buddhism Teaches That the Path to Salvation is the "Middle Way"

The "Middle Way" lies between worldly life and the extreme forms of asceticism practiced by Jain monks. Most Buddhists believe that to attain enlightenment it is necessary to renounce the world, but that religious practices that harm the body are counterproductive. Some—but not all—Buddhists are vegetarians. Many maintain that it is the act of killing and not eating meat that has negative karmic consequences.

The Most Basic Buddhist Teachings Are Those of the Four Noble Truths

These are: (1) Life is suffering, if for no other reason than that it will end; (2) suffering is caused by clinging to and craving worldly pleasures; (3) to end suffering, one must end the desire that leads to suffering; and (4) to eliminate desire, one must follow the Eightfold Path as taught by the Buddha.

Bodhisattvas Are Common to all Buddhist Schools, But Are Understood Differently

Bodhisattvas are future Buddhas. For Theravada Buddhists, they are beings traversing the path to Nirvana. They will come into the world, teach, and die, never to return. For Mahayana Buddhists, bodhisattvas are almost godlike beings who put off enlightenment until they can guide all beings to it. In Tibet, it is believed that the Dalai Lama and other reincarnated Lamas are actually bodhisattvas who constantly return to the Tibetan Buddhist community.

Sikhism—Basic Teachings

Sikhism Is Much Younger Than Other Religions That Originated in India

Sikhism emerged in the sixteenth century C.E. Although in some respects it resembles both Hinduism and Islam, Sikhs believe their faith to be based on the independent insights of their first teacher, Nanak.

Sikh Tradition Maintains That When Nanak Was Approximately Thirty Years Old, God Spoke to Him and Told Him That He Had Been Chosen as the Prophet of the True Religion

After receiving this message, Nanak and his companion wandered across India for many years teaching the unity of Hinduism and Islam. He accepted the teachings of monotheism and that of karma and rebirth.

Nanak Was Followed by a Series of Nine Teachers or Gurus—the Last of Whom Died in 1708 C.E.

Arjan, the fifth guru, was imprisoned and killed by Muslim authorities. Before he died he instructed his son to establish a core of armed guards. This militant tradition has continued because Sikhs have often been the victims of oppression and violence carried out by both Hindus and Muslims.

Sikh Devotions Are Very Simple

Nanak rejected the complicated ceremonies of both Hinduism and Islam. Sikh devotions include daily prayers and the singing of hymns. Sikhs gather for collective meals in a communal dining hall called a "langar," and the meal is free and open to all people.

Chapter 4
Hinduism

 Learning Objectives

After reading this chapter, you should be able to:

4.1 Understand the origins of Hinduism.

4.2 Analyze the significance of the Vedic era.

4.3 Discuss postclassical Hinduism.

4.4 Identify Muslim influences in India.

4.5 Discuss movements and issues in modern Hindiusm.

4.6 Name the Hindu holy days.

4.7 Discuss Hinduism today.

A Timeline of Hinduism

2500–1500 B.C.E.	Indus valley civilization
1750–1200	Aryan migration to South Asia; first Vedas compiled
400	Vedas completed
800–300	Upanishads compiled
200–200 C.E.	*Bhagavad Gita* compiled
300–300 C.E.	*Law of Manu* compiled; caste system formalized
600–1600	Rise of devotional and anti-caste movements
788–820	Shankara organizes Vedanta
1510	Portuguese conquest of Goa
1556–1857	Moghul Empire; with few exceptions, characterized by religious tolerance
1700	British emerge as major power in India
1774–1833	Life of Ram Mohan Roy
1836–1886	Life of Sri Ramakrishna
1869–1948	Life of Mahatma Gandhi
19th and 20th centuries	Emergence of large Hindu communities outside India; large numbers of Dalits (untouchables) convert to Buddhism and Christianity
1947	Independence from Britain; partition of British India into India and Pakistan sparks massive outbreaks of violence among Hindus, Muslims, and Sikhs
Late 20th–early 21st century	Growth of Hindu nationalism leads to increasing Hindu/Muslim/Christian tension and violence

KEY TERMS

Agni	moksha
atman	murti
Bhagavad Gita	Parvati
bhakti	prasad
Brahma	puja
Brahman	puranas
Brahmo Samaj	samsara
caste	Shiva
dharma	Trimurti
Ganesha	Upanishads
Indra	varna
Kali	Vedanta
karma	Vedas
Lakshmi	Vishnu
lingam	Vishnu
lingam	Vivekenanda
maya	yoni
Mohandas K. Gandhi	

> Perhaps the oldest and most complex of all the religions of the world is Hinduism. Whereas most of today's active religions seem to have begun sometime around the sixth century B.C.E. or later, Hinduism traces the beginnings of some of its religious themes and forms to the third millennium B.C.E. It is probably the most diverse and varied of all religions. One can find within the Hindu tradition almost any form or style of religion that has been conceived of or practiced. Its scope ranges from simple devotion to local deities to some of the most elaborate philosophical systems ever devised. In this vast diversity, Hinduism allows for literally millions of major and minor gods, their temples, and their priests. Therefore, for the Hindu, the possible religious views are virtually infinite.

Hinduism has also been the source of three other religions. In the sixth century B.C.E., two reform movements, Jainism and Buddhism, arose from within Hinduism and challenged traditional Indian religious concepts. For a time, it appeared that both movements might even replace Hinduism. Within a few centuries, however, their distinctive features were absorbed by Hinduism, which re-emerged as the major religion of India. Today, Jainism is a minority religion in India, and Buddhism, although having great influence in other Asian nations, has only a small following in India. In the fifteenth century C.E., after Muslim invasions of India, Sikhism arose as a religion with features resembling those of both Islam and Hinduism. However, it has never become more than a minority religion and is concentrated in the northwest of what is now modern India. Hinduism faced these challengers by absorbing them and adopting their distinctive features into the mainstream of Hindu thought.

Unlike most of the other major religions of the world, Hinduism has no identifiable founder. Although there have been many great teachers and leaders in its history, there has never been one whose teachings became the wellspring of all later Hindu thought.

The word *Hindu* comes from the Sanskrit name for the river Indus, *Sindhu*. Whereas the designation *Hindu* may refer to a great variety of religious beliefs and practices, it generally applies to the religion of the people of India. Only recently have the people we now know as Hindus begun to use the term to refer to their own religious beliefs and practices. It is believed that the Muslim conquerors of India were the first to use the word *Hindu* to describe religion. They called those Indians who did not convert to Islam "Hindus." The British picked up this usage from the Muslim rulers of India. From English it passed into other European languages. Although the vast majority of Hindus live in the modern nation of India, Hinduism flourished in much of Southeast Asia from the seventh to the fifteenth century C.E. and still survives on the Indonesian island of Bali. In the nineteenth and early twentieth centuries, Indian Hindus spread throughout the British Empire. Today, substantial Hindu communities exist in Europe, Africa, the Caribbean, and North America.

The Origins of Hinduism

4.1. **Understand the origins of Hinduism.**

Early Cultures in India

For years, scholars believed that the history of Hinduism began with the migratory waves of Aryan people into India during the second millennium B.C.E. It was thought that the religion that the Aryans brought with them mingled with the religion of the native people of the Indian subcontinent, and the culture that developed between them became classical Hinduism. Today, most scholars question the scope, and even the existence, of this migration. However, migration or not, there were people in ancient India whose religious and cultural traditions serve as a precursor to later Hinduism.

Actually, very little is known about the earliest inhabitants of the region. Prior to the 1920s, the only source that spoke of them was the Vedic literature of early Hinduism. References to these early natives of India were often negative, and the people were presented as uncivilized and barbaric. Beginning in the 1920s, however, archaeological excavations in northwestern India revealed an entire complex of cities along the Indus River. Contrary to the image presented in the **Vedas**, these excavations showed that as early as 2500 B.C.E. there was an advanced civilization in the Indus valley. The total complex of cities and villages in this area covered nearly one-half million square miles and may represent the largest political entity before the Roman Empire. The cities were laid out in rectangular blocks separated by broad streets with elaborate drainage systems, and they may have supported a population of 40,000 people per city. At the peak of this civilization, houses were made of fired brick, some two stories high, and they contained bathrooms with running water. Cities were supported by advanced agricultural communities. Evidence of complex irrigation systems exists. The cities often contained large granaries for the storage and distribution of food. Archaeologists also found that these early inhabitants of the Indus River valley had a written language. Unfortunately, this language has not yet been translated and the great amount of information that it could supply regarding the life and religion of these people remains hidden.

What we know of the religion of these people is revealed by numerous statues and amulets that archaeologists have found. Many of these bear the image of what have been interpreted as fertility gods and goddesses. Some of the figures sit in the lotus position that was later adopted by some Hindus and other meditative sects. In addition, archaeologists have found large ceremonial buildings that may have been places of worship. It is therefore assumed that far from being barbarians, these people were highly civilized city dwellers and that later Hinduism may have taken some of its gods and practices from this early period.[1]

Sometime between 1750 and 1200 B.C.E., the ancient cultures of the Indus River valley gave way to the peoples who were the immediate progenitors of modern Hinduism. Scattered references in the Vedic literature indicate that these people were basically nomads following their flocks and herds from place to place. They apparently had no

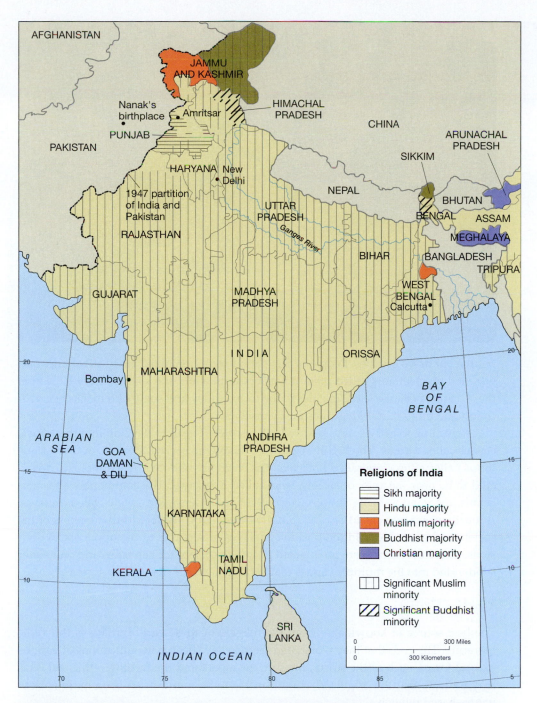

AFGHANISTAN

JAMMU
AND KASHMIR

Nanak's
birthplace • Amritsar
PUNJAB

HIMACHAL
PRADESH

CHINA

ARUNACHAL
PRADESH

SIKKIM

PAKISTAN

HARYANA New
• Delhi

BHUTAN

1947 partition
of India and
Pakistan

UTTAR
PRADESH

BENGAL

ASSAM

RAJASTHAN

Ganges River

MEGHALAYA

BIHAR

BANGLADESH

TRIPURA

GUJARAT

MADHYA
PRADESH

WEST
BENGAL
Calcutta •

I N D I A

ORISSA

20

20

Bombay •   MAHARASHTRA

*BAY
OF
BENGAL*

*ARABIAN
SEA*

GOA
DAMAN
& DIU

ANDHRA
PRADESH

15

15

KARNATAKA

Religions of India

Sikh majority

Hindu majority

Muslim majority

Buddhist majority

Christian majority

Significant Muslim
minority

Significant Buddhist
minority

KERALA

TAMIL
NADU

10

10

SRI
LANKA

0   300 Miles

0   300 Kilometers

INDIAN OCEAN

70   75   80   85   5

Tanah Laut, an oceanside Hindu
temple on the Indonesian island
of Bali.

Brahmins in yellow robes chanting the *Ramayana* in Varanasi, India.

John Henry Claude Wilson/Alamy

permanent bases or cities. People of this period were organized along tribal lines and were led by chieftains called *rajas*. It was not until about the sixth century B.C.E. that these people began to settle in cities in the Indus valley and some of the rajas began to collect and build minor kingdoms for themselves.

According to early sources, early Indian society began to develop into three basic classes called **varnas**. The highly regarded priests who served the cults of the various Indus valley cities were called *Brahmins*. The chieftains and their warriors, also considered to be near the apex of society, were called *Kshatriyas*. The commoners and merchants, regarded as being subservient to the two upper classes, were called *Vaishyas*. A fourth group was called *Shudras*. Shudras were not considered full members of the society and generally held the position of slaves or servants to the upper social divisions. These divisions were maintained in Indian society for centuries and were later subdivided into the multiple classes that became the basis of the caste system.

Vedic Religion

The best source of knowledge about the religion of these early Indians is the Vedic literature. The gods that they worshiped seem to have been personifications of various natural forces, such as the storm, the sun, the moon, and the fertility of the soil. This may indicate that the origins of Hinduism are to be found in an even more ancient nature-based religion.

The chief manner of worship of the gods was apparently sacrifice. Because the people were primarily nomadic in the early days of their civilization in India, they built no temples to their gods but rather offered sacrifices to them on altars built in open places. These offerings were frequently animal sacrifices, but they also included the sacrifices of dairy products like butter and libations of milk, which were poured out to the gods. Fire was the basic means through which sacrifices were offered to the gods. **Agni**, the god of fire, was the channel through whom offerings were presented to the other gods. Another liquid apparently used as a libation was the juice of the sacred soma plant. The exact identification of the soma plant is lost to the modern world. The ancient texts describe it as a sacred plant sent to Earth by the god Indra. Its juice was described as delicious and invigorating to the worshiper who drank it and shared it with the gods. The plant that modern Indians identify as soma is not delicious and invigorating but produces nausea. Naturally, there are those who suggest that the original soma may have been some form of mushroom or other plant that produced hallucinations.

The Vedas include an extravagant formula for sacrificial offerings. An expensive and elaborate sacrifice originated in this period—the horse sacrifice. Because of the expense and incredible detail involved, the horse sacrifice was limited to kings. This sacrifice was believed to have extraordinary effects in atoning and for giving religious power to those who participated in it. The horse sacrifice was also helpful to rulers who wished to expand their territory, and this, of course, was its major attraction to Indian rulers. A young male horse chosen for this sacrifice was set loose to roam the countryside for one year. The attendants of the ruler followed the horse wherever he went. If the horse covered any territory that was not in the domain of the ruler, that raja had the right to claim that land as his own. After one year, the horse returned. At that time, as many as 600 other animals, ranging from the bee to the elephant, were sacrificed to the gods. Finally, the sacred horse was strangled and the wives of the raja participated in fertility rites with the body of the horse. The carcass was ritually butchered and eaten by the ruler and his family. According to legend, if one man could perform 100 horse sacrifices he would become master over all of the gods and the universe. Unfortunately for those who aspired to this, such an act would have required over 100 years and incredible wealth. Consequently, there is no record of a ruler who could or would perform it 100 times. The horse sacrifice was last performed by an Indian ruler in the eighteenth century C.E.

The Vedic Era

4.2. **Analyze the significance of the Vedic era.**

The Vedas

The oldest sacred books of Hinduism are the Vedas. The Vedas are the basic source of the Hindu understanding of the universe. All later texts are seen as mere commentary upon them, even when they include new religious ideas. The Vedas were developed as the Aryans came into India, settled there, and mingled their religion with that of the native peoples. There is dispute over the exact period in which the Vedas were written. Some scholars believe that the earliest of the Vedic hymns may have developed before 2000 B.C.E., and that they were still developing as late as the sixth century C.E. Others contend that the bulk of the Vedic material came into being between 1500 and 400 B.C.E. As is true of much other ancient religious literature, there is no way of knowing the exact time of the origin and development of these books. Undoubtedly, they were first composed and transmitted orally for many generations before they were committed to writing; thus, centuries may have passed between their origin and completion.

There are four basic Vedic books. The first and most important is the *Rig-Veda* (*Veda* meaning "knowledge" or "sacred lore"), a collection of over 1,000 hymns to the Aryan gods, which contains the basic mythology of these gods.

The second book is the *Yajur-Veda* (knowledge of rites), a collection of materials to be recited during sacrifice to the gods. The third book, the *Sama-Veda* (knowledge of chants), is a collection of verses from the basic hymns recited by priests at sacrifices. The fourth book, second in importance only to the *Rig-Veda*, is the *Atharva-Veda* (knowledge given by the sage Atharva), which contains rituals to be used in the home and popular prayers to the gods, along with spells and incantations to ward off evil.

Each of the Vedic books is made up of four parts;[2] each contains a section of hymns (*mantras*) to the gods. As is the case in many ancient religions, hymns and religious poetry are to be regarded as the most ancient of all religious literature because they reflect the period when statements about and to the gods were memorized, chanted, and passed from one generation to the next without benefit of the written word. Each Vedic book also contains a section of ritual materials (*Brahmanas*) in which the worshipers are given instruction in the proper way to perform their sacrifices, and so on. The Brahmanas are considered to be later than the mantra sections. A third section in each of the Vedas is the so-called Forest Treatises (*Aranyakas*), which are materials for hermits in their religious pursuits. The fourth sections are called **Upanishads** and are made up of philosophical materials that reflect on earlier Vedic material. The Upanishads represent a systematization of the Vedas that reformed early sacrificial practices. It is important to note that the reforms suggested by the Upanishads occurred roughly during the same time period as the reforms to early Hinduism represented by Jainism and Buddhism.

Within the Vedas are basic descriptions and mythology of the various early Hindu gods. The god who receives the most attention in terms of numbers of hymns is **Indra**, the god of the thunderbolt, of clouds and rain, and the ruler of heaven. Indra is especially important because he is remembered as the conqueror of Vrtra, the personification of chaos. Contained within the *Rig-Veda* alone are over 250 hymns specifically addressed to him. One of these follows:

From the Source

That highest Indra power of thine is distant: that
which is here sages possessed aforetime.
    This one is on the earth, in heaven the other,
and both unite as flag with flag in battle.
    He spread the wide earth out and firmly fixed it,
smote with his thunderbolt and loosed the waters.
    Maghavan with his puissance struck down Ahi,
rent Rauhina to death and slaughtered Vyansa.
    Armed with his bolt and trusting in his prowess
he wandered shattering the forts of Dasas.
    Cast thy dart, knowing, Thunderer, at the Daysu:
increase the Arya's might and glory, Indra.
    For him who thus hath taught these human races,
Maghavan, bearing a fame-worthy title.
    Thunderer, drawing nigh to slay the Dasyus,
hath given himself the name of Son for glory.

    See this abundant wealth that he possesses,
and put your trust in Indra's hero vigor.
    He found the cattle, and he found the horses,
he found the plants, the forests and the waters.
    To him the truly strong, whose deeds are many,
to him the strong bull let us pour the Soma.
    The Hero, watching like a thief in ambush,
goes parting the possessions of the godless.
    Well didst thou do that hero deed, O Indra,
in waking with thy bolt the slumbering Ahi.
    In thee, delighted, Dames divine rejoiced them,
the flying Maruts and all gods were joyful.
    As thou hast smitten Sushna, Pipru,
Vrtra and Kuyava, and Samhara's forts, O Indra.
    This prayer of ours may Varuna grant, and Mitra,
and Aditi, and Sindhu, Earth and Heaven.[3]

Many other Aryan gods are also mentioned in the Vedic literature. Agni, the god of fire, is mentioned in over 200 hymns. He is basically regarded as the god of the priests and the priest of the gods. He leads the gods in proper sacrifice, and as the god of fire, he brings the burnt sacrifices to the other gods. The god Varuna also receives his share of hymns in the Vedic material. He is viewed as the god who presides over the order of the universe and the god who forgives those who have sinned.

From the Source

May we be in thy keeping, O thou Leader,
wide-ruling Varuna, Lord of many heroes.

    O sons of Aditi, forever faithful, pardon us,
Gods, admit us to your friendship.[4]

Vishnu is mentioned briefly in the Vedas, but at the time they were composed, he was not the important deity he was to become in later Hinduism. Another of the gods whose function and name was to change in later Hinduism was Rudra, later known as **Shiva**, the god of death and destruction. In later times, Shiva and Vishnu become two of the most popular gods in Hinduism. The god of the dead who receives attention in the Vedas is Yama, who was supposed to have been the first man to die.

From the Source

Honor the King with thine oblations, Yama,
Vivasvan's Son, who gathers men together,
   Who travelled to the lofty heights above us,
who searches out and shows the path to many.

Yama first found for us a place to dwell in:
this pasture never can be taken from us.
   Men born on earth tread their own paths that lead
them whither our ancient Fathers have departed.[5]

In addition to hymns to the many gods of the early Hindu pantheon, the Vedas also contain legendary and mythological material from early Indian life. One of the most interesting of these is the story of Manu, which speaks of the origin of women and the subsequent growth of the human race. As in other Vedic texts, sacrifice plays an important role in the story.

From the Source

They brought water to Manu for washing, as it is now usual to bring it for washing hands. When he was washing, a fish came into his hands.

It said to him in words, "Bring me up, I shall save you." "From what will you save me?" "A flood will carry away all the creatures. I shall save you from that flood." "How can I bring you up?"

"Fish swallow fish. So long as we remain small, destruction awaits us. Keep me first in a jar. When I outgrow it, dig a pond and keep me in it. When I outgrow that also, take me to the sea. Then I shall be beyond danger."

It quickly became a Jhasa, which become the largest. Then it said, "The flood will come in such and such a year. Take my advice then, and build a ship. Enter it when the flood rises, and I shall save you from the flood."

After rearing the fish thus, Manu took it to the sea. In the year indicated to him by the fish, he acted according to the advice of the fish and built a ship. When the flood rose, he entered it. The fish then swam to him. He tied the rope of the ship to the horn of the fish and thus reached swiftly the Northern Mountain there.

The fish then said, "I have saved you. Tie the ship to a tree and do not let the water leave you stranded when you are on the mountain. Descend as the water subsides." Thus gradually he descended, hence that slope of the Northern Mountain is called "Manu's Descent." The flood carried off all the creatures, Manu alone survived.

Wishing for a progeny, he began to worship and do penance. Then he performed a sacrifice of cooked meal. In the waters he offered melted butter, buttermilk, whey, and curd as oblations. In a year, a woman was created out of them. She rose dripping, melted butter collected at her footprints.

Wishing for progeny, he continued to worship and perform penance along with her. Through her this race was generated by him. This is the race of Manu. Whatever blessings he desired through her were all conferred on him.[6]

In modern Hinduism, the Vedic literature is held in high regard, but its texts are known by only a few scholars. Indeed, it is not accurate to think of Hinduism as a religion based on sacred writings, as most Hindus have little interaction with scripture reading or study. In addition, some of the gods mentioned in the Vedas are no longer worshiped. This ancient sacred literature serves mainly as background for other developments in Hinduism; later sacred writings tell the stories of contemporary Hindu deities.

The Upanishads

As noted earlier, the fourth section of each of the Vedas is the Upanishads.[7] Within these materials, one finds the early philosophical statements that became the basis for later Hindu philosophy and worldview. Although there originally may have been more of these treatises, there are currently about 200 Upanishads, varying in length from one to over fifty pages. Of these, fourteen are called the principal Upanishads. Scholarly research indicates that the earliest Upanishads probably originated in the ninth century B.C.E.

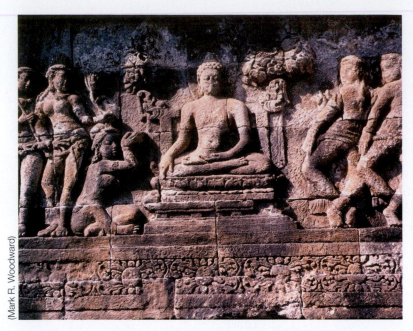

The Buddha and lay devotees at Borobudur, a ninth-century Buddhist stupa near Yogyakarta, Indonesia.

(Mark R. Woodward)

Some scholars contend that the Upanishads are an integral part of the Vedas and that they are a natural commentary on the early hymns and ritual texts. These scholars tend to see the Upanishads as the philosophical expression of what one finds in the rest of the Vedas. Others disagree and point out the basic disharmony between the two. Whereas the hymns, chants, legends, and rituals in the rest of the Vedic material are clearly polytheistic, giving instruction on the proper worship of myriad gods, the Upanishads operate from a monistic presupposition. The gods of the earlier Vedic literature are not very important. The Upanishads assume that there is only one reality, the impersonal god-being called Brahman. All other beings are but an expression of Brahman. All that is not Brahman is not real. Humans have a false knowledge (*maya*) when they believe that this life and our separation from Brahman are real. Not only is there this basic distinction between the Upanishads and the rest of the Vedic material, but the Upanishads also seem to have been written as a reaction to the priestly form of worship prescribed by the other Vedic books. Whereas most of the Vedas seem to teach that the proper way to worship is by sacrifice to the various Vedic gods, the Upanishads emphasize meditation as a means of worship. They teach that people's real problem is ignorance (*avidya*) of their plight and that only when people realize this ignorance and come to true knowledge will they find release. Those scholars who point to these essential differences between the Upanishads and other portions of the Vedas believe that the Upanishads may have had a different origin and became attached to the Vedic literature at a later time. It probably is fair to say that although the Upanishads have been tremendously influential as the basis for later Hindu philosophy, they have never been extremely popular, except among intellectuals. They are complicated and difficult discussions, and they require the acceptance of a worldview that is not easily understood. Nevertheless, their movement away from the priestly and sacrificial religion of the Vedas toward a more philosophical reflection on divine reality reflects an important change in Hinduism.

As indicated, the fundamental assumption of the Upanishads is that there is but one true reality in the universe—**Brahman**. Brahman is eternal, infinite, unknowable, sexless, without a past, present, or future, and totally impersonal.

From the Source

In the beginning Brahman was all this. He was one, and infinite; infinite in the East, infinite in the South, infinite in the West, infinite in the North, above and below and everywhere infinite. East and the other regions do not exist for him, nor across, nor below, nor above. The Highest Self is not to be fixed, he is unlimited, unborn, not to be reasoned about, not to be conceived.[8]

The living beings that inhabit our world are really only expressions of the Brahman. They are souls (*atman*) that are a part of the great ocean of souls that make up the Brahman. Therefore, all phenomenal existence is illusion (maya) arising from ignorance of the true nature of reality. A person's individuality apart from the Brahman—the world in which one lives, that which one sees, hears, touches, and feels—is all an illusion, a dream.

From the Source

That from which the maker sends forth all this—the sacred verses, the offerings, the sacrifices, the panaceas, the past, the future, and all that the Vedas declare—in that the other is bound up through that mâyâ (illusion).[9]

The plight of human beings is that they are bound up in this world of illusion and ignorance, thinking that it is real, unaware of their true identification with Brahman. "All who worship what is not real knowledge (good works), enter into blind darkness: those who delight in real knowledge, enter, as it were, into greater darkness."[10] This ignorance is often illustrated by the parable of the tiger who was orphaned as a cub and reared by goats. All of his life, he believed that he too was a goat; he ate grass and bleated like a goat. One day he met another tiger who took him to a pool where the first tiger saw his true image. The second tiger then forced him to eat meat for the first time, and he slowly came to realize his tiger nature. In a similar manner, humans are deceived about their true nature. It is the task of religion to reveal the divine within us and to show us how to live on the new plane.

In discussing the nature of life, the Upanishads introduce the concept of **karma**. What makes one person different from another? Why is one person kind, intelligent, talented, or wise, and a brother or sister the opposite? Modern answers to these questions often center on a debate over the effects of heredity or environment. Ancient Indian thinkers preferred to attribute virtue or evil to choices made by the individual. They introduced the concept of karma into religious language. The Sanskrit word *karma* comes from a root that means "to do or act." In the classical period, Indians came to believe that every action and every thought had its consequence, marking the individual internally, an effect felt either in this life or in a succeeding one. Therefore, the person who seems to have positive innate qualities is merely a demonstration of positive actions in the past. Likewise, the person who is criminal is acting out the consequences of choices made in the past.

Along with the idea of karma, Indian thinkers introduced the concept of *samsara*, literally "to wander across." Indian religions believe that the life force of an individual does not die with the death of the body, but instead "wanders across." The life force moves on to another time and body, where it continues to live. Many Western thinkers have proposed this idea as "reincarnation" or the "transmigration of souls." Some see this process as a blessing; but in Indian thought, samsara may be thought of as a curse. One is bound to live in ignorance and pain, living over and over again through countless generations. Indeed, the goal of most Indian religions is to break the cycle of karma and samsara and be free from the burden of life. This breaking free from life is called *moksha*.

In the Upanishads, release from life comes when there is true knowledge of the illusion of life. "That god, the maker of all things, the great Self, always dwelling in the heart of man, is perceived by the heart, the soul, the mind; they who know it become immortal."[11] When true knowledge of the illusion of life is realized, one can be freed from the bondage of life and achieve unity with the Brahman. This is difficult. It comes only after much study, and requires many lifetimes. "Rise, awake! having obtained your boons, understand them! The sharp edge of a razor is difficult to pass over; thus the wise say the path (to the Self) is hard."[12]

Within the Upanishads, one finds a collection of materials. Various legends and tales are used to illustrate the philosophical material of these books. They are frequently cast in the form of a student's discussion with a guru and apparently have been collected over centuries of use. The Chandogya-Upanishad records a conversation between a son and his father. The father instructs his son in the following manner:

From the Source

"Place this salt in water, and then wait on me in the morning."
The son did as he was commanded.
The father said to him: "Bring me the salt, which you placed in the water last night."
The son having looked for it, found it not, for, of course, it was melted.
The father said: "Taste it from the surface of the water. How is it?"
The son replied: "It is salt."
"Taste it from the middle. How is it?"
The son replied: "It is salt."

"Taste it from the bottom. How is it?"
The son replied "It is salt."
"The father said Throw it away and then wait on me."
He did so; but salt exists for ever.
Then the father said: "Here also, in this body, forsooth, you do not perceive the True (Sat), my son; but there indeed it is."
"That which is the subtle essence, in it all that exists has its self. It is the True. It is the Self, and thou, O Svetaketu, art it."
"Please, Sir, inform me still more," said the son.
"Be it so, my child," the father replied.[13]

The *Law of Manu*

Another piece of traditional Indian literature produced during the classical era is the ethical *Law of Manu*. This law, which was probably written at some point between 300 B.C.E. and 300 C.E., is of value not only because of its religious teachings but also because of what it reveals about Indian life during the period. Within this book, the student finds the ethical and social standards that were held as ideals during the classical era of Indian history and the effects that the religious and philosophical teachings of the Vedas had on Indian society. Furthermore, one finds here the roots of many of the social and religious traditions that characterize modern Hinduism.

One of the basic assumptions of the *Law of Manu* is the varna, or **caste**, system, which had apparently developed from the early Aryan divisions of society. The description of the varna system included in this text is based on an earlier account in the *Rig-Veda* that describes the gods' sacrifice of the cosmic man Purusa as the origin of Hindu society.

From the Source

When they divided Purusa, into how many parts did they separate him?

What did his mouth become? What his two arms? What are declared to be his two thighs, his two feet?

The Brahman [priest] was his mouth. His two arms became the Raja [ruler]; his two thighs are the Vaishya [artisans, merchants and farmers], from his two feet the Sudra [servant] was produced.[14]

The *Law of Manu* is more explicit concerning the duties of the four varna. It specifies particular occupations for each of the four social groups, which are seen as being divinely ordained.

For the growth of the worlds, (Brahman) created Brahmanas (Brahmins), Kshatriyas (warriors), Vaishyas (traders) and Shudras (manual workers) from his face, arms, thighs, and feet respectively.[15]

The first three are called "twice born" and the fourth, the Shudras, "once born." Members of each group have specific duties (**dharma**) and opportunities and must obey them only.[16]

From the Source

For the Brahmanas (Brahmins), he created teaching, studying, sacrifice, officiating at sacrifice, giving gifts, and accepting gifts.

For the Kshatriya, he created in short the protection of people, giving gifts, performing sacrifices, studying, and nonattachment to sense pleasures.

For the Vaishya, he created the protection of cattle, charity, performance of sacrifices, studying, trading, lending on interest, and agriculture.

The Lord created only one profession for the Shudra: service without envy of the above three castes.[17]

(Mark R. Woodward)

Mountaintop Hindu temple dedicated to Vishnu and Lakshmi found in Central Bali, Indonesia.

At this time, Brahmins were expected to lead a religious life and to devote themselves to the study of the Vedas and the practice of their teachings. Members of the other varna were expected to perform their duties faithfully and to move gradually through the system, incarnation by incarnation. Even at this early stage, Indian society was stratified into fixed classes. Mobility through the system could be achieved only through reincarnation.

The *Law of Manu* also demonstrates the state of the understanding of rebirth in this period.

From the Source

Man obtains the life of motionlessness (of plants, and so on) as a result of the evil committed by the body, the life of birds and beasts because of the evil committed by speech, and the life of the lowest born because of the evil committed by mind.

If a man performs only good actions, he will be born a god; if he performs mixed actions, he will be born a man; and if he performs only evil actions, he will be born a bird or an animal. The result of evil speech is the destruction of knowledge, that of evil mind is the loss of the supreme destiny; and that of the evil body is the loss of the worlds. So let one protect the three in every way. The punishment prescribed for evil speech is silence; that for evil mind is fasting; and that for evil action is breath control.[18]

Conceptually, the idea that karma decides how one is reborn depends to a certain extent on a society with different status levels or states of being. The *Law of Manu* clearly articulates this connection between karma, caste, and rebirth.

Religion and Public Life

Another central teaching of the *Law of Manu* is the various stages of life through which upper-caste men were expected to pass. In the first stage of life, the typical upper-caste Indian male is supposed to be a student, studying the Vedas and giving careful attention to a teacher. In the second stage, he is to become a householder and marry within his caste. In the ideal marriage described in the *Law of Manu*, the man is to be considerably older than his wife. The role of householder and provider is one of the most important, for the householder is seen as one of the cornerstones of society. This is also the time when a man enjoys whatever wealth and pleasure may come into life. When his duties as a householder are finished (typically when the grandchildren are grown), a Hindu man may retreat to the forest and live there for some years as a hermit, meditating and offering sacrifices. During this time, he learns non-attachment to the things of the world. Finally, when the hermit life is completed, Hindus may become wandering beggars (*sannyasi*). These four stages are only the ideals of the twice-born males (the three higher castes); the role of the Shudra is to serve the higher castes. And, indeed, it should be accentuated that these were ideals; the greatest majority of Hindus, then and now, do not expect to move beyond the householder stage of life. Women are generally depicted as inferior and subservient to men in the *Law of Manu*. For the most part, women's role is to support men as they progress through the various stages of life.[19] However, it should again be noted that the *Law of Manu* represents a "snapshot," as it were, of social ideals at the time of its compilation. It is reasonable to think, however, that the role of women in Hindu society was and is more complex than allowed for in this text. As discussed later in this chapter, Hindus venerate a number of very powerful goddesses, and several women have become legendary holy people.

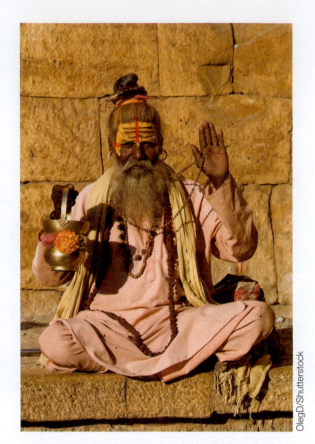

Sadhu, Hindu holy man in Bombay, India. This man has entered the final stage of life and has given himself totally to meditation and acts of devotion.

SOURCE: (Zzvet/Dreamstime)

Jainism and Buddhism

In the sixth century B.C.E., two new religions arose in India and offered alternative paths within the Indian worldview. They are discussed in detail in later chapters, but it is worth noting at this point in our discussion of classical Hinduism that they did arise as serious challenges to the mother religion.

Both Jainism and Buddhism rejected the sacrifice system taught in the Vedas. Both taught that one achieved release from life not by offering sacrifices to the gods or by any form of worship but through accomplishments in one's own life. Both rejected the Vedas as sacred scripture, and both taught that anyone of any caste who lived properly might find release.

Jainism taught that one found release from life through asceticism. The more one denied pleasures and satisfactions to the body, the more likely that person was to achieve freedom from the endless cycle of birth and rebirth. In addition, the founders of Jainism expanded on the traditional Indian concern for cattle and taught that all forms of life were sacred and were to be loved and preserved whenever possible. *Ahimsa*, the Jain term for this nonviolent regard for all living things, was taken originally from a similar idea in Hinduism. Although Jainism had its moments of popularity, it demanded too much of the average person for it to become a mass movement. In the centuries following Jainism's origin, Hinduism re-absorbed its concern for asceticism and ahimsa. Today, Jainism has only about four million followers in India out of a population of more than a billion.

Buddhism grew out of many of the same longings and beliefs that formed the basis for Jainism. However, it taught that although one could find release from life without priests and a sacrifice system, the extremes of asceticism were not necessary. For a time, Buddhism, with its more moderate ways, appeared to have become the religion of India. It became a missionary religion, sending its preachers to other Asian nations. However, Hinduism eventually reasserted itself and absorbed the distinctive features of Buddhism. Gautama Buddha, founder of Buddhism, was made a member of the Hindu pantheon, and some of his teachings became a part of Hinduism. He is said by some to have been an incarnation of the god Vishnu. By the fifteenth century C.E., few Buddhists were left in India. Buddhism did, however, become the dominant religion of many other Asian nations and survives in them today. The rise and popularity of Jainism and Buddhism in the sixth century C.E. demonstrates that not all Indians found satisfaction in the teachings of classical Hinduism.

Bhagavad Gita

Perhaps the concluding statement on classical Hinduism is the great epic poem of Indian culture and religion, the **Bhagavad Gita**. The *Gita* is about a great battle; it relates the stories of the struggles of notable heroes and gods and contains much of the basic philosophy of the culture.

Krishna dancing the Dance of Life (Rasa Lila) with Radha and the cowherd women. Krishna is worshiped by Hindus as the eighth avatar (incarnation) of the Hindu god Vishnu. As a youth, Krishna was a cowherd who made a reputation for himself as a lover, and when he played the flute, the gopis (wives and daughters of the cowherds) came to dance with him.

The *Bhagavad Gita* is found within the text of a longer epic called the *Mahabharata*.[20] The *Mahabharata* is the story of the struggles between the two leading families from the beginning of Indian history. Finally, these two families come together in the battle of Kurukshetra, which historians roughly place between 850 and 650 B.C.E. Just prior to this battle, one of the warriors, Arjuna, contemplates his fate and the struggle before him. His charioteer, Krishna, enters into the dialogue with him. Their conversation, found between chapters 25 and 42 of the *Mahabharata*, makes up the *Bhagavad Gita*.

Although the *Mahabharata* is believed to have been composed over a very long period, beginning perhaps as early as the ninth or eighth century B.C.E., the *Gita* is believed to have been composed at some point between the second century B.C.E. and the third century C.E. The eighteen chapters that make up the *Gita* are divided into three sections of six chapters each. In the first section, Arjuna (the young warrior) looks out on the battlefield and contemplates the coming war and his part in it.

From the Source

There as they stood the son of Pritha saw fathers, grandsires, teachers, uncles, brothers, sons, grandsons, and comrades, fathers-in-law and friends in both armies, and seeing them, all his kinsmen, [thus] arrayed, the son of Kunti was filled with deep compassion and, desponding, spoke these [words]:

"Krishna, when I see these mine own folk standing [before me], spoiling for the fight, my limbs give way, my mouth dries up, trembling seizes my body, and my [body's] hairs stand up in dread. [My bow,] Gandiva, slips from my hand, my very skin is all ablaze; I cannot stand and my mind seems to wander. Krishna, adverse omens too I see, nor can I discern aught good in striking down in battle mine own folk. Krishna, I do not long for victory nor for the kingdom nor yet for things of pleasure. What should I do with a kingdom? What with enjoyments or [even] with life?

"O let the sons of Dhritarashtra, arms in hand, slay me in battle though I, unarmed myself, will offer no defense; therein were greater happiness for me."[21]

Thus, like other warriors in all ages, Arjuna ponders the folly of war, particularly interfamily war, and contemplates going into battle unarmed and thus committing suicide. Arjuna's contemplation is answered by his charioteer, Krishna. The remainder of the poem is the conversation between Arjuna and Krishna about the nature of life and one's duties in life. These duties, in Hinduism, are known as one's *dharma*. In the second section of the poem, Krishna reveals that he is the incarnation of the god **Vishnu**. As such, he has come to earth to help mortals who are struggling with their problems. In the third section, Krishna and Arjuna continue to discuss the problems of life that confront mortals.

Much of the advice and teaching that Krishna gives Arjuna is a reflection of the philosophy of the Upanishads, that most of what mortals see as life and its problems is merely illusion. The most direct teaching that Krishna gives to Arjuna is that he should not dread going into battle because he is a member of the Kshatriya class and as such it is his dharma to be a warrior and to kill. If Arjuna were a member of another class, such as the Brahmin, he might have reason to reject the battlefield. However, battle is the dharma of the Kshatriya, and Arjuna has an obligation to obey that duty.

From the Source

No man shall 'scape from act by shunning action; nay, and none shall come by mere renouncements unto perfectness. Nay, and no jot of time, at any time, rests any actionless; his nature's law compels him, even unwilling, into act..[22]

The basic teachings and religious implications of the *Bhagavad Gita* are many. The obvious teaching is that individuals should perform the duty of their caste and thus avoid karma, the force that binds people to the endless cycle of birth, death, and rebirth. The obligations that are placed upon each caste are raised to the level of religious duties, or dharma.

A second feature of Indian religion apparent in the *Gita* is its openness to a variety of means of religious expression. People can achieve release from life (moksha) through asceticism, meditation, devotions to and worship of the gods, or obedience to the rules of caste. It is for this reason that Hinduism is often described as the most tolerant of all the world religions.

Perhaps the most lasting teaching of the *Gita* is its picture of Vishnu as a god who loves and is concerned about human beings. Indeed, loving devotion, or **bhakti**, for the gods becomes the pre-eminent path to moksha in Hinduism. Much of this loving devotionalism is rooted in the *Gita*. Vishnu's concern for humankind is such that he takes various forms and comes to Earth at certain times to aid mortals in their struggles. As Krishna says:

From the Source

When Righteousness declines, O Bharata! when Wickedness is strong, I rise, from age to age, and take visible shape, and move a man with men.[23]

In postclassical Hinduism, Vishnu became one of the most popular gods. The *Bhagavad Gita* makes clear that, in addition to meditation and fulfilling one's dharma, devotion (bhakti) to gods like Vishnu is a path to moksha and utter communion with the divine.

From the Source

Arjuna, be sure of this: none who worships Me with loyalty and love is lost to Me. For whosoever makes Me his haven, base-born though he may be, yes, women too, and artisans, even serfs, theirs it is to tread the highest way. How much more, then, Brahmans pure and good, and royal seers who know devoted love. Since your lot has fallen in this world, impermanent and joyless, commune with Me in love. On Me your mind, on Me your loving service, for Me your sacrifice, to Me be your prostrations: now that you have thus integrated self, your striving bent on Me, to Me you will [surely] come.[24]

Postclassical Hinduism

4.3. **Discuss postclassical Hinduism.**

With the completion of the *Bhagavad Gita*, the classical era in Indian religion came to a close. This period included the development of the Vedas and other religious literature, such as the *Law of Manu*, the Upanishads, and the *Bhagavad Gita*. This material, its philosophy, and the pantheon of gods that it presented became the basis for later Hinduism.

Some scholars distinguish between the religion of the classical era and that of the postclassical period by referring to the earlier religion as Brahminism and the later as Hinduism. Within Brahminism, the religion of the Indian people was much based on sacrificial rites carried out by specialist priests. In this context, gods were worshiped with sacrifices offered on altars built in the open. Priests who were experts in rituals and methods of sacrifice were very important.

After the close of the classical period, subtle changes gradually were introduced into the religion of India. Although the existence of many gods was still acknowledged, interest tended to center on the worship of a few major deities, who were, however, worshiped in many forms. Worship came to be love and devotion to those gods. Temples were built to honor them, and hymns were composed about their outstanding qualities. Whereas the literature of the classical period tended to deal with the great epics of Indian history, the literature of the postclassical era tended to center on gods and goddesses. These writings, called **puranas**, are comprised of devotional verses about the exploits and attributes of popular Hindu deities. The major gods are seen as taking various forms and becoming involved in the affairs of humans. Female goddesses were particularly important in postclassical Hinduism, and many of the people of India became devotees of these goddesses, developed cults about them, and built temples for their worship. Particularly in south India, major temple festivals celebrate the marriages of gods and goddesses. Hindu gods and goddesses have many human qualities, but on a grand scale. They can be kind and loving or cruel and violent; they can be erotic and life-affirming or practice severe austerities. Some of the tales of the gods and goddesses are romances that tell of love and desire; others concern battles between gods and demons.

Some scholars also point to the change that occurred in the basic attitude toward life in India between the classical and postclassical eras. By the beginning of modern Hinduism, one sees certain meditative forces emerging in Hindu philosophy. If the basic worldview of Hinduism is that life is an endless cycle of birth, life, death, and rebirth, and that the goal of religion is to cease living, then this is essentially a negative and world-denying religion. The ascetic who refuses the pleasures and comforts of this life (and not the warrior) becomes the religious and cultural hero.

None of these changes occurred overnight or even over one century. Their roots appear even in the Vedas. By the beginning of the Common Era, however, certain changes in the basic religious structure did appear.

Devotion to the Gods

Hinduism offers its devotees many paths. Most Hindus practice their religion through devotion to one or more of the Indian gods. They may give full religious attention to each of these gods or goddesses by worshiping at their temples, offering sacrifices, praying, supporting the priests of the temple, and so on. In this manner, the gods or goddesses may look with favor upon the devotees, support the believers in life, and help in the struggles of life. This path is called *bhakti-marga* ("the way of devotion").

Brahman, who is ultimate reality, is at the core of Hindu thought. He is one and undivided. Yet postclassical Hinduism sees him in terms of three forms or functions. These three (called the **Trimurti**) are creation, destruction, and preservation. Each of these three functions of Brahman is expressed by a god from the classical literature: Brahma, the creator; Shiva, the destroyer; and Vishnu, the preserver. Devotees of any of these three gods tend to see all of the functions of Brahman in their chosen deity. Devi, the great goddess, represents the feminine principle in Hindu thought. She is the creative power worshiped in female form and is believed to be the all-pervasive energy (*shakti*) of the gods as well as the slayer of demons. Other goddesses are thought to be manifestations of Devi in much the same sense that the gods can be seen as manifestations of the supreme god Brahman.

(Mark R. Woodward)

A Hindu goddess in a temple in Kuala Lumpur, Malaysia. Hindus are a substantial minority in the predominantly Muslim country in Southeast Asia.

BRAHMA   Of the three leading deities of the Trimurti, **Brahma** receives the least attention.[25] Although Brahma is widely respected and recognized as being the creator of the world, only two temples are specifically dedicated to him in all of India, and he has no cult of devotees. When Brahma is depicted in Indian art, he is shown as red, with four bearded faces and four arms. His chief wife, Sarasvati, is the goddess of knowledge, speech, poetry, and wisdom. In Hindu Bali she is also regarded as the primary patron of the performing arts. Although Brahma is not mentioned in the Vedas, considerable mythology has accumulated during the post–Vedic era about him and his work of creation.

SHIVA   Among the most popular gods in postclassical Hinduism is Shiva, known as "the destroyer." Shiva is the god of death, destruction, and disease. Like Brahma, Shiva does not appear in Vedic literature, but he is believed to have been developed from the Vedic god Rudra.

The functions of Shiva are many. Not only is he the god of death, disease, and destruction, he is also the god of the dance. In the mythology connected with Shiva, there is frequently some statement about his dancing. He is a special god to Hindu ascetics, probably because in the process of tormenting and destroying their flesh, this terrible deity is the one who is closest to reality for them. One of the most common symbols of Shiva is the **lingam**. A lingam is a cylindrical pillar, sometimes considered to have phallic imagery. The lingam is often found atop a **yoni**, a stylized dish or round receptacle that symbolizes the feminine shakti. Together, they represent energy and regeneration.

Perhaps the most important reason for Shiva's popularity is that he is also the god of vegetable, animal, and human reproduction. In Indian thought, death is but the prelude to rebirth. Therefore, it follows that the god of death will also be a god of reproduction and sexuality. Thus Shiva becomes the special deity of those who seek fertility.

Devotees of Shiva are known as Shaivites. Several sects of Shaivism exist in Hinduism today. All regard the Vedas and special Shaivite texts as scriptures. Their philosophical stance is that Shiva is ultimate reality; he is creator, preserver, and destroyer. Humans are thought to be separated from Shiva because of ignorance, karma, and illusion. To achieve union with Shiva, people must follow a prescribed path and worship and attend Shiva in his temples. They must also meditate and study under the direction of a guru. Some Shivaites require the repetition of a special mantra. All of these acts culminate in a union between Shiva and the worshiper and ultimately result in moksha (release from the death–rebirth cycle).

Fully as popular as Shiva are several goddesses related to Shaivite worship. The most important and most popular are **Kali** or, as she is sometimes called, Durga, and Parvati. Kali is, if anything, more terrible than Shiva. She is frequently depicted as wearing a necklace of human skulls, tearing away the flesh of sacrificed victims, and drinking blood. Mythology connects her with the founding of the modern city of Calcutta.

From the Source

When Kali died, Shiva was both grief-stricken and angry. He placed her corpse on his shoulders and went stamping round the world in a dervish dance of mourning which became more furious the longer it lasted. The other gods realized that unless Shiva was stopped the whole world would be destroyed by his rage, which was unlikely to end as long as he had his wife's body on his shoulders. So Vishnu took up a knife and flung it at the corpse, dismembering it into fifty-two pieces which were scattered across the face of the earth. By the side of a great river in Bengal the little toe of the right foot landed, and a temple was built there, with an attendant village, and the people called this place Kalikata.[26]

(Mark R. Woodward)

Ganesha is one of the most popular Hindu gods. He is the son of Shiva and Paravati. He is known as the patron of scribes and accountants and as "the remover of obstacles." Every Hindu divinity is associated with an animal. Ganesha's is the rat, pictured here.

Parvati is very nearly the opposite of Kali. She is the daughter of the Himalayas and the female element of the perfect loving couple when paired with the gentler aspect of Shiva. Parvati is often depicted as the perfect wife and mother. Because of her desire to marry Shiva, she undertakes the practice of asceticism. It is her responsibility to persuade Shiva to stop his meditation and use his powers for the benefit of the world. She is also a fertility goddess. Like that of Shiva, the mythology of Parvati emphasizes the ascetic as well as the erotic aspects of her personality. In her destructive mode, she is often depicted riding a lion.[27]

Another extremely popular god related to the Shaivite worshiping community is **Ganesha.** Easily recognized by his elephant head, Ganesha is revered as a remover of obstacles and is called upon to assist in many endeavors. He is also considered to oversee the obtaining of knowledge and many other creative pursuits. Most stories about him relate that he is the son of Shiva and Parvati, although some believe that he was created by Parvati. When Shiva saw her new baby, he was enraged and cut off his head, which greatly upset Parvati. To console her, he sent out for a head from the closest available being, which turned out to be an elephant. In any case, Ganesha remains one of the most important and common gods in contemporary Hinduism.

VISHNU The third god of the postclassical Hindu triad is Vishnu, the preserver. In contrast to Shiva, Vishnu is known as a god of love, benevolence, and forgiveness. One of his chief characteristics is his love of play. He plays and joins humanity in play. He enjoys tricks and pranks. The chief feature of Vishnu is his concern for humanity, which he expresses by appearing on Earth a number of times in various forms (*avatars*). According to mythology, Vishnu has appeared on Earth in nine forms. In some incarnations, he has come as a man. According to the *Bhagavad Gita*, he appeared as Krishna. As Hinduism absorbed the distinctive features of Buddhism, it was taught that Vishnu had appeared as Gautama, the Buddha. He has purportedly also come to Earth as various animals and creatures involved in helping people. For example, it is believed that Vishnu appeared as Matsya, the fish who saved Manu from the great flood. In every case, he has come to aid humankind because he is the preserver and the restorer. The tenth avatar of Vishnu will occur at the end of the age, when he will appear as Kalkin on a white horse. He will bring time to an end, punish the wicked, and reward the virtuous.

Devotees of Vishnu are known as Vaishnavites. In India, they are noted for their deep love of God and for the poems and songs they write in his praise. Kabir and Nanak, the founders of Sikhism, were poets in this tradition. Like the Shaivites, the worshipers of Vishnu regard their god as ultimate reality. Generally, they emphasize the love and grace of Vishnu rather than the actions of devotees.

Lakshmi is the wife of Vishnu. She is believed to have risen from the ocean to ensure the fertility and welfare of the world. She is the goddess of fertility and wealth and also of victory. On the Indonesian islands of Java and Bali, where she is known as Sri, she is worshiped as the goddess of rice. She is often seen as a mediator between humans and Vishnu, who is sometimes too remote for humans to approach directly. Lakshmi is also known for her complete devotion to her husband, despite his frequent extramarital affairs. The love of Vishnu and Lakshmi is the central theme in the second of the great Indian epic poems, the *Ramayana*. In this tale, Vishnu and Lakshmi are born in the world as Rama and Sita. The story focuses on Rama's quest to find and rescue his beloved Sita when she is kidnapped by Rawana, the king of the demons.

An extreme example of devotion to one god has become familiar in many major American cities in the past few decades—the so-called *Hare Krishna* movement. This group of devotees of the god Krishna traces its origin to the appearance of Krishna in human form, as recorded in the *Bhagavad Gita*. From that time onward, groups of people in India have devoted themselves totally to the worship and adoration of Krishna.

The act of worship to the gods is known as **puja**. Puja occurs both in households, where it is often practiced by women, as well as in Hindu temples, and it tends to be a sensory experience. Puja is made to a god or to various gods as they are represented as **murtis**, or sacred statues or images. During the course of the puja, special lamps are lit, incense is often burned, and the murtis are bathed with milk. Often food, known as **prasad**, is offered to the murtis during puja. In temple worship, this prasad is often distributed to devotees after the puja and is considered to be blessed. Other offerings can also be made to the gods—flowers and colorful pastes and powders are common. During puja, prayers are said, and sometimes hymns from the Vedas are sung. Finally, puja often includes "aarti," a practice in which lit lamps or candles are moved in a circle in front of the murti as an act of devotion.

Vishnu, the preserver, one of the three most important gods of Hinduism, is depicted with Garuda, a mythological bird, at a Balinese temple, ca. 1600 C.E.

Devotion to Knowledge

As we have seen, postclassical Hinduism developed in such a way that most people practiced their religion through devotion to one or more of the gods. No doubt, this was the most acceptable and convenient path for most people. An equally acceptable way for those who could follow it was the so-called way of knowledge (*jnana-marga*). For the wealthy or the intellectual who had the time to spend studying the various philosophical implications of sacred writings, the way of knowledge had merit.

Generally, when one speaks of the way of knowledge in Hinduism, one refers to the various systems of philosophy (*darshan*). These systems are Sankhya, Yoga, Mimansa, Vaisheshika, Nyaya, and Vedanta. All claim to be based on the Vedas, all aim at release, and all believe in rebirth and pre-existence. Two of the more well known of these systems are discussed next.

THE YOGA SYSTEM   Of all the Hindu philosophies, Yoga is the best known to Westerners, although they tend to think only of physical (*Hatha*) Yoga, or of the various extremes of asceticism that the Yogin may achieve. The word *Yoga* is derived from the root *yuj*, "to yoke" or "to join." Yoga basically follows the philosophical views of the Sankhya system, viewing the world as a dualism and teaching that one should attempt to yoke or join the individual spirit to god, the atman, to Brahman.

Statues and seals depicting persons in various yogic positions have been found in the remains of the pre-Vedic cities dating back to the third millennium B.C.E. However, the philosophy of Yoga as it is known today was developed by the sage Patanjal, who lived in the second century B.C.E. and codified the teachings of Yoga in his *Yoga Sutra*.

The main feature of all Yoga is meditation. Meditation is necessary even for the gods if they are to find release from the cycle of birth, death, and rebirth. There are several forms of Yoga, each having several features and each emphasizing a different one. Raja Yoga stresses mental and spiritual development. In this form of yogic discipline, one works through various stages to free the mind from anger, lust, hatred, greed, and so on. According to the *Yoga Sutra*, there are eight steps one must take to achieve trance or the superconscious level in Raja Yoga:

1. Before one can progress, one must take certain vows of restraint (*yama*). These are vows against harming living creatures and against unchastity.
2. At this stage, one attempts to achieve internal control, calmness, and equanimity (*niyama*).
3. In the third stage, one learns and practices certain bodily postures (*asana*) designed to help one achieve the aims of Yoga.[28]
4. Once the postures have been mastered, one works on breath control (*pranayama*).
5. The fifth stage is control of the senses (*pratyahara*), in which one seeks to shut out the outside world.
6. The sixth stage is extreme concentration on a single object (*dharana*).
7. Then, one seeks to achieve meditation (*dhyana*).
8. Finally, the Yogin seeks a trance (*samadhi*), in which the Yogin becomes one with the Brahman.

Those who work through these steps achieve great physical powers and remarkable abilities of concentration. The ascetics who master Yoga are those who perform the outstanding feats of asceticism that have come to be identified with Yoga in the Western mind.

THE VEDANTA SYSTEM   The term *Vedanta* is usually translated "the end of the Vedas," thus indicating that the major materials in these systems are taken from the Upanishads, which are placed at the end of the Vedic literature. The term is also translated as "the acme of the Vedas," indicating that the Vedanta philosophy is the very peak of the religious teaching found in the Vedas. Regardless of the interpretation, Vedanta philosophy is based on the Upanishadic writings and their outlook on life. It is believed that the Vedanta philosophy was first formulated by a sage named Badarayana, who may have lived during the first century B.C.E. and may have written the *Vedanta Sutra*.

The Vedanta is monistic and assumes only one true essence in the universe. This essence may be called God, or Brahman. Nothing else exists but Brahman. The world of humankind, its bodies, souls, and material substances, does not really exist. The world as we perceive it is based on false knowledge (maya), which conceals the reality of Brahman. Humans do not recognize Brahman but instead try to cling to the objects of life, which are like mirages—they keep slipping from our grasp. In truth, only Brahman is real. Therefore, humankind's basic problem is not wickedness but ignorance. People are ignorant about the true nature of reality and believe that they are separated from Brahman. This ignorance thus binds them endlessly to the cycle of birth and rebirth until they can achieve liberation through knowledge.

One branch of Vedanta that developed in the ninth century C.E. is called *Advaita*, which means "non-dual" and indicates its monistic viewpoint. Its founder was Shankara (788–820 C.E.), who was perhaps the most outstanding scholar of medieval Hinduism. Although he was a famous ascetic and teacher in his time, he is best known for his philosophical approach in interpreting the Upanishads. His most outstanding literary contribution is a commentary on the *Vedanta Sutra*. This commentary has become such a classic in Hindu literature that it has been the object of several commentaries. In his commentary, Shankara asserted the absolute oneness of Brahman in the classic manner of the Upanishads. Brahman is all there is. All else in the universe is

Prambanan, a tenth-century Hindu temple dedicated to the three major gods, Brahma, Vishnu, and Shiva, near Yogyakarta, Indonesia.

(Mark R. Woodward)

an illusion, and people are bound up in endless reincarnations until they rip aside the veil of this illusion. Shankara himself was a devotee of Shiva, because he believed that Shiva was the best representation of the true nature of Brahman.

Shankara is also remembered for his fierce opposition to Buddhism. It is thought that his leadership against Buddhism was a major factor in destroying this religion in India and restoring Hinduism to its dominant position.

According to one story, Shankara did not die; he simply disappeared. Consequently, some Shaivites believe that the great scholar was actually an avatar of Shiva.

A second philosopher of the medieval period in Hinduism, who represents a side in the debate over the true meaning of the Vedas, was Ramanuja (ca. 1056–1137 C.E.). Ramanuja believed that devotion to the gods was extremely important. He was himself devoted to the worship of Vishnu. He reasoned that if Shankara were correct and if each person were merely a part of the god Brahman, then devotion to god would not be possible, for how can one be devoted to oneself? Although he could not move away from the traditional Vedanta position of the oneness of god, Ramanuja taught a qualified dualism in which he asserted that the human soul and the divine soul were united and yet somehow separate. The analogy that he used was the human body and spirit—one cannot exist without the other, but they are separate entities.

The third point of view in this debate was presented by the philosopher Madhva (1199–1278 C.E.). Like Ramanuja, Madhva was devoted to the god Vishnu and believed strongly in devotion to the gods as the only proper religious expression. He was willing to go further than Ramanuja, however. He took the side of dualism even though he remained in the general school of Vedanta. He abandoned completely the notion that god was all and that all else was illusion. To him, the world and individual souls were completely separate from Brahman and separate from one another. Thus, each individual and separate soul is able to worship properly the separate nature of god.

Muslim Influences in India

4.4. **Identify Muslim influences in India.**

In the seventh century C.E., a new and vital religion sprang from the deserts of Arabia. Within a few decades, the religion of Islam had spread, through conquest and conversion, across the entire Middle Eastern world. By the eighth century, it was on the verge of moving into Europe. Muslims also moved eastward and by the eighth century had conquered Persia and Afghanistan and made occasional raids into India.

Portions of northwest India were conquered by Muslim leaders as early as 712 C.E. In the eleventh century, the Turkish general Mahmud of Ghazni invaded India seventeen times and brought a vast treasure to his headquarters in Afghanistan. By the thirteenth century, Islam was so well entrenched in India that there was a Sultanate of Delhi. In the sixteenth century, a dynasty of Turkish rulers, known as the Mughals, established an empire and ruled most of the subcontinent of India. Most of the Mughal emperors sought to accommodate their Hindu subjects. By the eighteenth century, however, this empire had run its course and had decayed into many small warring states that became easy prey for the invading British armies. Despite its political and economic decline, the Mughal Empire retained its symbolic importance until its final destruction in 1857.

Religion and Public Life

In 1857, Hindu and Muslim *sepoys* (soldiers) of the British East India Company joined together in a rebellion against the British when they began to use a combination of beef suet and lard to grease rifles. The beef suet was considered to be defiling by Hindus and the lard equally so by Muslims. This led to one of the deadliest outbreaks of religious violence in history. Hindus and Muslims massacred Christians and were in turn massacred by them with the aid of Sikhs. Strangely, the British spared the last of the Mughal emperors, Bahadur Shah Zafar II. He was sent to Rangoon, Burma, in exile, where he died in 1862. He was buried in an unmarked grave. The location was not discovered until 1991. It has since become an important pilgrimage site for Indian Muslims, particularly politicians.

Today, India has the world's second-largest Muslim population. Only Indonesia's is larger. Relations between Hindus and Muslims have always been touchy. Indeed, it would be difficult to find two religions more different than Hinduism and Islam. Whereas Muslims staunchly worship only one God, Hindus tend to have many gods; whereas Muslims disdain the representation of Allah in any form, Hindus have richly decorated temples, their homes, and in modern times their cars and trucks with images portraying their many gods; whereas Muslims sacrifice cattle and other animals in commemoration of the biblical and Quranic account of Abraham's willingness to sacrifice his son at God's command, Hindus regard the cow as a sacred animal and seek to protect it from any harm; and whereas Muslims regard every person as equal before Allah, Hindus have traditionally followed a caste system that divides society into classes, with the upper classes having more religious privileges than the lower.

Early Muslim visitors to India were amazed at the openness of Hindu theology. Al-Biruni, a Muslim writer from the eleventh century, described the Hindus in the following terms:

From the Source

They totally differ from us in religion, as we believe in nothing in which they believe, and vice versa. On the whole there is very little disputing about theological topics among themselves; at the utmost, they fight with words, but they will never stake their soul or body or their property on religious controversy.[29]

Despite these vast differences, Hindus and Muslims have managed to live side by side for more than 1,000 years. Hinduism has not altered its basic theology in light of its contacts with Islam, but Indian society has adopted many of the elements of the Muslim culture. Particularly during the years of the Mughal Empire, Indian society was influenced by the art, architecture, sciences, and even the dress styles of the Muslim world. Over the centuries, Hinduism and Islam have also converged in important ways. Many Muslims have adopted the caste system as a mode of social organization. There are also shrines and saints that both members of both communities venerate.

In the fifteenth century, there arose the most notable attempt at reconciliation between Islam and Hinduism: the religion of Sikhism. Sikhism is discussed in detail in Chapter 7; however, it must be said at this point that Sikhism managed to attain a harmony between the uncompromising monotheism of Islam and the doctrines of illusion and rebirth of Hinduism. It must also be said that whereas Hindus and Muslims have somehow managed to live together in India, the religious and political differences between the two peoples are one of the major problems facing India today.

Movements and Issues in Modern Hinduism

4.5.   **Discuss movements and issues in modern Hinduism.**

Hinduism, like all major religions, has had to face the rigors of the modern age, with its nationalistic movements, its social reforms, its encounters between religions, and its scientific revolutions. Of the factors of the modern era that have affected Hinduism, one of the most important has been its encounter with Christianity and its European and American representatives. According to tradition, Christianity was brought to India by the disciple Thomas in the first century C.E. Christian communities existed in southern India many centuries before the arrival of the Europeans. However, Christianity had little effect on the vast majority of Indian people until more recent times. In premodern times, Christians were treated as simply another caste, in much the same way Muslims were in large parts of India. However, when Christianity was encountered in conjunction with the political power of the British Empire and modern scientific knowledge, it had to be taken as a more serious challenge.

The first significant encounter between India and the modern European nations came in 1510, when the Portuguese conquered Goa. In the seventeenth century, the British invaded India and established the British East India Company. This began three centuries of British rule in India. Although the British were present in India as merchants and soldiers, it was not until the nineteenth century that they allowed missionaries to enter the country to try to convert the Indians. One of the reasons for this late entry was that many Protestant denominations did not actively seek to send missionaries earlier.

One of the British missionaries to enter India was the Baptist William Carey (1761–1834). Like many other missionaries of the nineteenth century, Carey was concerned not only with preaching the gospel of his faith but also with raising the living and educational standards of the people to whom he ministered. He was the first to begin modern printing in India, and he also initiated many new educational programs for the Indian people. Carey, along with other missionaries, was alarmed at several practices he felt were inhuman and harmful within Indian social life. One of these was the *suttee*, in which an Indian widow was expected to be placed on the funeral pyre of her dead husband and be destroyed with his remains. Suttee was more social than religious in origin. Indeed, passages in Hindu sacred literature speak against the practice. Suttee had also been rejected by many Hindu reformers, such as Ram Mohan Roy. At the insistence of Christians and reform-minded Hindus, the British government outlawed the practice in 1829. Another practice that was abhorrent to the European missionary was child marriages. It had become common in India for parents to betroth their young children to ensure a suitable marriage. One of the primary concerns of parents in arranging marriages was that their children should marry within their caste. Frequently, this meant the betrothal of very young children and the marriage of nine- and ten-year-olds, which was particularly harsh for girls, who might have been promised by their parents to men twenty or thirty years their senior. This practice tended to ensure that when a husband died he left behind a fairly young widow who was not allowed to remarry and in some cases was expected to destroy herself. Eventually, child marriage also was officially outlawed in India.

The late nineteenth and twentieth centuries saw several reform movements in Hinduism. One of the earliest reformers was Ram Mohan Roy (1774–1833), who was called "the Father of Modern India." As noted, Roy opposed suttee and pressured the British government to outlaw the practice. He saw in Christianity many elements he appreciated, although he did not accept the divinity of Jesus. For example, Roy adopted monotheism and sought to suppress what he perceived to be the idolatry of Hinduism. To continue his work after his death, Roy organized the **Brahmo Samaj** (The Society of God), which became a force for Western-style reforms in Hinduism in the nineteenth and twentieth centuries.

Perhaps the greatest religious reformer of the nineteenth century was Sri Ramakrishna (1836–1886). Once a priest of Kali in Calcutta, Ramakrishna was philosophically a follower of non-dualistic Vedanta. He later became convinced that behind all religions was a single reality that might be called God. His religious experience

Images of gods and goddesses in a Hindu shop in Singapore.

(Mark R. Woodward)

with Christians and Muslims, as well as Hindus, convinced him that truth was essentially one. The teachings of Ramakrishna might have died with him in India had it not been for one of his disciples, Narendranath Dutt (1863–1902), who was later known as **Vivekananda**. Vivekananda became a member of the Brahmo Samaj early in life. Later, he met Ramakrishna and became his apostle. After a period of several years of retreat in the Himalayas, he set forth to be the first Hindu missionary to the modern world. Vivekananda traveled widely, lecturing about the virtues of Vedanta Hinduism, which he described as "the mother of all other religions." He made his greatest impression at the Parliament of Religions in Chicago in 1893 as the representative of Hinduism. Wherever he went, this spokesman for the oneness of God captivated audiences and produced converts. Vivekananda was followed by Paramahansa Ananda (1893–1952), who came to the United States in 1920 and founded the Self Realization Fellowship, which teaches a form of Vedanta philosophy that draws its inspiration from the Christian gospels as well as the sacred texts of Hinduism. The Fellowship is particularly active in California, and also has branches in India, Europe, and most of the major cities of the United States.

The best-known Indian reformer of the twentieth century was **Mohandas K. Gandhi** (1869–1948). Gandhi is chiefly remembered for his work in bringing political and social benefits to the Indian people near the end of British rule, through a combination of religious idealism and civil disobedience. In his childhood, Gandhi was deeply influenced by Hinduism, its literature and ideals. He also encountered Jains, Muslims, and Parsis. Gandhi was originally trained as a lawyer in England, where he came into contact with many of the social and political ideas of the nineteenth century. He also was introduced to Christianity, especially to Jesus's Sermon on the Mount. These factors, along with the ideals of his Hindu heritage, molded Gandhi. As the leader of the Indian people in their struggle for freedom from British rule, he personally led many fasts and strikes against various British policies and usually was victorious. In addition to espousing civil disobedience and nonviolence, Gandhi also was influenced by the Jain community's interpretation of non-injury of life (*ahimsa*). Thus, he was a vegetarian and stoutly defended the Indian practice of cow protection. Gandhi also read the works of the American Henry David Thoreau (1817–1862), who advocated passive resistance to civil authority. In turn, Gandhi became one of the models for the political thinking of Martin Luther King Jr., who led the civil rights movement in the United States during the 1960s. Gandhi, who advocated nonviolence, was assassinated by an extremist Hindu Nationalist in 1948, just a few months after his people won their independence.

An object of special concern for internal and external reformers is the caste system. Although the ancient Hindu literature spoke of society's being divided into four *varnas* (colors), the full-blown caste system is a relatively modern development. In early Hinduism, there is evidence of social intercourse among classes. At some point after 700 C.E., the modern caste system began to develop. The four basic social groups proceeded to divide into literally thousands of castes. Most frequently, these castes are based on vocations. There are castes of metal workers, weavers, warriors, priests, and many other professions. Other castes developed along ethnic or religious lines. Tribal communities, as well as Muslims, Christians, and Jews, were incorporated into Hindu society as distinct caste groups. Ultimately, more than 3,000 separate castes emerged in Indian society. When the Portuguese came to India in the sixteenth century, they gave their word *casta* (breed, race) to these divisions.[30]

Dalits, the lowest caste, who are sometimes referred to as untouchables, perform such tasks as sweeping streets, cleaning latrines, handling the dead, tanning leather, and washing clothes, which bring them into constant contact with sources of pollution. With these vocations come the lowest wages, the worst living conditions, and little hope of improvement. Generally speaking, members of higher castes have few, if any, social contacts with members of these groups. They will give gifts to or accept gifts from them. Traditionally, they were forced to live in segregated compounds on the east sides of villages for fear that the prevailing westerly winds might expose other castes to airborne pollution. It is, however, important to note that despite the fact that the untouchables are thought of as defiled, Hindu society cannot function without them because their work enables members of the higher castes to live without coming into contact with polluting substances.[31]

Traditional Hinduism seems to justify the status of the outcasts. Because the untouchables are in this situation in life, it must be because their karma from a previous life dictates it. If the outcasts accept the dharma (duty) of this life and do not rebel against it, they may hope for a better caste in the next life. As a result of the efforts of reformers like Gandhi, discrimination against the outcasts was officially forbidden in the 1948 *Constitution of the Republic of India*. Gandhi referred to the untouchables as *harijan* (children of God) and taught that because of their long and quiet suffering they had earned the respect and affection of both the gods and humans. Many lower-caste Hindus have converted to Islam or Christianity. Conversion is not a fully effective remedy for the inequalities of caste because upper-caste Hindus continue to treat the converts as they always have. The long-standing, firmly entrenched rules of caste die slowly in modern India.

Hindu Holy Days

4.6. Name the Hindu holy days.

Because Hindus worship a variety of gods and goddesses, there are a tremendous variety of festivals, fasts, feasts, and pilgrimages in Hinduism. Millions of Hindus make pilgrimages to the holy Ganges River each year to bathe in its waters and to fulfill their vows. In addition to the holy days dedicated to the various deities and holy places, festivals are held in relation to the seasons. It would be impossible to describe all of these holy days in one brief chapter; however, several general festivals that are celebrated throughout India will be discussed.

Holi

Holi is the most popular festival. It is celebrated each year during February/March to welcome spring. Holi is dedicated to the god Krishna, and it was once a fertility ceremony. This festival also celebrates the destruction of demons. During the days of Holi, many of the caste and taboo restrictions are set aside and pleasure is emphasized.

Divali

In November, Hindus welcome the new year, which is also a festival of lights. The goddesses Kali and Lakshmi, the goddess of good fortune, are connected to Divali. Devotees may choose to make pilgrimages to the holy sites connected to the story of Kali at this season. Lakshmi visits every house that is lit with a lamp and brings to it prosperity and good fortune.

Dasehra

Nine days in October are reserved for this celebration in honor of Durga, a consort of Shiva. Dasehra celebrates Durga's victory over the Buffalo demon. Presents are exchanged, and dances and processions are held to honor the goddess.

Lakshmi puja, worship of the goddess of prosperity and fertility in central India.

John Henry Claude Wilson/Alamy

Hinduism Today

4.7. **Discuss Hinduism today.**

Like all religions, Hinduism today must struggle with the issue of modernity. Its primary home, India, is the world's largest democracy; therefore, the demands of its people must be heard. Perhaps for the first time in its history, Hinduism must deal with such issues as birth control and the problems raised by urbanization. In the past, people were taught to accept their lots in life and not complain, in that the next life might be better. If problems became so severe that one could not endure them, there was always the alternative of life as an ascetic.

Hinduism, while principally practiced in India, has also spread around the world with Indian immigrants to other nations. Today, millions of Hindus live and worship outside of India, especially in the British Isles and North America. One change that has occurred in Hinduism because of these new contexts has to do with the worship of gods in temples. In India, temples are often devoted to the worship of a relatively small number of locally popular deities. However, when a temple is built in the United States or in another nation where Hindus are not the majority, oftentimes the temple will be dedicated to the worship of many gods from various regions of India. Of course, this is to meet the needs of Indian immigrants and their families who come from all over the vast and religiously diverse country of India. Hinduism is an ancient religion and has withstood many challenges over the centuries. New religions have been established and absorbed by Hinduism. Social changes have come and gone, and Hinduism remains a viable force in the lives of millions of people. Its temples, gods, and festivals continue to fulfill a need in the lives of Indians and Hindus throughout the world.

Think About It

1. Discuss the origins of Hinduism and why Vedic literature is the best source of knowledge about Hinduism.

2. What are the four basic Vedic books? Briefly summarize what each book contains.

3. What subtle changes were introduced gradually into the religion of India after the close of the classical period?

4. Compare and contrast Hindu religious practice and Muslim religious practice.

5. What were some of the reform movements in Hinduism in the late nineteenth and twentieth centuries? Who was the best-known Indian reformer of the twentieth century and why?

6. Briefly summarize the Hindu holy days.

7. What are some of the issues and struggles faced by modern-day Hindus?

Suggested Reading

Chaudhuri, Nirad C. *Hinduism*. New York: Oxford University Press, 1979.

Dalrymple, William. *The Last Mughal: The Fall of a Dynasty: Delhi 1857*. London: Knopf, 2006.

Dimmitt, Cornelia, and J. A. B. van Buitenen. *Classical Hindu Mythology. A Reader in the Sanskrit Puranas*. Philadelphia: Temple University Press, 1978.

Dirks, Nicholas B. *Castes of Mind: Colonialism and the Making of Modern India*. Princeton: Princeton University Press, 2001.

Eck, Diana. *Darsan: Seeing the Divine Image in India*. Chambersburg: Anima Books, 1985.

Feldhaus, Anne. *Water and Womanhood. Religious Meaning of Rivers in Maharashtra*. New York: Oxford University Press, 1995.

Hopkins, Thomas J. *The Hindu Religious Tradition*. Encino, Calif.: Dickenson, 1971.

Hume, Robert Ernest. *The Thirteen Principal Upanishads*. New York: Oxford University Press, 1971.

Koller, John M. *The Indian Way*. New York: Macmillan, 1982.

Zaehner, R. C., trans. *The Bhagavad-Gita*. New York: Oxford University Press, 1969.

Source Material

Selections from the *Rig-Veda*

The basis of all later Hindu scripture is the *Rig-Veda*, the ancient collection of hymns to the Vedic gods. The following are representative selections from this book.

Varuna and Indra

Rig-Veda, IV. 42, 1–7, 10

1. I am the royal Ruler, mine is empire, as mine who sway all life are all the Immortals. Varuna's will the Gods obey and follow. I am the king of men's lofty cover.

2. I am King Varuna. To me was given these first existing high celestial powers. Varuna's will the Gods obey and follow. I am the King of Men's most lofty cover.

3. I Varuna am Indra; in their greatness, these the two wide deep fairly fashioned regions. These the two world-halves have I, even as Tvashtar knowing all beings, joined and held together.

4. I made to flow the moisture shedding waters, and set the heaven firm in the seat of Order. By Law, the son of Aditi, Law-Observer, hath spread abroad the world in threefold measure.

5. Heroes with noble horses, fain for battle, selected warriors, call on men in combat. I Indra Maghavan, excite the conflict; I stir the dust, Lord of surpassing vigour.

6. All this I did. The god's own conquering power never impedeth me to whom none opposeth. When lauds and Soma juice have made me joyful, both the unbounded regions are affrighted.

7. All beings know these deeds of thine; thou tellest this unto Varuna, thou great Disposer! Thou art renowned as having slain the Vritras. Thou madest flow the floods that were obstructed. . . .

10. May we, possessing much, delight in riches, Gods in oblations and the kine in pasture; And that Milch-cow who shrinks not from the milking, O Indra-Varuna, give to us daily.[32]

"What God Shall We Adore with Our Oblation?"

Rig-Veda, X. 121, 1–10

1. In the beginning rose Hiranyagarbha, born Only Lord of all created beings. He fixed and holdeth up this earth and heaven. What God shall we adore with our oblation?
2. Giver of vital breath, of power and vigour, he whose commandments all the gods acknowledge; The Lord of death, whose shade is life immortal. What God shall we adore with our oblation?
3. Who by his grandeur hath become Sole Ruler of all the moving world that breathes and slumbers; He who is Lord of men and Lord of cattle. What God shall we adore with our oblations?
4. His, through his might, are these snow-covered mountains, and men call sea and Rasa his possession; His arms are these, his are these heavenly regions. What God shall we adore with our oblation?
5. By him the heavens are strong and earth is steadfast, by him light's realm and sky-vault are supported; By him the regions in mid-air were measured. What God shall we adore with our oblation?
6. To him, supported by his help, two armies embattled look while trembling in their spirit. When over them the risen Sun is shining. What God shall we adore with our oblation?
7. What time the mighty waters came, containing the universal germ, producing Agni, Then sprang the Gods' one spirit into being. What God shall we adore with our oblation?
8. He in his might surveyed the floods containing productive force and generating Worship. He is the God of gods, and none beside him. What God shall we adore with our oblation?
9. Ne'er may he harm us who is earth's Begetter, nor he whose laws are sure, the heaven's creator, he who brought forth the great and lucid waters. What God shall we adore with our oblation?
10. Prajapati! thou only comprehendest all these created things, and none beside thee. Grant us our heart's desire when we invoke thee; may we have store in riches in possession.[33]

Selections from Upanishads

Upanishads are philosophical writings from the classical teachers of Hinduism. The following is a description of the moment of death.[34]

Now when that Self, having sunk into weakness, sinks, as it were, into unconsciousness, then gather those senses (prânas) around him, and he, taking with him those elements of light, descends into the heart. When that person in the eye turns away, then he ceases to know any forms. "He has become one," they say, "he does not see." "He has become one," they say, "he does not smell." "He has become one," they say, "he does not taste." "He has become one," they say, "he does not speak." "He has become one," they say, "he does not hear." "He has become one," they say, "he does not think." "He has become one," they say, "he does not touch." "He has become one," they say, "he does not know." The point of his heart becomes lighted up, and by that light the Self departs, either through the eye, or through the skull, or through other places of the body. And when he thus departs, life (the chief prâna) departs after him, and when life thus departs, all the other vital spirits (prânas) depart after it. He is conscious, and being conscious he follows and departs. Then both his knowledge and his work take hold of him, and his acquaintance with former things. (Brihadâranyaka Upanishad IV, 4, 1–2)

When the person goes away from this world, he comes to the wind. Then the wind makes room for him, like the hole of a carriage wheel, and through it he mounts higher. He comes to the sun. Then the sun makes room for him, like the hole of a Lambara, and through it he mounts higher. He comes to the moon. Then the moon makes room for him, like the hole of a drum, and through it he mounts higher, and arrives at the world where there is no sorrow, no snow. There he dwells eternal years. (Brihadâranyaka Upanishad V, 10)

Selections from the *Law of Manu*

Asceticism has been associated with forms of Hinduism from its beginning. The following is a description of the life of an ascetic.

Law of Manu, VI. 33–36, 41–43, 45–49, 60–65[35]

33. But having thus passed the third part of (a man's natural term of) life in the forest, he may live as an ascetic during the fourth part of his existence, after abandoning all attachments to worldly objects.
34. He who after passing from order to order, after offering sacrifices and subduing his senses, becomes, tired with (giving) alms and offerings of food, an ascetic, gains bliss after death.
35. When he has paid the three debts, let him apply his mind to (the attainment of) final liberation; he who seeks it without having paid (his debts) sinks downwards.

36. Having studied the Vedas in accordance with the rule, having begat sons according to the sacred law, and having offered sacrifices according to his ability, he may direct his mind to (the attainment of) final liberation.

41. Departing from his house fully provided with the means of purification (Pavitra), let him wander about absolutely silent, and caring nothing for enjoyments that may be offered (to him).

42. Let him always wander alone, without any companion, in order to attain (final liberation), fully understanding that the solitary (man, who) neither forsakes nor is forsaken, gains his end.

43. He shall neither possess a fire, nor a dwelling, he may go to a village for his food, (he shall be) indifferent to everything, firm of purpose, meditating (and) concentrating his mind on Brahman.

45. Let him not desire to die, let him not desire to live; let him wait for (his appointed) time, as a servant (waits) for the payment of his wages.

46. Let him put down his foot purified by his sight, let him drink water purified by (straining with) a cloth, let him utter speech purified by truth, let him keep his heart pure.

47. Let him patiently bear hard words, let him not insult anybody, and let him not become anybody's enemy for the sake of this (perishable) body.

48. Against an angry man let him not in return show anger, let him bless when he is cursed, and let him not utter speech, devoid of truth, scattered at the seven gates.

49. Delighting in what refers to the Soul, sitting (in the postures prescribed by the Yoga), independent (of external help), entirely abstaining from sensual enjoyments, with himself for his only companion, he shall live in this world, desiring the bliss (of final liberation).

60. By the restraint of his senses, by the destruction of love and hatred, and by the abstention from injuring the creatures, he becomes fit for immortality.

61. Let him reflect on the transmigrations of men, caused by their sinful deeds, on their falling into hell, and on the torments in the world of Yama,

62. On the separation from their dear ones, on their union with hated men, on their being overpowered by age and being tormented with diseases,

63. On the departure of the individual soul from this body and its new birth in (another) womb, and on its wanderings through ten thousand millions of existences,

64. On the infliction of pain on embodied (spirits), which is caused by demerit, and the gain of eternal bliss, which is caused by the attainment of their highest aim, (gained through) spiritual merit.

65. By deep meditations, let him recognize the subtle nature of the supreme Soul, and its presence in all organisms, both the highest and the lowest.

Selections from the *Bhagavad Gita*

The *Bhagavad Gita,* "The Song of the Blessed Lord," is the classic poem of India. In this massive poem about a great battle, the gods take human forms and talk with mortals. In the following sections, the god Krishna speaks with the poem's hero, Arjuna, about the nature of life, death, and the gods.[36]

II. 16–27

That which is can never cease to be; that which is not will not exist. To see this truth of both is theirs who part essence from accident, substance from shadow. Indestructible, learn thou! The Life is, spreading life through all; it cannot anywhere, by any means, be anywise diminished, stayed, or changed. But for these fleeting frames which it informs with spirit deathless, endless, infinite, they perish. Let them perish, Prince! And fight! He who shall say, "Lo! I have slain a man!" He who shall think, "Lo! I am slain!" those both Know naught! Life cannot slay. Life is not slain! Never the spirit was born; the spirit shall cease to be never; Never was time it was not; End and Beginning are dreams! Birthless and deathless and changeless remaineth the spirit for ever; Death hath not touched it at all, dead though the house of it seems! Who knoweth it exhaustless, self-sustained, Immortal, indestructible—shall such Say, "I have killed a man, or caused to kill?" Nay, but as when one layeth His worn-out robes away, And, taking new ones, sayeth, "These will I wear to-day!" So putteth by the spirit Lightly its garb of flesh, And passeth to inherit A residence afresh. I say to thee weapons reach not the Life; Flame burns it not, waters cannot o'erwhelm, Nor dry winds wither it. Impenetrable, Unentered, unassailed, unharmed, untouched, Immortal, all-arriving, stable, sure, Invisible, ineffable, by word And thought uncompassed, ever all itself, Thus is the Soul declared! How wilt thou, then—knowing it so—grieve when thou shouldst not grieve?

XI. 15–21, 24, 25, 31–34

The gods are in Thy glorious frame! The creatures of earth, and heaven, and hell in Thy Divine form dwell, and in Thy countenance shine all the features of Brahma, sitting lone upon His lotus-throne; Of saints and sages, and the serpent races Ananta, Vasuki; Yea! mightiest Lord! I see Thy thousand thousand arms and breasts, and faces, and eyes—on every side perfect, diversified; and nowhere end of Thee, nowhere beginning, nowhere a centre! Shifts—wherever soul's gaze lifts—Thy central Self, all-wielding, and all-winning! Infinite King! I see the anadem on Thee, the club, the shell, the discus; see Thee burning in beams insufferable, lighting earth, heaven, and hell with brilliance blazing, glowing, flashing; turning darkness to dazzling day, look I whichever way; Ah, Lord! I worship Thee, the Undivided, the Uttermost of thought, the Treasure-Palace wrought to hold the wealth of the worlds; the Shield provided to shelter Virtue's laws; the Fount whence Life's stream draws all waters of all rivers of all being: The One Unborn, Unending: Unchanging and Unblending! With might and majesty, past thought, past seeing! Silver of moon and gold of sun are glories rolled from Thy great eyes; Thy visage, beaming tender throughout the stars and skies, doth to warm life surprise Thy Universe. The worlds are filled with discus; see Thee burning in beams insufferable, wonder. Unnumbered eyes, vast arms, members tremendous, flanks, lit with sun and star, teet planted near and far, adore, as I adore Thee, quake, as I quake, to witness so much splendour! Arise! Obtain renown! Destroy thy foes! Fight for the kingdom waiting thee when thou hast vanquished those. By Me they fall—not thee! The stroke of death is dealt them now, even as they show thus gallantly; My instrument art thou! Strike, strong-armed Prince, at Drona! At Bhishma strike! Deal death on Karna, Jyadratha; stay all their warlike breath! 'Tis I who bid them perish! Thou wilt but slay the slain; Fight! they must fall, and thou must live, victor upon this plain!

Chapter 5
Jainism

 ## Learning Objectives

After reading this chapter, you should be able to:

5.1 Understand the life of Mahavira and its connection to the origins of Jainism.

5.2 Explore Jain religious teachings.

5.3 Identify and discuss Jain sects.

5.4 Name the Jain festivals and their significance.

5.5 Discuss Jainism today.

A Timeline of Jainism

599–527 B.C.E	Life of Mahavira
1st century B.C.E	Distinction between Svetambara and Digambara sects emerges
9th–11th century C.E	Digambara Jains supported by South Indian kings
1700	British emerge as major power in India
19th–21st century	Jains are among India's best-educated and most prosperous communities
20th century	Emergence of Jain communities worldwide, especially in former British colonies

Key Terms

Agamas	**Mahavira**
ahimsa	**moksha**
ajiva	**Siddhantas**
Digambara	**Svetambara**
jiva	**Tirthankaras**

In the sixth century B.C.E., two protests arose in India against Hinduism. These were Jainism and Buddhism, and each offered an alternative to that presented in the Vedic literature and taught by the Brahmins. Unlike the Upanishads, which represented an internal reform to Vedic religion, both Jainism and Buddhism denied the validity of the Vedas as inspired scripture, and both rejected the religious implications of the Indian caste system. Of these two new religions, Jainism was probably the first.

The Life of Mahavira

5.1. Understand the life of Mahavira and its connection to the origins of Jainism.

It is difficult to determine precisely the origin of Jainism, although Nataputta Vardhamana, who became known to his followers as **Mahavira** ("great hero"), has traditionally been identified as its founder. The story of Mahavira's life, however, has been covered with legend. In orthodox Jainism, Mahavira was only the last in a long line of founders. It is believed that over enormously long periods of time the truth is discovered, fades and is lost, and is found again. Theravada Buddhists and Jains share this understanding of time and religion. Twenty-three figures preceded Mahavira in the establishment of Jainism. These people, together with Mahavira, are called **Tirthankaras**, or "crossing builders." They are believed to be those ideal persons who forged a bridge between this life and moksha. A total of twenty-four Tirthankaras receive the veneration of Jains in their temples.

Most sources suggest that Mahavira lived between 599 and 527 B.C.E., although some authorities place his death as late as 467 B.C.E. This means that he was contemporary with Siddhartha Gautama, Confucius, Lao-tzu, and the great Hebrew prophets of the sixth century B.C.E. (Jeremiah, Ezekiel, and the anonymous author or authors of Isaiah 40–66).

The reported details of the life of Mahavira are similar in many respects to those of the life of the Buddha, and some suggest that these details are taken from Buddhism. Others suggest that Buddhists borrowed them from Jains. Like the Buddha, Mahavira was born in the sixth century B.C.E. to parents of the Kshatriya caste; his father was a minor ruler. Mahavira was the second of two sons. According to legend, the family possessed great wealth and lived in luxury. They resided in Vaisali, the capital city of the region of Magadah in north India. At the proper age, Mahavira married and had a daughter. Despite his position and wealth, he was not happy and sought a religious answer to this unhappiness. When a group of wandering ascetics came to dwell in his village, Mahavira became interested in them and longed to join their order. Being a dutiful son, however, he waited until his parents died and the business affairs of the family had been taken over successfully by his older brother.[1] Then he bade farewell to his family, turned his back on his wealth and luxury, tore out his hair and beard by the handfuls, and went off to join the ascetics.

Mahavira did not find what he had sought among this group of ascetics. He came to believe instead that one must practice a more severe asceticism than they practiced to find release of the soul from this life. In addition to his concern for extreme asceticism, Mahavira eventually felt that one must also practice **ahimsa** (non-injury to life) to find release. Therefore, he went forth on his own path.

The legends concerning this period of Mahavira's life emphasize the extreme measures of asceticism that he imposed on himself. Because he did not wish to become attached to people or things, he never stayed more than one night in any place when he traveled. During the rainy season, he stayed off the roads to avoid walking where he might inadvertently step on an insect. During the dry season, he swept the road before him as he walked to avoid crushing insects. He strained all the water he drank to prevent swallowing any creature it might contain. Like any true ascetic, he begged for his food; but he refused to eat raw food and preferred to eat only that which had been left over from the meal of some other person, so that he might not be the cause of death. To better torment his body, he sought out the coldest spots in the winter months and the hottest climates in the summer, and he always went about naked. Whenever angry or cruel persons sent their dogs after him, Mahavira allowed himself to be bitten rather than resist them. Legend also tells of a time when Mahavira was meditating and some people built a fire beneath him to see if he would resist; he did not. After twelve years of the harshest forms of asceticism, he achieved release (**moksha**) from the bonds that tie one's soul to the endless cycle of birth, death, and rebirth. Thus, he became known to his followers as a *Jina* (conqueror) because he had heroically conquered the forces of life. Although he had achieved moksha, Mahavira lived for another thirty years and died at the age of seventy-two.

The Teachings of Jainism

5.2. **Explore Jain religious teachings.**

Like other Indian religions, Jainism views life in terms of endless rebirth. People are born, live out their lives, die, and are born again. This is the problem around which Indian religions revolve. How does a person get off the wheel of lives and cease to live? Hinduism offers a variety of answers, as do Buddhism and Sikhism. Jainism views people as bound to life because of the karma they acquire.

From the Source

All living beings owe their present form of existence to their own Karma; timid, wicked, suffering latent misery, they err about (in the Circle of Births), subject to birth, old age and death.[2]

Mahavira taught that karma was built up in an individual as the result of activity of any sort. Thus, the ideal life for a Jain might simply be to do as little as possible and thereby escape karma and be freed from life.

From the Source

Liberation is absolute from the totality of actions through the absence of the causes of bondage and exhaustion (of past karmas).[3]

Jain pilgrims on the road to Ranakpur in Rajasthan, India (photo)/Private Collection/Ann & Bury Peerless Picture Library/ The Bridgeman Art Library

A Jain pilgrim wears a mask to prevent swallowing of insects as he walks and sweeps the road before him with a broom to prevent crushing of life. Thus he adheres to the principles of ahimsa (non-injury of life).

The philosophical worldview of Jainism is dualistic. According to Jainism, the world is comprised of essentially two substances—soul (**jiva**) and matter (**ajiva**). Soul is life; it is eternal and valuable. Matter is lifeless, material, and evil. The entire universe can be identified as either soul or matter. All persons are seen as soul encased in matter. Matter clings to the soul because of past actions (karma). As long as soul is enmeshed in matter, it can never be free and is bound to remain in the endless cycle of lives. Thus, it is the goal of Jainism to liberate the soul from matter. This philosophical basis views the flesh as being evil, because it traps the spirit. If the flesh is evil, then the ascetic answer is to release the soul by tormenting the flesh in some manner. This answer to the human plight is found in some form in Hinduism, Buddhism, Christianity, Islam, and nearly every other major religion in the world. Whereas these religions also have other solutions to the problem of humankind's plight, Jainism is consistent and single-minded. It views the world as a dualism. Its answer to the dualistic nature of the world is severe asceticism. Because not all Jains can be free from the responsibilities of life and dedicate themselves to the ascetic life, it is believed that the Jains who do are closest to release from the cycle of birth, life, and death. Mahavira set the pattern by turning his back on the wealth and pleasures of his home and submitting his body to the rigors of asceticism; thus, he found release.

Jainism maintains that release from the cycle of life, death, and rebirth must be accomplished by the individual. The soul can be freed from matter only by the actions of the person involved, and that person cannot receive help from outside. Therefore, the gods are of little consequence in Jainism. Jains have no need for a creator god because they believe that matter is eternal. Thus there never was a creation of the world. It has been here forever and will continue to exist forever. Jains recognize heavenly beings, but they are simply creatures living on a different plane from that of humankind and are also yet bound by karma. These gods cannot help humans in their search for release. Therefore, prayer and worship are worthless. So, although Jainism acknowledges the existence of gods, it does not rely on them.

In the practice of their religion, Jains tend to divide themselves into two distinct groups: the majority, who cannot afford to leave their homes and accept the rigors of the ascetic life, and the minority, who can and do become monks. The latter group represents the ideal life of a Jain. Jain monks take five vows to guide their lives.

From the Source

1. *They vow non-injury of life (ahimsa).* According to Jain tradition, Mahavira taught:
   He who injures these (animals) does not comprehend and renounce the sinful acts; he who does not injure these, comprehends and renounces the sinful acts. Knowing them, a wise man should not act sinfully toward animals, nor cause others to act so, nor allow others to act so. He who knows these causes of sin relating to animals, is called a reward-knowing sage. Thus I say.[4]
2. *Jain monks vow to always speak the truth.* Because of this vow, they are widely respected for their truthfulness. In its search for truth, however, Jainism has tended to view truth as relative rather than absolute.[5]
3. *Jain monks vow to refrain from taking anything that is not given to them.* This too has added to the Jains' reputation for honesty.
4. *They renounce sexual pleasures.* In keeping with traditional asceticism, which views the pleasures of the flesh as evil, because sex is one of the greatest pleasures of the flesh, it must be forsaken. (Mahavira went even further, by not only renouncing sexual pleasures but by also renouncing women in general. He is said to have declared that "women are the greatest temptation in the world").
5. *They renounce all attachments.* Attachments to and love for other persons or things is one of the elements that keep humans bound to life. (It was for this reason that Mahavira renounced his family and possessions and refused to stay in any place longer than one day, lest he form new attachments.)[6]

The first vow concerning ahimsa has become the most dominant characteristic of all Jains and the mark by which they are known to the world. A Jain will go to great lengths to avoid harming any living creature; thus, they are vegetarians and avoid leather products, which necessitate killing. Some Jains are so concerned with avoiding meat products that they will not eat food that has been cooked in pans previously used to cook meat. Jain monks, following Mahavira's example, sweep the path before them when they walk to avoid treading on insects, and they strain the water they drink to protect whatever life may have been in it. In certain extreme cases, Jains have been known to extend this care to rats.[7] Most Jains avoid occupations, including agriculture, that involve even the possibility of harming a person or other living creature. For this reason, Jainism is almost exclusively an urban religion. The Jain principle of not injuring life has had widespread influence among non-Jains, such as Mohandas Gandhi and Martin Luther King, Jr. There have, however, been Jain kings who have waged war. Jainism does not require complete pacifism. Some Jains hold the view that it is permissible to use weapons but only in self-defense, although monks are not permitted to use them under any circumstances.

Generally, all Jains seek to follow the first three vows as much as possible; those who enter the monastic life keep all five. Thus, a Jain layperson may marry and have a family and possessions—with the understanding that he or she is not leading the ideal life and may not expect release in this life.

The scriptures of the Jains are called **Agamas**, or "precepts," or **Siddhantas**, or "treatises." Orthodox Jains believe these Agamas are the actual sermons or teachings Mahavira gave to his disciples. The various Jain sects differ regarding the number of Agamas they consider genuine and authoritative.

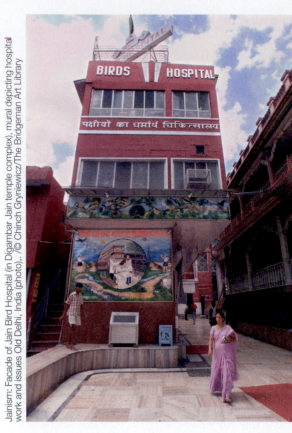

Jainism: Facade of Jain Bird Hospital (in Digambar Jain temple complex), mural depicting hospital work and issues Old Delhi, India (photo).. /© Chinch Gryniewicz/The Bridgeman Art Library

An expression of Jain care and compassion for all life, the famous hospital for birds in Delhi adjoins a Jain temple. Thousands of sick and injured birds are treated here every year.

Jain Sects

5.3. **Identify and discuss Jain sects.**

By 80 B.C.E., the Jains were severely divided over what was to be the true meaning of Jainism, and they split into two sects that exist today. The sect that interprets Jain teachings more liberally is the **Svetambara** (literally, "the white-clad"). This group is now located mainly in the northern part of India. They are liberal in their interpretation of Mahavira's teachings regarding the wearing of clothing and are called "white-clad" because they reject the necessity of nudity and allow their monks to wear a white garment. They are also liberal in that they allow women into the religion and into their monasteries and even accept the possibility that a woman may find release. Of the two sects, the Svetambara is the more popular.

The second sect, the **Digambara** (literally, "the sky-clad"), is the more conservative of the two, and its members live mainly in southern India. The Digambaras require their monks to go about nearly nude; total nudity is reserved only for those of greatest holiness. In addition, they believe women have no chance of achieving release and are to be regarded as the greatest of all temptations to a man. Therefore, women are prohibited from entering the monasteries and temples. The Digambaras even refuse to believe that Mahavira was ever married.

Jain Festivals

5.4. **Name the Jain festivals and their significance.**

Although Jains do not place heavy emphasis on corporate worship and rituals, they do celebrate certain major annual festivals. These festivals are connected with the five major events in the life of each of the Tirthankaras. They coincide with Tirthankaras' entering into the womb, birth, renunciation, attainment of great knowledge, and final release from this life. Mahavira's birthday is celebrated in early April.

Paijusana

This celebration comes at the end of the Jain year, usually in the month of August or September, and it is the most popular festival. During this eight-day period, each Jain fasts and attends special worship. All Jain laity are encouraged to live as monks for at least one twenty-four-hour period. During this time, the layperson is to live in a monastery, fast, and meditate. At the conclusion of this period, Jains perform acts of penance and seek forgiveness to begin the new year with a clean slate. The festival ends with a procession of adherents carrying the image of a Tirthankara through the village and giving alms to the poor.

Divali

Jains observe the Hindu holiday of Divali, which is celebrated in November. Instead of worshiping the Hindu goddess, Kali, Jains use this period to remember the liberation of Mahavira by the lighting of lamps. In addition to these festivals, Jains fast at each full moon and make pilgrimages to various holy sites.

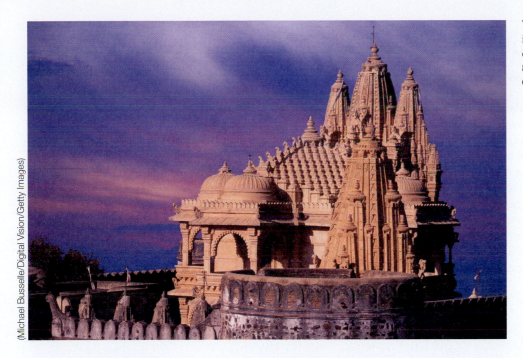

The Shatrunjaya Hill in Palitana is an important pilgrimage for the followers of Jainism. This site contains over 863 temples of worship. Palitana, Gujarat, India.

Jainism Today

5.5. **Discuss Jainism today.**

Hinduism was affected by Jain teaching and was moved to accept its emphasis on asceticism and ahimsa. Although Jainism and its ascetic movement may have been very popular in India at one time, today it is a minority religion.

Worldwide, there are an estimated four million Jains, most of whom live in urban areas in western India. There are fewer than 6,000 Jain monks. Because of their overwhelming concern for the sacredness of life, Jains are strict vegetarians and are forbidden from entering certain occupations.

A Statue of Mahavira. In this portrayal, the founder of the Jain path of purification and release exhibits the serenity of Jain who has "conquered" samsara.

Religion and Public Life

No Jain can belong to any profession that takes a life or profits from slaughter. For example, they cannot be soldiers, butchers, leather workers, exterminators, or even farmers, as farmers regularly plow the soil and might kill worms and insects that live in it. In the past, however, there have been Jains who were soldiers and emperors. These prohibitions have forced Jains to enter the commercial professions. This fact, along with their reputation for honesty and morality, has made them excellent businesspeople. It is paradoxical that a sect that began with the intention of asceticism and poverty has become, by virtue of its respect for life, one of the wealthiest classes in India. Jains have not actively participated in the religious and ethnic violence that is all too common in modern India, although some have been caught in the crossfire.

Although Jains have no need for gods, they do venerate the twenty-four Tirthankaras and have erected over 40,000 temples in India to worship these figures. Many of these temples are renowned for their beauty; the temple on Mount Abu is considered one of the seven wonders of India. Apart from adoring the Tirthankaras in temples, Jain worship includes many rituals in the home. This may include reciting the names of the *Jinas* (saints from the past), bathing idols, and offering flowers and perfumes to them. Worship also may include meditation and the observance of vows during the worship.

Think About It

1. Discuss the origins of Jainism. How does the story of Mahavira relate to the establishment of this religious practice?

2. Discuss the dualistic philosophical worldview of Jainism.

3. What are the two major Jain sects? Where are each located and how does their religious practice differ?

4. What are the major Jain festivals?

5. How do modern-day Jains practice their religion?

Suggested Reading

Jaini, Jagmanderlal. *Outlines of Jainism*. Cambridge: Cambridge University Press, 1940.

Jaini, Padmanabh. *The Jaina Path of Purification*. Berkeley: University of California Press, 1979.

Mahapragya, Nathamal. *Jain Ethics and Morality*. London: Amol, 2000.

Rankin, Adian. *The Jain Path: Ancient Wisdom for the West*. Winchester UK: O Books, 2006.

Shah, Bharat. *An Introduction to Jainism*. Charlestown, S.C.: BookSurge, 2003.

Source Material

A Jain Parable: The Man in the Well

Jainism, along with many other Indian religions, has historically taught that there are few yes-or-no answers to the problems of life. This has never been better illustrated than in the Jain parable of the man in the well. The story also is found in many other cultures and literatures.[8]

Haribhadra, 'Samara-dityakatha,' II. *55–88*

A certain man, much oppressed by the woes of poverty,
Left his own home, and set out for another country.
He passed through the land, with its villages, cities, and harbors,
And after a few days he lost his way.

And he came to a forest, thick with trees . . . and full of wild beasts. There, while he was stumbling over the rugged paths, . . . a prey to thirst and hunger, he saw a mad elephant, fiercely trumpeting, charging him with upraised trunk. At the same time there appeared before him a most evil demoness, holding a sharp sword, dreadful in face and form, and laughing with loud and shrill laughter. Seeing them he trembled in all his limbs with deathly fear, and looked in all directions. There, to the east of him, he saw a great banyan tree . . . .

And he ran quickly, and reached the mighty tree.
But his spirits fell, for it was so high that even the birds could not fly over it,
And he could not climb its high unscalable trunk . . . .
All his limbs trembled with terrible fear,
Until, looking round, he saw nearby an old well covered with grass.
Afraid of death, craving to live if only a moment longer,
He flung himself into the well at the foot of the banyan tree.
A clump of reeds grew from its deep wall, and to this he clung,
While below him he saw terrible snakes, enraged at the sound of his falling;
And at the very bottom, known from the hiss of its breath, was a black and mighty python
With mouth agape, its body thick as the trunk of a heavenly elephant, with terrible red eyes.
He thought, "My life will only last as long as these reeds hold fast,"
And he raised his head; and there, on the clump of reeds, he saw two large mice,
One white, one black, their sharp teeth ever gnawing at the roots of the reed clump.
Then up came the wild elephant, and, enraged the more at not catching him,

Charged time and again at the trunk of the ban-
yan tree.
At the shock of his charge a honeycomb on a large
branch
Which hung over the old well, shook loose and fell.
The man's whole body was stung by a swarm of
angry bees,
But, just by chance, a drop of honey fell on his
head,
Rolled down his brow, and somehow reached his
lips,
And gave him a moment's sweetness. He longed
for other drops,
And he thought nothing of the python, the snakes,
the elephant, the mice, the well, or the bees,
In his excited craving for yet more drops of honey.
This parable is powerful to clear the minds of
those on the way to freedom,
Now hear its sure interpretation.
The man is the soul, his wandering in the forest
the four types of existence.
The wild elephant is death, the demoness old age.
The banyan tree is salvation, where there is no
fear of death, the elephant,
But which no sensual man can climb.
The well is human life, the snakes are passions,
Which so overcome a man that he does not know
what he should do.
The tuft of reed is man's allotted span, during
which the soul exists embodied;
The mice which steadily gnaw it are the dark and
bright fortnights.
The stinging bees are manifold diseases,
Which torment a man until he has not a mo-
ment's joy.
The awful python is hell, seizing the man be-
mused by sensual pleasure,
Fallen in which the soul suffers pains by the
thousand.
The drops of honey are trivial pleasures, terrible
at the last.
Now can a wise man want them, in the midst of
such peril and hardship?

Jain Respect for Life

Ahimsa (the vow of non-injury to life) is one of the primary doctrines of Jainism and may be its chief contribution to other religions. The selection from the *Akaranga-Sutra* details Jain respect for all life.[9]

Akaranga-Sutra, *I. 1*

Earth is afflicted and wretched, it is hard to teach, it has no discrimination. Unenlightened men, who suffer from the effect of past deeds, cause great pain in a world full of pain already, for in earth souls are individually embod-ied. If, thinking to gain praise, honour, or respect . . . or to achieve a good rebirth . . . or to win salvation, or to escape pain, a man sins against earth or causes or permits oth-ers to do so, . . . he will not gain joy or wisdom. . . . Injury to the earth is like striking, cutting, maiming, or killing a blind man. . . . Knowing this, man should not sin against earth or cause or permit others to do so. He who under-stands the nature of sin against earth is called a true sage who understands karma.

And there are many souls embodied in water. Truly water . . . is alive. He who injures the lives in water does not understand the nature of sin or renounce it. . . . Knowing this, a man should not sin against water, or cause or per-mit others to do so. He who understands the nature of sin against water is called a true sage who understands karma.

By wicked or careless acts one may destroy fire-beings, and moreover, harm other beings by means of fire. . . . For there are creatures living in earth, grass, leaves, wood, cowdung, or dustheaps, and jumping creatures which . . . fall into a fire if they come near it. If touched by fire, they shrivel up . . . lose their senses and die. . . . He who understands the nature of sin in respect of fire is called a true sage who understands karma.

And just as it is the nature of a man to be born and grow old, so is it the nature of a plant to be born and grow old. . . . One is endowed with reason, and so is the other; one is sick, if injured, and so is the other; one grows large, and so does the other; one changes with time, and so does the other. . . . He who understands the nature of sin against plants is called a true sage who understands karma.

All beings with two, three, four, or five senses, . . . in fact all creation, know individually pleasure and displeasure, pain, terror, and sorrow. All are full of fears which come from all directions. And yet there exist people who would cause greater pain to them. . . . Some kill animals for sacrifice, some for their skin, flesh, blood, . . . feathers, teeth, or tusks; . . . some kill them intentionally and some unintentionally; some kill because they have been previously injured by them, . . . and some because they expect to be injured. He who harms animals has not understood or renounced deeds of sin. . . . He who understands the nature of sin against animals is called a true sage who understands karma.

A man who is averse from harming even the wind knows the sorrow of all things living. . . . He who knows what is bad for himself knows what is bad for others, and he who knows what is bad for others knows what is bad for himself. This reciprocity should always be borne in mind. Those whose minds are at peace and who are free from passions do not desire to live (at the expense of others). . . . He who understands the nature of sin against wind is called a true sage who understands karma.

In short, he who understands the nature of sin in respect of all the six types of living beings is called a true sage who understands karma.

Chapter 6
Buddhism

 ## Learning Objectives

After reading this chapter, you should be able to:

6.1 Discuss the life of the Buddha.

6.2 Summarize the teachings of Buddha and the role of enlightenment in Buddhist practice.

6.3 Discuss the development of Buddhism over time.

6.4 Understand the basic teachings of Theravada Buddhism.

6.5 Identify the tenets of Mahayana Buddhism.

6.6 Name the Buddhist festivals and holy days.

6.7 Discuss Buddhism today.

A Timeline of Buddhism

480–405 B.C.E.	Life and teaching of the Buddha
405	First Buddhist Council
350	Second Buddhist Council
297	Spread of Buddhism in India encouraged by Emperor Asoka
247	Transmission of Buddhism to Sri Lanka
250	Third Buddhist Council distinction between Theravada and Mahayana schools emerges
200–200 C.E.	Development of Theravada Buddhism
1st century C.E.	Transmission of Buddhism to Southeast Asia and China
4th century	Transmission of Buddhism to Korea
550	Transmission of Buddhism to Japan
700	Transmission of Buddhism to Tibet
845	Persecution of Buddhists in China
1200	Growth of Zen in Japan
1250	Decline of Buddhism in India
1617–1682	Life of the fifth Dalai Lama; beginning of monastic rule in Tibet
19th century	Initial transmission of Buddhism to Europe and North America
1949–1976	Communist persecution of Buddhism in China

1950	Tenzin Gyatso becomes Dalai Lama; China invades Tibet and begins persecution of Buddhists
1975–1979	Severe persecution of Buddhists by the Communist Khmer Rouge in Cambodia
1976–present	Buddhist revival in China
1959–present	Dalai Lama in exile; spreads message of Tibetan Buddhism throughout the world
1963–present	Buddhism used to justify military rule and human rights abuses in Burma
1950–present	Rapid growth of Buddhism in Europe and North America
1980s–present	Emergence of Socially Engaged Buddhism
2008	Hundreds killed in pro-independence demonstrations in Tibet

Key Terms

anatman	**Lotus Sutra**
arhat	**Mahayana**
bodhisattva	**Nirvana**
Buddha	**Sangha**
dharma	**Theravada**
Four Noble Truths	**Vajrayana**
lama	

Buddhism began in India in the sixth century B.C.E. as another interpretation of the Hindu religious system. In many respects, it resembled Jainism because it rejected the authority of the Vedas and offered a vision of salvation based on individual effort. It differed from Jainism in that the Buddha taught a "middle way" between worldliness and the extreme asceticism of Mahavira. As such, it held great appeal in India for several centuries. By the third century B.C.E., Buddhism developed something unusual for any version of Hinduism: a missionary imperative. The rulers of India, who were enamored of this new religion, sent Buddhist missionaries into neighboring Asian countries. At the same time, Buddhism was developing new philosophies that became more and more attractive to the Asian peoples. This combination of missionary thrust and new philosophies made it a sweeping success in China, Japan, Korea, and Southeast Asia. Yet while Buddhism was becoming a success in these regions, it was slowly being pushed aside in India by a resurgent Hinduism. The Muslim conquest of India led to the further decline of Buddhism there. Although new converts have emerged in the twentieth and twenty-first centuries, particularly among lower-caste Hindus and many Tibetan refugees who now live in India, today the vast majority of Buddhists are found in East and Southeast Asia.

The Life of Gautama

6.1. **Discuss the life of the Buddha.**

The founder of Buddhism was a man named Siddhartha, who was a member of the Gautama clan. The dates usually given for his life are 560–480 B.C.E.; however, the life of Gautama, as he has come to be known, is surrounded by legend and the exact dates

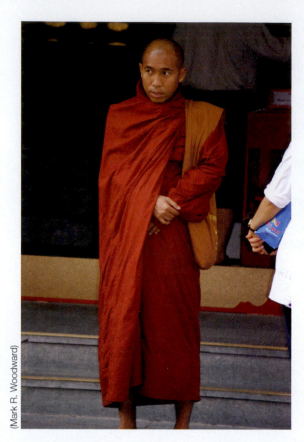

Theravada Buddhist monk, Burma.

(Mark R. Woodward)

of his life are subject to question.[1] Nevertheless, he probably lived during the sixth century B.C.E. and was a contemporary of Mahavira.

Gautama was the son of a Kshatriya raja (king) called Suddhodana and his wife, Maya. The legends say that the birth of the child was surrounded by extraordinary events and portents. According to one story, a soothsayer predicted that the child would either become a great king, who would rule the entire world, or a great **Buddha** (Enlightened One). Gautama's mother died soon after his birth, and he was reared by his maternal aunt, who became his father's second wife.

When Gautama was born, it was predicted that he could become a great king, but that if he ever saw the sights of human misery or the tranquility of a monk, he would grow up to be a religious teacher. Because his father did not wish this, he sought to protect him from the ugliness and distress of humanity. The raja specifically sought to keep the young prince from seeing four sights: a dead body, an aged person, a diseased person, and an ascetic monk. Thus, Gautama grew up surrounded by youth, beauty, and health. He received a normal education for a prince of that era. He studied the arts and warfare and received some training in philosophy. When he was nineteen, he married his cousin and they shared a happy home. They had one child, a son, Rahula.[2]

As Gautama neared his thirtieth birthday, he gradually became aware of the ugliness of the real world. One by one, he began to see the things his father had forbidden. He saw a wrinkled and bent elderly person, a man with a loathsome disease, a rotting corpse, and finally a peaceful monk, who had renounced the world in search of a release from his suffering. Gautama, reaching his mature years, became aware that life always involves suffering and pain. It is said that he once entered his harem room where there were some of the most beautiful young women in the kingdom. There he received a vision that these women would soon become wrinkled, gray, and stooped. These revelations made it impossible for the young prince to continue to live in his palace surrounded by ease and plenty; one night, he decided to leave his home. He crept into his wife's bedroom and said farewell to her and their infant son. Then he took his best horse and rode off into the night. After riding a certain distance, he clipped off his hair and beard and sent his horse back. He changed clothes with a beggar and began a period of searching for answers to life's miseries.

At first, Gautama thought the answers to the questions that troubled him were to be found in the various schools of philosophy. Therefore, he attached himself to a guru and studied with him for some time, but he received no satisfaction in his studies. A second avenue Gautama tried was asceticism. As a solution to the problems of life, asceticism was an acceptable pursuit in the sixth century B.C.E., as can be seen from the life of Mahavira and his followers. Gautama joined five other monks and with them began a life of severe asceticism that lasted six years. The ascetic measures Gautama took were as severe as any recorded in the history of religion. According to legend, he became something of a champion ascetic. Gautama sought out anything that was unpleasant, painful, or disagreeable as a means by which he might find release. He is supposed to have practiced fasting until he reached the point of living on a single grain of rice per day.

At this time in his life, Gautama reportedly became so thin that when he grasped his stomach he touched his backbone. He wore irritating garments and sat in awkward and painful positions for hours. He sat on thorns and for a time slept in a cremation ground among rotting corpses. In the tradition of many ascetics, Gautama allowed filth and vermin to accumulate on his body. But despite these heroic efforts at asceticism, he did not find the enlightenment he was seeking.

Apparently, the turning point in Gautama's quest came one day when he was walking near a stream. Because he had been terribly weakened by his ordeals, he fainted and fell into the stream. The cold water revived him; when he was able to contemplate his situation, he realized that although he had done everything that could be expected of an ascetic, he still had not found satisfaction. He therefore arose, walked to a nearby food stand, and ate a meal. Another tradition states that he received his first meal from a village woman named Sujata.[3] His five friends happened to pass by; when they saw him eating and drinking and enjoying himself, they spurned him as a traitor. When Gautama had finished his meal, he went to the banks of a river and sat down under the shade of a fig tree and began to meditate.[4] He decided to meditate until he received enlightenment. At last, after a period of meditation, Gautama was enlightened; from then on, he was known as the Buddha (Enlightened One). In his meditation, the Buddha had a vision of the endless cycle of birth and death that is the lot of humankind. It was revealed to him that people were bound to this cycle because of desire, which is what causes karma and thus fetters people. The Buddha had desired enlightenment and had sought it through asceticism and knowledge, but it had eluded him. When he had ceased to desire it, he found enlightenment.

The first step the Buddha took after his enlightenment was to travel to the holy city of Varanasi and locate the five ascetic friends who had spurned him. He found them in Deer Park; although at first they had contempt for him, they listened as he preached. In his first sermon, the Buddha taught that neither the extreme of indulgence nor the extreme of asceticism was acceptable as a way of life and that one should avoid extremes and seek to live in the middle way. The five ascetics noted the change that had come over the Buddha, and they accepted his teachings. These five formed the first **Sangha** (the Buddhist community, especially referring to those in monastic orders).

The Buddha became enlightened when he was about thirty-five years old. He spent the remaining years of this life teaching his growing band of disciples. Unlike orthodox Hindus, he taught that any person of any caste or sex could find the same enlightenment he knew.[5] Therefore, his followers included a wide variety of persons. When women asked to join his group, the Buddha was at first reluctant, but he eventually relented and allowed them to form an order of nuns. According to legend, the Buddha's stepmother and former wife were among the first women to seek admission to this group. Unlike orthodox Hinduism and Jainism, early Buddhism taught that women as well as men could achieve enlightenment. People who seriously joined the Buddha as monks shaved their heads and wore coarse yellow robes. Their only possession was a bowl they carried when they begged for food. Their creed was, and continues to be, "I take refuge in the Buddha; I take refuge in the **dharma** (the teachings of the Buddha); and I take refuge in the *Sangha*." Lay Buddhists supported the Sangha with gifts of food, clothing, and other necessities of life.

Lay Buddhists also were expected to observe five basic rules of moral conduct: abstain from killing, stealing, lying, engaging in improper sexual conduct, and partaking of intoxicants. The monks sought to observe both these prohibitions and the following rules of conduct, as described in the Pali Sermons (an early collection of the Buddha's teachings):

A statue of the Buddha carved in Java, which was located in the Southeast Asian island nation of Indonesia during the ninth century. Although today Java is overwhelmingly Muslim, it was, at that time, home to Buddhist and Hindu civilizations. (Mark R. Woodward)

From the Source

"And how, Maharaja, is the Bhikkhu [monk] attained to right conduct?

"The Bhikkhu, refraining from all taking of life, Precepts, shuns taking the life of anything that lives. Putting away club and sword, he is mild and merciful, kind and compassionate toward every living creature. He abstains from the taking of what has not been given him, shuns taking things ungiven. Taking only what is offered him, awaiting such gifts, he abides heart-free from all thievish intent. Refraining from unchastity, he lives the pure, the chaste life. He shuns the sexual act, the vulgar, the common. Abstaining from lying, he shuns the speech of untruth. He speaks the truth, holds by the truth. Staunch and trustworthy, he is no worldly deceiver. Abstaining from tale-bearing, he shuns slanderous speech. What he hears in this quarter he does not repeat in that, so as to make trouble for the people here. And what he hears in that quarter be does not repeat in this, so as to make trouble for the people there. Those at variance he brings together; and those already at one he fortifies. Concord pleases him; concord rejoices him; in concord is all his delight. The words of his mouth all make

for concord. Refraining from speech that is harsh, he avoids rough speech. Whatsoever words are harmless, pleasant to the ear, affectionate, heart-moving, courteous, charming and giving delight to all that hear them—such are the words that he speaks. Refraining from idle chatter, he shuns unprofitable conversation. Speaking in proper season, in accordance with fact, to the purpose, agreeable with the Doctrine and Discipline, his words are a precious treasure, full of appropriate comparisons, discriminating, and to the point. Such is the Bhikkhu's right conduct.[6]

The Buddha reportedly died at the age of eighty after eating spoiled food. According to tradition, his final words were, "Subject to decay are all component things. Strive earnestly to work out your own salvation."

The Teachings of the Buddha

6.2. **Summarize the teachings of Buddha and the role of enlightenment in Buddhist practice.**

There is nothing in the life and teachings of the Buddha to indicate that he intended to found a new religion. He understood life in Hindu religious categories and taught his followers using those categories and vocabulary. The Buddha was opposed to many of the various existing forms of religious worship; he certainly was opposed to the Vedic system of animal sacrifice. In addition, he rejected the authority of the Vedas. The Buddha accepted many Hindu teachings concerning the gods but considered them as similar to mortal beings, subject to the laws of karma and rebirth. Although Buddhism teaches that gods have great powers, the Buddha was much more concerned that people find their own enlightenment than appeal to the gods for help and support.

Enlightenment, or **Nirvana**, for Buddhists—as with Hindus—involves escaping from samsara. Upon his own enlightenment, the Buddha came to understand both the plight of humankind and the way to move beyond the eternal cycle of birth, karma, death, and rebirth. His insight is referred to as the **Four Noble Truths**; these truths form the core of Buddhist teaching:

1. To live is to experience suffering.
2. Suffering comes from desire and attachment.
3. The way to eliminate suffering is to eliminate desire.
4. This is possible if one follows the Eightfold Path.

The Eightfold Path is another key element in the Buddha's teaching, and focuses on the proper way of living one's life.

From the Source

And what, monks, is the Middle Path, of which the Tathagata has gained enlightenment, which produces insight and knowledge, and tends to calm, to higher knowledge, enlightenment, Nirvana?[7] This is the noble Eightfold Way, namely right view, right intention, right speech, right action, right livelihood, right

effort, right mindfulness, right concentration. This, monks, is the Middle Path, of which the Tathagata has gained enlightenment, which produces insight and knowledge, and tends to calm, to higher knowledge, enlightenment, Nirvana.[8]

The person who follows the Eightfold Path will break the bonds that tie one to life and will achieve release from the cycle, that is, Nirvana. Thus the goal of basic Buddhist practice is not the achievement of a state of bliss in some heaven but the extinguishing of craving and desire. When all desire is extinguished, one is released from the cycle of life that includes birth, suffering, death, and rebirth. One who has followed the Eightfold Path and has arrived at the point of achieving Nirvana is called **arhat**.

Among the unique teachings of the Buddha is that the soul does not exist. According to Buddha, people live in a state of **anatman** (the absence of enduring souls). Likewise, the Buddha taught that all things are impermanent. Indeed, one of the principal insights of Buddhist enlightenment is that suffering occurs when one falls prey to the illusion of permanence. If one considers life, the soul, or anything else to be permanent, one can easily develop attachments and desires. To live in the proper way for the Buddhist, then, is to follow the Eightfold Path and embrace impermanence. This impermanence extends to one's own self; hence, instead of acknowledging the reality of a permanent soul, the Buddha taught the concept of anatman. Unlike Hindu rebirth, which carries the soul of the person from one life to the next, the Buddhist concept of anatman allows for the transfer of one's karma if not one's soul during rebirth. A common metaphor is that Buddhist rebirth is like the flame of a candle that lights another candle. When the first candle is extinguished, its flame lives on in the second candle. Neither the flame nor the second candle is identical to the original burning candle, but the energy of the first flame somehow persists.

The teachings of the Buddha became the basis for an organization that took on many of the components of a religion. His followers organized themselves into a monastic order, the Sangha. His teachings became codified in the laws of that order and in various forms of scripture. The Buddha himself came to be regarded as the greatest of beings. The rules under which early Buddhist monks were expected to live are noteworthy because they demonstrate the practical outworking of the Buddha's teachings.

The Development of Buddhism

6.3. Discuss the development of Buddhism over time.

The teachings of the Buddha differed radically from those of the Indian religions of his day. He denied the relevance of the gods and the necessity of worship or sacrifice. Although the Buddha shared the Indian idea that the goal of life was release from the cycle of rebirth, he taught that release depends totally on the works of the individual. However, as Buddhism developed into a religion practiced by millions of people, it developed and diversified. As it entered different historical and geographical contexts, like other religions, it adapted to meet the needs of its many adherents. In the twenty-first century, Buddhism is one of the major religions of the world. Its devotees are found in nearly every Asian nation and in many other parts of the world. The path by which Buddhism was transformed from a small group of disciples following one man into one of the largest religions is fascinating.

As in the case of almost every other founder of a religion, before the Buddha had been dead very long his followers were debating the meaning of his teachings. According to one tradition, a schism occurred between the disciples the day after his death. Within a year of his death, his followers called a council to try to determine the true meaning of his teachings. This council failed to bring unity; within a short period, there were four major Buddhist factions. During the next ten years, the number increased to more than sixteen.

In 390 B.C.E., a second council was called and a conservative minority declared the majority of Buddhists to be heretics. From this point onward, Buddhism has been divided into these two major camps, which have in turn subdivided into numerous sects. The smaller and more conservative wing of Buddhism is known as Hinayana (the exclusive way). At one time, there may have been as many as eighteen schools within the Hinayana movement. Today, the only remaining Hinayana school is **Theravada** (the tradition of the elders). The larger and more liberal segment is known as **Mahayana** (the expansive way). The basic differences between these two divisions are discussed later in this chapter.

Buddhism received its greatest impetus when the emperor of India, Asoka, converted to the new religion. Asoka, who ruled from 268 to 232 B.C.E., became convinced that, unlike other religions of India, Buddhism was potentially the religion for all the peoples of the world. Thus, he was the first Buddhist to send out missionaries to carry the teachings of Gautama and urge non-Indians to accept them. Asoka sent his son Mahinda to Ceylon (present-day Sri Lanka), where the king and his court were converted. Today, Sri Lanka boasts the longest history of Buddhism of any country except India. Other emissaries carried the Buddhist message to Burma. One of Asoka's edicts claims that the missionaries went as far west as Syria and Greece.[9] Asoka's decision to spread his religion proved to be the salvation of Buddhism, because Buddhism virtually ceased to exist in India centuries later. Asoka also called the third council of Buddhism in 247 B.C.E. to determine the authoritative list of Buddhist scriptures.

Despite the enormous unifying work of Asoka and others, by the first century C.E. many major and minor sects existed within Buddhism. The most distinct split was along the lines of the differences between Theravada and Mahayana.

Theravada Buddhism

6.4. **Understand the basic teachings of Theravada Buddhism.**

Theravada Buddhism is the less embellished of the two major divisions within this religion. As such, it believes itself to be closer to the original teachings of the Buddha. The major locations of Theravada Buddhism today are Sri Lanka and the Southeast Asian nations of Burma, Thailand, Cambodia, and Laos. There are also growing communities of Theravada Buddhists in Europe, Australia, and North America.

According to Theravada Buddhism, people must achieve enlightenment for themselves without reliance on the gods or on any force beyond human beings who are faithfully following the teachings of the Buddha. For this reason, the monk is the ideal figure. It is he who shaves his head, puts on the yellow or orange robe, takes up a begging bowl, and seeks release from life through meditation and self-denial. His home is the Sangha, as it was in the days of the Buddha. When a monk achieves the goal he is seeking, he becomes an arhat and when he dies is released from the cycle of birth, death, and rebirth—the common lot of humankind.

From the Source

There is no suffering for him who has finished his journey, and abandoned grief, who has freed himself on all sides, and thrown off all fetters.

They exert themselves with their thoughts well-collected, they do not tarry in their abode, like swans who have left their lake, they leave their house and home.

Men who have no riches, who live on recognized food, who have perceived void and unconditioned freedom [Nirvana], their path is difficult to understand, like that of the birds of the air.

He whose appetites are stilled, who is not absorbed in enjoyment. . . .

The gods even envy him whose senses, like horses well broken in by the driver, have been subdued, who is free from pride, and free from appetites;

In a hamlet or in a forest, on sea or on dry land, wherever venerable persons [Arananta] dwell, that place is delightful.[10]

If a Theravada Buddhist cannot or will not join the Sangha and become a monk, then that person must be content to lead the life of a layperson, supporting the needs of the monks and hoping to be in a better position in another life. One need not make a lifelong commitment to the monastic life. Most Theravada men become monks as a rite of passage from youth to adulthood. Many Theravada Buddhists temporarily "put on the robes," as ordination is called, for a period of weeks or months to mark critical stages in the course of life, or when life's pressures become too much to bear. Monks are free to leave the Sangha at any time.

However, there are many ways for lay Theravada Buddhists to make merit even if they are not able to join the Sangha permanently. Sponsoring the ordination of a monk or novice is thought to be a source of good karma, or merit, as it is commonly known. Because they cannot be ordained themselves, many women encourage their sons, grandsons, and even husbands to join the Sangha and sponsor their ordinations. Offering food to monks is among the most important ways of making merit for Theravada Buddhists.

Theravada Buddhism, like that of the Buddhism of Gautama, teaches that the goals of religion are reached through the efforts, meditation, and achievements of the individual. The gods, sacrifice, and prayer are of minor consequence. However, certain traditional religious elements have evolved. For example, relics of the life of the Buddha have become important to Theravadins. His bones and possessions have become objects of veneration at many important Theravada shrines. Paying homage to these relics is considered to be almost as meritorious as paying homage to a living Buddha. Control and veneration of relics also plays an important role in the legitimation of Theravada Buddhist politics. This is as true in modern states as it was in traditional kingdoms, and plays a role in international affairs as well as in domestic politics. China, for example, periodically sends a tooth relic on tours of other Buddhist countries, allowing local Buddhists to make large stores of merit "good karma" and presumably incurring the gratitude and support of their governments.

As Jains believe that there were many Tirthankaras in the past, Theravada and other Buddhists believe that there have been many Buddhas in the past and that there will be more in the future. A Buddha, after all, is only a human being who has discovered the path to Nirvana through his or her own efforts. There are also many stories concerning the former lives of the Buddha Gautama known as *Jatakas*. The Jatakas are among the most common themes in Buddhist art and are the subject of sermons and popular religious texts in all Theravada societies.[11]

Religion in Public Life

Burma, also known as Myanmar, has been a Theravada Buddhist stronghold for centuries, and monks represent a vital segment of society. Not only do they provide opportunities to Burmese for worship and religious activities, they also help to meet social and educational needs.

Unfortunately, Burma has been under some form of military rule since 1962. In September of 2007, large pro-democracy protests broke out across the country to call for reform. Tens of thousands of Buddhist monks joined these protests, which many commentators believe lent a powerful public and moral uplift to the protest movement. A group called the All Burma Monks Alliance stated, "In order to banish the common enemy evil regime from Burmese soil forever, united masses of people need to join hands with the united clergy forces."[12] When the government cracked down on the protests, monks were some of the victims of the violence, and many were exiled or imprisoned.

Since the time of the protests, now sometimes referred to as the "Saffron Revolution" because of the color of the monks' robes, modest democratic reforms have occurred in Burma. The monks continue to call for peaceful reform and democracy.

The characteristic physical structure of Theravada Buddhism is a complex of buildings that in Thai is called a *wat*.[13] The most important building in the wat is the *bot* or *vihara*, a hall used for teaching, preaching, and meditation. Usually, this hall contains a statue of the Buddha, with attending altars, candles, and incense. Another portion of the hall may have raised seats for lecturing teachers and preachers. Other buildings include the living quarters for the monks and a number of graceful towers known as *stupas* or *pagodas*. Some speculate that the pagodas may have begun as relic mounds, but today they serve as worship or festival centers for the Buddhist community. Some of these pagodas are believed to contain relics of the Buddha or arhats. Others contain manuscript copies of Buddhist texts or large images of the Buddha. Laypeople often visit and make offerings at these shrines. Their purpose, however, is not to worship the Buddha or the enlightened saints, but to pay respect to the ideas of Buddhahood and Nirvana and dedicate themselves to the quest for liberation. These devotional acts are also said to produce merit.

The wealthy also make merit by constructing or repairing pagodas and monasteries. In the past, Buddhist kings and nobles engaged in massive Buddhist building programs, erecting hundreds of shrines and dedicating tax revenues for their maintenance. Today politicians and wealthy businesspeople continue this practice, although on a lesser scale. Even the poor can engage in this type of merit making by dropping a few coins in the collection boxes found in most pagodas.

Monks should not be concerned with making merit. Monastic life is structured in ways that block the acquisition of either merit or de-merit—both of which lead to rebirth and impede progress toward enlightenment. Instead, through meditation and the study of Buddhist scriptures, they cultivate the types of mental states and knowledge that lead toward enlightenment. Pagodas are used as places of meditation by both monks and lay Buddhists. Today there are meditation centers that are used as retreats for those who want to devote themselves fully to the practice for a period of time. There are two types of Theravada meditation. *Sammatta* meditation involves intense concentration, the purpose of which is the attainment of the spiritual states that open the path to enlightenment. *Vipassana* is insight meditation; its purpose is the sudden, intuitive realization of Buddhist truths, and it is modeled on the experience of the Gautama under the bo tree.

Mahayana Buddhism

6.5. **Identify the tenets of Mahayana Buddhism.**

The Principles of Mahayana

In the third century B.C.E., while King Asoka was spreading the teachings of Buddhism through his missionary efforts, certain subtle changes began to occur in the religion. One of the basic assumptions underlying these new developments was that, in addition to what the Buddha had openly taught his disciples, there were many other principles he had secretly taught, but only to a select group who could properly understand them. A favorite story of the Mahayanists is that, as the Buddha was teaching, he took a handful of leaves from the forest floor and explained to his disciples that as the leaves in his hand were less than the total leaves of the forest, so were the teachings that he had given them openly less than the total amount of truth that could be imparted in secret. Mahayana Buddhism simply picked up a few more leaves. Once this assumption was accepted, it was possible to accept fresh and expansive interpretations of basic Buddhist concepts as part of the Buddha's original teachings.

A second principle that began to develop in Mahayana Buddhism between the third century B.C.E. and the first century C.E. was that Gautama was really more than a man. In contrast to the teachings of early Buddhism and those of the Theravada school, the Mahayanists began to teach that the Buddha was really a compassionate, eternal, and almost divine being who came to Earth in the form of a man because he loved humankind and wished to be of assistance.

The third principle the Mahayanists put forth was that Gautama was not the only Buddha to whom people could appeal. If Gautama was an eternal being who had come to Earth to help people, the Mahayanists maintained that there must be many others. The Mahayana teaching is that there are many Buddhas located in different parts of the cosmos, all of whom are capable of helping people on the path to enlightenment.[14] This new idea did more than anything else to broaden the appeal of Buddhism: If there were many such eternal beings who were compassionate and had come to Earth to help suffering people, then these beings were worthy of veneration and respect. Whereas Gautama had been unconcerned about the gods and worship had meant little in his scheme of things, Mahayanists could now focus their devotion on these many eternal Buddhas. They could study their lives and build temples for them. Clergy could be trained in worshiping them; and cultic systems of ritual, sacrifice, hymns, and the like could be established on their behalf. It also meant that people could appeal to them for assistance. This remains an important part of Mahayana devotionalism.

This development also was essential to the Buddhist missionary movement. When Buddhist missionaries entered a new country, they did not have to ask the natives to give up their old gods; these gods were seen as various incarnations of the Buddha, and their cults could continue. In the same way that Hinduism absorbed Buddhism by saying that Gautama was really an avatar of Vishnu, Buddhism absorbed many other religions by saying that their gods were really incarnations of one of the Buddhas.

Mahayanists also developed a class of beings called **bodhisattvas**, who could provide help for humans struggling with the problems of life. It was taught that certain beings had taken vows to become bodhisattvas (future Buddhas) at some point during their lifetimes. Then, by living exemplary lives, they could acquire merit. Following death, these bodhisattvas postponed their achievement of Nirvana until such time as all living beings could attain it and shared their merit with humankind. Some of the bodhisattvas were thought to reside in heaven, while others continued to be incarnated as human beings. They were all believed to respond to the prayers of those who needed their help. One of the most popular bodhisattvas is Avalokiteshvara, who is venerated as the bodhisattva of compassion. He is also known as Guanyin, a female bodhisattva common in China. Avalokiteshvara, under his various guises, is first discussed in the **Lotus Sutra**, a key Mahayana text. Another popular bodhisattva is Maitreya, who is revered as the Buddha of the age to come.

The Spread of Mahayana Buddhism

The teachings of the Buddha were carried over the Himalayas into China soon after they became popular in India. There is some evidence that Theravada Buddhism had achieved a foothold in China by the first century C.E. However, it was not until the third century, when Mahayana was introduced, that Buddhism really began to make inroads there. From that era onward, Buddhism became one of the three major religions of China, alongside the native Confucianism and Daoism.

From China, Mahayana Buddhism spread to other East Asian nations. Because of its close ties to China, Korea was brought under the influence of Buddhism as early as the fourth century C.E. The spread to the east continued in the sixth century, when Buddhism entered Japan. The Japanese at first refused to accept this new religion; but after a short time, they embraced it to the point that it came to share religious leadership with the native Shinto. Mahayana Buddhism also spread to the Indonesian islands of Java, Sumatra, and Bali. Chinese pilgrims en route to India often stopped for a period of months or even years in Southeast Asia to improve their knowledge of Sanskrit and Buddhist doctrine. Other Asian nations, such as Mongolia and Tibet, also accepted versions of Mahayana Buddhism. Because of the remote location of these countries, their versions of the religion developed along slightly different lines than it did in other places, and today they remain unique.

While Buddhism was becoming a great success as a missionary religion in the East and Southeast Asia, it was gradually dying in India. Buddhism declined there because

Quan Yin, the Chinese bodhisattva of compassion. Quan Yin, or Guanyin, is an important female figure in Chinese Buddhism.

Getty Images, Inc.- Photodisc./Royalty Free

Hinduism was able to absorb the distinctive qualities of the major challenging religions of Jainism and Buddhism. By the seventh century, it had absorbed many Buddhist features—simply by stating that Gautama was an avatar of Vishnu. Therefore, anything new, important, or distinctive about Buddhism came to be understood as an expression of Vishnu within the Hindu scheme of things. In predominately Buddhist countries, images of the Buddha can be found in Hindu temples, often with inscriptions describing him as an avatar of Lord Vishnu. Waves of invasions, particularly the Islamic invasions in the eleventh through thirteenth centuries, destroyed many Indian centers of Buddhist learning. In those times, many Buddhists converted to Islam. With the destruction of Buddhist kingdoms, monasteries and temples found it difficult to survive. Although Hinduism somehow had the resiliency to survive the transition to Muslim rule, Buddhism—in India—did not.

Mahayanist Groups

Mahayana Buddhism began as a religion open to innovation and change. As it spread and developed in various Asian nations, it acquired many new concepts from these peoples. Therefore, we do not speak of Buddhism today as a single religion but as a family of religions; within this family, many forms of religious expression may be found.

THE PURE LAND SECT (CHING-T'U, JODO) One of the most popular and widespread branches of Mahayana Buddhism is the so-called Pure Land school. The goal of its adherents after death is to be reborn in a paradise called "the Land of Bliss." Mahayanists believe there have been many Buddhas and bodhisattvas. Among these are the Dhyani Buddhas, who preside over heavenlike Buddha-lands, in which it is possible to cultivate Buddhist virtues and in which evil does not exist. One of the most popular of these cosmic Buddhas is Amitabha.[15] Amitabha presides over a western paradise called "the Pure Land." His followers believe that living a virtuous life and reciting Amitabha's name will lead to rebirth in his world.

From the Source

[The Pure Land,] Ananda, which is the world system of the Lord Amitabha, is rich and prosperous, comfortable, fertile, delightful and crowded with many Gods and men. And in this world system, Ananda, there are no hells, no animals, no ghosts, no Asuras and none of the inauspicious places of rebirth. And in this our world no jewels make their appearance like those which exist in the world system Sukhavati.

And that world system Sukhavati, Ananda, emits many fragrant odors, it is rich in a great variety of flowers and fruits, adorned with jewel trees, which are frequented by flocks of various birds with sweet voices, which the Tathagata's miraculous power has conjured up. And these jewel trees, Ananda, have various colors, many colors, many hundreds of thousands of colors. They are variously composed of the seven precious things, in varying combinations, i.e., of gold, silver, beryl, crystal, coral, red pearls or emerald. Such jewel trees, and clusters of banana trees and rows of palm trees, all made of precious things, grow everywhere in the Buddha field.[16]

To the Pure Land Buddhist, the emphasis is on faith in Amitabha. Some members of this sect believe that simply uttering the name *Amitabha* many times during the day will aid in one's achieving the Land of Bliss. With faith in Amitabha as its central premise and eternity in the Pure Land as its goal, this version of Buddhism is quite different from that originally taught by the Buddha. It is possible for the Pure Land monk to marry, have children, and live in the world in a manner very similar to that of the laity. Worship for the Pure Land devotee often occurs in congregations; in fact, some Pure Land congregations in Western nations have adopted worship styles and institutional structures that are roughly analogous to those of Christian churches. Pure Land Buddhists may have "Sunday schools" for the religious instruction of their children, meet for worship in congregations, hear sermons from their clergymen, and offer prayers to Amitabha.

THE INTUITIVE SCHOOLS (CH'AN, ZEN)   There has always existed a group within Buddhism that has emphasized that the truths of religion do not come through rational thought processes, study of scripture, or faith, but rather through a sudden flash of insight. These groups usually trace their origin to the experience of the Buddha under the bo tree. Recall that here the Buddha realized he had not found the truth he sought through study with the Brahmin gurus, or after five years of extreme asceticism. He therefore resolved to meditate. He sat under the bo tree for several weeks and the truth came to him in a flash of inspiration. Advocates of this position maintain that the intuition or inspiration that comes after a period of meditation is the key to Buddhist truth. These groups have been known throughout the Buddhist world as being meditative or intuitive Buddhists. In India, the word for meditation is *dhyana*; in Theravada countries, it is associated with Vipassana meditation schools; in China, it is Ch'an; and in Japan, it is Zen.

The basic principle behind all of the intuitive sects of Buddhism is that enlightenment is an individual matter and therefore one cannot receive much help from other persons or institutions. Individuals find enlightenment through meditation and the realization that the Buddha nature is within themselves. Although the externals of religion, including the study of texts, monastic discipline, temples, and images, are important in Zen Buddhism, only direct insight can yield enlightenment. Zen teaches that all people must learn the real truth about religion and life for themselves, through their own experience. One can become enlightened while sitting under a tree or sweeping a floor.

According to the intuitive sects, reason is to be distrusted because it cannot possibly lead people to real truth. In fact, people must deliberately confuse reason before they can find the truth. Therefore, Zen Buddhism uses riddles that are carefully constructed to go beyond reason or confuse reason in order to lead the initiates into enlightenment. Such riddles of Zen are called *koans*. Entire books have been filled with these riddles, tales, and short statements used by Zen masters to aid their pupils. Perhaps best known to Westerners is the simple statement, "You have heard the sound of the clapping of two hands, but what is the sound of one hand clapping?" This question makes no sense, but it is designed to induce the initiate to go beyond sense or reason and to ponder. Another koan frequently given to students is, "What was your face before your parents were born?" Still another is, "From where you are stop the distant boat from moving across the water."

The pupil of Zen first meditates. When the pupil's mind is cleared of day-to-day matters and is ready to be released from reason, the master gives the student a riddle. It is hoped that while the novice meditates on one of these nonsense statements a flash of enlightenment (*satori*) will lead the initiate to the truth beyond reason.

THE RATIONALIST SCHOOL (T'IEN-T'AI, TENDAI)   Whereas the intuitive schools, Ch'an and Zen, tended to distrust the rational process and felt they had little need for scripture in their search for enlightenment, another group that arose in China in the sixth century taught that, in addition to meditation, one should use reason and study the scriptures to discover the truth about Buddhism. This sect, which was called T'ien-t'ai, was founded by a monk named Chih-I. According to Chih-I, the Buddha had used various methods during his lifetime to teach his truths. At one point, he taught the Theravada doctrines; at another time, he felt he could communicate better by teaching the Mahayana doctrines; and at still another point, he taught in a manner similar to that used by the intuitive sects. In reality, there is only one true Buddhist teaching; individuals must study the scriptures of Buddhism to know this truth. Therefore, although meditation may be helpful at certain times, it is not the only path, and rational thought and study should not be disregarded. In the ninth century, the teachings of Chih-I were introduced into Japan, where this sect became known as Tendai.

THE SOCIOPOLITICAL SCHOOL (NICHIREN)   From time to time, the various sects of Buddhism have come to have great effect on the social and political life of

Young Theravada Buddhist monks and novices at the Shwedagon Pagoda in Rangoon, Burma.

(Alison Wright/Corbis)

various nations. One such sect is the so-called Nichiren (sun lotus) Buddhist group, which is a purely Japanese phenomenon. The founder of Nichiren lived in Japan in the thirteenth century. The son of humble parents, at age fifteen he entered a Tendai Buddhist monastery. During his ten years there, he came to believe that all of the current sects of Buddhism were a perversion of the true teachings of the Buddha. He also came to believe that the Lotus Sutra was the only scripture a person needed to study to become a correct Buddhist. While meditating on this sutra, he underwent a conversion. He changed his name to Nichiren, took a vow to faithfully follow and teach the Lotus Sutra, and set forth on a career of preaching and polemics with great fervor. He preached that he alone understood the truth of pure Buddhism and that the other Japanese sects—Zen, Pure Land, and so on—were preaching falsehoods and leading people to hell. Because most Japanese people followed these "false" sects, the nation was suffering from internal and external woes. Naturally, this kind of preaching aroused powerful enemies; Nichiren was twice deported and twice condemned to death by the Japanese authorities.

Throughout its history, Nichiren Buddhism has expressed hostility toward the rituals and teachings of other Buddhist sects. Consequently, it has always been a small, persecuted minority. Nichiren has also stressed a simpler form of Buddhism and uncompromising patriotism and loyalty to Japan. It teaches that when Buddhism becomes purified in Japan, it will reach out to the rest of the world. Although Nichiren has only slightly over 2 million followers today, it was the source of another Buddhist sect, Soka Gakkai, that has a large international following.

Nichiren Buddhists are especially known for their practice of repeatedly chanting to the Lotus Sutra as a form of devotion. Although the teachings of the sutra are important to many Mahayana Buddhists, the followers of Nichiren revere the Lotus Sutra itself as worthy of veneration.

Tibetan Buddhism

Tibetan Buddhism is variously regarded as another form of Mahayana Buddhism and as its own major division, referred to as **Vajrayana**, or "the Diamond Vehicle." Similar to the Mahayanists, Tibetan Buddhists are deeply devoted to the Lotus Sutra. But, Buddhism in Tibet is characterized by ornate ritual practices, chants, esoteric teaching, and the centrality of monastic leadership.

The indigenous religion of Tibet, called *Bon*, emphasized incantations and spells to protect people from the demons and spirits that lurked in the shadows and dark places of that harsh land. When Buddhism entered Tibet in the seventh century, it absorbed this concern for magic and protection from demons as a major emphasis even as it reconceptualized many of these Tibetan spirits as Buddhas and bodhisattvas. Today, Tibetan Buddhism remains concerned with the spiritual dimensions and struggles of daily life as well as with the more orthodox Buddhist commitment to enlightenment.

Vayjrayana Buddhism is much like the Buddhism found throughout the Mahayana world, but because of the isolation of Tibet, many unique features have been developed and maintained. The most important practical feature of Tibetan Buddhism is its concern for spoken formulas, divination, and daily rituals as a means of coping with the problems of life. Tibetan Buddhism is sometimes referred to as Tantric Buddhism because of its heavy reliance on manuals (*tantras*) that teach the various words and spells that help one deal with the unknown and are believed to guide the quest for positive rebirth and eventually enlightenment.

Another feature of Tibetan Buddhism is its use of the phrase *Om mani padme hum*, which means, "Om, the jewel in the lotus, hum." This expression is used to invoke the Bodhisattva Avalokiteshvara, a figure first known in the Lotus Sutra. Avalokiteshvara

(Mark R. Woodward)

Chinese Mahayana Buddhist laywoman chanting sutras. Buddha Tooth Relic Temple (Singapore).

(Mark R. Woodward)

Tibetan Buddhist prayer wheel. The cylinder contains a prayer text. Spinning it is thought to yield as much positive karma as reciting the text.

is venerated in many schools of Mahayana Buddhism, but he is particularly important in Tibet. He is revered as the patron of the Tibetan people and is worshiped because of his great compassion and ability to rescue his disciples from the perils of the world, as well as to guide them on the path to enlightenment.

Another unique feature of Tibetan Buddhism is the prayer wheel. No one knows the origin of this device, but it has been used primarily among Tibetans. One form of the prayer wheel is a cylinder that contains the text of the Lotus Sutra; within this cylinder is an agitator. It is believed that by turning the agitator and stirring the prayers, they are somehow prayed. The most common form of the prayer wheel is a small model that can be carried on one's person and activated regularly. Other larger models are found in monasteries. Inventive Tibetan Buddhists have even been known to set up prayer wheels near streams, where they are turned by water power.

Still another distinctive feature of Tibetan Buddhism is its clergy, the **lamas**. The word *lama* basically means "superior one." From the earliest days, Tibetan men who have spurned the normal pursuits of life to enter monasteries have been unusually powerful. As early as the ninth century, the kings of Tibet gave the lamas certain land for their monasteries and with these lands the power to gather funds from the people. By the fourteenth century, the leaders of the monasteries had become more powerful than the kings. The kings disappeared, and for all practical purposes, the country was ruled by the lamas. Although the lamas had originally taken vows of celibacy, by the fourteenth century they had rejected it and lived in lordly splendor with their wives and children. During that same century, however, reforms were introduced and celibacy was restored.

The lamas of Tibetan Buddhism are divided into orders, but two orders dominate. The larger of the two is identified by Western scholars as the Yellow Hat school; the other is identified as the Red Hat school. One of the most interesting contributions of the Red Hat school is the scriptural book of its adherents, the *Bardo Thodol* (The Book of the Dead). It is believed that this book came to written form sometime in the eighth century C.E., although it may contain materials that are centuries older. Of course, it contains some teachings that are pre-Buddhist in nature. It teaches essentially that after death the human soul abides for forty-nine days in a dreamlike state called the Bardo. During this period, the ultimate destiny of the soul is determined. Individuals who have lived virtuous lives will achieve Nirvana from the Bardo; if, on the other hand, a karmic pull has built up during an individual's life, then that person will be drawn again to rebirth.[17] It also is believed that the immediate predeath hours can influence the soul in its stay in the Bardo. Therefore, Tibetan Buddhist monks are trained to help the dying through this experience.

The leader of the Yellow Hat group has been known for centuries as the Dalai Lama and by virtue of his position essentially has been the ruler of Tibet.[18] When one Dalai Lama dies, an extensive search is made for his successor. A group of monks scours Tibet for a child who seems to have the qualities and characteristics of the dead Dalai Lama, because it is believed that following his death he will reincarnate himself in the body of his successor. When the group has found such a child and agrees that this is the new Dalai Lama, the boy begins a long period of preparation for leadership of the nation.

By the twentieth century, Tibet had become a nation in which the lamas ruled the land. The Dalai Lama served as both spiritual and temporal leader, and the position of lama became so popular and so important that it was estimated in 1950 that almost 20 percent of the male population lived in monasteries.

Religion and Public Life

This came to an abrupt end in 1950, when China invaded Tibet. For centuries, Tibet was claimed by China, but because the claim was rarely pressed, Tibet enjoyed a virtually independent existence. In 1950, China occupied Tibet and set up a puppet government. In 1959, under the leadership of the young Dalai Lama, the Tibetans attempted to overthrow Chinese rule, but their revolution was crushed. The Dalai Lama and many of his followers escaped to India. In exile, the Tibetan Buddhists have maintained their identity and carried on missionary work in India, Europe, and North America. The Dalai Lama has become an international spokesman for peace and human rights and has received the Nobel Prize. He is particularly adept at translating the message of Buddhism into terms that Western people can understand easily. The Dalai Lama has held talks with the Chinese government since 2002 concerning the future of Tibet. Little has been accomplished and China continues its repressive policies. Worldwide protests by Tibetans and their supporters during the period leading up to the 2008 Olympic Games in Bejing actually led to increased repression in Tibet itself. There is no hope that the Dalai Lama will be allowed to return to his homeland.

Buddhist Festivals and Holy Days

6.6. **Name the Buddhist festivals and holy days.**

Because Buddhism is divided in many ways according to philosophy and geography, there is great variety in its holy days. Some Theravada Buddhist monks have as many as forty holy days each year, but they are not celebrated by all Buddhists. The major festivals recognized by most Buddhists follow.

New Year

In Theravada Buddhist countries, the new year is celebrated in April. This holiday often lasts three days and has a certain carnival-type atmosphere. During the first two days, there is a time of washing, cleaning, and preparing for the new year. On the third day, there is a rededication to the Buddhist way of life; worshipers visit the temples and make offerings in preparation for the new year.[19]

Buddha's Birthday

The birth of Gautama is celebrated on April 8 in China and Japan and on the last full moon in May in Southeast Asia. Japanese Buddhist temples have a flower festival during this holiday. Other Buddhist communities celebrate by washing the statue of the

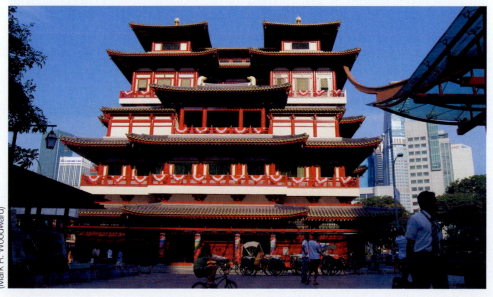

(Mark R. Woodward)

The Singapore Buddha Tooth Relic Temple. The veneration of relics plays an important role in Buddhist piety that crosses sectarian divides. In this case the temple was built by a Chinese Mahayana monk who obtained the relic from a Burmese Theravada monk. In Buddhist countries, relics play a significant role in public diplomacy, as they are periodically sent on tour to foster goodwill among Buddhists abroad. China, India, Singapore, and Sri Lanka have all sponsored relic tours.

infant Buddha in a basin of fragrant water filled with flower petals to honor the gods who bathed the Buddha immediately after his birth. Sometimes, there is a procession of images of the Buddha through the streets, accompanied by cheers and firecrackers. Buddhist children dress up as the little Buddha on this holiday.

The Festival of Souls (Ullambana)

During July (in Japan) or August (in China), Buddhists believe realms of the dead are opened and the souls of the dead are allowed to wander about this world. Out of compassion, families leave gifts of food for these wandering spirits. During the middle of the month, elaborate rituals are performed by priests to provide comfort and release for the souls of the dead.

The Robe Offering

In November, at the end of the rainy season, Theravada Buddhists celebrate the sending forth of the first Buddhist missionaries in the days of Asoka. The laity present new yellow robes to the monks of their region, as well as other gifts. A public feast and display of the robes on a "wishing tree" make up the ceremony. The season ends with the making and presentation of the *mahakathina* (great robe). This robe is one that has been made in a single day or night—from spinning the thread to stitching the cloth. The robe commemorates the act of the Buddha's mother, who, upon hearing that the Buddha was to renounce his worldly life, wove his first mendicant robe in one night.

Buddhism Today

6.7. **Discuss Buddhism today.**

After the great missionary movements in the first fifteen centuries of its existence, and after such Asian nations as Sri Lanka, Burma, Thailand, China, Japan, and Korea had been converted, Buddhism slipped into a state of quiescence. For centuries, there were no great movements or changes. Within the twentieth century, however, Buddhism began to revive and grow again. There are several reasons for this revival.

Ironically, one of the factors in renewed interest in Buddhism has been the work of Christian missionaries and other Western travelers. As Europeans entered Asian nations in the nineteenth and twentieth centuries, they felt the need to know more about Buddhism. They therefore initiated translations of ancient Buddhist texts. Some actually converted to Buddhism.[20] This marked the beginning of Western fascination with Buddhism, which has continued until the present day.

A second factor that has contributed to the revival of Buddhism, particularly Theravada Buddhism, has been the rise of Asian nationalisms. With the collapse of the colonial empires after World War II, many new Asian nations began to take pride in being Buddhist. In the past, it was in vogue to be Western, to speak a European language, and to study Christianity. After World War II, Theravada Buddhism attracted renewed attention in such nations as Burma and Thailand. Some modernist interpretations of Buddhism and Hinduism claim that their theories of endless ages are much more in tune with science than is the Judeo-Christian story of creation. Furthermore, Buddhism's message of peace and tolerance seemed to fit the needs of the nuclear age. Therefore, some Buddhists have come to see their religion as being the religious option for the modern world. These concerns have led to a renewed emphasis on missionary efforts, as well as to an ecumenical Buddhist movement known as Socially Engaged Buddhism, which minimizes sectarian differences and emphasizes such universal Buddhist teachings as nonviolence and compassion for all living beings.

Historically, the chief locations for Mahayana Buddhism have been China, Japan, Vietnam, and Korea. Following World War II, Buddhism suffered severe losses in China. With the establishment of the People's Republic of China in 1949, Buddhism was suppressed. It suffered even more serious repression during the so-called Cultural Revolution (1966–1971). In recent years the Chinese government has relaxed some of its policies toward religion and there has been renewed Buddhist activity. In Japan, Korea, Singapore, and Taiwan, Mahayana Buddhism remains a vital force in people's lives. Today Buddhist temples and shrines are found in all of these countries, and Buddhist literature is widely read.

Buddhism, it would seem, is in the process of another great missionary outreach. During and after American involvement in the Vietnam War (1965–1975), many Vietnamese, Thai, Lao, and Khmer Buddhists emigrated to the United States and other Western countries. Zen, Nichiren, and Tibetan Buddhism have attracted many converts in America and Europe since the 1950s. The 1958 publication of *Dharma Bums* by Beat Generation writer Jack Kerouac (1922–1969) helped to raise interest in Buddhism. Today it is not unusual to find large communities of Buddhists of many sects and varieties in major American urban centers. American Buddhism is beginning to acquire its own unique characteristics and divisions. On the one hand, "ethnic" Buddhists are descended from Asians who immigrated to North America. On the other, "convert" Buddhist communities include those who have adopted Buddhism not as part of their ancestral heritage but as a choice in the religious marketplace. Popular Buddhist magazines like *Tricycle* cater to this latter group of Buddhists and emphasize the study and practice of meditation and social and ecological responsibility. They focus less on monastic life and more on meditation. In contrast, ethnic Buddhist communities continue typical Asian Buddhist practices such as merit making and reverence for bodhisattvas. These trends are contemporary examples of the ways in which Buddhists have tried to apply the teachings of the Buddha in widely different cultural, social, and historical contexts.

Think About It

1. Briefly discuss the life of Guatama and the origins of Buddhism.

2. Summarize the teachings of Buddha, discussing what role the idea of enlightenment plays in these teachings and the practice of Buddhism in general.

3. How did the teachings of Buddha differ radically from those of the other Indian religions of his day? Over time, how did Buddhism develop and diversify?

4. Describe the basic teachings of Theravada Buddhism.

5. What are the principles of Mahayana Buddhism?

6. What are the major Buddhism festivals and holy days?

7. Why has there been a renewed interest in Buddhism in last the hundred years?

Suggested Reading

Beyer, Stephen. *The Buddhist Experience.* Encino, Calif.: Dickenson, 1974.

Conze, Edward. *Buddhist Scriptures.* New York: Penguin, 1959.

de Bary, William Theodore, ed. *The Buddhist Tradition.* New York: Vintage, 1972.

Fields, Rick. *How the Swans Came to the Lake. A Narrative History of Buddhism in America.* Boston: Shambala Publications, 1992.

Gyatso, Tenzin.*The Buddhism of Tibet and the Key to the Middle Way.* London: George Allen and Unwin, 1975.

Kuah, Pearce. *State Society and Religious Engineering: Towards a Reformist Buddhism in Singapore.* Singapore: Eastern Universities Press, 2003.

Robinson, Richard H., and Willard L. Johnson. *The Buddhist Religion.* Belmont, Calif.: Wadsworth, 1997.

Spiro, Melford. *Buddhism and Society. A Great Tradition and Its Burmese Vicissitudes.* Berkeley: University of California Press, 1982.

Strong, John. *The Experience of Buddhism. Sources and Interpretations.* Belmont, Calif.: Wadsworth, 1995.

Suzuki, Daisetz T. *Zen and Japanese Buddhism.* Boston: Charles E. Tuttle, 1958.

Source Material

Gautama Speaks of His Ascetic Practices

Before Gautama achieved enlightenment under the bo tree, he had struggled for many years. One of his paths led him to practice extreme asceticism. In the following passage, Gautama relates his experiences to one of his disciples.[21]

Majjhima-Nikaya. XII

Aye, Sariputta, I have lived the fourfold higher life;—I have been an ascetic of ascetics; loathly have I been, foremost in loathness, scrupulous have I been, foremost in scrupulosity; solitary have I been, foremost in solitude.

i. To such a pitch of asceticism have I gone that naked was I, flouting life's decencies, licking my hands after meals, never heeding when folk called to me to come or to stop, never accepting food brought to me before my rounds or cooked expressly for me, never accepting an invitation, never receiving food direct from pot or pan or within the threshold or among the faggots or pestles, never from (one only of) two people messing together, never from a pregnant woman or a nursing mother or a woman in coitu, never from gleanings (in time of famine) nor from where a dog is ready at hand or where (hungry) flies congregate, never touching flesh or spirits or strong drink or brews of grain. I have visited only one house a day and there take only one morsel; or I have visited but two or (up to not more than) seven houses a day and taken at each only two or (up to not more than) seven morsels; I have lived on a single saucer of food a day, or on two, or (up to) seven saucers; I have had but one meal a day, or one every two days, or (so on, up to) every seven days, or only once a fortnight, on a rigid scale of rationing. My sole diet has been herbs gathered green, or the grain of wild millets and paddy, or snippets of hide, or water plants, or the red powder round rice-grains within the husk, or the discarded scum of rice on the boil, or the flour of oil-seeds, or grass, or cow-dung. I have lived on wild roots and fruit, or on windfalls only. My raiment has been of hemp or of hempen mixture, of cerements, of rags from the dust-heap, of bark, of the black antelope's pelt either whole or split down the middle, or grass, of strips of bark or wood, of hair of men or animals woven into a blanket or of owl's wings. In fulfillment of my vows, I have plucked out the hair of my head and the hair of my beard, have never quitted the upright for the sitting posture, have squatted and never risen up, moving only a-squat, have couched on thorns, have gone down to the water punctually thrice before nightfall to wash (away the evil within). After this wise, in divers fashions, have I lived to torment and to torture my body—to such a length in asceticism have I gone.

ii. To such a length have I gone in loathness that on my body I have accumulated the dirt and filth of years till it dropped off of itself—even as the rank growths of years fall away from the stump of a tinduka-tree. But never once came the thought to me to clean it off with my own hands or to get others to clean it off for me;—to such a length in loathness have I gone.

iii. To such a length in scrupulosity have I gone that my footsteps out and in were always attended by a mindfulness so vigilant as to awake compassion within me over even a drop of water lest I might harm tiny creatures in crevices;—to such a length have I gone in scrupulosity.

iv. To such a length have I gone as a solitary that when my abode was in the depths of the forest, the mere glimpse of a cowherd or neatherd or grass cutter, or of a man gathering firewood or edible roots in the forest, was enough to make me dart from wood to wood, from thicket to thicket, from dale to dale, and from hill to hill,—in order that they might not see me or I them. As a deer at the sight of man darts away over hill and dale, even so did I dart away at the mere glimpse of cowherd, neatherd, or whatnot, in order that they might not see me or I them;—to such a length have I gone as a solitary.

When the cowherds had driven their herds forth from the byres, up I came on all fours to find a subsistence on the drippings of the young milch-cows. So long as my own dung and urine held out, on that I have subsisted. So foul a filth-eater was I.

I took up my abode in the awesome depths of the forest, depths so awesome that it was reputed that none but the passionless could venture in without his hair standing on end. When the cold season brought chill wintry nights, then it was that, in the dark half of the months when snow was falling, I dwelt by night in the open air and in the dank thicket by day. But when there came the last broiling month of summer before the rains, I made my dwelling under the baking sun by day and in the stifling thicket by night. Then there flashed on me these verses, never till then uttered by any:

> Now scorched, now froze, in forest dread, alone.
> Naked and fireless, set upon his quest.
> The hermit battles purity to win.

In a charnel ground I lay me down with charred bones for pillow. When the cowherds' boys came along, they spat and staled upon me, pelted me with dirt and stuck bits of wood into my ears. Yet I declare that never did I let an evil mood against them arise within me.—So poised in equanimity was I.

(80) Some recluses and Brahmins there are who say and hold that purity cometh by way of food, and accordingly proclaim that they live exclusively on jujube-fruits, which, in one form or other, constitute their sole meat and drink. Now I can claim to have lived on a single jujube-fruit a day. If this leads you to think that this fruit was large, in those days, you would err; for, it was precisely the same size then that it is today. When I was living on a single fruit a day, my body grew emaciated in the extreme; because I ate so little, my members, great and small, grew like the knotted joints of withered creepers; like a buffalo's hoof were my shrunken buttocks; like the twists in a rope were my spinal vertebrae; like the crazy rafters of a tumble-down roof, that start askew and aslant, were my gaunt ribs; like the starry gleams on water deep down and afar in the depths of a well, shone my gleaming eyes deep down and afar in the depths of their sockets; and as the rind of a cut gourd shrinks and shrivels in the heat, so shrank and shriveled the scalp of my head,—and all because I ate so little. If I sought to feel my belly, it was my backbone which I found in my grasp; if I sought to feel my backbone, I found myself grasping my belly, so closely did my belly cleave to my backbone;—and all because I ate so little. If for ease of body I chafed my limbs, the hairs of my body fell away under my hand, rotted at their roots;—and all because I ate so little.

> Other recluses and Brahmins there are who, saying and holding that purity cometh by way of food, proclaim that they live exclusively on beans—or seasamum—or rice—as their sole meat and drink.

(81) Now I can claim to have lived on a single bean a day—on a single seasamum seed a day—or on a single grain of rice a day; and (the result was still the same). Never did this practice or these courses or these dire austerities bring me to the ennobling gifts of super-human knowledge and insight. And why?—Because none of them lead to that noble understanding which, when won, leads on to Deliverance and guides him who lives up to it onward to the utter extinction of all ill.

The Buddha Explains the Four Noble Truths to His First Disciples

At the heart of Buddha's teaching about the nature of life and death and the proper way to live are the Four Noble Truths. The following selection from his first sermon to his disciples contains the Buddha's explanation of these truths.[22]

Then the Lord addressed the five brethren: "These two extremes, brethren, are not to be practised by one who has given up the world. What are the two? The one, devotion to lusts and pleasures, base, sensual, vulgar, ignoble, and useless, and the other, devotion to self-mortification, painful, ignoble, and useless. By avoiding these two extremes, brethren, the Tathagata [the Buddha himself] has gained perfect knowledge of the middle path, which produces insight and knowledge, and conduces to tranquillity, to transcendent knowledge, to complete enlightenment, to Nirvana. What is this middle path, brethren? It is the Noble Eightfold Path, that is, right views, right aspiration, right speech, right action, right livelihood, right endeavour, right watchfulness, and right meditation. This, brethren, is the middle path, of which the Tathagata has gained perfect knowledge, which produces insight and knowledge, and conduces to tranquillity, to supernatural faculty, to complete enlightenment, to Nirvana. This, brethren, is the noble truth of suffering: birth is suffering, old age is suffering, illness is suffering, death is suffering. Union with unpleasant things is suffering, separation from pleasant things is suffering, not obtaining what we wish is suffering, in short the fivefold clinging to existence is suffering. And this, brethren, is the noble truth of the cause of suffering: craving, which causes rebirth, accompanied by pleasure and lust, and rejoices at finding delight here and there, that is, craving for pleasure, craving for existence, and craving for prosperity. And this, brethren, is the noble truth of the destruction of suffering: which is the complete and trackless destruction of that thirst, its abandonment and relinquishment, liberation, and aversion. And this, brethren, is the noble truth of the path that leads to the destruction of suffering, that is, right views, right aspiration, right speech, right action, right livelihood, right endeavour, right watchfulness, and right meditation."

The Infinite Compassion of the Bodhisattva

One of the important figures in Mahayana Buddhism is the bodhisattva. These beings may have lived as humans and have delayed their achievements of Nirvana because of their compassion for humankind. This passage from *Shikshasamuccaya* (pp. 280–82) is a statement about the compassion of the bodhisattva.[23]

A Bodhisattva resolves: I take upon myself the burden of suffering. I am resolved to do so, I will endure it. I do not turn or run away, do not tremble, am not terrified, nor afraid, do not turn back or despond.

And why? At all costs I must bear the burdens of all beings. In that I do not follow my own inclinations. I have made the vow to save all beings. All beings I must set free. The whole world of living beings I must rescue, from the terrors of birth, of old age, of sickness, of death and rebirth, of all kinds of moral offense, of all states of woe, of the whole cycle of birth-and-death, of the jungle of false views, of the loss of wholesome dharmas, of the concomitants of ignorance,—from all these terrors I must rescue all beings. I walk so that the kingdom of unsurpassed cognition is built up for all beings. My endeavors do not merely aim at my own deliverance. For with the help of the boat of the thought of all-knowledge, I must rescue all these beings from the stream of Samsara, which is so difficult to cross, I must pull them back from the great precipice. I must free them from all calamities, I must ferry them across the stream of Samsara. I myself must grapple with the whole mass of suffering of all beings. To the limit of my endurance I will experience in all the states of woe, found in any world system, all the abodes of suffering. And I must not cheat all beings out of my store of merit, I am resolved to abide in each single state of woe for numberless aeons; and so I will help all beings to freedom, in all the states of woe that may be found in any world system whatsoever.

And why? because it is surely better that I alone should be in pain than that all these beings should fall into the states of woe. There I must give myself away as a pawn through which the whole world is redeemed from the terrors of the hells, of animal birth, of the world of Yama, and with this my own body I must experience, for the sake of all beings, the whole mass of all painful feelings. And on behalf of all beings I give surety for all beings, and in doing so I speak truthfully, am trustworthy, and do not go back on my word. I must not abandon all beings.

And why? There has arisen in me the will to win all-knowledge, with all beings for its object, that is to say, for the purpose of setting free the entire world of beings. And I have not set out for the supreme enlightenment from a desire for delights, not because I help to experience the delights of the five-sense qualities, or because I wish to indulge in the pleasures of the senses. And I do not pursue the course of a Bodhisattva in order to achieve the array of delights that can be found in the various worlds of sense-desire.

And why? Truly no delights are all these delights of the world. All this indulging in the pleasure of the senses belongs to the sphere of Mara.

The Importance of Sitting

In that branch of Mahayana Buddhism known in Japan as Zen, meditation is the key to enlightenment. The following text from Shobogenzo Zuimonki speaks of the importance of meditation in Zen.[24]

When I stayed at the Zen lodge in T'ien-t'ung (China), the venerable Ching used to stay up sitting until the small hours of the morning and then after only a little rest should rise early to start sitting again. In the meditation hall we went on sitting with the other elders, without letting up for even a single night. Meanwhile many of the monks went off to sleep. The elder would go around among them and hit the sleepers with his fist or a slipper, yelling at them to wake up. If their sleepiness persisted, he would go out to the hallway and ring the bell to summon the monks to a room apart, where he would lecture to them by the light of a candle.

"What use is there in your assembling together in the hall only to go to sleep? Is this all that you left the world and joined holy orders for? Even among laymen, whether they be emperors, princes, or officials, are there any who live a life of ease? The ruler must fulfill the duties of the sovereign, his ministers must serve with loyalty and devotion, and commoners must work to reclaim land and till the soil—no one lives a life of ease. To escape from such burdens and idly while away the time in a monastery— what does this accomplish? Great is the problem of life and death; fleeting indeed is our transitory existence. Upon these truths both the scriptural and meditation schools agree. What sort of illness awaits us tonight, what sort of death tomorrow? While we have life, not to practice Buddha's Law, but to spend the time in sleep is the height of foolishness. Because of such foolishness Buddhism today is in a state of decline. When it was at its zenith monks devoted themselves to the practice of sitting in meditation (zazen), but nowadays sitting is not generally insisted upon and consequently Buddhism is losing ground."

Upon another occasion his attendants said to him, "The monks are getting overtired or falling ill, and some are thinking of leaving the monastery, all because they are required to sit too long in meditation. Shouldn't the length of the sitting period be shortened?" The master became highly indignant. "That would be quite wrong. A monk who is not really devoted to the religious life may very well fall asleep in a half hour or an hour. But one truly devoted to it who has resolved to persevere in his religious discipline will eventually come to enjoy the practice of sitting, no matter how long it lasts. When I was young I used to visit the heads of various monasteries, and one of them explained to me, 'Formerly I used to hit sleeping monks so hard that my fist just about broke. Now I am old and weak, so I can't hit them hard enough. Therefore it is difficult to produce good monks. In many monasteries today the superiors do not emphasize sitting strongly enough, and so Buddhism is declining. The more you hit them the better,' he advised me."

Chapter 7
Sikhism

Learning Objectives

After reading this chapter, you should be able to:

7.1 Discuss the lives of Nanak and the other Sikh gurus.

7.2 Understand how Sikhism stands between Islam and Hinduism on many issues.

7.3 Summarize some of the important historical developments in Sikhism.

7.4 Discuss the ceremonies important to Sikhs.

7.5 Name the Sikh holy days.

7.6 Understand Sikh life in modern-day India.

A Timeline of Sikhism

1491–1539 C.E.	Life of Guru Nanak
1577–1604	Construction of the Harimandir Sahib, the "Golden Temple," in Amritsar
1658–1707	Persecution of Sikhs during reign of Emperor Arungzeb
1666-1708	Life of Guru Gobind Singh
1699	Founding of the Khalsa
1700	British emerge as major power in India
1780–1839	Ranjit Singh rules Sikh kingdom in the Punjab; encourages religious tolerance
	British occupy the Punjab; end of Sikh independence
19th and 20th centuries	Sikh immigration to Britain, Africa, North America, and other English-speaking colonies/countries
1947	Independence from Britain; Sikh demands for independent state ignored; partition of British India into India and Pakistan sparks massive outbreaks of violence among Hindus, Muslims, and Sikhs
1983	Sikh militants occupy Golden Temple; Indian army storms the temple and thousands die in outbreak of Hindu rioting
1984	Assassination of Indian Prime Minister Indira Gandhi triggers Hindu violence in which thousands of Sikhs are killed
2004	Manmohan Singh, a Sikh, becomes first non-Hindu prime minister of India

Key Terms

Adi Granth

Golden Temple

gurdwara

guru

Khalsa

langar

Nanak

The True Name

Vaisakhi

Sikhism originated in the sixteenth century C.E. in the Punjab in northwestern India. Sikhs believe their faith to be a new and independent religion based on the insights of their first teacher, Nanak. Scholars have long held that Sikhism developed in the context of a religious conversation between devotional Hinduism and Islamic mysticism. Like Buddhism and Jainism, Sikhism takes much of its worldview from and seeks to reform certain elements of Hinduism. Unlike other reform movements in Hinduism, however, Sikhism endeavors to accommodate elements from another major world religion, Islam. Many Sikh spiritual leaders have, by necessity, also been warriors.

Sikhism has always been a minority religion in India. Today, there are approximately 30 million Sikhs around the world, and most are found mainly in the Punjab, although substantial communities also are found in other regions of India, Europe, North America, and Southeast Asia.

The Life of Nanak

7.1. **Discuss the lives of Nanak and the other Sikh gurus.**

From the tenth century onward, various Muslim groups invaded India from their bases to the west. These invasions eventually resulted in the domination of India by the Moghul rulers. Although all of India faced Muslim conquest at one time or another, the northwest section was invaded most frequently. Here, Islam made its greatest number of converts and established its strongest bases. Because Islam and Hinduism were basically so different in so many areas, the encounters between Muslims and Hindus often were hostile and violent.

From the earliest days, however, there were teachers who did not believe the two religions had to be antagonistic and thought a synthesis could be reached. The reformer best remembered for attempting to bring Hinduism and Islam together was Kabir (1440–1518 C.E.). By this time, Hinduism and Islam had grown closer than they had been at the time of the initial Muslim conquest. Hindus and Muslims revered many of the same holy men and sometimes shared shrines and other places of religious devotion. This was possible because Hinduism teaches that gods appear in many forms, and Sufism, the mystical branch of Islam, believes in saints whose tombs become objects of veneration. There were some, Hindu and Muslim alike, who took these similarities as a sign that the two religions pointed to a common sacred reality.

Kabir was born a Muslim, but he found it possible to worship with his Hindu neighbors. While worshiping the Hindu deities, he was also teaching that the true God was one. The oneness of God is the most basic Muslim teaching. Kabir was later accepted as a holy man or saint by Hindus and Muslims and made a profound impression on the Sikhs and their literature.

The founder of Sikhism was a man named **Nanak** (1469–1538 C.E.), a later contemporary of Kabir. Nanak was born into a Hindu home in the Punjab about forty miles from the city of Lahore. Because of the mixed nature of the region, Nanak's schoolmaster was a Muslim and surely influenced him.

Nanak is remembered as a dreamer who had little grasp of the day-to-day world of business or practicality. His interests and talents leaned more toward poetry and religion. His father tried to place him in a variety of occupations, but Nanak failed at all of them. He was betrothed to a young woman when he was twelve, and their marriage was consummated when he was nineteen. Two sons were born of this marriage. Nanak eventually left his wife and sons and went to the city of Sultanpur to earn his living. Here he was a bit more successful in his business pursuits.

During his stay in Sultanpur, when he was about thirty years old, Nanak received a vision from God that was to change his life. According to some stories, God spoke to him while he was meditating in the forest. The message of the vision was that Nanak had been singled out as a prophet of the true religion. His message was to be, "There is no Muslim and there is no Hindu." Thus, he was to become an evangelist, preaching a gospel of unity between these two religions. Along with his constant companion, a Muslim named Mardana, Nanak became a wandering preacher of this new message. The two traveled widely in India over the next decades, preaching the essential unity of Islam and Hinduism. To emphasize his message, Nanak wore a mixed costume, made up of the clothing of both Hindus and Muslims. Wherever he went, he sought to organize communities of people who accepted his teachings. Each of his followers became known as a Sikh, a Punjabi word for "disciple." In his travels, Nanak even made the pilgrimage to Mecca, although he antagonized the people there because of his unwillingness to display the proper respect for Muslim shrines.

After many years of wandering, Nanak returned home to northwest India, where he continued to teach and form communities of Sikhs. According to a Sikh legend, as Nanak was about to die, his followers were still divided over their basic religious loyalties. Those who originally had been Hindus planned to cremate his remains, whereas those who originally had been Muslims wished to bury him. Nanak, aware of this dispute over his body, requested that each group place flowers beside him, and the group whose flowers were still fresh on the following day could have his body. When the two factions agreed and placed their flowers beside him, Nanak covered himself with a sheet and died. When the sheet was removed the next morning, the Sikhs found that both sets of flowers were still fresh but that Nanak's body had disappeared. Thus, according to this legend, the peaceful and loving Nanak, even in death, sought to bring harmony between Muslims and Hindus.

The Teachings of Nanak

7.2. **Understand how Sikhism stands between Islam and Hinduism on many issues.**

Nanak, like Kabir and others, had a vision to reconcile differences between Islam and Hinduism. Following the revelations he received from God, he took from each religion what he believed to be of most importance. From Islam he took the teaching that there is but one God. Hindus may also recognize the oneness of God, but Muslims and Sikhs are generally far more insistent on this point. Sikhs refer to this God as **The True Name**.

Nanak also taught that The True Name is the creator of the entire universe and that human beings are God's supreme creation. Thus Nanak rejected the teaching of *ahimsa*, or non-injury, which is so important to many Indian religions. Because people are the primary creation, they are free to kill and eat animals.

Nanak did adopt several elements of Hinduism. He accepted the principle of rebirth, which is basic to many Indian religions. Sikhs came to believe that the spirit of Nanak was reborn in the bodies of those gurus who succeeded him as the leaders of Sikhism. Nanak also taught the Indian principle of karma and believed that people continue to acquire karma and live again and again until they are freed from this cycle by The True Name.

Nanak rejected the ceremonialism and rituals of both Hinduism and Islam. He taught a very plain and simple form of religion that distrusted and rejected ritual.

From the Source

The Musalamans [Muslims] praise the Sharia, read it, and reflect on it:

But God's servants are they who employ themselves in His service in order to behold him.

The Hindus praise the Praised One whose appearance and form are incomparable;

They bathe in holy streams, perform idol-worship and adoration, use copious incense of sandal.

The Jogis meditate on God the Creator, whom they call the Unseen,

Whose form is minute, whose name is the Bright One, and who is the image of their bodies.[1]

According to one story, Nanak was once ejected from Muslim worship because he laughed aloud during the sermon of the imam. When asked why he was so disrespectful to Muslim worship, he replied that he had perceived that the imam was not really thinking about God while he was preaching but was in fact thinking about his horse and worrying lest the horse fall into a well. This perception struck Nanak as being so ludicrous that he burst into laughter.

Another element in the religion of Nanak was his pacifism. In all of his travels and with all of the rejection he received, Nanak maintained the stance of a pacifist. He never struck out at his enemies and apparently taught his disciples to follow this pattern. In contrast to the teachings of Nanak, Sikhs, in their later history, became known as the most militant of warriors. Many Sikh spiritual leaders have also been warriors.

The Historical Development of Sikhism

7.3.   Summarize some of the important historical developments in Sikhism.

Upon the death of Nanak, the leadership of the new movement was taken over by Angad, who ruled until 1552. Nanak and Angad were the first two in a series of ten **gurus** who led Sikhism until the eighteenth century. Usually, the word *guru* in Indian religions carries the connotation of "teacher," but to the Sikhs, it means "leader." The first four of the ten gurus of Sikhism tended to follow the teachings of Nanak and be rather pacific toward their enemies. Angad is remembered because he devised a new script and began to compile the Sikh scriptures. Other gurus followed similar paths.

In the sixteenth century, Sikh leaders built a beautiful house of worship in the Punjabi city of Amritsar. Called the Harimandir Sahib, or **Golden Temple**, the structure still serves as a place of pilgrimage and gathering for Sikhs all over the world.

Archenova/Alamy

The Golden Temple (Harimandir) in Amritsar.

With the ascension of the fifth guru, Arjan Dev (1581–1606), both the office and the religion underwent significant changes. Arjan is remembered for beginning the compilation of the official scriptures of Sikhism, the **Adi Granth**. The *Granth* has become increasingly important in Sikhism since the days of the gurus. Basically, it is a collection of hymns, a large portion of which came from Nanak. The remainder of the hymns that make up the *Granth* came from Kabir and other gurus. The *Granth* contains 3,384 hymns and is roughly three times the size of the *Rig-Veda*. Although copies of the *Granth* are distributed across the globe, the text is especially honored and housed in the Golden Temple. In addition to his contribution as the compiler of the *Granth*, Arjan is recognized for giving Sikhism its militant aspect, in direct contrast to the pacifism of Nanak and the earlier gurus. Between the time of Nanak and Arjan, the Sikh movement had grown and was beginning to be recognized as a threat by the Muslim authorities. The Muslim emperor ordered Arjan to remove from the *Granth* any doctrine that was contrary to the teachings of the Qur'an. When Arjan refused, he was jailed and tortured to death. Before his death, however, he instructed his son Har Gobind, who was to become the sixth guru (1606–1645), to arm and surround himself with bodyguards. The advice of Arjan was accepted, and henceforth the Sikhs were more militant and aggressive in their attitude toward their enemies.

The last of the human Sikh gurus was Gobind Singh (1666–1708). He assumed the leadership of the Sikhs when he was only a boy because his father, the ninth guru, had been imprisoned and executed by the Muslims. It was Gobind Singh, more than any other guru, who organized and prepared the Sikhs for self-defense and war. He also established the *Granth* as the final word for Sikhs and named it their guru. Because Sikhs were to be governed by the *Granth*, now typically referred to as the Guru Granth Sahib, human gurus did not exist after Gobind Singh's death.

To strengthen his people further and prepare them for war, he developed an elite class of Sikhs who made unusually fine warriors and loyal supporters of the community. This corps was known as the **Khalsa** and was distinguished in the following ways (often called the 5 Ks): They wore the *kes,* or uncut hair, on their heads and faces and adorned their hair with the *kangha* (comb); they wore *kachera* (short trousers) under their clothing; they wore a *kara* (steel bracelet); and they were equipped with a *kirpan* (steel dagger). The members of this corps were not allowed to use wine, tobacco, or any other form of stimulant. The Khalsa has been open to both men and women since its foundation; men in the Khalsa are given the last name Singh, which means "lion," and women receive the last name Kaur, or "princess."

Sikh women and children make bread near the Golden Temple in Amritsar.

Sylvain Leser/Haytham Pictures/Alamy

Religion in Public Life

Gobind Singh was assassinated in 1708. From that time until the present, the Sikhs have been governed by their scripture, the *Granth*, and their history has been full of strife. At certain times, the Sikhs have been the victims of violence; at other times, they have been the aggressors. By the early nineteenth century, they controlled most of the Punjab region. When the British sought to enter that area, the Sikhs fought bloody wars against them but were finally subdued. Because of the Sikhs' valor as warriors, the British came to admire and use the Sikhs as soldiers and policemen throughout India. Even today Sikhs are employed as bank security guards as far away from the Punjab as northern Burma and southwestern China. With the departure of the British in the 1940s and with the partition of India into Hindu and Muslim states by the United Nations in 1947, the Sikhs were located in the Indian state of Punjab. There, their numbers were only slightly larger than those of the Hindus.

Sikh Religious Life

7.4. **Discuss the ceremonies important to Sikhs.**

The religious life of the modern Sikh tends to be simple, probably because of the distrust of elaborate ceremonies that moved the early founders of this religion. One joins the Sikhs not by being born into a Sikh family but by undergoing a ritual of baptism when one is mature enough to accept it. In this ritual, a bowl of sweetened water is stirred by a dagger; the water is then sprinkled on the initiate as the initiate is instructed in the truths and prohibitions of the faith. Just as the initiatory ceremony of Sikhism is simple, so are the ceremonies surrounding marriage and death.

Daily rituals for a Sikh include an early-morning bath, followed by the reading of certain hymns and the recitation of prayers. At night, there is another ritual involving hymns and prayers. When Sikhs gather for congregational worship, they meet in temples called **gurdwaras**. In these temples, the central object of worship is a copy of the sacred Guru Granth Sahib. Congregational worship involves prayers to the *Granth*, various hymns, a sermon, and a communion meal. There are no Sikh priests, and the group services may be led by any member of the community. In addition, there are no caste or gender differentiations in worship.

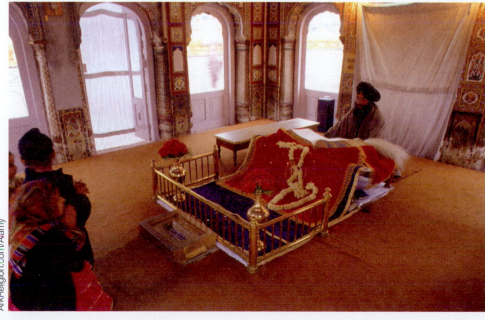

ArkReligion.com/Alamy

The *Adi Granth* is the perpetual Guru of the Sikh community and is treated with great respect and care.

Gurdwaras always include a **langar**, or community dining hall. A principal religious duty of Sikhs is to feed the poor, and langars provide free meals to people without regard to their religious tradition or status in life.

An object of special attention to Sikhs all over the world is the *Takht* (throne) of Sikhism at Amritsar. Although there are three other such thrones throughout the Sikh world, the one at Amritsar, within the Golden Temple, is central. It is here that the authorities of the Sikh world make decisions regarding the worship and practice of their people. Although Nanak specifically prohibited pilgrimages as being worthless for true religion, most Sikhs like to go to Amritsar and plan to visit there at least once in their lives.

Sikh Holy Days

7.5. Name the Sikh holy days.

Because of the extreme simplicity and personal nature of Sikhism, this religion does not have an elaborate calendar or set of festivals. As residents of northern India, the Sikhs celebrate Holi and Divali with their Hindu neighbors. In June, the Sikhs celebrate the martyrdom of Guru Arjan, the compiler of the *Adi Granth* and the builder of the Golden Temple at Amritsar. The Sikhs also celebrate annually the birthdays of Nanak in November and Guru Arjan in December or January. These celebrations include communal processions and meals in the langar. Another important Sikh holiday is **Vaisakhi**. Celebrated by Hindus as the new year, for Sikhs it holds special importance as the day on which Guru Gobind Singh founded the Khalsa.

Sikhism Today

7.6. Understand Sikh life in modern-day India.

The life of the Sikhs has become increasingly precarious in modern India. In the Punjab region, the growth of Hindus and other religious groups has once again made the Sikhs a minority group. Because they are neither Hindu nor Muslim, Sikhs lack the political strength of the major religions of India. Therefore, radical factions in Sikhism have begun to demand that the Punjab be declared an independent Sikh nation. This combination of factors has sometimes led to armed conflict with the government of India. In 1984, when Indian Prime Minister Indira Gandhi was assassinated by her Sikh bodyguards, there were anti-Sikh riots in Delhi in which large numbers of innocent people were killed.

Religion in Public Life

Today large communities of Sikhs live in Canada and the United States. Tragically, several Sikhs have been the targets of misguided violence, especially following the terrorist attacks of September 11, 2001. Often, the attackers mistake turban-wearing Sikh men for Muslims. A particularly grave example of this kind of violence occurred in 2012 at the Oak Creek Gurdwara in suburban Milwaukee, Wisconsin.

A gunman entered the gurdwara during Sunday worship and killed six Sikhs as well as himself. In the aftermath, community member Baljander Khattra said, "I don't know what that person thinks. . . . We are peaceful. The Sikh temple is open to anybody."[2] Sikhs have been united in the face of these attacks, calling for an end to all prejudice and violence against both Sikhs and Muslims.

Think About It

1. Who is Nanak and what role did he play in the development of Sikhism?

2. Discuss Sikhism's connections to Hinduism and Islam. Which features has it taken from each religion?

3. Briefly summarize some of the important historical developments in Sikhism along with some of the more important historical figures who influenced its development.

4. What are some of the ceremonies related to initiation, marriage, and death in Sikhism? Describe them.

5. What are the most important Sikh holy days?

6. Why has the life of Sikhs become increasingly precarious in modern India?

Suggested Reading

Archer, John Clark. *The Sikhs*. Princeton, N.J.: Princeton University Press, 1946.

Banerjee, Anil Chandra. *Guru Nanak and His Times*. Columbia, Mo.: South Asia Books, 1971.

Mann, Gurinder Singh. *Sikhism*. Upper Saddle River, N.J.: Prentice Hall, 2004.

Singh, Harbans. *The Heritage of the Sikhs*. New York: Asia Publishing House, 1964.

Source Material

The Japji

The following material, which is a selection from a text called the Japji, is extremely important to Sikhs and comprises the first section of the *Adi Granth*. According to tradition, the Japji was written by Nanak, the founder of Sikhism.[3]

One Universal Creator God. The Name Is Truth. Creative Being Personified. No Fear. No Hatred. Image Of The Undying, Beyond Birth, Self-Existent. By Guru's Grace ~

Chant And Meditate:

True In The Primal Beginning. True Throughout The Ages.

True Here And Now. O Nanak, Forever And Ever True.

By thinking, He cannot be reduced to thought, even by thinking hundreds of thousands of times.

By remaining silent, inner silence is not obtained, even by remaining lovingly absorbed deep within.

The hunger of the hungry is not appeased, even by piling up loads of worldly goods.

Hundreds of thousands of clever tricks, but not even one of them will go along with you in the end.

So how can you become truthful? And how can the veil of illusion be torn away?

O Nanak, it is written that you shall obey the Hukam of His Command, and walk in the Way of His Will.

By His Command, bodies are created; His Command cannot be described.

By His Command, souls come into being; by His Command, glory and greatness are obtained.

By His Command, some are high and some are low; by His Written Command, pain and pleasure are obtained.

Some, by His Command, are blessed and forgiven; others, by His Command, wander aimlessly forever.

Everyone is subject to His Command; no one is beyond His Command.

O Nanak, one who understands His Command, does not speak in ego.

Some sing of His Power-who has that Power?

Some sing of His Gifts, and know His Sign and Insignia.

Some sing of His Glorious Virtues, Greatness and Beauty.

Some sing of knowledge obtained of Him, through difficult philosophical studies.

Some sing that He fashions the body, and then again reduces it to dust.

Some sing that He takes life away, and then again restores it.

Some sing that He seems so very far away.

Some sing that He watches over us, face to face, ever-present.

There is no shortage of those who preach and teach.

Millions upon millions offer millions of sermons and stories.

The Great Giver keeps on giving, while those who receive grow weary of receiving.

Throughout the ages, consumers consume.

The Commander, by His Command, leads us to walk on the Path.

O Nanak, He blossoms forth, Carefree and Untroubled.

True is the Master, True is His Name-speak it with infinite love.

People beg and pray, "Give to us, give to us", and the Great Giver gives His Gifts.

So what offering can we place before Him, by which we might see the Darbaar of His Court?

What words can we speak to evoke His Love?

In the Amrit Vaylaa, the ambrosial hours before dawn, chant the True Name, and contemplate His Glorious Greatness.

By the karma of past actions, the robe of this physical body is obtained. By His Grace, the Gate of Liberation is found.

O Nanak, know this well: the True One Himself is All.

He cannot be established, He cannot be created.

He Himself is Immaculate and Pure.

Those who serve Him are honored.

O Nanak, sing of the Lord, the Treasure of Excellence.

Sing, and listen, and let your mind be filled with love.

Your pain shall be sent far away, and peace shall come to your home.

The Guru's Word is the Sound-current of the Naad; the Guru's Word is the Wisdom of the Vedas; the Guru's Word is all-pervading.

The Guru is Shiva, the Guru is Vishnu and Brahma; the Guru is Paarvati and Lakhshmi.

Even knowing God, I cannot describe Him; He cannot be described in words.

The Guru has given me this one understanding:

there is only the One, the Giver of all souls. May I never forget Him!

If I am pleasing to Him, then that is my pilgrimage and cleansing bath. Without pleasing Him, what good are ritual cleansings?

I gaze upon all the created beings: without the karma of good actions, what are they given to receive?

Within the mind are gems, jewels and rubies, if you listen to the Guru's Teachings, even once.

The Guru has given me this one understanding:

there is only the One, the Giver of all souls. May I never forget Him!

Even if you could live throughout the four ages, or even ten times more,

and even if you were known throughout the nine continents and followed by all,

with a good name and reputation, with praise and fame throughout the world-

still, if the Lord does not bless you with His Glance of Grace, then who cares? What is the use?

Among worms, you would be considered a lowly worm, and even contemptible sinners would hold you in contempt.

O Nanak, God blesses the unworthy with virtue, and bestows virtue on the virtuous.

No one can even imagine anyone who can bestow virtue upon Him.

Part III
Religions Originating in China and Japan

Unlike religions originating in the Middle East or South Asia, East Asian religions have never had a strong missionary spirit. Thus, their influence has long been limited to the East Asian nations of China, Japan, Korea, Mongolia, and Vietnam. However, in the last century, increased political, cultural, and commercial contacts with East Asia and the Christian missionary movement have brought to a global audience the texts and traditions of Daoism, Confucianism, and Shinto, along with East Asian forms of Buddhism, and within these a deep and modern love for the beauty of nature and the family. Today there are substantial populations of people of East Asian heritage throughout Europe, the Americas, and Southeast Asia.

Chinese Religion—Basic Teachings
Chinese Religions Work Together and Overlap

Most Chinese people see no conflict between Daoism, Confucianism, Buddhism, and the practices of divination and ancestor veneration.

Each set of practices and beliefs is part of a total religious and social system and serves its own purposes.

Yinyang Is a Basic Philosophical Concept

Yin is dark, cool, and female. *Yang* is light, warm, and male. The two forces must be in balance for life to flow smoothly. Indeed, these forces cannot be considered separately and may best be understood as *yinyang*.

Ancestor Veneration and Family Reverence Are Important Social and Religious Concepts

The Chinese believe that children have an obligation to take care of their parents in their old age and even after they are dead. There are small shrines dedicated to the ancestors in most Chinese homes. Offerings are made to them in Buddhist and Daoist temples. These may include food, incense, and even reproductions of paper money, credit cards, cars, and houses.

Daoism Emerged from the Teachings of Laozi, Who Is Believed to Have Lived in the Sixth Century B.C.E.

The most basic Daoist teaching is that the course of life is governed by a force known as the Dao. Ideally, people should strive to flow with the Dao, and not to struggle against it. Accordingly, life itself is the greatest of all possessions. Life should be lived simply—ideally in small communities. Wealth and social position are to be rejected. Many believe that those who truly master the Dao will become immortal.

Confucianism Provided the Moral Basis for Most Historical and Some Contemporary Chinese Societies

Confucius lived in the sixth century B.C.E. He was as much a social and political thinker as he was a religious thinker. His teachings emphasize order, propriety, and respect for authority. Over time, he came to be regarded as a religious figure and temples were dedicated to him. Confucianism and all other forms of religious thought were severely repressed after the Communist Revolution. There has been a religious revival in China since the end of the Cultural Revolution in 1976. All forms of Chinese religion have continued to flourish in Hong Kong, Singapore, and Taiwan.

Shinto—Basic Teachings
Shinto Is the Indigenous Religion of Japan

For centuries, some variants of Shinto have been closely associated with the Japanese Imperial House. Japanese mythology maintains that the emperor of Japan is a descendant of the Sun Goddess Amaterasu. Shinto also includes elements of ancestor veneration and worship of the kami. Some Shinto rituals are conducted in the numerous shrines found throughout the country and others in private homes.

Although the Term Is Hard to Define—Even for the Japanese—Kami Play a Central Role in Shinto Religious Beliefs and Practices

Kami can be viewed as spiritual beings, but they are more than that. The term also refers to the spiritual beings and forces that give life to the natural world. They have the power to inflict pain and suffering as well as to come to the aid of humans.

Some Variants of Shinto Have Been Militaristic

Bushido, or the "way of the fighting knight," was important during the Tokugawa period. It emphasized loyalty, bravery, respect for authority, and benevolence. State Shinto was instituted in 1868. The newly modernizing Japanese state took over 110,000 shrines and used State Shinto to encourage patriotism and support for military adventurism. It was abolished after World War II.

Sectarian Shinto Is the Public Dimension of Japanese Popular Religion

There are at least thirteen sects emphasizing mountain and other forms of nature worship, shamanism, divination, and Japanese mythology.

Domestic Shinto Is the Household Religion of Many Japanese

Almost every Japanese home has a kami-dana, or household altar. It usually contains plaques inscribed with the names of ancestors, objects bought at national shrines, and images of divinities who have helped the family in the past. Offerings include food, drink, and flowers.

Chapter 8
Chinese Religions

 Learning Objectives

After reading this chapter, you should be able to:

8.1 Explain how Chinese religion combines elements of Chinese tradition, Daoism, Confucianism, and Buddhism, and explain the basic teachings of each of these traditions.

8.2 Discuss Daoism as a philosophy of nature, a religion, and a system of ritual practices.

8.3 Identify the basic tenets of Confucianism and understand how it is inextricably interwoven into the total philosophy of the Chinese people.

8.4 Name the traditional Chinese holidays.

8.5 Discuss religion in China today.

A Timeline of Chinese Religion

11th century B.C.E.	Development of belief in Shangdi
6th century	Life of Laozi
4th century	Composition of *Daodejing*
551–479	Life of Confucius
468–390	Life of Mozi
3rd century	Buddhism enters China
298–238	Life of Mencius
195	Ritual veneration of Confucius begins
1503 C.E.	Ritual veneration of Confucius suppressed
1851–64	Tai Ping Rebellion
19th century	Large-scale Christian missionary activity
1949	Communist Revolution; founding of People's Republic of China
1966	Cultural Revolution; severe repression of religions
1977	Death of Chairman Mao; relaxation of restrictions on religions

Key Terms

Analects	**ren**
ancestor veneration	**Shangdi**
Dao	*shu*
Daodejing	**wu wei**
li	**yinyang**

An important feature of religions in China is that they are by no means mutually exclusive. It is perfectly acceptable for the traditional Chinese to be a Buddhist, Daoist, and Confucian. This is illustrated in the story of the emperor who asked a Buddhist scholar if he was a Buddhist. The scholar pointed to his Daoist cap. "Are you then a Daoist?" the emperor asked, and the scholar pointed to his Confucian shoes. "Are you then a Confucian?" the emperor asked, and the scholar pointed to his Buddhist scarf. It is not at all unusual for a Buddhist priest to attend a Daoist temple and to memorize the teachings of Confucius. Many Chinese temples are shared by adherents of all of these religions. Another important feature of Chinese religions is that for the past fifty years the government of China has been at best neutral and sometimes hostile to any form of religion. Missionaries have been excluded, and the teachings of Laozi and Confucius were often suppressed as hostile to modern China. In recent years, the government of China has softened its attitude toward religion, which has led to a resurgence of religion. Even during the period when the Chinese government was most hostile toward religion, millions of Chinese living outside of their ancestral homeland continued to practice traditional Chinese religions.

The history of religion in China falls into several broad categories. From the earliest recorded history until the end of the Shang dynasty in the eleventh century B.C.E., the Chinese people apparently followed a religion of nature deities intermingled with ancestor worship. From the development of the Zhou dynasty in the eleventh century B.C.E. until the beginning of the Common Era, a portion of the Chinese literati concluded that there was one Supreme God above all other gods and spirits. The second period also was characterized by an emphasis on morality, particularly the morality of the rulers. This was the era that produced Laozi (the legendary founder of Daoism) and Confucius. From the beginning of the Common Era until the eleventh century C.E., Buddhism and religious Daoism developed in China; for the first time, fully developed religious institutions were found. The fourth general period of religious development extends from the eleventh century to the present. In this period, we find an eclectic movement, bringing about a synthesis among Buddhism, Daoism, and Confucianism for most of the Chinese people.

Basic Chinese Religious Concepts

8.1. **Explain how Chinese religion combines elements of Chinese tradition, Daoism, Confucianism, and Buddhism, and explain the basic teachings of each of these traditions.**

From earliest times, the Chinese have held certain religious concepts and practices that later played a part in the development of the philosophies of Daoism and Confucianism. Although the ancient records are sketchy in their description of these concepts, we must examine them first to better understand Chinese religions.

Recognition of Multiple Gods and Spirits

As already stated, the earliest religion of the Chinese people seems to have been based on the recognition of many gods and spirits that controlled the universe. The gods of the heavens and the Earth received particular attention and sacrifice. In the spring and fall, the emperors of ancient China performed elaborate and expensive sacrifices to the gods of the heavens and the Earth. Many of these rituals were intended to ensure the fertility of the soil and bountiful harvests. Lesser rulers and the common people also performed sacrifices to these spirits.

Yinyang

In searching for a principle to explain the true nature of the universe, the ancient Chinese philosophers developed the concept of **yinyang**. What made the universe operate the way it did was understood to be a balance between these two forces. The yin was the negative force in nature. It was seen in darkness, coolness, femaleness, dampness, the Earth itself, the moon, and the shadows. The yang was the positive force in nature. It was seen in lightness, brightness, warmth, maleness, dryness, and the sun.

The inseparability of yinyang was understood as one of the factors in the operation of the universe. Except for a few objects, such as the sun or the Earth, which were clearly yin or yang, all the rest of nature, humankind, and even events were a combination of both forces. When these two forces were at work in harmony, life was what it should be.

Family Reverence and Ancestor Worship

A characteristic of the Chinese people throughout history has been their respect for and even veneration of aged members of the family, known as **ancestor veneration**. The legendary founder of Daoism was Li-poh-yang, but his disciples called him *Laozi*, which means "Old Master" or "Old Boy."

To the Chinese, the term *old* or *aged* is not the sign of disrespect that it often is in many Western countries; rather, it is the ultimate term of respect. Historically, it is the aged father, mother, grandfather, or grandmother who dominates the Chinese home. It is the obligation of the children to support the elderly, to obey them, and to give them proper burial after death. Even after the parents' death, the child is obligated to maintain their grave site, to remember them and their deeds, and to offer sacrifices to them.

There is a religious aspect to these practices: Individuals revere their parents while they are alive and after they are dead. While they are alive, the aged represent the wisdom of the family; after their deaths, they may be in a position to help the family further because of their contact with the spirit world. Therefore, support of the dead ancestors with remembrance and sacrifices is essential. The Chinese who forget their ancestors are disgraced and will one day become homeless ghosts. It is also commonly believed that those lacking family reverence will be afflicted by dangerous spirits. Historically, the Chinese home has tended to have a small shrine or altar at which the names and deeds of many previous generations of the family are remembered and where small sacrifices of rice and wine may be offered. Imitation paper money is another common offering. Ancestral tablets are also often placed in Chinese temples and lineage meeting centers.

Divination

The early Chinese believed that the unity of the universe allowed future events to be predicted by some means. Whereas certain ancient religions sought out the future in the patterns of the flight of birds, in the entrails of sacrificed animals, or in the sayings of various oracles, the ancient Chinese sought the future in the patterns of the shell of the tortoise or in stalks of grain. The shell of the tortoise was thought to be especially in tune with the rhythms of the universe because of the long life of its inhabitant. Frequently, the shell was heated and the future was divined by the cracks that appeared in it. Divination among the ancient Chinese probably reached its peak in the development of a book called the *Yijing* (The Book of Changes), which was edited by Confucius and is still used today. With the casting of coins or stalks of a plant, certain patterns emerge. By identifying these patterns among some sixty-four hexagrams presented in the *Yijing*, a statement or prediction is evoked.

Mark R. Woodward

Central altar of a Chinese temple, Semarang, Java, Indonesia.

Development of Belief in Shangdi

Chinese religion recognized many deities, as previously described. However, in
the eleventh century B.C.E., certain political events affected the religious thinking
of the Chinese, perhaps for all time. In that century, the Zhou clans rebelled against
the ruling Shang dynasty. By the end of the century, the Zhou warriors had effectively completed the rebellion and had begun a new dynasty that was to rule
China for several centuries. The Zhou rulers began to assert that the right to rule
had to be based on morality and religion. They further asserted that one Supreme
God controlled the destinies of all humankind. This God was **Shangdi**, who had
previously been regarded as the patron ancestor of the Shang dynasty. The Zhou
rulers asserted that Shangdi was more than an ancestor; he was the Supreme God,
and he had been responsible for the fall of the Shang dynasty because of their immorality. Shangdi was seen as the rewarder of good morality and the punisher of
immorality, particularly among rulers. Therefore, government had to be founded
upon virtue. Although Shangdi might delight in elaborate sacrifice and ritual, he
still loved morality more; all the sacrifices in the world could not cover up evil. We
read of his concern for morality in the ancient *Shujing* (Book of Documents). Eventually, Shangdi would come to be associated with Tian, or "heaven." Later Chinese
thought exalted heaven as the source of goodness and order.

Decline of the Feudal System

During the Zhou dynasty, China had been organized and governed by a feudal system. The empire was divided into vassal states whose princes were subject to the
emperor. The states in turn were subdivided into districts ruled by governors who
were vassals to the princes. Each substate supported its lord financially, while the
lord in turn provided protection for the state. Society was then stratified into ranks.
Members of the society knew their ranks and duties. They also knew who was above
and below them.

In the five centuries between the eighth and third centuries B.C.E., the feudal system in China began to break down. Lords were no longer able to protect their vassals
from invading armies. This led to the development of warlords who could provide

protection and command respect. Serfs sometimes became landowners in these upsetting times. Merchant classes began to appear in the cities, and their economic power began to be felt. Old aristocratic families began to find themselves without either wealth or power. In general, the feudal world turned upside down. Into this era came the great Chinese schools, each with its own distinctive answer to the problems facing the nation. The Confucians dreamed of a restored idealized form of feudalism as the best government; the Legalists wanted nothing to do with feudalism but wished for a strong centralized government; the Daoists wanted no government at all, or at least as little government as possible. It was out of this confused milieu that the great Chinese philosophy-religions were born.

Daoism

8.2. **Discuss Daoism as a philosophy of nature, a religion, and a system of ritual practices.**

The origins of Daoism are lost in the mists of Chinese antiquity. Little is known of its founder; indeed, there are those who even deny his existence. Its sacred book is more a brief poetical statement of philosophy than a scripture. The name *Daoism* is taken from the title of this book, *Daodejing*, and it is often translated as "the way" or "the way of nature." But, the Dao is not so much an essence as a dynamic and relational view of the universe. The earliest teachers of Daoism were only vaguely theistic in their beliefs. By the early centuries of the Common Era, however, Daoism had evolved into a religion complete with gods, priests, temples, and sacrifices. In modern China, Daoism is mainly associated with charms, exorcisms, and ritual attempts to prolong life. A philosophy of nature, a religion, a system of ritual practices—Daoism is all of these.

The Life of Laozi

Traditionally, the founder of Daoism is thought to be Laozi, who lived in the sixth century B.C.E., although the basic philosophy of Daoism is probably much

This lush interior of the Zushi Daoist Temple (China) contains statues of numerous Daoist deities. Like human beings, the gods of the Daoist pantheon are subject to the Dao.

older. Little is known about Laozi, and some scholars doubt that he was a historical figure. Legends about him state that he was born approximately fifty years before Confucius; according to Confucian sources, there was a meeting between the two. His original name was Li-poh-yang, but he was given the title Laozi (Old Master or Old Boy) by his disciples as a title of respect. It is said that he was the keeper of royal archives in the court of the Zhou dynasty during the tumultuous period when order was breaking down. He tired of the artificial life in court and retired from his post. Journeying westward, he reached a pass in the mountains at the northwest boundaries of China, where he sought to leave the country. The guard of the pass recognized the wise man and refused to allow him to leave until he had committed to writing the sum of his wisdom. Thereupon, Laozi sat down and wrote the *Daodejing*. When this was completed, he was allowed to leave the country and was never seen again. The truth of this story has never been verified. Certainly, we know less about the founder of Daoism than we know about any of the other founders of world religions.

The *Daodejing*

The book that Laozi was supposed to have written in the sixth century B.C.E., the *Daodejing*, has become the most influential book in Chinese literature, except for the *Analects of Confucius*. The title literally means "The Classic of the Dao and Its Power or Virtue." It is a small book, made up of slightly more than 5,000 words contained in eighty-one chapters, and it is usually translated in poetic form. It has been the object of at least a thousand commentaries and has been translated into English more than forty times. In fact, it has been translated more times than any other book in the world except the Bible and thus is probably the best known of all Chinese books.

Mark R. Woodward

Guardian Spirit in a Chinese temple in Malacca, Malaysia.

Top Photo/Asia Photo Connection/Henry Westheim Photography/Alamy

A statue of Laozi seems to rise like a boulder from the land.

That the *Daodejing* was written by Laozi in the sixth century B.C.E. as he waited to be allowed to leave China has been the subject of much scholarly debate for some time. It is generally agreed that the book was developed over many centuries and evolved into its present form around the fourth century B.C.E. Arthur Waley suggests that the book was written in the third century B.C.E. as a polemic against the Confucians and Legalists who wished for either an idealized form of feudalism or some strong central government.[1] The theme of the *Daodejing* is that all human achievements are folly, especially elaborate government.

Teachings of the Early Daoist Philosophers

The beliefs of the early Daoists are difficult to ascertain. Our two major sources for Daoism before the Common Era are the *Daodejing* and the work of a fourth-century B.C.E. disciple of Laozi, Zhuangzi. Zhuangzi covered the field of Daoism as it was practiced by the early devotees. He collected this material into a book and with it tried to convince the Chinese to accept Laozi instead of Confucius as their main teacher. The teachings of early Daoism center on the following themes:

1. *The basic unity behind the universe is a mysterious and undefinable force called the Dao.* Usually the word **Dao** is defined as "the way," yet the true Dao is impossible to define. The *Daodejing* begins with the following admonition:

From the Source

The dao that can be described
is not the eternal Dao.
The name that can be spoken
is not the eternal Name.

The nameless is the boundary of Heaven and Earth.
The named is the mother of creation.

Freed from desire, you can see the hidden mystery.

By having desire, you can only
see what is visibly real.

Yet mystery and reality
emerge from the same source.
This source is called darkness.

Darkness born from darkness.
The beginning of all understanding.[2]

The Dao is often compared to a stream or a moving body of water as it progresses endlessly and inexorably. As water wears away the hardest stone or metal and carries off buildings in its path, it is useless to struggle against the Dao. Therefore, the ancient Daoist philosophers believed that all humankind's accomplishments and monuments will sooner or later be destroyed by the Dao. The greatest buildings will fall into decay, hard-won knowledge will be superseded, wealth will fail, and even the sharpest sword will become dull. For this reason, it behooved people not to struggle against the Dao but to seek to blend with it and be guided by it. True Daoists live quiet and simple lives. They avoid any achievement except that of seeking to understand the Dao.

2. *Life is the greatest of all possessions.* Because of their belief in the Dao as the source of all life and their belief in the folly of achievement, the early Daoist philosophers taught that life itself was the greatest of possessions; all others were doomed to decay. Fame, wealth, power, and education were mere fleeting, transient illusions. If people were not interested in the acquisition of goods, power, or education, then they could give their full attention to the enrichment of their

own lives. This led the Daoists to search for a way to lengthen life; eventually, they employed various alchemical practices in an attempt to prolong and enrich life.

3. *Life is to be lived simply.* Believing that all life originated from the Dao, which would ultimately destroy people's achievements, the early Daoists turned their backs on civilization with all of its ills and benefits and sought to live life as simply as possible. One term that describes this Daoist principle is **wu wei**, which can be translated as "non-action" or "effortlessness." The Daoist practitioner diminishes his or her actions that are not in harmony with the Dao. The Daoist philosophers may have carried this objective to its greatest extreme. They considered education, wealth, power, and family ties worthless, in fact, impediments to living.

From the Source

Forget about knowledge and wisdom,
and people will be a hundred times better off.
Throw away charity and righteousness,
and people will return to brotherly love.
Throw away profit and greed,
and there won't be any thieves.

These three are superficial and aren't enough
to keep us at the center of the circle, so we must also:

Embrace simplicity.
Put others first.
Desire little.[3]

Ideally, individuals should turn their backs on the advancements of civilization and live as simply and as quietly as possible. The word *innocence* characterizes the ideal state. Like the plants and creatures of the Earth, innocent human beings are content with what the Dao has ordained for them. According to early Daoist philosophers, there should be little government in the ideal state. In fact, it was an axiom of Daoists that the least government is the best government. Laozi is remembered for saying, "Govern a great nation as you would cook a small fish"—do not overdo it.[4] The small village is the ideal unit of society. The best ruler is the one who rules least and is virtually anonymous. If all this were realized, all striving, quarrels, and wars would cease. Daoism is pacific, not out of any moral commitment to pacifism but because warring is useless and wasteful. If a larger, stronger state wished the territory of the quiet Daoist village, the village should simply submit to the larger state. In the long run, there would be no grief due to this decision and the village ultimately would conquer the large state with its humility.

The early Daoists looked upon the innocence of the child as an ideal toward which all human beings should strive. The infant knows no craft and has no ambitions but to live; yet the child is cared for, fed, and clothed. The weakness and softness of the infant are the ideals of Daoism.

4. *Pomp and glory are to be despised.* Because the Daoists were concerned with living according to the path of nature (i.e., as simply as possible), they despised the fame, pomp, and glory that most people seek. They saw such things as the cause of strife and discord in society. If each person were only content to live as the Dao intended, without seeking to rise above other people, then life would be as it was intended. This attitude also contained a condemnation of pride. It was a Chinese belief, perhaps older than Daoism, that pride invited destruction,

that the tree that stood taller than its neighbors would be the first felled by the woodsman. Therefore, better to be humble, small, or imperfect than to stand out from all the rest.

From the Source

If you want to become whole,
first let yourself become broken.
If you want to become straight,
first let yourself become twisted.
If you want to become full,
first let yourself become empty.
If you want to become new,
first let yourself become old.
Those whose desires are few get them,
those whose desires are great go astray.

For this reason the Master embraces the Dao,
as an example for the world to follow.
Because she isn't self centered,

people can see the light in her.
Because she does not boast of herself,
she becomes a shining example.
Because she does not glorify herself,
she becomes a person of merit.
Because she wants nothing from the world,
the world can not overcome her.

When the ancient Masters said,
"If you want to become whole,
then first let yourself be broken,"
they weren't using empty words.
All who do this will be made complete.[5]

Perhaps the best example of the Daoists' contempt for pomp, glory, rank, and wealth is the story of Zhuangzi, the fourth-century B.C.E. Daoist philosopher. Zhuangzi was widely regarded for his wisdom and was offered the position of prime minister by Prince Wei of Chu. When the messengers of the prince brought this offer, Zhuangzi is said to have replied in the following manner:

From the Source

You offer me great wealth and a proud position indeed; but have you never seen the sacrificial ox? When after being fattened up for several years, it is decked with embroidered trappings and led to the altar, would it not willingly then change places with

some uncaring pigling? . . . Begone! Defile me not! I would rather disport myself to my own enjoyment in the mire than be a slave to a mire of a state. I will never take office. Thus I shall remain free to follow my own inclinations.[6]

History does not record the response of the prince whose offer was spurned with such contempt.

There is little worship of deities or spirits in early Daoism. The Dao itself is certainly not a god in any traditional sense of the word. In one translation of the *Daodejing*, the word *god* is used only once; in many translations, it does not appear at all.[7] Only rarely does the term *heaven* appear. The Dao is not conceived of as a force to which one can pray or sacrifice, and the early Daoists seem to have had no rituals for worship. In fact, they may have been rejecting religion and all of its accoutrements as part of their rejection of the Confucians, who placed a very high value on rituals.

The early Daoists also seem to have had little concern for life after death. One of the most frequently remembered tales of Zhuangzi concerns an occasion following his wife's death. His disciples sought to comfort him in his time of mourning but found him singing and beating time on a wooden bowl.

From the Source

"To live with your wife," exclaimed Hui-tzu, "and see your eldest son grow up to be a man, and then not to shed a tear over her corpse—this would be bad enough. But to drum on a bowl and sing; surely this is going too far!"

"Not at all," replied [Zhuangzi]. "When she died I could not help being affected by her death. Soon, however, I remembered that she had already existed in a previous state before her birth, without form or even substance; that while in that unconditioned condition, substance was added to spirit; that this substance then assumed form and that the next state was birth. And now, by virtue of a further change she is dead, passing from one phase to another like the sequence of spring, summer, autumn and winter. And while she is thus lying asleep in eternity for me to go about weeping and wailing would be to proclaim myself ignorant of these natural laws. Therefore I refrain."[8]

In general, the early Daoists were concerned about the quality of life as it is lived on a day-to-day basis, without much interest in the heavens, the gods, rituals, or life after death.

Schools That Rivaled the Early Daoists

The fourth and third centuries B.C.E. were eras of chaos in China. The old governmental structure of feudalism was breaking down, invaders regularly made inroads into the country, the social order was in a state of flux, and the ancient systems of values were seriously being questioned. The Daoist philosophers and their challenge to existing values and structures were, of course, a part of that era. Other philosophers, politicians, and teachers held other views of life and government and toured the nation. In this period, courts throughout China were replete with traveling philosophers, each making his own claim concerning the proper way to rule.

In addition to the Daoists, three major schools of thought were dominant in those days: the Confucians, the Legalists, and the Mohists.

THE CONFUCIANS. More will be said about the school of Confucius in a later section. However, it must be noted here that its members were rivals of the Daoists in the fourth and third centuries B.C.E. in advising the rulers of China on government. Whereas the Daoists believed that the least government was the best government, the disciples of Confucius believed that a hierarchical and stratified system was the best form of government. Whereas the Daoists had little use for formal religion, the Confucians at least believed that the rites and rituals of religion served the function of uniting the people and teaching them about proper social order. Whereas the Daoists believed that the best society was one with little structure, the Confucians taught that society needed an elaborate structure, reinforced by etiquette, to be effective.

THE LEGALISTS. A second group that vied for the attention of the rulers of China during this period was a large one that followed no specific teacher; its members were known as Legalists or Realists. They believed that human nature and the condition of China at the time demanded strong leadership. To them, human nature tended to be wicked and lazy. People followed the path of least resistance. Left to their own devices, people made decisions that were bad for society as a whole. Therefore, government should not be affected by morality or pity. People did not need love or pity, they needed food and houses. Thus, leaders of government should determine what would be best for the majority of society and take the difficult steps necessary to achieve these ends. Any resulting hardship for the minority should not affect decisions. Legalists had no room for religion. Money and time spent on sacrifices to the gods were better spent on good government. Naturally, these teachers had little in common with Daoist sages who embraced wu wei.

THE MOHISTS.   The third group that sought to influence government during the fourth and third centuries B.C.E. was the Mohists. These teachers were disciples of Mozi, who lived in the fifth century B.C.E. (ca. 468–390 B.C.E.). Mozi began his career as a Confucian but later broke away to form his own distinctive philosophy. He and his disciples believed that the best government operated under the direction of the traditional Chinese religions. Under these religions, people were taught to love one another; thus, the government would operate from a position of love. The Mohists were pacifists, yet they recognized the necessity of self-defense and allowed the building of fortifications.

Although there were probably many representatives of each of these distinct philosophies, it is doubtful that any of them had serious influence on the governors of China, except perhaps the Legalists. Nevertheless, the teachings of the Daoists, the Confucians, and the Mohists have been held as ideals for the Chinese people for thousands of years.

Later Development of Daoism

Basically, Daoism as it is seen in the *Daodejing* and in the essays of Zhuangzi was concerned with living life in harmony with the basic force behind nature, the Tao. As a pure philosophy, this appealed to a small group of persons, malcontent with the intricacies of society and government, but it probably never had wide appeal for the populace.

After the period of the early philosophers, however, Daoism did develop wide appeal for the masses and is frequently listed among the major religions of the world. This development from a philosophy for the few, to a religion for the many, is a fascinating story.

Following the period of the early Daoist philosophers, two kinds of Daoists developed. One group followed the philosophical writings of Laozi and Zhuangzi. The second group was searching for immortality, not in the sense of life after death, as taught by many other religions, but in an endless extension of the present life through various devices. The philosophers had taught that life was the greatest of all possessions and that the person whose life was properly attuned to the Dao might have a long life. This appealed to the Chinese, who look forward to old age and the relative ease and honor that it has traditionally brought in Chinese culture. Taking up this aspect of Daoism, scholars, priests, and magicians began to seek the means whereby life could be extended indefinitely. They sought every possible means, including special dietary regulations. Some came to believe that all foods, particularly solid foods, were poisonous; thus they tried to train their bodies to live on very little liquid food. Some claimed that eventually they were able to live on only saliva and air. Others practiced fasting and breath control, in a manner similar to that of the Indian ascetic.

Still another popular means of extending life was alchemy. Some believed that because dead meat could be preserved from decay by salt, living flesh might be preserved by some other mineral, such as gold. One can only guess at the outcomes of some of these experiments in longevity. Nevertheless, the hope that immortality might be achieved did not die out among the Chinese.

The Daoist alchemist seeking to work his craft soon became concerned with gods that might be involved in the process. Because the alchemists worked at the stove, they began to offer sacrifices to the god of the stove, Zaojun. Thus it is said that Zaojun, by the third century C.E., became the first god of Daoism. The process of apotheosis continued until there were many Daoist gods. And so a philosophy that began by essentially denying personal gods developed its own gods.

By the second century C.E., the *Daodejing* had been officially recognized as a Chinese classic and was soon on its way to becoming the Daoist scripture. Those seeking immortality came to believe that the only way they could achieve it was through the practice of morality and virtuous deeds toward their fellow human beings.

Also in the second century C.E., the Han dynasty, which had ruled China for several centuries, began to break down. During this time of chaos, certain charismatic Daoist leaders appeared. Several of them not only led the search for immortality but also gathered great armies of followers and participated in wars in a most un-Daoist fashion. With the organization that these people brought, the concern for faith healing, the search for immortality, and the other accoutrements of gods, morality, temples, priests, rituals, and so on, Daoism became one of the religions, if not the religion, of the masses of the Chinese people by the beginning of the third century C.E.

Because there were contacts between India and China from very early times, and because Buddhism under the influence of Asoka had become a missionary religion, no doubt there were Buddhist missionaries and traders in China as early as the third century B.C.E. However, early Chinese contacts with Buddhism were with the Theravada branch. It is likely that this version of Buddhism, with its emphasis on the monastic life, was far too Indian for the Chinese; therefore, it made little headway in China. In later years came the development of Mahayana Buddhism, with its elaborate rituals and many gods and bodhisattvas. Extraordinary missionaries also came, such as the legendary Bodhidharma, who brought Mahayana Buddhism from India to China in the fifth century C.E. In China, as in most other Asian nations, this version of the teachings of the Buddha appealed tremendously to the masses.

By the fourth century C.E., Mahayana Buddhism was a force to be reckoned with by the Daoists. At first, there seems to have been no rivalry between the two religions. The Daoists helped the Buddhists translate their texts into Chinese, and the Buddhists used Daoist terms to explain Buddhist concepts. As Buddhism became more popular among the Chinese, however, the Daoists began to recognize it as a threat. Fierce struggles arose between the two groups to determine who would have influence with the various rulers and thus control the provinces. In a most uncharacteristic fashion, each religion became hostile to the other and persecution developed. In the ninth century C.E., Emperor Wuzong, who was greatly influenced by Daoist priests, persecuted the Buddhists on a vast scale, destroying numerous temples. At other times, Buddhists influenced the rulers to discriminate against the Daoists.

The struggle between the Buddhists and Daoists was settled more by mutual accommodation than by persecution. Each religion borrowed from the other until both became associated, along with the teachings of Confucius, with the common religion of the people. Daoism borrowed widely from the Mahayana teachings of an afterlife, with heavens and hells and judgment. The Buddhists followed their traditional pattern of accepting the native gods and heroes of the land as Buddhist bodhisattvas, and the Daoists sought to turn the tables by asserting that Laozi and others were created before the foundations of the Earth and thus were superior to the Buddha. All in all, the Daoists seem to have absorbed the most. By the sixth century C.E., the Daoists had taken up the Buddhist pattern of monasticism. Their priests could now live in monasteries and in some cases were commanded to be celibate. Nunneries were established for Daoist women who desired celibacy. By the tenth century, the shape of Daoism was established; it changed little during the next ten centuries.

Daoism, with its religious side fully developed and its traditional emphasis on an alchemical means of extending life, continued to have a hold on the common people into the twenty-first century. The Chinese upper classes and intellectuals continued to read the *Daodejing* and other classics of philosophical Daoism, but they tended to regard the religion itself as being fit only for the masses.

Confucianism

8.3. **Identify the basic tenets of Confucianism and understand how it is inextricably interwoven into the total philosophy of the Chinese people.**

Because Confucianism is generally considered one of the major religions of the world, it might be appropriate to discuss it in a separate chapter rather than to include it as part of a general chapter on the religions of China. However, in its origins and development, Confucianism, like Daoism, is inextricably interwoven into the total philosophy of the Chinese people. Therefore, to discuss Confucianism in a chapter separate from Daoism and Chinese religious thinking would be to present it in an unreal setting.

Some contend that the teachings of Confucius and his disciples were never intended to be a religion, that Confucius was probably a non-theist who discouraged prayer to the gods as worthless and that his main concern was the nature of human society. If Confucianism is a religion, it is a very different kind of religion. It has no priesthood; its sacred writings, although important, have never been considered a divine revelation like the Vedas or the Qur'an; it has frowned upon asceticism and monasticism; and it has no doctrine of an afterlife. In spite of all of these "non-religious" aspects, there have been some cultic developments in the history of Confucianism, and its philosophy has deeply affected the Chinese character.

The Life of Confucius

The man whom the West knows as Confucius was really named Kong. When he became a famous teacher, his disciples referred to him as *Kongzi* (Kong, the master). As his teachings became known to Western missionaries and scholars, the name was latinized to "Confucius."

Although Confucius was born in the sixth century B.C.E., the biographical material about him is extensive and fairly reliable because of the influence that he and his disciples had on the Chinese people. This is in marked contrast to the life of Laozi, who also lived in the sixth century B.C.E. but about whom we know almost nothing. The earliest and most authentic material about Confucius is contained in the *Analects*, a collection of his teachings compiled about seventy years after his death. In addition to the biographical material in Confucian literature, Confucius is mentioned in the writings of contemporary Daoists and Mohists. No one seriously doubts the historicity of Confucius.

Confucius was born in 551 B.C.E. in the state of Lu (now in modern Shandong). He was the child of an aristocratic family that had lost its wealth and position in the decline of the feudal states of China during that chaotic period. His father was said to have been a famous warrior of gigantic size and strength who was seventy years old when Confucius was conceived. The father died shortly before the birth of the child, and Confucius was reared in poverty by his widowed mother. Although his mother had to struggle for survival, she was determined to provide her son with an education. Therefore, Confucius was allowed to study with the village tutor. The biographies say he studied subjects that were the traditional fare of Chinese students of his time: poetry, Chinese history, music, hunting, fishing, and archery. Even as a youth, he seems to have been extremely interested in the interworkings of society, particularly in what constituted good government. This was to be his main theme for the rest of his life.

In his late teens, he accepted a minor position in government, where he closely observed the ruling process. He married and fathered one son, but the marriage ended in divorce. We know little about the wife or family of Confucius beyond these scanty facts. However, there are still Chinese today who claim to be the physical descendants of Confucius. While Confucius was in his mid-twenties, his mother died; being a devoted son, Confucius mourned her for three years.

During his twenties, Confucius began his true career, that of teacher. His reputation as a man of learning allowed him to establish himself as a teacher of young people. In the following years, his reputation spread widely, and he attracted many students. They lived in his home and followed him on his journeys. He taught them history, the principles of good government, and divination.[9]

Legend has it that at the age of fifty, Confucius was finally able to put into practice some of his principles of good government when he was asked to join the government of the Duke of Lu as its prime minister. According to these Confucian legends, Confucius's government was ideal. During his leadership, the state was so well governed that the crime rate dropped to almost nothing. People stopped locking their doors, and a wallet that was dropped on the street was left untouched for days. However, the enemies of Confucius became jealous of his success and conspired against him. Consequently, he was forced to retire from government at the age of fifty-five.

During the next twelve years of his life, Confucius held no position. He wandered from place to place with a few of his faithful disciples. Sometimes he was accepted by the populace and treated hospitably. At other times he and his friends were jeered and even jailed. Finally, when he was sixty-seven years of age, a position was found for him as an adviser to the Duke of Ai. Although this was not as important as the position he had formerly held, it at least gave Confucius a home for himself and his disciples. During the next years, he taught and compiled some of the classical Chinese texts. The master died in the year 479 B.C.E. and was widely mourned by his disciples. According to one tradition, his most faithful disciple built a hut beside the grave and stayed to mourn Confucius for three years.

The Teachings of Confucius

Confucius's attitude toward religion has been a point of great debate; on the one hand, some regard him as the founder of one of the world's great religions; on the other hand, some believe he was an agnostic, if not an atheist. The truth about Confucius's teachings on religion probably lies somewhere between the two extremes. Relative to his contemporaries, he was somewhere in the middle of the spectrum, with Laozi on the left, denying the validity of religions, and Mozi on the right, advocating a return to the ancient religions of China.

Confucius seems to have believed that although the gods existed and worship and rituals were of value in bringing people together, these things were of secondary importance to an equitable social order. Praying to the spirits should not interfere with one's proper social duties. His attitude seems to have been that, ideally, one should respect the spirits but keep them at a distance.[10] Even

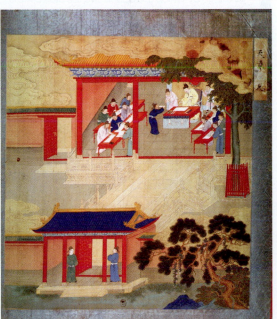

Chinese civil service examination. For many years, a knowledge of the writings of Confucius was required for entry into Chinese civil service.

though Confucius was not an atheist or anti-religious, no evidence suggests that he was interested in starting a religion. Rather, he developed a system of ethics, a theory of government, and a set of personal and social goals that deeply influenced the Chinese for almost twenty-five centuries.

The teachings of Confucius are based on certain central themes. One of these themes is represented by the word **li**, variously translated as "propriety," "rites," "ceremonies," or "courtesy." Originally, it may have meant the grain found in wood or the pattern in jade. Basically, *li* seems to mean "the course of life as it is intended to go"; of course, it has religious and social connotations. When society lives by li, it moves smoothly: men and women respect their elders and superiors; the proper rituals and ceremonies are performed; everything and everyone is in its proper place.

Naturally, the principle of li was most closely followed when an idealized form of hierarchical government existed. In such a state, all people know their superiors and inferiors and are able to act in the genteel manner that Confucius believed was necessary for a smoothly functioning society. Furthermore, Confucius believed that China in his day was in a state of chaos because the people were no longer living according to the principles of li.

One of the Confucian classics, the *Li Ji*, whose primary subject is li, records the following conversation:

From the Source

Duke Ai asked Confucius, saying, "What do you say about the great rites [li]? How is it that superior men, in speaking about them, ascribe so much honour to them?" Confucius said, "I, Khiu, am a small man, and unequal to a knowledge of the rites." "By no means," said the ruler. "Tell me what you think, my Master." Then Confucius replied, "According to what I have heard, of all things by which the people live the rites are the greatest. Without them they would have no means of regulating the services paid to the spirits of heaven and earth; without them they would have no means of distinguishing the positions proper to father and son, to high and low, to old and young; without them they would have no means of maintaining the separate character of the intimate relations between male and female, father and son, elder brother and younger, and conducting intercourse between the contracting families of a marriage, and the frequency or infrequency (of the reciprocities between friends). These are the grounds on which superior men have honoured and reverenced (the rites) as they did."[11]

According to Confucius, there are five basic relationships in life. If li were present in these relationships throughout society, the social order would be ideal. These five relationships are as follows:

1. *Father to son.* There should be kindness in the father and filial piety in the son.
2. *Elder brother to younger brother.* There should be gentility in the elder brother and humility in the younger.
3. *Husband to wife.* There should be righteous behavior in the husband and obedience in the wife.
4. *Elder to junior.* There should be consideration among the elders and deference among the juniors.
5. *Ruler to subject.* There should be benevolence among the rulers and loyalty among the subjects.

In Confucian ideals, the principle of li is the outward expression of the superior individual toward others in society. The inward expression of Confucian ideals is called **ren**. Ren is frequently translated as "love," "goodness," or "human-heartedness." According to Confucius, only the great sages of antiquity truly possessed ren, but it is a quality that all should seek to develop. The pursuit of this quality is mentioned many times in the *Analects of Confucius.*

From the Source

The Master said, "Virtue [ren] is more to man than either water or fire. I have seen men die from treading on water and fire, but I have never seen a man die from treading the course of virtue."[12]

The Master said, "To subdue one's self and return to propriety, is perfect virtue. If a man can for one day subdue himself and return to propriety, all under heaven will ascribe perfect virtue to him."[13]

Thus, Confucius taught that people should love one another and practice respect and courtesy toward each other in their daily lives. He instructed that society was best served when people acted with reciprocity (*shu*) toward each other.

From the Source

Tsze-kung asked, saying, "Is there one word which may serve as a rule of practice for all one's life?"

The Master said, "Is not reciprocity [shu] such a word? What you do not want done to yourself, do not do to others."[14]

If the principles of li and ren were present and operative in a person, the end product would be the Confucian goal, the superior human being.

Apparently, Confucius believed in the natural goodness, or at least in the natural perfectibility, of humankind, although it is not as clear in his teachings as it is in the work of his disciple Mencius. Confucius apparently believed that under the proper circumstances it was possible for individuals to achieve goodness and eventually to achieve the status of the superior human being.

One requirement for people to achieve goodness is good government. Confucius believed that poor government with bad laws caused people to do evil, and that a generation of good rulership could cure most of the moral ills of people. A good example set by the ruling classes will bring out the true morality of people. Because of the natural morality of humanity, Confucius believed that it was unnecessary to offer people rewards or punishments to induce them to good conduct. Good conduct is its own reward. Therefore, whatever Confucius might have believed about the gods, he never spoke of an afterlife in heaven or hell to reward good deeds or punish evil. Under the proper conditions, people simply grow and develop into what Confucius called the "Superior Person."

The Development of Confucianism

When Confucius died in 479 B.C.E., his teachings were remembered and followed by only a small group of disciples. He had not had the success as a ruler that he had hoped for, and his teachings had not received widespread support—nor did the rulers of China open their doors to his immediate disciples. During the following 500 years, however, the disciples of Confucius began to take a major part in training and advising the rulers of China, to such an extent that his teachings became an integral part of Chinese culture.

After the death of Confucius, approximately seventy of his disciples scattered across the empire. Some sought positions as advisers to rulers and others tried to establish their own schools. They were not spectacularly successful in either of these attempts for at least two reasons. First, they faced the opposition of rival schools—Daoists, Legalists, and later Mohists—who all claimed to have the key to good government for the official who would listen. Second, the disciples of Confucius taught that the best form of government was an idealized feudalism—and they were teaching this in a time when the feudal society was breaking down all over China; they were out of step with their time. Nevertheless, the disciples did manage to reach a few receptive ears with their teaching and advising; Confucius's teaching was thereby perpetuated. In the fourth and third centuries B.C.E. arose two of the most outstanding Confucians of all times, Mencius and Xunzi, who did much to popularize and spread the teachings of Confucius.

In Chinese thought, the Chinese sage second only to Confucius is his latter-day disciple, Mencius.[15] Mencius was born approximately 100 years after the death of Confucius and lived from 372 to 289 B.C.E. We are not certain about a great many details in his life; but as is true of many of the ancients, there is an abundance of legend about him. Much of this legendary material apparently is intended to draw parallels between him and Confucius. We are told that, like Confucius, Mencius was the only child of a poor widow who struggled to support her son and provide him with an education. As did Confucius, Mencius became a teacher and sought a position as a political adviser. Also as was true for his master, his advice was not wanted; he too wandered about teaching his disciples. More substantial tradition says that Mencius studied under the disciples of Cunsi, the grandson of Confucius, and was in fact an ineffective adviser to some of the Chinese rulers of his day.

The teachings of Mencius have been maintained in the *Book of Mencius*. From this text and others, his contribution as a Confucian scholar can be learned. Like Confucius, Mencius was not terribly interested in religion. Little is said about the gods in his writings, and no attempt is made to influence people to return to the worship of the traditional Chinese gods. Mencius's major ethical position was a reinforcement of Confucius's teaching of the natural goodness of human beings. Whereas this teaching had not been terribly clear in the writings of Confucius, it became crystal clear in those of Mencius. The latter strongly asserted that human nature was basically good. He observed that not all people act virtuously, but that this is because of their environment. Given the proper environment, he taught, it is possible for all people to be virtuous. Naturally, the best environment for a Confucian scholar features a government based on paternalistic feudalism operated for the benefit of the people.

Because war destroyed the possibility of the kind of just and honorable conditions under which human goodness could develop, Mencius opposed war. On the other hand, because people were the most important element in any state, Mencius believed that people had the right to revolt against an oppressive government. In many ways, Mencius sharpened the focus of Confucius's teachings; in other ways, he added his own distinctive ideas to the Confucian canon.

The second most famous Confucian interpreter was Xunzi, who lived in the generation after Mencius (298–238 B.C.E.). Whereas Mencius has come to be regarded as the orthodox interpreter of Confucius, Xunzi is regarded as the heterodox interpreter; however, Xunzi had a greater impact in his time. Some authorities even give him credit for the development of Confucianism during the Han dynasty (206 B.C.E. to 220 C.E.).[17] He was a native of Zhao and a widely respected and revered scholar. In his later years, he served as a magistrate of the city of Lan-Ling. Beyond these bare facts, we know little about him.

Xunzi is remembered for two major contributions to Confucian thought. First, even more than Confucius himself, he believed in the worth of rites (li) as devices to bring people together and educate them. He taught that ancient Chinese rulers had dealt with social disorder by establishing common rites that would regulate the various desires and competing interests of the population. In this sense, li functions as a type of social control and order.

The second contribution of Xunzi, and the one for which he is more famous, is his denial of the basic goodness of humankind. In direct contradiction of the teachings of Mencius, Xunzi contended that people were basically evil in nature. He believed that goodness comes only through proper training. Therefore, training, laws, and restraint are necessary so that society might survive. This made rites even more important, because it is through rites that people are trained in proper living. Added to this teaching was Xunzi's belief that the spirits of the heavens were basically impersonal forces. For this reason, Xunzi appears as the most non-religious of all of the early Confucian scholars.

The rise of the Han dynasty marked a new era in Chinese history. The period preceding it had been one of political upheaval. When the Han rulers came to power, they needed great numbers of new administrators and advisers. This new market for political theorists attracted many scholars who had been trained by the disciples of Confucius. The Confucians' position was further strengthened when in 136 B.C.E. they were placed in charge of the education of Chinese youth, particularly those youths who would eventually govern. The civil service examinations were based on the teachings of Confucius. From that date until 1905 C.E., Chinese education included a study of the teachings of Confucius. Master Kong himself could not have devised a system in which his philosophy would have had more influence over the future of China.

In addition to the development of Confucianism as the leading educational theory of China, a cult of Confucius himself developed during the years of the Han dynasty. The ruler of the state of Lu is said to have mourned Confucius after his death and built a shrine to him. With the coming of the Han rulers and the ascendancy of the Confucian scholars, however, reverence for him increased dramatically. In 195 B.C.E., the first of the Han emperors visited the grave of Confucius and offered a pig, a sheep, and an ox as sacrifices. Fifty years later, a temple was built to honor Confucius in his native town. By 8 B.C.E., titles and land were given to his descendants. The practice of awarding posthumous titles to Confucius himself began, and he was given the title of Duke. Gradually, the temples and ceremonies increased all over China. By the sixth century C.E., every prefecture in China had a temple to Confucius and some people came to look upon him as a god. However, no popular religion developed about Confucius. He was generally regarded as the patron saint or ancestor of the Chinese scholar, and he was remembered and revered as one would remember any ancestor.

The growth of the Confucian cult was set back in 1503, when the government ordered the removal of the images of Confucius from the temples and replaced them with wooden tables on which his teachings were inscribed. In addition, all of the titles that had been given were removed, and he was known simply as "Master Kong, the perfect teacher of antiquity." In 1906, an attempt was made to restore the Confucian cult to some of its original glory, but with the birth of the People's Republic of China, the sacrifices to Confucius, along with the other "great sacrifices," were abandoned.

Religion in Public Life

Confucianism and Daoism were greatly curtailed following the Communist rise to power in China in 1949. However, in recent years the Chinese government has been slowly making space for religions and for the ancient Chinese traditions. Several Chinese are looking to Confucius and his principles to help guide the nation as it expands its position in the global marketplace. Confucian schools for children are enjoying a renaissance, and even some economists and politicians are turning to Confucian thought. A pro-privatization economist named Sheng Hong buttressed his own position with Confucian values, claiming that "'Confucius' theory is very similar to the invisible hand of Adam Smith," says Sheng. "People will [naturally] seek their own benefit, the government doesn't have to interfere, and the economy will flourish."[19]

Henry Westheim Photography/Alamy

Students at a Confucian temple and school celebrate Teachers' Day. After years of oppression, Confucian education is enjoying a resurgence in China.

Traditional Chinese Holidays

8.4. **Name the traditional Chinese holidays.**

Holidays in Chinese communities are based on various religious and secular foundations. Ancient holidays associated with the various agricultural seasons and other holidays are connected to Daoism, Confucianism, and Buddhism. Some holidays celebrate the births of the various gods and the founders of Chinese religions. A list of some of the traditional festivals celebrated in Chinese communities follows. The Chinese year is based on a lunar calendar, and festival dates vary from year to year in relation to a solar calendar.

Chinese New Year

The New Year is celebrated at the end of January or the beginning of February. Each year is associated with a particular animal. The New Year celebrations' emphasis is on cleansing and renewal to prepare for the new year and the coming planting in the spring. Often, businesses are closed for several days. Houses are cleansed in preparation for feasts and guests. On the eve of the New Year, families gather to worship various gods and to venerate ancestors. The acts of worship are followed by a feast of many courses. This is also a time of new clothes and presents for children. Firecrackers and parades are a part of this holiday. Chinese New Year celebrations continue until the full moon of the first month.

Pure and Bright Festival

In early April, Chinese people celebrate another festival that involves the ancestors. This celebration includes ritual baths and the building of new fires that symbolize the newness of the spring season and the renewal of the yang forces in nature. Families also use this season as an occasion to clean and redecorate the graves of ancestors. Food is offered to the departed family members at the graves, and the living family enjoys a picnic.

The Dragon Boat Festival

In June, the Chinese people celebrate the beginning of summer with the Dragon Boat Festival. This season is celebrated with dragon boat races and the eating of rice cakes. The beginning of summer is believed to be the high point of yang power in the Earth (the longest day of the year) and the beginning of yin power. Daoist rituals exorcise pestilent spirits during this season.

All Souls' Day

The festival of All Souls' Day occurs in late August. It is the Chinese version of the Buddhist Ullambana. The Buddhist idea of purgatory is combined with traditional Chinese concern for the welfare of the ancestors. It is believed that souls are released from purgatory in a kind of amnesty. Money and other offerings are made to the spirits of the ancestors. Food and flower offerings are left outside for wandering spirits. Some people light fires in the streets to drive spirits and ghosts away. On this day, families join together for another feast.

Autumn Harvest Festival

The Chinese celebrate the autumn harvest during the full moon of the eighth lunar month (September). This holiday includes the enjoyment of the full moon and the eating of fresh fruits and sweet pastries, called moon cakes. The festival also features the reading of poetry and a general spirit of thanksgiving for the autumn harvest.

Winter Holidays

The winter season includes the Daoist holiday of the renewal of the universe (*Chiao*) at the time of the winter solstice. During the late autumn and early winter days, there are also celebrations of the birthdays of various heroes, gods and goddesses, and patron saints.

Religion in China Today

8.5. **Discuss religion in China today.**

Throughout the centuries, Chinese governments have attempted to manage or control religion, in part because in traditional China religion and politics were so closely intertwined. While religion provided the basis for political authority, it also contained the seeds of rebellion. The nineteenth and twentieth centuries were difficult times for religion in China. During the mid-nineteenth century, natural disasters and political and military intervention by European powers yielded social and economic chaos in much of the country. There were many religious responses that offered hope of a return to peace and prosperity.

The most disastrous of these was the Taiping Rebellion, which raged between 1851 and 1864. Its leader, Hung Hsiu-chuan, combined elements of traditional Chinese religion and Protestant Christianity in a revolutionary ideology. Hsiu-chuan believed that he was the younger brother of Jesus Christ and that he had been sent by God to destroy demons and those who worshiped them. These included Buddhists, Daoists, and Confucians. Hsiu-chuan was also dedicated to the destruction of the ruling Qing dynasty. He declared a new "Kingdom of Heavenly Peace," of which he would be the "Heavenly King." In his teachings, he combined Christian notions of Christ as the king of heaven with Chinese concepts of the authority of heaven. The rebellion attracted an enormous following and spread rapidly over much of southeastern China. By the time it ended in 1864, nearly thirty million people had died.

In 1949, China underwent a revolution and became the People's Republic of China, under the direction of a Marxist government. The official attitude of this government toward religion was that it was a vestige of the feudal past and would gradually fade away from a modern society. Theoretically, at least, the government allowed freedom of religious belief. However, Daoism and Confucianism were regarded with great suspicion because Confucianism seemed so clearly tied to the feudalism of the past and Daoism was seen as superstition. Buddhism was viewed as an imported religion and was therefore suspect. Large numbers of Buddhist monks fled the country, contributing to the development of more sophisticated communities in Taiwan, Hong Kong, Singapore, and the West. Christianity was associated with the imperialistic Western nations. Therefore, Christian missionaries were expelled from China by 1952. Islam was a more delicate matter for the new government. Most Muslims in China live in the western part of the nation and are members of various minority ethnic groups related to the Turkic peoples of central and western Asia. Even though Islam had been brought in from outside China, the government of the People's Republic did not suppress it; however, Islamic education was severely restricted. Despite the official government position, many temples, mosques, and churches closed or were converted to other uses in the years following 1949. Christians were required to join together in the so-called Three-Self Movement[20] to protect themselves against foreign intervention or control. Those who refused and formed independent Christian communities (often called "house churches" in English) suffered persecution. The Chinese government refused to recognize the authority of the pope to appoint bishops. Generally, post-1949 China was not a healthy place for organized religions, although some adherents of all five faiths maintained their practices.

During the period of the Cultural Revolution, which began in August 1966, all religions in China were severely repressed. For three years, the leaders of the Cultural Revolution moved actively against anything that represented the four "olds": old ideas, old culture, old customs, and old habits. The remnants of religion were inviting targets. Temples and churches that had managed to survive until 1966 were closed. Buddhist temples were especially singled out to be plastered and painted with slogans. Their statues were smashed and dragged through the streets. Confucius was called "the number one criminal of feudal thinking." His birthplace was raided, and the temple there was destroyed. People who dared to celebrate Daoist festivals were arrested and accused of wrong thinking. Many Daoist shrines, tablets, altars, and relics were destroyed in the purge.

In 1977, after the death of Mao and with the thawing of relationships between China and Western nations, the government became more open to religions. In 1982, the Chinese Communist Party declared its respect for religion—and continues to hope that it will disappear. Churches and temples were allowed to reopen and hold services. The University of Nanking established a Center for Religious Studies in 1979. Chinese students are now enrolled in religious studies departments at several American universities. The Chinese government is paying the costs for a translation and publication of the Bible and subsidizing the studies of Chinese Muslim students in Egypt. Despite these liberalizing trends, the position of religion in Chinese society remains precarious. The government tolerates only those religious organizations willing to accept strict regulation. Religions must be free from foreign influence. To be officially recognized, religious organizations must accept government censorship of religious writings and guidance in the selection of clergy, and limit religious activities to approved locations. Only five religions are officially recognized: Daoism, Buddhism, Roman Catholicism, Protestant Christianity, and Islam. The government does not recognize individual Protestant denominations.

Religion and Public Life

Unrecognized religious organizations and those the government declares to be "cults" are subject to severe repression. Roman Catholics who remain loyal to the pope, Protestant "house churches," and conservative Muslims who refuse government regulation continue to suffer. Demonstrations by Tibetans calling for independence and the return of their spiritual leader, the Dalai Lama, from exile are violently suppressed. The latest of these took place in March of 2008. According to the Tibetan government in exile, approximately 130 people were killed by security forces. Officials are also concerned about the possible development of political Islamic movements, especially in Muslim-majority regions in the western part of the country. This concern motivated the government to limit "Year of the Pig" celebrations in 2007 to avoid angering Muslims who might consider images of pigs to be offensive. What the future holds for religion in China is unclear.

Think About It

1. Explain how Daoism and Confucianism emphasize different aspects of Chinese culture and worldview.

2. Who was Laozi and what is his significance in the development of Daoism? Also, discuss the three major themes of early Daoism.

3. The text refers to Confucianism as a "very different kind of religion." Why? What makes it different from other religions in practice?

4. Identify three important traditional Chinese holidays and when and how they are celebrated.

5. What political difficulties do religions face in China today?

Suggested Reading

Bush, Richard C. *Religion in Communist China*. Nashville, Tenn.: Abingdon Press, 1970.

Giles, Herbert A. *Religions of Ancient China*. Salem, N.H.: Books for Libraries Press, 1969.

Hung Lou Meng. *The Dream of the Red Chamber*. West Stockbridge, Mass.: Anchor, 2003.

Kohn, Livia. *Daoism and Chinese Culture*. Cambridge, Mass.: Three Pines Press, 2001.

Overmyer, Daniel C. *Religion in China Today*. Cambridge, Mass.: Cambridge University Press, 2003.

Reilly, Thomas H. *The Taiping Heavenly Kingdom: Rebellion and the Blasphemy of Empire*. Seattle: University of Washington Press, 2004.

Smith, D. Howard. *Chinese Religions*. New York: Holt, Rinehart and Winston, 1968.

Thompson, Laurence G. *The Chinese Religion: An Introduction*, 3rd ed. Belmont, Calif.: Wadsworth, 1979.

Waley, Arthur, trans. *The Analects of Confucius*. New York: Vintage, 1938.

———, Trans. *The Way and Its Power*. London: George Allen & Unwin, 1956.

Source Material

Selections from Sacred Chinese Literature

The source book for Daoism is the *Daodejing*. Passages from the *Daodejing* occur earlier in this chapter. Zhuangzi, one of the most important early interpreters of Daoism, is known for his whimsical reflections on the nature of reality. In this passage, the great Daoist philosopher Zuangzi reflects provocatively on the concepts of action, dependence, and distinction.[21]

The penumbra said to the shadow, "First you were walking, then you were standing still. First you were sitting, then you were upright. Why can't you decide on a single course of action?"

The shadow said, "Do I depend on something to make as I am? Does what I depend on depend something else? Do I depend on it as a snake does on its skin, or a cicada on its shell? How would I know why I am so or not so?"

Once Zhuang Zhou dreamt he was a butterfly, fluttering about joyfully as a butterfly would. He followed his whims exactly as he liked and knew nothing about Zhuang Zhou. Suddenly he awoke, and there he was, the startled Zhuang Zhou in the flesh. He did not know if Zhou had been dreaming he was a butterfly, or if a butterfly was now dreaming it was Zhou. Surely, Zhou and a butterfly count as two distinct entities! Such is what we call the transformation of one thing into another."

The *Analects of Confucius*

The *Analects* are a collection of the sayings of Confucius and his disciples, dating from the fifth century B.C.E. The following selections are representative of its concern for a well-ordered society.[22]

Book III

CHAP. I. Confucius said of the head of the Chi family, who had eight rows of pantomimes in his area, "If he can bear to do this, what may he not bear to do?"

CHAP. II. The three families used the Yung ode, while the vessels were being removed, at the conclusion of the sacrifice. The Master said, "'Assisting are the princes;—the son of heaven looks profound and grave:'—what application can these words have in the hall of the three families?"

CHAP. III. The Master said, "If a man be without the virtues proper to humanity, what has he to do with the rites of propriety? If a man be without the virtues proper to humanity, what has he to do with music?"

CHAP. IV. 1. Lin Fang asked what was the first thing to be attended to in ceremonies.

2. The Master said, "A great question indeed!"

3. "In festive ceremonies, it is better to be sparing than extravagant. In the ceremonies of mourning, it is better that there be deep sorrow than a minute attention to observances."

CHAP. V. The Master said, "The rude tribes of the east and north have their princes, and are not like the States of our great land which are without them."

CHAP. VI. The chief of the Chi family was about to sacrifice to the T'ai mountain. The Master said to Zan Yu, "Can you not save him from this?" He answered, "I cannot." Confucius said, "Alas! will you say that the T'ai mountain is not so discerning as Lin Fang?"

CHAP. VII. The Master said, "The student of virtue has no contentions. If it be said he cannot avoid them, shall this be in archery? But he bows complaisantly to his competitors; thus he ascends the hall, descends, and exacts the forfeit of drinking. In his contention, he is still the Chun-tsze."

CHAP. VIII. 1. Tsze-hsia asked, saying, "What is the meaning of the passage— 'The pretty dimples of her artful smile! The well-defined black and white of her eye! The plain ground for the colours?'"

2. The Master said, "The business of laying on the colours follows (the preparation of) the plain ground."

3. "Ceremonies then are a subsequent thing?" The Master said, "It is Shang who can bring out my meaning. Now I can begin to talk about the odes with him."

CHAP. IX. The Master said, "I could describe the ceremonies of the Hsia dynasty, but Chi cannot sufficiently attest my words. I could describe the ceremonies of the Yin dynasty, but Sung cannot sufficiently attest my words. (They cannot do so) because of the insufficiency of their records and wise men. If those were sufficient, I could adduce them in support of my words."

CHAP. X. The Master said, "At the great sacrifice, after the pouring out of the libation, I have no wish to look on."

CHAP. XI. Some one asked the meaning of the great sacrifice. The Master said, "I do not know. He who knew its meaning would find it as easy to govern the kingdom as to look on this";— pointing to his palm.

CHAP. XII. 1. He sacrificed to the dead, as if they were present. He sacrificed to the spirits, as if the spirits were present.

2. The Master said, "I consider my not being present at the sacrifice, as if I did not sacrifice."

CHAP. XIII. 1. Wang-sun Chia asked, saying, "What is the meaning of the saying, 'It is better to pay court to the furnace than to the south-west corner?'"

2. The Master said, "Not so. He who offends against Heaven has none to whom he can pray."

CHAP. XIV. The Master said, "Chau had the advantage of viewing the two past dynasties. How complete and elegant are its regulations! I follow Chau."

CHAP. XV. The Master, when he entered the grand temple, asked about everything. Some one said, "Who will say that the son of the man of Tsau knows the rules of propriety! He has entered the grand temple and asks about everything." The Master heard the remark, and said, "This is a rule of propriety."

CHAP. XVI. The Master said, "In archery it is not going through the leather which is the principal thing;— because people's strength is not equal. This was the old way."

CHAP. XVII. 1. Tsze-kung wished to do away with the offering of a sheep connected with the inauguration of the first day of each month.

2. The Master said, "Ts'ze, you love the sheep; I love the ceremony."

CHAP. XVIII. The Master said, "The full observance of the rules of propriety in serving one's prince is accounted by people to be flattery."

Book IV

CHAP. I. The Master said, "It is virtuous manners which constitute the excellence of a neighborhood. If a man in selecting a residence, do not fix on one where such prevail, how can he be wise?"

CHAP. II. The Master said, "Those who are without virtue cannot abide long either in a condition of poverty and hardship, or in a condition of enjoyment. The virtuous rest in virtue; the wise desire virtue."

CHAP. III. The Master said, "It is only the (truly) virtuous man, who can love, or who can hate, others."

CHAP. IV. The Master said, "If the will be set on virtue, there will be no practice of wickedness."

CHAP. V. 1. The Master said, "Riches and honours are what men desire. If it cannot be obtained in the proper way, they should not be held. Poverty and meanness are what men dislike. If it cannot be avoided in the proper way, they should not be avoided."

2. "If a superior man abandon virtue, how can he fulfil the requirements of that name?"

3. "The superior man does not, even for the space of a single meal, act contrary to virtue. In moments of haste, he cleaves to it. In seasons of danger, he cleaves to it."

CHAP. VI. 1. The Master said, "I have not seen a person who loved virtue, or one who hated what was not virtuous. He who loved virtue, would esteem nothing above it. He who hated what is not virtuous, would practise virtue in such a way that he would not allow anything that is not virtuous to approach his person."

2. "Is any one able for one day to apply his strength to virtue? I have not seen the case in which his strength would be insufficient."

3. "Should there possibly be any such case, I have not seen it."

CHAP. VII. The Master said, "The faults of men are characteristic of the class to which they belong. By observing a man's faults, it may be known that he is virtuous."

CHAP. VIII. The Master said, "If a man in the morning hear the right way, he may die in the evening without regret."

CHAP. IX. The Master said, "A scholar, whose mind is set on truth, and who is ashamed of bad clothes and bad food, is not fit to be discoursed with."

CHAP. X. The Master said, "The superior man, in the world, does not set his mind either for anything, or against anything; what is right he will follow."

CHAP. XI. The Master said, "The superior man thinks of virtue; the small man thinks of comfort. The superior man thinks of the sanctions of law; the small man thinks of favours which he may receive."

CHAP. XII. The Master said: "He who acts with a constant view to his own advantage will be much murmured against."

CHAP. XIII. The Master said, "Is a prince is able to govern his kingdom with the complaisance proper to the rules of propriety, what difficulty will he have? If he cannot govern it with that complaisance, what has he to do with the rules of propriety?"

CHAP. XIV. The Master said, "A man should say, I am not concerned that I have no place, I am concerned how I may fit myself for one. I am not concerned that I am not known, I seek to be worthy to be known."

CHAP. XV. 1. The Master said, "Shan, my doctrine is that of an all-pervading unity." The disciple Tsang replied, "Yes."

2. The Master went out, and the other disciples asked, saying, "What do his words mean?" Tsang said, "The doctrine of our master is to be true to the principles of our nature and the benevolent exercise of them to others,— this and nothing more."

CHAP. XVI. The Master said, "The mind of the superior man is conversant with righteousness; the mind of the mean man is conversant with gain."

CHAP. XVII. The Master said, "When we see men of worth, we should think of equalling them; when we see men of a contrary character, we should turn inwards and examine ourselves."

CHAP. XVIII. The Master said, "In serving his parents, a son may remonstrate with them, but gently; when he sees that they do not incline to follow his advice, he shows an increased degree of reverence, but does not abandon his purpose; and should they punish him, he does not allow himself to murmur."

CHAP. XIX. The Master said, "While his parents are alive, the son may not go abroad to a distance. If he does go abroad, he must have a fixed place to which he goes."

CHAP. XX. The Master said, "If the son for three years does not alter from the way of his father, he may be called filial."

CHAP. XXI. The Master said, "The years of parents may by no means not be kept in the memory, as an occasion at once for joy and for fear."

CHAP. XXII. The Master said, "The reason why the ancients did not readily give utterance to their words, was that they feared lest their actions should not come up to them."

CHAP. XXIII. The Master said, "The cautious seldom err."

CHAP. XXIV. The Master said, "The superior man wishes to be slow in his speech and earnest in his conduct."

CHAP. XXV. The Master said, "Virtue is not left to stand alone. He who practises it will have neighbors."

CHAP. XXVI. Tsze-yu said, "In serving a prince, frequent remonstrances lead to disgrace. Between friends, frequent reproofs make the friendship distant."

The Meaning and Value of Rituals

One of the greatest interpreters of Confucius was Xunzi. In the following section, Xunzi states the Confucian view of the value rituals have for a society.[23]

Rites (li) rest on three bases: Heaven and earth, which are the source of all life; the ancestors, who are the source of the human race; sovereigns and teachers, who are the source of government. If there were no Heaven and earth, where would life come from? If there were no ancestors, where would the offspring come from? If there were no sovereigns and teachers, where would government come from? Should any of the three be missing, either there would be no men or men would be without peace. Hence rites are to serve Heaven on high and earth below, and to honour the ancestors and elevate the sovereigns and teachers. Herein lies the threefold basis for rites.

In general rites begin with primitive practices, attain cultured forms, and finally achieve beauty and felicity. When rites are at their best, men's emotions and sense of beauty are both fully expressed. When they are at the next level, either the emotion or the sense of beauty oversteps the others. When they are at still the next level, emotion reverts to the state of primitivity.

It is through rites that Heaven and earth are harmonious and sun and moon are bright, that the four seasons are ordered and the stars are on their courses, that rivers flow and that things prosper, that love and hatred are tempered and joy and anger are in keeping. They cause the lowly to be obedient and those on high to be illustrious. He who holds to the rites is never confused in the midst of multifarious change; he who deviates therefrom is lost. Rites—are they not the culmination of culture?

Rites require us to treat both life and death with attentiveness. Life is the beginning of man, death is his end. When a man is well off both at the end and the beginning, the way of man is fulfilled. Hence the gentleman respects the beginning and is carefully attentive to the end. To pay equal attention to the end as well as to the beginning is the way of the gentleman and the beauty of rites and righteousness.

Rites serve to shorten that which is too long and lengthen that which is too short, reduce that which is too much and augment that which is too little, express the beauty of love and reverence and cultivate the elegance of righteous conduct. Therefore, beautiful adornment and coarse sackcloth, music and weeping, rejoicing and sorrow, though pairs of opposites, are in the rites equally utilized and alternately brought into play. Beautiful adornment, music, and rejoicing are appropriate on occasions of felicity; coarse sackcloth, weeping, and sorrow are appropriate on occasions of ill-fortune. Rites make room for beautiful adornment but not to the point of being fascinating, for coarse sackcloth but not to the point of deprivation or self-injury, for music and rejoicing but not to the point of being lewd and indolent, for weeping and sorrow but not to the point of being depressing and injurious. Such is the middle path of rites.

Funeral rites are those by which the living adorn the dead. The dead are accorded a send-off as though they were living. In this way the dead are served like the living, the absent like the present. Equal attention is thus paid to the end as well as to the beginning of life.

Now the rites used on the occasion of birth are to embellish joy, those used on the occasion of death are to embellish sorrow, those used at sacrifice are to embellish reverence, those used on military occasions are to embellish dignity. In this respect the rites of all kings are alike, antiquity and the present age agree, and no one knows whence they came.

Sacrifice is to express a person's feeling of remembrance and longing, for grief and affliction cannot be kept out of one's consciousness all the time. When men are enjoying the pleasure of good company, a loyal minister of a filial son may feel grief and affliction. Once such feelings arise, he is greatly excited and moved. If such feelings are not given proper expression, then his emotions and memories are disappointed and not satisfied, and the appropriate rite is lacking. Thereupon the ancient kings instituted rites, and henceforth the principle of expressing honour to the honoured and love to the beloved is fully realized. Hence I say: Sacrifice is to express a person's feeling of remembrance and longing. As to the fullness of the sense of loyalty and affection, the richness of ritual and beauty—these none but the sage can understand. Sacrifice is something that the sage clearly understands, the scholar-gentleman contentedly performs, the officials consider a duty, and the common people regard as established custom. Among gentlemen it is considered the way of man; among the common people it is considered as having to do with the spirits.

Chapter 9
Shinto

 Learning Objectives

After reading this chapter, you should be able to:

9.1 Discuss the kami and their significance to Shinto.

9.2 Talk about the history of Shinto.

9.3 Identify the three forms of Shinto.

9.4 Describe the traditional Japanese festivals.

9.5 Analyze the practice of Shinto today.

A Timeline of Shinto

522	The term *Shinto* is used to distinguish Buddhism from local religion
8th century	Composition of Shinto classics
800–1700	Shinto is practiced in concert with other religions
1700	Revival of Shinto as an expression of Japanese nationalism
1889	Meiji rulers institute State Shinto
1946	As part of World War II peace treaties, State Shinto is abolished

Key Terms

Amaterasu	*Kojiki*
Bushido	samurai
kami	Tenrikyo
kami-dana	torii

Shinto is a native Japanese religion that embraces a wide variety of beliefs and practices. It is especially known for its profound connections to the natural landscapes, history, and people of the Japanese islands. Indeed, in one sense, Shinto is a religious form of Japanese nationalism. Its mythology describes the formation of Japan as a land greater than all other lands, and its shrines commemorate the heroes and events in the history of Japan. For centuries, Shinto taught the Japanese people that their emperors were descendants of the sun goddess.

Shinto is more than religious nationalism, however. It also involves the Japanese in a worshipful attitude toward the beauties of their land, particularly its mountains and forests. It includes aspects of nature and ancestor worship. Large-scale, public Shinto rituals take place in shrines throughout Japan. Private family rituals are carried out in small shrines in Japanese homes. Highly organized and active religious sects also have developed from basic Shinto. Thus, the term *Shinto* may refer to a multitude of varying Japanese religious and cultural practices.

The word *Shinto* itself was not officially coined until the sixth century C.E. It was developed then to distinguish native Japanese religion from the newer religions— Buddhism, Daoism, and Confucianism—being imported from China and Korea during the period. The word *Shinto* actually comes from the Chinese words *shen* and *dao*, which may be roughly translated in this context as "the way of the gods." The preferred Japanese term that describes this native religion is *kami-no-michi*, which also may be defined as "the way of the gods."

The Kami

9.1. **Discuss the kami and their significance to Shinto.**

To understand Japanese religion before the sixth century C.E., we must look at some of the traditional myths surrounding the origin of Japan, its native gods, and its early history. In the beginning, there were the **kami**, usually defined as "gods," which is inexact. There are thousands of kami. A few of them appear as personified beings in Japanese mythology, but the vast majority are unnamed entities who inhabit specific places in the Japanese landscape. Other kami are the spirits of deceased ancestors and national figures. Kami have power to help people and are often called on to protect and oversee those who worship them. However, their essence continues to defy easy classification and definition. Eighteenth-century Japanese Shinto scholar Motoori Norinaga confessed, "I do not yet understand the meaning of the term kami."[1]

The major source for our knowledge of Japanese mythology is the *Kojiki*, "Chronicles of Ancient Events." These chronicles were collected in the seventh and eighth centuries C.E. as a response to the entrance of Chinese culture and religions. In these centuries, the Japanese, although willing to accept the advanced culture of the Chinese, sought to define and celebrate their own heritage. The results of this search yielded the chronicles, which contain a section called "The Age of the Gods." In this material, one finds the mythological background of Japanese culture. The *Kojiki* includes stories that describe the special creation of the Japanese islands by two kami, Izanagi and his consort Izanami. These two become the divine parents of the other kami in Japanese mythology. The chief of these spirits is **Amaterasu**, the sun goddess. All of the Japanese emperors are believed to have descended from the line of Amaterasu.

From the Source

Hereupon all the [kami] commanded the two deities His Augustness the Male-Who-Invites and Her Augustness the Female-Who-Invites, ordering them to "make, consolidate, and give birth to this drifting land." Granting to them a heavenly jeweled spear, they thus deigned to charge them. So the two deities, standing upon the Floating Bridge of Heaven pushed down the jeweled spear and stirred with it, whereupon, when they had stirred the brine till it went curdle-curdle, and drew the spear up, the brine that dripped down from the end of the spear was piled up and became an island. This is the Island of Onogoro.

Having descended from Heaven on to this island, they saw to the erection of a heavenly august pillar, they saw to the erection of a hall of eight fathoms. Then Izanagi, the Male-Who-Invites, said to Izanami, the Female-Who-Invites, "We should create children"; and he said, "Let us go around the heavenly august pillar, and when we meet on the other side let us be united."[2]

The History of Shinto

9.2.   **Talk about the history of Shinto.**

Shinto Prior to 300 C.E.

According to tradition, the first Japanese emperor was enthroned in the seventh century B.C.E., but most modern scholars agree that the actual history of Japan does not begin until the third century C.E. At that point, the Japanese became known to other nations and began to keep historical records. Therefore, Japan's is among the youngest cultures of all of the Asian nations.

It is difficult to say what the exact worship of the Japanese was prior to this period. The coming of Buddhism in the sixth century C.E. caused the Japanese to collect their various myths and rituals under the title of *kami-no-michi* to distinguish native religion from those religions brought in by the Chinese and Koreans. Prior to this, Japanese worship probably consisted of a loosely organized, widely varying collection of practices. The myths allowed for a limitless number of gods, goddesses, and spirits; ancestor worship; and various forms of animism. Shrines were established throughout the Japanese islands for the worship of the various kami, and shrines were built in individual homes for ancestor and kami worship. Amaterasu and Susa-No-O, the kami of the sea and storms, were probably the most popular kami and received more than their share of attention at the shrines built for them and in private homes. Beyond these very general statements, it is difficult to say anything about Japanese worship in its prehistoric period.

Chinese Influence on Shinto

Early in its history, Japan became an object of interest to Chinese and Korean merchants and missionaries. These persons brought with them much of the older culture of China, including its arts, language, system of writing, and, of course, its various religions and ethical systems. After the fourth century C.E., the Japanese came under the influence of Buddhism, Daoism, and Confucianism. All of these had a lasting effect on Japanese civilization. The *Kojiki* records the entrance of Chinese culture into Japan.

In the years that followed, intercourse between China and Japan greatly increased. Before this period, the Japanese had no written language. They subsequently adopted the Chinese script and many other elements of Chinese culture. Confucian ethics were welcomed because Japan was governed by a feudal system, and Confucianism provided an ethical foundation for the Japanese political system. Ancestor worship had always been practiced in Japan; thus, the Confucian and Daoist elements that emphasized family reverence were readily accepted. The Chinese arts, particularly those connected to Buddhist ritual, were also adopted. Altogether, the period between the fourth and eighth centuries C.E. was one of dramatic change for Japan.

The introduction of Chinese and Korean Buddhism was extremely important in the development of Japanese religion. According to the Japanese chronicles, the emperor was presented with an image of the Buddha and several volumes of Buddhist scripture in 522 C.E. The emperor was delighted, but his advisers warned him that the introduction of a foreign god might arouse the anger of the native kami. Shortly after the introduction of the Buddha, a plague broke out in Japan. The emperor was afraid that the plague was the work of vengeful kami. He had the Buddha image thrown into a canal and the temple built to house it burned. The chronicles explain that the emperor's rejection of the foreign religion brought the plague to an end.

Buddhism could not so easily be turned away from Japan, however. In succeeding generations, other statues of the Buddha were introduced, as well as prayers and rituals. By the end of the sixth century C.E., Mahayana Buddhism had taken a firm foothold in Japan.

Japanese reaction to Buddhism was fourfold. First was the introduction of the name *Shinto* or *kami-no-michi* to distinguish the native Japanese religion from the new foreign religion. This was probably the time at which the Japanese actually began to think of their native worship as a distinct religion.

The second reaction was for the Japanese advocates of Shinto to recognize the many Buddhas and bodhisattvas of Buddhism, but to think of them as the revelation of the kami to the Indian and Chinese people. Naturally, the Buddhists tended to reverse this line of thinking and to identify the kami as Japanese revelations of the Buddhas and bodhisattvas.

The third reaction was Ryobu ("Two-Aspect Shinto"), a combination of Shinto and Buddhism that developed in Japan between the sixth and ninth centuries C.E. An identification gradually developed between the various Shinto kami and the Buddhist deities. Little by little, the boundaries between the two religions disappeared. Buddhist priests began to officiate at Shinto shrines. The rituals performed in these sanctuaries made little distinction between the two religions. Buddhist architectural elements were added to Shinto temples. Generally, Japanese life began to be divided into two spheres. The concerns of day-to-day life became the domain of the Shinto side of the religion, and concerns for the afterlife were served by the Buddhists. Thus, a traditional citizen of Japan might be said to have been born a Shintoist but to have died a Buddhist. For ten centuries, Shinto and Buddhism lived side by side in Japan, each serving a special need of the people.

The fourth reaction of the Japanese to Buddhism was the development of some distinctively Japanese forms of Buddhism. Mahayana Buddhism is an extremely elastic religion, allowing for variations to such a degree that it may be considered a family of religions rather than a single branch of Buddhism. Within a few centuries of the time that Buddhism came to Japan, new variations on the Buddhist theme began to develop. Buddhism had emphasized meditation (*dhyana*) as a means of insight into religious truth. The Chinese Buddhists had picked up this emphasis through the missionary work of Bodhidharma and called their branch of Buddhism Ch'an. The Japanese developed meditative Mahayana Buddhism even further under the name Zen. The Japanese also originated or developed other forms of Buddhism, such as Pure Land and Nichiren.[3] These and other forms of Buddhism became so popular in Japan that even though Shinto was intermingled with them, it was almost forgotten as a viable religion for the Japanese people.

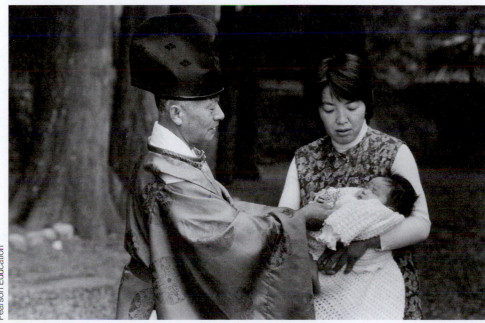

Shinto priest with a mother and child for ceremony after the birth of a baby, Kiso Province, Japan.

Pearson Education

The Revival of Shinto

From the eighth century C.E. onward, Shinto and Buddhism merged to the point that Shinto almost disappeared as an independent religion. Nevertheless, many reformers wished to revise and revitalize the native religion of Japan. As early as the fourteenth century, various scholars tried to point out the strengths of Shinto and restore it to a place of prominence. However, it was not until the seventeenth century and the rise of the Tokugawa regime (1600–1867) that Shinto received official support. In this era, the Japanese were unified by tough-minded military leaders who sought to isolate the nation from outside influences.

The Modern Era

During the Tokugawa era, Japan did its best to avoid foreign influence in any form. It closed itself off from foreign trade, diplomatic missions, and foreign religions. During this period, it attempted to draw only from its native resources. In the meantime, the rest of the world, particularly the West, moved toward industrialization. In 1853, Japan was brought to a sudden confrontation with the modern world when Commodore Perry of the U.S. Navy appeared in Tokyo Bay and asked that the Japanese ports be opened and trade relations established between the United States and Japan. In 1854, Perry appeared again with more ships, troops, and cannons; the Japanese rulers were forced to open their nation to foreigners.

Religion and Public Life

Because Buddhism and Christianity were foreign-born, they were pushed aside; since Shinto was native to Japan, it was given new strength and support by the national government. Large numbers of Christians were executed when they refused to renounce their faith. A Japanese version of Confucianism was the only foreign system that was allowed support during this period, because Confucian ethics were supportive of the militaristic Tokugawa regime.

One of the most colorful aspects of Japanese life during the Tokugawa era was the feudal knight, called **samurai**. Throughout the history of Japan, individual warriors hired themselves out as bodyguards or mercenary soldiers to lords; but in the Tokugawa era, the samurai was idealized and a code of conduct was established for him. In the seventeenth century, the government set up the Chu Hsi (*Shushi*) School of Confucianism as the orthodox model for the conduct of the upper classes. A leader of this school, Yamaga Soko (1622–1685), led in combining Shinto and Confucianism to develop the warrior code called **Bushido**, "the way of the fighting knight." The standard of conduct established for the Japanese feudal knight was similar in many respects to that of the idealized Christian knight of medieval Europe, except for the absence of romantic love. Generally, Bushido may be summarized under the following categories:

1. *The samurai is bound to be loyal to his master in the hierarchy of the feudal system.* The extremes to which this loyalty was carried are best illustrated by one of the most famous stories in Japanese literature, the tale of the forty-seven ronin. In 1702, a certain lord was insulted by a government official. He drew his sword and wounded the official. For this act, the lord was required to commit suicide and his property was confiscated by the government. He had in his employ forty-seven samurai who, because their lord was dead, were officially known as ronin (men without a master). These knights took a vow of vengeance for the injustice brought against their master. To avoid suspicion, they disbanded and acted publicly as if they had no concern for their master. When their enemies ceased to be watchful, they gathered together, attacked the castle of the one who had humiliated their master, and killed him. Then they quietly waited for the government to order them to commit suicide. Thus, the forty-seven ronin became the ideal examples of the loyalty that samurai are to have toward their masters.

2. *The samurai must have great courage in life, in battle, and in his willingness to lay down his life for his master.*

3. *Above all, the samurai is to be a man of honor.* He prefers death to dishonor and is expected to take his own life rather than face a situation in which he is dishonored.

4. *Like a true Confucian, the samurai is expected to be polite to his master and to people in a position of authority.* However, this politeness and gentility did not extend to everyone in

society. There are stories of samurai who felt quite justified in trying out the edge of their swords on peasants if there was no battle at hand. The age-old story of the man who struck a peasant with his sword seven times and had no apparent effect until the peasant fell into eight pieces probably originated in samurai lore.

5. *Despite his attitude toward peasants, the samurai is expected to be a gentleman in every sense of the word.* He is supposed to be benevolent, to right wrongs, and to bring justice to the victims of injustice.

The willingness of the proper samurai to commit suicide rather than face dishonor and the attitude of the Japanese people toward suicide as a whole have long amazed Westerners. Many European religious traditions forbid suicide. In Japan, however, suicide has often been encouraged as a means of avoiding dishonor, as a means of escaping a bad situation, as a means of protest, and in World War II as a very effective means of destroying enemy warships.

In Bushido, the warrior is expected to kill himself in a slow, painful manner called *seppuku*. This is suicide by disembowelment. At the proper time, the warrior is expected to slit open his abdomen so his intestines fall out. This form of death was reserved for warriors and nobility. Women and peasants are forbidden to commit seppuku and were expected to kill themselves in a quicker manner by stabbing themselves in the throat.

The willingness of warriors to die in such a manner for personal honor or for the good of the Japanese nation may seem out of place to the Westerner trained in the sacredness of life and the evils of suicide, but in the coming together of the Shintoist's love of and worship for the nation and its heroic figures and the Confucian's high sense of honor, seppuku is considered very religious.

After a period of some confusion over what role religion was to play in the new Japan, it was decided, in the Constitution of 1889, that the nation would follow the pattern of many Western nations in that there would be a state-supported religion but that all other religions would be allowed to exist and propagate. There would be state-supported Shinto that would essentially consist of patriotic rituals at certain shrines. In addition, those who wished could develop Shinto sects, which would be supported by their adherents. Further, Shinto could be carried on in every home around simple domestic shrines. Beyond these forms of Shinto, any other religion—Buddhism, Christianity, and so on—was free to exist in Japan. However, only the patriotic rituals at the state shrines would receive financial support from the government of Japan.

Torii gate at Hiroshima-Miyajima. The symbol for Shinto is the torii.

Three Forms of Shinto

9.3. **Identify the three forms of Shinto.**

State Shinto

Following the Constitution of 1889, the state took over the support of some 110,000 Shinto shrines and approximately 16,000 priests who tended these shrines throughout the nation. This version of Shinto (sectarian) became known as *Jinja* (shrine) to distinguish it from the more religious *Skuha* versions.

Each shrine supported by the state was dedicated to some local deity, hero, or event; the grand imperial shrine at Ise was dedicated to the mother goddess of Japan, Amaterasu. The visitor approaches the shrine through a distinctive Japanese archway, called a **torii**, which is so inseparably connected to Shinto that it has become known worldwide as its symbol.

A torii and building at the famous Ise Shrine.

The typical major shrine consists of two buildings, an inner and an outer shrine. Both are built of unpainted wood and must be torn down and rebuilt once every twenty years. Anyone may visit the outer shrine, but the inner one is reserved for priests and government officials. The inner shrine contains objects of importance to the deity or event it commemorates. For example, at the grand imperial shrine, the sacred objects are a mirror, sword, and string of beads, all of which are important to the myth of Amaterasu. On certain occasions or holidays, these relics are publicly displayed.

The visitor who enters the outer shrine meditates on the importance of the deity or the event celebrated there and offers a modest offering and perhaps a brief prayer. No one is obligated to visit the shrine, but it is an unwritten assumption that every loyal Japanese citizen will try to visit the shrine at Ise at least once during his or her lifetime.

Religion and Public Life

State Shinto was established to engender patriotism and loyalty toward the nation of Japan. It established a religious foundation for the Japanese nation but had no other religious functions. After the 1889 Constitution, the Japanese government forbade the priests who tended the state shrines and were supported by the state from performing any religious act, such as conducting funerals. The Constitution of 1889 began with these words: "The Empire of Japan shall be reigned over and governed by a line of Emperors unbroken for ages eternal. . . . The Emperor is sacred and inviolable."[4] This constitution also made the military leaders responsible to the emperor rather than to the parliament. State Shinto therefore became an instrument of support for the military in the wars in which Japan participated during the last part of the nineteenth century and the first part of the twentieth. It was particularly supportive of the Japanese war effort during World War II. Shinto had become such an inseparable part of Japanese militarism that the American occupation forces felt it necessary to abolish state support for Shinto in December 1945. In January 1946, the occupation forces directed the emperor to issue a statement declaring that he was not divine.[5]

Since 1945, the shrines once supported by the Japanese government have continued to exist but are now sustained by the financial support of private citizens. Immediately following World War II, attendance at these shrines dropped off and many fell into disuse. In the ensuing years, however, interest in them revived.

Sectarian Shinto

With the developments of the Meiji era (1868–1912), specifically when the government treated Shinto as a nationistic and militaristic institution, the religious side of Shinto was forced to identify itself separately and find its own support, as were all other religions in Japan.

The major sects of Shinto may be divided into three categories. First are the sects whose primary emphasis is on mountain worship. The beautiful, graceful mountains of Japan have always been objects of reverence to its people. At some point in time, it became popular for people to climb the mountains during seasonal pilgrimages, in a combination of nature worship and asceticism. Some made exhausting climbs from the valleys to the peaks, while others took up temporary dwellings in the mountains for ascetic purposes. Mountains Ontake and Fuji were the special favorites for these purposes. During the Meiji era, three groups dedicated to nature worship and asceticism became established Shinto sects.

A second category developed from the basic practices of shamanism and divination of the Japanese peasants. The basic appeal of these sects in modern Japan is their promise of faith healing. Representative of such sects is **Tenrikyo** (Teaching of Heavenly Reason). Tenrikyo was founded in the nineteenth century by a peasant named Nakayama Miki (1798–1887). When she was forty-one years old, she felt she was possessed by the kami of Divine Reason. She believed she had been miraculously healed from a serious illness and began to teach others as a result of this experience. Her religion emphasized various elements that had always been a part of the basic religion of the Japanese peasant, such as shamanism, ecstatic dance, and faith healing. Today, this sect emphasizes volunteer labor for public charity and, of course, faith healing.

A third type of sectarian Shinto includes sects that focus on personal purification. When the rulers of Japan took over the shrines of Shinto in the Meiji era and used them for political purposes, this left behind a basic residue of the religious tradition of Shinto, its mythology, and its rituals. Three major sects developed to emphasize these religious elements and revived the myths of the origin of Japan from the ancient chronicles. They believed that there were religious, ethical, and political aspects to Shinto. They emphasized purification of the body through fasting, breath control, bathing in cold water, and chanting. Today, these sects seem to be losing ground among the people of Japan, whereas groups like Tenrikyo are growing.

Domestic Shinto

In addition to the organized forms of sectarian State Shinto is another, more basic form that takes place in many Japanese homes. The basic unit or symbol of domestic Shinto is the **kami-dana** (god shelf), which is found in many Japanese homes. The kami-dana, whether it is elaborate or simple, contains the symbols of whatever may be of religious significance to the family. It usually contains the names of the ancestors of the family, because a part of the religion of the household is filial piety. The kami-dana might contain statues of the kami that have been beneficial to the family or are highly regarded. In the homes and shops of many Japanese artisans are the images of the various patron deities. The literature of Japan contains many stories of skilled workers creating masterpieces under the direction of an unseen patron kami.

The traditional kami-dana contains objects that have been bought at the great shrines, such as the one at Ise. Any object the family considers sacred is fit for veneration at the god shelf. There is a story that the kami-dana in one household contained the cast-off shoes of a man who had been a benefactor of the household when it was in trouble. The shoes were believed to be symbolic of the friend's goodness or to contain the *kami* that prompted the good deeds. At any rate, they became objects of veneration.

Paul Fusco/Magnum Photos

Fortune prayers are tied to a fence at the Shinto temple in Kyoto.

Worship at the kami-dana in the Japanese home is a simple affair. Offerings of flowers, lanterns, incense, food, and drink may be placed before this altar each day. A simple daily service in which the worshipers wash their hands, make an offering, clap their hands as a symbol of communication with the spirits, and offer a brief prayer may also be held here. On such special occasions as holidays, weddings, or anniversaries, more elaborate ceremonies may be held at the kami-dana. However, if the occasion is decidedly religious—a funeral, for example—the Japanese family turns not to the Shinto deities or priest but to the Buddhist priest. In the special religious environment of Japan, Shinto is for this life but Buddhism is for the life beyond. Therefore, in addition to their kami-dana, many Japanese homes have a *butsu-dan*, a Buddhist household altar, where worship of the Buddhist deities is also held.

As we have seen, Shinto, the native religion of Japan, is many things to many people. To some Japanese, it is a set of myths and rituals that remind them of the special origin of their nation. They are occasionally reminded of these myths and rituals on national holidays or during visits to a national shrine. Religion in terms of more regular worship and a concern for the future life is likely to be Buddhism. To those who are members of specific Shinto religious sects, Shinto may be related to faith healing, ascetic practices, or purification of the body. To many rural families of Japan, Shinto includes the daily worship that is carried on in the home at the kami-dana and contains elements of ancestor worship and animism.

Japanese Festivals

9.4. **Describe the traditional Japanese festivals.**

Traditional Japanese holidays are a combination of secular, agricultural, Buddhist, and Shinto celebrations. At times, one tradition or religion dominates; at others, all sources blend together. Various festivals are held at local Shinto shrines throughout the year.

New Year (Shogatsu)

The most widely celebrated holiday is the Japanese New Year. In the past, when a lunar calendar was used, this holiday was kept in February, but today, it is celebrated January 1 through January 6. During this period, businesses close and people gather with their families. Each family purifies and cleans the house in preparation for the new year. On New Year's Eve, special food is eaten and offerings are made to the ancestors. At Buddhist temples at midnight, gongs are struck 108 times for 108 kinds of passions to be purged in the new year. On New Year's Day, families visit places of worship. Some go to Buddhist temples, but most go to Shinto shrines. At the end of the season, the New Year's decorations are burned in bonfires.

Buddha's Birthday

In Japan, Buddha's birthday is celebrated on April 8. At Buddhist temples, the priests pour flowers and sweet tea over the statues of the Buddha as a remembrance that on the day of his birth flowers and sweet tea came down from heaven. December 8 is celebrated as the traditional day of the Buddha's enlightenment. Zen Buddhists participate in an all-night meditation to welcome this day.

All Souls' Day (Ullambana)

Among Japanese Buddhists, Ullambana (the festival for dead ancestors) is celebrated in mid-July. As in other Buddhist nations, this holiday is an occasion to welcome the spirits of the dead into homes. In this season, the graves are swept and decorated. It also is a time of parades, dancing, and bonfires.

Autumn Festival (Niiname-sai)

A combination agricultural and Shinto holiday is Niiname-sai, celebrated on November 23 and 24. At this time, the emperor offers the first fruits of the autumn harvest to Amaterasu and the other kami at Ise. Although this is the national festival of the harvest, various local thanksgiving ceremonies are held throughout Japan during October and November.

Shinto Today

9.5.   **Analyze the practice of Shinto today.**

Following the defeat of Japan at the end of World War II, several events occurred that made the future of Shinto uncertain. The most direct threat to this religion was the removal of official government support for state Shinto. The second threat came from Japan's rapid industrialization. Within a few decades, Japanese industry and science caught up to most Western nations and, in many cases, surpassed it. In this environment of quick movement into the twentieth, and now the twenty-first, centuries, it would seem that an ancient religion like Shinto would have little chance of survival. In addition to a struggle with the modern world, Shinto faced its old rival, Buddhism. Most Japanese think of themselves as being primarily Buddhist. Shinto is viewed as a secondary practice. Therefore, one might think that Shinto, with its ancient myths, rituals, and shrines, would quickly fade away.

But Shinto has not faded at all. It is as strong as ever in Japan today. It has survived the withdrawal of support by the state and continues to exist on private donations. New Shinto sects, which emphasize faith healing, positive thinking, and chanting, have been accepted by millions of Japanese. In some cases, adherents of these new forms of Shinto have entered politics and taken up the causes of certain labor unions. The new forms of Shinto have also provided an outlet for the religious aspirations of urban people, helping them cope with the day-to-day stress of modern life. Therefore, Shinto, in its many forms, still remains an important force in Japanese culture.

Think About It

1. Who are the kami, and what is their significance to Shinto?
2. What effect did the entrance of the Chinese and of Buddhism into Japan have on Shinto?
3. What are the three forms of Shinto? Describe each.
4. Describe two of the traditional Japanese holidays and their individual characteristics.
5. List the three forms of Shinto in modern Japan.

Suggested Reading

Anesaki, Masaharu. *Religious Life of the Japanese People.* Tokyo: The Society for International Cultural Relations, 1961.

Davis, Winston. *Dojo Magic and Exorcism in Modern Japan.* Stanford: Stanford University Press, 1980.

de Bary, William I., ed. *Sources of Japanese Tradition.* New York: Columbia University Press, 1958.

Earhart, H. Byron, ed. *Religion in the Japanese Experience: Sources and Interpretations.* Encino, Calif.: Dickenson, 1974.

_____, ed. *Japanese Religion: Unity and Diversity*, 2nd ed. Encino, Calif.: Dickenson, 1974.

Kitagawa, Joseph M. *Religion in Japanese History.* New York: Columbia University Press, 1966.

Nelson, John. *A Year in the Life of a Shinto Shrine.* Seattle: University of Washington Press, 1996.

Ross, Floyd Hiatt. *Shinto, the Way of Japan.* Boston: Beacon Press, 1965.

Yamamoto, Yukitaka. *Way of the Kami.* Stockton, Calif.: Tsubaki American Publications, 1987.

Source Material

Shinto Myths

The *Kojiki* (The Records of Ancient Matters) contain the myths of ancient Japan. These chronicles were compiled in the seventh and eighth centuries C.E. at a time when Japan was being deeply influenced by Chinese Buddhism. At that time, the Japanese felt a need to remember their own heritage.[6]

Myths Regarding the Plain of High Heaven

BIRTH OF KAMI The names of the Deities [kami] that were born in the Plain of High Heaven when the Heaven and Earth began were the Deity Master-of-the-August-Centre-of-Heaven, next the High-August-Producing-Wondrous Deity, next the Divine-Producing-Wondrous-Deity. These three Deities were all Deities born alone, and hid their persons. The names of the Deities that were born next from a thing that sprouted up like unto a reed-shoot when the earth, young and like unto floating oil, drifted about medusa-like, were the Pleasant-Reed-Shoot-Prince-Elder Deity, next the Heavenly-Eternally-Standing-Deity. These two Deities were likewise born alone, and hid their persons.

The names of the Deities that were born next were the Earthly-Eternally-Standing-Deity, next the Luxuriant-Integrating-Master-Deity. These two Deities were likewise Deities born alone, and hid their persons. The names of the Deities that were born next were the Deity Mud-Earth-Lord next his younger sister the Deity Mud-Earth-Lady; next the Germ-Integrating-Deity, next his younger sister the Life-Integrating-Deity; next the Deity Elder-of-the-Great-Place, next his younger sister the Deity Elder-Lady-of-the-Great-Place; next the Deity Perfect-Exterior, next his younger sister the Deity Oh-Awful-Lady; next the Deity the Male-Who-Invites [Izanagi], next his younger sister the Deity the Female-Who-Invites [Izanami].

BIRTH OF OTHER KAMI When [Izanagi and Izanami] had finished giving birth to countries, they began afresh giving birth to Deities. So the name of the Deity they gave birth to was the Deity Great-Male-of-the-Great-Thing; next they gave birth to the Deity Rock-Earth-Prince; next they gave birth to the Deity Rock-Nest-Princess; next they gave birth to the Deity Great-Door-Sun-Youth; next they gave birth to the Deity Heavenly-Blowing-Male; next they gave birth to the Deity Great-House-Prince; next they gave birth to the

Deity Youth-of-the-Wind-Breath-the-Great-Male; next they gave birth to the Sea-Deity, whose name is the Deity Great-Ocean-Possessor; next they gave birth to the Deity of the Water-Gates, whose name is the Deity Prince-of-Swift-Autumn; next they gave birth to his younger sister the Deity Princess-of-Swift-Autumn.

The Conflict between Amaterasu and the Storm God Susa-No-O

The following selection from the Nihongi, I, 40NN45, relates the tale of a struggle between Amaterasu and her kinsman, Susa-No-O. It explains some of the features of the cult of Amaterasu.[7]

> After this, Susa-No-O Mikoto's behavior was exceedingly rude. In what way? Amaterasu (the Heaven-shining Deity) had made august rice fields of Heavenly narrow rice fields and Heavenly long rice fields. Then Susa-No-O, when the seed was sown in spring, broke down the divisions between the plots of rice, and in autumn let loose the Heavenly piebald colts, and made them lie down in the midst of the rice fields. Again, when he saw that Amaterasu was about to celebrate the feast of first-fruits, he secretly voided excrement in the New palace. Moreover, when he saw that Amaterasu was in her sacred weaving hall, engaged in weaving garments of the Gods, he flayed a piebald colt of Heaven, and breaking a hole in the roof tiles of the hall, flung it in. Then Amaterasu started with alarm, and wounded herself with the shuttle. Indignant of this, she straightway entered the Rock cave of Heaven, and having fastened the Rock-door, dwelt therein in seclusion. Therefore constant darkness prevailed on all sides, and the alternation of night and day was unknown.
>
> Then the eighty myriads of gods met on the bank of the tranquil River of Heaven, and considered in what manner they should supplicate her. Accordingly Omoio-kane no Kami, with profound device and far-reaching thought, at length gathered long-singing birds of the Eternal Land and made them utter their prolonged cry to one another. Moreover he made ta-ji-kara-o to stand beside the Rock door. The Ame no Koyane no Mikoto, ancestor of the Nakatomi Deity Chieftains, and Futo-dama no Mikoto, ancestor of the Imibe Chieftains, dug up a five-hundred branched True Sakaki tree of the Heavenly Mount Kagu. On its upper branches they hung an august five-hundred string of Yasaka jewels. On the middle branches they hung an eight-hand mirror. On its lower branches they hung blue soft offerings and white soft offerings. Then they recited their liturgy together.
>
> Moreover Ama no Uzume no Mikoto, ancestress of the Sarume Chieftain, took in her hand a spear wreathed with Eulalia grass, and standing before the door of the Rock-cave of Heaven, skillfully performed a mimic dance. She took, moreover, the true Sakaki tree of the Heavenly Mount Kagu, and made of it a head-dress, she took club moss and made of it braces, she kindled fires, she placed a tub bottom upwards, and gave forth a divinely-inspired utterance.
>
> Now Amaterasu heard this, and said: "Since I have shut myself up in the Rock-cave, there ought surely to be continual night in the Central Land of fertile reed-plains. How then can Ama no Uzume no Mikoto be so jolly?" So with her august hand, she opened for a narrow space the Rock-door and peeped out. Then Ta-jikara-o no Kami forthwith took Amaterasu by the hand and led her out. Upon this the Gods Nakatomi no Kami and Imibe no Kami at once drew a limit by means of a bottom-tied rope (also called a left-handed rope) and begged her not to return again (into the cave).
>
> After this, all the gods put the blame on Susa-No-O, and imposed on him a fine of one thousand tables, and so at length chastised him. They also had his hair plucked out, and made him therewith expiate his guilt.

Part IV
Religions Originating in the Middle East

Two religions considered in this section, Christianity and Islam, have more adherents than any other religions, sharing almost half of the world's population between them. Their influence on the values and aspirations of humanity is therefore enormous, and a basic knowledge of them is essential. These two giant missionary religions arose from the milieu of the ancient Middle East, which first produced Judaism. It was from this religion that Christianity and Islam drew much of their worldview, ethics, and especially their concept of world history, beginning with a creation and ending with a divine judgment. Baha'i grew out of Islam in the nineteenth century. Study of these religions is essential for the student to be truly aware of the past and future of many of the people of planet Earth.

Judaism—Basic Teachings

Judaism Is Based on the Assumption That There Is a Covenant between God and the Jewish People

Over the centuries, interpretations of this teaching have taken many forms. The Hebrew Bible mentions God appearing to or talking with Abraham and other patriarchs. It also describes the ways in which he destroys the enemies of the Jewish people and punishes them when they are disobedient. The covenant is also interpreted politically because the Hebrew Bible describes the territory on the east shore of the Mediterranean Sea as the "Promised Land."

Prophets Were the Moral Voice of Ancient Israel

Prophets often denounced the wicked ways of all classes of people, including kings, and called on them to comply with the term of the covenant. They also offered hope in troubled times, including the period of the Babylonian exile.

Contemporary Judaism Has a Complex Legal Tradition

Part of this tradition concerns the Sabbath and dietary laws. Jews are forbidden to work on the Sabbath (Saturday). For some, this means that even simple acts such as turning on lights is prohibited. Dietary laws regulate the ways in which animals are slaughtered and what foods can be eaten. Pork and shellfish are prohibited, as is mixing milk and meat. Foods that are allowable are known as Kosher.

Jews Have Suffered from Oppression—Primarily by Christians—for Centuries

In Europe during the Middle Ages, there were restrictions on where Jews could live and what work they could do. They were expelled from several European countries. Many moved to Muslim lands to avoid persecution. Zionism, a movement seeking a Jewish homeland, developed as a result of continued persecution in the nineteenth and twentieth centuries. The worst case was the Holocaust, in which the Nazis murdered approximately six million Jews.

Contemporary Judaism Is Extremely Diverse

Orthodox Judaism is a variant that stresses dietary laws and the Sabbath. It requires that men and women be separated in the synagogue. Reform Judaism is the most liberal variant. Few Reform Jews are concerned with dietary laws. They do not require separation of the sexes in worship services. Conservative Judaism is located between these extremes. Some Conservative Jews "keep Kosher." Their Sabbath restrictions are milder than those of the Orthodox, and they make more extensive use of vernacular languages in worship services. There are also large numbers of secular Jews, for whom Judaism is a cultural rather than religious identity.

Christianity—Basic Teachings
Christianity Is Based on a Belief in the Unique Character of Jesus of Nazareth, and That by His Death and Resurrection He Provided for the Redemption of Humanity

Jesus's life story and teachings are the subject of the four Gospels. They place him in the context of the first-century C.E. Judaism. His ministry is described as a combination of preaching, healing, and teaching. It is not clear that Jesus saw himself as the founder of a new religion. Many Christian rituals, including baptism and the Lord's Supper, are based on episodes in his biography.

Paul Was among the Most Important of the Early Christian Missionaries

Paul was at first strongly anti-Christian and joined in early persecutions. He was converted when he was struck down by a light from Heaven. He did much to establish Christianity as a distinct religion and carried its message to non-Jews.

In 313 C.E., Christianity Was Legalized by the Roman Emperor Constantine

It rapidly became the official religion of the Roman Empire. As the empire collapsed in western Europe, the bishop of Rome, or the pope, came to be increasingly important.

His authority was not accepted by the churches of the eastern part of the empire. This and ritual differences led to the division of the church into Eastern Orthodox and Roman Catholic branches in 1054 C.E.

The Protestant Reformation Initiated by Martin Luther in 1517 Split the Western Church, and Led Ultimately to the Formation of Thousands of Protestant Denominations

Martin Luther sought to purify the church, which in his day was notoriously corrupt. He taught that the Scripture and reason were the only sources of religious authority, and that all Christians should read and interpret the Bible. He also taught that faith was the only source of salvation and that rituals were useless. He rejected the veneration of saints, an important part of the Roman Catholic and Orthodox faiths. A second great reformer was John Calvin, who broke with the Roman Catholic Church in 1534. His teachings emphasized the utter sovereignty of God and the depravity of human beings.

Islam—Basic Teachings

Islam Is Based on the Life and Teachings of the Prophet Muhammad

Islam means "Submission to God." *Allah* is the Arabic word for God, the same God worshiped by Jews and Christians. The Prophet Muhammad was born about 570 C.E. Tradition holds that he received his first revelation from God in 610, a process that continued until his death in 632 C.E. Together, these revelations are the Qur'an, which Muslims believe to be the speech of God.

Muhammad Was the Political Leader of the Muslim Community as Well as a Prophet

Following years of persecution, he led the Muslim community from Mecca to Medina in what is now Saudi Arabia in 622 C.E. For the next eight years, there was intense and often violent conflict with the people of Mecca, who sought to destroy the new religion. Mecca was taken in 630 C.E. and Islam rapidly became the religion of almost all Arabs.

Following the Death of the Prophet Muhammad, Islam Entered a Period of Expansion That Continues Today

Although it originated in Arabia, today only a small minority of Muslims are Arabs. Most Muslims are found in South and Southeast Asian countries. Today, Islam is expanding in Africa, Europe, and North America.

Like Judaism, Islam Has a Rich Tradition of Dietary Laws

Muslims are prohibited from eating pork, birds of prey, dogs, donkeys, and mules, and from drinking alcohol and gambling. They must also abstain from eating, drinking, and engaging in sexual acts between dawn and sunset during the month of Ramadan.

The Most Basic Sectarian Dispute Is That between Sunnis and Shi'ites

This division is based on an early dispute concerning leadership of the Muslim community. The Sunni maintain that decisions about leadership are the prerogative of the Muslim community; the Shi'ites believe that it should be in the hands of imams, who were descendants of the Prophet Muhammad. Since the death of Husayn, the grandson of the Prophet Muhammad, in the Battle of Karbala in 680 C.E., the division between them has been bitter, often sparking sectarian violence. Approximately 85 percent of Muslims are Sunni; 15 percent are Shi'ite. The Shi'ite are concentrated in Iran and Iraq.

The Most Basic Aspects of Muslim Ritual Are the Five Pillars

The first is accepting the confession of faith: There is no God but God and Muhammad is the messenger of God. The others are the five daily prayers, fasting during the month of Ramadan, charity, and pilgrimage to Mecca (for those who can afford it).

Baha'i—Basic Teachings

Baha'i Began as a Sect of Shi'ite Islam

It was founded in 1863 C.E. in Persia (Iran) by Husayn Ali. The Baha'i have been persecuted in Iran throughout their history. In part because of flight from persecution, and in part from missionary ventures, the faith has spread throughout the world.

The Baha'i Quickly Began to Think of Themselves as a Distinct, Universal Religion

The most basic Baha'i teaching is that all religions come from the same source. It teaches the revelation is a continuous process. It maintains that there have been numerous revelations in the past, including those of the Buddha, Jesus, and Muhammad, and that there will be more in the future.

Baha'i emphasizes modernity and social reform. All forms of religious persecution are condemned. Gender equality, the harmony of religion and science, modern education, social and economic justice, and the establishment of world peace are emphasized.

Baha'i Ritual Practices Are Similar to Those of Islam

There are three required daily prayers. In another sense, the totality of life should be understood as prayer. There is an annual fasting period of nineteen days, during which eating and drinking are prohibited between dawn and sunset. Marriage requires the consent of both sets of parents.

Chapter 10
Judaism

Learning Objectives

After reading this chapter, you should be able to:

10.1 Discuss in detail the ancient Israelite religion and the history of the growth of the Hebrew Bible.

10.2 Analyze the influence of the period during which Hebrew worship was centralized by the Hebrew monarchy and the building of the temple.

10.3 Understand the impact of the exile of the Jewish people and their return to Jerusalem after the Babylonian captivity.

10.4 Analyze the Diaspora and the development of rabbinic Judaism.

10.5 Understand how Islam impacted Judaism during the medieval era.

10.6 Discuss Judaism after the fifteenth century and why many Jews became refugees.

10.7 Analyze Jewish responses to modernity.

10.8 Recognize the modern divisions and religious practices in Judaism.

10.9 Identify and explain the significance of Jewish festivals and holy days.

10.10 Understand the issues faced by modern Jews and Judaism as a whole.

A Timeline of Judaism

1812	Traditional date for the birth of Abraham
1312	Traditional date of the Exodus from Egypt
1000–586	Approximate dates of the biblical Israelite kingdoms
1200–400	Period in which the Torah was compiled
825	Construction of First Temple completed
586	Destruction of First Temple; beginning of Babylonian exile
537	Persians allow return from exile
352	Construction of Second Temple
63	Roman conquest of Israel
70 C.E.	Romans destroy Second Temple; Jewish population dispersed the Roman Empire
219	Completion of the Mishnah
499	Completion of the Talmud
1492	Jews expelled from Spain; many find refuge in Muslim lands
1791–1917	Emancipation of Jews from legal discrimination in most of Europe

1938	Beginning of the Holocaust
1948	Establishment of the modern state of Israel; many Palestinian Muslims flee or are forced into exile
1948–present	Political conflict between religious and secular Jews in Israel
1967	Israel occupies East Jerusalem and the West Bank territories
1972	First female rabbis ordained

Key Terms

anti-Semitism

Bible

Diaspora

Exodus

Holocaust

Mishnah

rabbi

synagogue

Talmud

temple

Torah

One of the most perplexing problems that arises in any discussion of Judaism is its definition. If we were to define Judaism as we define any other religion, we might say that a Jew is anyone who adheres to a certain set of Jewish religious beliefs or practices. Indeed, in many cases this may be a very effective definition. Unfortunately, the issue has been clouded, so it is not always so simple. Alan W. Miller, in his introduction to *The God of Daniel S.: In Search of the American Jew*, lists eight different types of persons who are called Jews in American society. These range all the way from the extremely orthodox Hasidic Jew to the person whose parents or grandparents happened to be born Jewish. In the modern nation of Israel, a continuing and perplexing problem is "Who is a Jew?"

Judaism cannot be defined primarily in terms of religious beliefs, because some people are called Jews but consider themselves atheists. Adolf Hitler found it expedient to define Judaism in terms of race, but Jewish people display the physical characteristics of nearly every race. There are European Jews, African Jews, and Asian Jews. Nor can Judaism be defined in linguistic or ethnic terms. Jewish people have spoken and written many languages and have acquired much of the cultures of the lands in which they have dwelt.

If we cannot define Judaism in terms of all people who might be called Jews, we can speak of those people who identify themselves with the religion of Judaism. Although religious practices differ widely among Jews, generally the unifying feature among all Jews is a belief in the oneness of a God who works in and through historical events and who has in some manner chosen the Jewish people as agents. Numerous forms of Judaism are built around this basic principle.

Ancient Israelite Religion

10.1. **Discuss in detail the ancient Israelite religion and the history of the growth of the Hebrew Bible.**

Because Judaism is concerned with God's activity in history, it is necessary to describe Jewish beliefs and practices historically. According to Jewish sacred writings, known as the **Bible**, God found it necessary to call out one man and woman and their family from all the people on Earth. This calling of Abraham and Sarah is recorded in Genesis 12. It came after a series of disastrous dealings with all humankind (Adam and Eve, Cain and Abel, the Flood, the Tower of Babel, and so on). Because of these disasters, God chose to communicate with only one nation, the descendants of Abraham and Sarah.

According to the book of Genesis in the Bible, Abraham was promised that he would become the father of a great nation, possess a land, and become a blessing to all people if he were faithful to his part of a covenant with God. Abraham is succeeded in this covenant by his son Isaac, his grandson Jacob (or Israel), and Jacob's twelve sons. The biblical narratives present these ancient Israelites, as they came to be known, as nomads, following their flocks from place to place.

The Bible does not give the reader a systematic presentation of the religious beliefs and practices of the ancient Israelites, but it does reveal a great deal about their theology. They worshiped one God who guided their destinies. The generic name for God among ancient Semitic peoples was El. This name is frequently used in various combinations in the patriarchal literature to refer to their God. The God is called El Shaddai (God of the mountains), El Elyon (God Most High), El Olam (God Everlasting), and most frequently, Elohim (Gods).[1] This God was worshiped by burning animal sacrifices on altars built in the open. The Israelites apparently did not worship their God in a building or temple until the time of Solomon (961–922 B.C.E.).

From very early on in the worship of the ancient Israelites, male circumcision was practiced. Genesis traces the ritual back to a commandment of God to Abraham (Genesis 17:10, 11). However, circumcision is a very ancient and widespread religious custom, which probably did not originate with Abraham. In addition, the practice of keeping a Sabbath may have been a part of the worship of the ancient Israelites. Genesis attaches the custom to the days of creation, when God rested on the seventh day after laboring for six days (Genesis 2:2).

Exodus

Whatever their religious practices may have been, and whatever gods they may have worshiped, the stories of the first Israelites exist in Genesis to provide the reader with the context of the most important event in Judaism—the **Exodus**. God promised Abraham and Sarah that a great nation would arise from them, that this nation would have a homeland (Canaan), and that the entire world would be blessed by this nation. The Book of Genesis closes with a great nation springing up from the descendants of Abraham and Sarah, but they were not in Canaan. They were in Egypt, where they were bound in slavery. Therefore, the Exodus from Egypt and their slavery, the journey back to Canaan, and the conquest of the land had to be accomplished before God's promise could be fulfilled. The events and characters of the Exodus became the heart and soul of the Jewish religion. God acted to save his chosen people, the Israelites, miraculously delivered them from slavery (from the most powerful nation in the world at that time), revealed to the leaders the divine name and laws, and finally brought the former slaves, as a conquering army, into Canaan. These events are remembered annually in the various major holidays of Judaism. The legal material, which is attributed to the Sinai experience, became the most important material in the Hebrew Bible.

The Book of Exodus opens with the descendants of Abraham and Sarah, the Israelites, crying out for deliverance from their enslavement by the Egyptians.[2] The key figure in this drama of salvation is Moses.

Menorah in front of the Knesset, Israel's parliament. The seven-branched candelabrum is one of the oldest symbols of Judaism.

Fabian von Poser/imagebroker/Alamy

Ancient Israel

Modern Israel and Neighboring Nations

Like many great figures in religion, Moses was endangered as an infant by the forces of evil and was miraculously delivered. He was rescued and reared by the daughter of the pharaoh of Egypt. After recognizing his Israelite heritage and killing an Egyptian in defense of a slave, Moses was exiled to the Sinai Desert, where he lived for forty years as a shepherd. In the desert, the God of Abraham was revealed to Moses and spoke through a bush that burned but was not consumed. The God declared that his name was YHWH and commanded Moses to lead the Israelites from their slavery. At this stage of Israelite history, many scholars think that YHWH was the Israelites' tribal god in at least some competition with other nearby deities. Moses returned to Egypt and, after a series of ten miraculous plagues upon the Egyptians, was able to gain the release of the Israelites and thus prove the power of the Israelites' god over that of their rivals. The final plague was death to the firstborn of every house in Egypt. Israelites who ate a sacred meal of roasted lamb, bitter herbs, and unleavened bread and who smeared lamb's blood on their doorposts were passed over by the angel of death.

When the Israelites fled Egypt, they were pursued by the pharaoh, who had changed his mind about their release. The waters of the Sea of Reeds were parted by YHWH, and the Israelites crossed through on dry land.[3] When the Egyptians attempted to follow them, the waters returned and the Egyptians were trapped and drowned. This event, along with the Passover, became a part of Jewish history—an act in which God intervened to deliver his chosen people.

Sinai and the Law

The next significant event was the giving of the law on Mt. Sinai. After crossing the Sea of Reeds, the Israelites came to Mt. Sinai on their journey to Canaan. From this mountain, YHWH communicated the law to the Israelites through Moses. Ten absolute laws that are basic to Jewish life—the Ten Commandments—are found in Exodus 20:1–17 and in Deuteronomy 5:6–21. They may be summarized as follows:

From the Source

1. I am the LORD* your God, who brought you out of the land of Egypt, out of the house of bondage. You shall have no other gods before me.
2. You shall not make for yourselves an idol
3. You shall not take the name of the LORD your God in vain, for the LORD will not hold him guiltless who takes his name in vain.
4. Remember the Sabbath day, to keep it holy.
5. Honor your father and your mother.

6. You shall not murder.
7. You shall not commit adultery.
8. You shall not steal.
9. You shall not give false testimony against your neighbor.
10. You shall not covet your neighbor's house . . . nor anything that is your neighbor's.[4]

*Bible verses in this chapter have been modified from the World English Bible. "Yahweh" has been changed to "LORD".

Basically, these commandments stress obedience and loyalty to YHWH and proper behavior toward members of the community. The books of Exodus and Leviticus and portions of Numbers and Deuteronomy elaborate codes of law that regulate every area of life. These laws are purported to have been given by God through Moses during the wilderness experience, but many of them reflect a community that has been established in agricultural life for centuries.

Whenever they may have been codified, the legal material in the **Torah** (the first five books of the Bible) became the single most important part of the Bible for Judaism. It is to this material that Jews have turned for centuries, looking for inspiration and guidance. This material became the basis for the later Mishnah and **Talmud**, which in turn became central for Judaism. It is at this point that Judaism is defined as a religion of the law and Jews as a people primarily concerned with obedience to the laws of God.

Post-Sinai Religious Institutions

In addition to the laws of God, the years in the Sinai wilderness gave the Israelites two other religious institutions, the Ark of the Covenant and the Tent of Meeting. The Ark of the Covenant was an ornate chest that contained the sacred relics of the Exodus and may have been the portable throne of YHWH. The ark was the most treasured sacred possession of the Israelites and was eventually placed in Solomon's temple, in the Holy of Holies, in the tenth century B.C.E. It presumably remained there until the temple was destroyed by the Babylonians in 586 B.C.E. The Tent of Meeting was not as popular or long-lived as the Ark. It was literally a tent that could be moved from place to place with the nomadic Israelites. It provided a place to worship YHWH. After the Israelites entered Canaan, it is mentioned only once in connection with the cult at Shiloh.

After their period of wandering in the wilderness, the Bible records that the Israelites conquered the territories on the East Bank of the Jordan River. Then, under the leadership of Joshua, Moses's successor, they crossed the Jordan and conquered the cities of Canaan. Two conflicting accounts are given. According to the Book of Joshua, the Israelites swept across the country and destroyed the Canaanites. The Book of Judges tells another story, however. Here we have a picture of the worshipers of YHWH living side by side with the native dwellers of Canaan, and sometimes even being subject to them. Later events seem to support the second story.

When the Israelites settled in Canaan, they renewed their covenant with YHWH. The cult of YHWH, its ark, its priests, and its sacrifices were centered in Shiloh. Worship at this time seems to have been

Rafael Ben-Ari/Alamy

An Israeli family prays at the start of their Seder dinner celebrating the traditional week-long festival of Passover, which commemorates the Israelite Exodus from Egypt.

a rather informal matter. The cultic priests attended to those who came on special days to the sanctuary for special needs. They were in turn supported by the gifts of those who came to worship and perhaps by the donations of the various tribal groups surrounding the cult center.

The Hebrew Monarchy and the Temple

10.2. **Analyze the influence of the period during which Hebrew worship was centralized by the Hebrew monarchy and the building of the temple.**

The religion of Israel took a more formal turn when David became the first truly effective king of the Israelites. David, who was from the southern portion of the country, needed a central capital and a cult to unify his nation. He captured Jerusalem in the central hill country and made it his capital. Jerusalem had little to recommend it except its location, its easily defended hills, and perhaps a history as a sacred site. David's decisions and actions, as well as later historical events, parlayed these features and made Jerusalem one of the most important, most disputed cities in the world. David's abilities as a military leader and administrator helped Israel develop into a fairly powerful and wealthy small nation of the ancient Middle East. Hebrew scripture indicates that David wished to build a magnificent **temple** in Jerusalem but was forbidden by YHWH.

It remained for Solomon, David's son and successor, to build the temple. With all the wealth his father had amassed, Solomon built a palace for himself and a temple for his God. The temple not only centralized worship of Israel's god YHWH, it also had the effect of consolidating the monarchy's political seat of power in Jerusalem. The Ark of the Covenant was placed in the temple, and a class of priests was attached to the temple. Worship of YHWH thus took on a more formal status. The main form of worship remained the animal sacrifice, with its flesh burned in the courtyard. In the temple, prayers were offered to YHWH, and if the example of David is typical, there may also have been sacred dancing before the Ark (II Samuel 6:14).

The Prophetic Movement

In addition to the priests who oversaw worship at the Jerusalem temple, prophets also arose in this period. Unlike the priests, whose duties involved the proper offerings of sacrifices, the prophets of ancient religions danced, sang, breathed incense, and worked themselves into an ecstatic state to hear the voices of their gods. The prophets of Israel may have begun in this fashion.[5] They healed the sick, cursed, blessed, and produced food for their followers, and worked other miracles.[6] One of the prophets' most important roles in ancient Israelite religion was to point out infractions of the law and to plead for a return to justice. The language they used often threatened exile and destruction for the people if they did not return to righteous adherence to proper observance of the law. Likewise, blessings were promised for those who upheld the proper standards, cared for the poor and the oppressed, and recalled their reliance on YHWH.

From the Source

The LORD says:

"For three transgressions of Israel, yes, for four,
"I will not turn away its punishment;
because they have sold the righteous for silver,
and the needy for a pair of shoes;
They trample on the dust of the earth on the head of the poor,
and deny justice to the oppressed."[7]

Seek good, and not evil,
that you may live;
and so the LORD, the God of Armies, will be with you,
as you say.
Hate evil, love good,
It may be that the LORD, the God of Armies, will be gracious to the remnant of Joseph.[8]

These are not the words of seers predicting the future but of people who were busy speaking the word of God to their people. Later prophets who addressed the people's exile from the land of Israel and the destruction of the temple would also promise eventual divine deliverance for the people. A *messiah*, a powerful and saving figure, would arise and restore the fortunes of Israel. The prophetic movement of ancient Israel stands out as one of the major moral and literary contributions to any religion of the world.

Exile and Return

10.3. **Understand the impact of the exile of the Jewish people and their return to Jerusalem after the Babylonian captivity.**

In 922 B.C.E., after the reign of Solomon, a rebellion split the nation of Israel into two nations. The northern nation, called Israel, was the larger and more productive of the two. It was destroyed by the Assyrians in 721 B.C.E., and its people disappeared from history. Its population was either killed or deported and enslaved. Whatever their fate, they were never to be a distinctive people of Israel again; they are known as the ten lost tribes.

The southern nation, called Judah (from which the words "Jew" and "Judaism" derive), was made up of the remainder of David's kingdom. Judah survived the Assyrian years but was eventually destroyed by the Neo-Babylonian Empire in 586 B.C.E. With the Babylonian conquest, the city of Jerusalem was destroyed, Solomon's temple was torn down, and the citizens of Judah were either killed or deported. Whereas the northern nation had simply ceased to exist after its destruction, the people of Judah held on to their identity, customs, and religion while in captivity. They were led by a man who was both a prophet and a priest, Ezekiel. Ezekiel and others so forged the identity of the Jews in captivity that when the Persians captured Babylon in 538 B.C.E., many Jews were freed and returned to Jerusalem to re-establish their lives and their temple there.

During the Babylonian captivity, certain theological changes were forced upon the Jews. Previously, they had thought of YHWH as their local deity, perhaps residing in the temple at Jerusalem. Now the temple was destroyed and the people were scattered in a strange land. An unknown poet of that period wrote of their sadness:

From the Source

By the rivers of Babylon, there we sat down.
Yes, we wept, when we remembered Zion.
On the willows in that land,
we hung up our harps.

For there, those who led us captive asked us for songs.
Those who tormented us demanded songs of joy:
"Sing us one of the songs of Zion!"
How can we sing the LORD's song in a foreign land?[9]

Ezekiel answered that YHWH was mobile and was available to his people in Babylon as easily as in Jerusalem.[10] Another prophet, Isaiah, stated that YHWH was no longer just the God of the Israelites but was in fact the one true God for all the people of all the world.[11] Indeed, the mission of the Jews as YHWH's chosen people is to present his message to all the nations of the world.

From the Source

I will also give you as a light to the nations,   that you may be my salvation to the end of the earth.[12]

Among the most influential Jews to return from Babylon to Jerusalem was Ezra (ca. 428 B.C.E.). Ezra was a priest who brought with him a copy of Scripture that he read to the citizens of the rebuilt Jerusalem. The nature and exact content of this book are unknown, but it had a profound effect on the people. They reformed their lives according to the laws in this book. For all times, Jews became identified not only as a people of God's laws but as a people centered around a book. Ezra probably began the process of canonizing books as the word of God. From this time onward, it was believed that God no longer spoke through the prophets but through his book. It remained only for the followers of YHWH to read this book and interpret it for their own lives.

In addition to the growth of a scriptural canon, the religion of the period of the second temple (520 B.C.E. to 70 C.E.) included sacrifices at the rebuilt temple, with a cult of priests, singers, and attendants. At first, the temple (which was rebuilt in the sixth century B.C.E.) was a rather simple structure. In the time of Herod the Great (37–4 B.C.E.), and later, it was restored and decorated to a magnificent state, far beyond the glory of Solomon's temple. Just a few years after the second temple was finally finished, it was destroyed by the Romans in 70 C.E.

Diaspora and Rabbinic Judaism

10.4. Analyze the Diaspora and the development of rabbinic Judaism.

The years following the Assyrian destruction of the northern kingdom of Israel (721 B.C.E.) saw the beginning of the **Diaspora**, the scattering of the Jewish people all over the world. Sometimes it was forced on them, as in 586 B.C.E., when the Babylonians destroyed the first temple and took many of the people of Judah into exile. In other cases, Jews moved by choice to other nations or stayed by choice in such nations as Babylon and Persia. By the year 250 B.C.E., there was such a large Jewish community in Alexandria, Egypt, that it was necessary to translate the Hebrew Bible in to Greek.[13] Jews in Babylon apparently lived well under Persian rule. According to the Book of Esther, a young woman from the Jewish community actually became queen of Persia in the fifth century B.C.E. In later years, Jews were found in such prominent cities as Toledo, Lyons, Cologne, Bonn, and most major cities throughout the Roman Empire.[14]

In 66 C.E., the cup of bitterness between Jews and Romans in the Roman-controlled province of Judea overflowed into violent revolution. At first, the Jews were successful, but by 68 C.E., the tide had turned. The Romans gradually subdued the land and finally besieged Jerusalem. By the summer of 70 C.E. the city was defeated. Jewish revolutionaries were slaughtered or enslaved by the thousands. Worst of all, the magnificent temple was looted and burned, never to be rebuilt. This was surely the most severe blow of all to the Jews.

The Synagogue

Judaism away from the land of Israel was forced to accept a new concept of God and new institutions of worship. The notion of YHWH as the only God of all the peoples of the world, as enunciated by Isaiah, was accepted; various books were accepted as Scripture. Because they were separated by great distances from the temple in Jerusalem, the Jews of the Diaspora developed the institution of the **synagogue** as a local center for prayer and study.

The English word *synagogue* is derived from the Greek word *synagoge*, or "assembly." The synagogue is literally an assembly. A synagogue can exist wherever there is a copy of the Scripture (Torah) and ten adult (over thirteen years of age) Jewish males. Ten adult males constitute a quorum, or a *minyan*. Whenever this combination exists,

A rabbi and other men read from an open Torah at Temple Beth Or, Everett, Washington, United States.

Bill Aron/Photo Edit

there can be prayer and instruction. Synagogue may be held in many kinds of places. It can be under a tree, in the back room of a home, or in an elaborate building set aside for the purpose. No one knows exactly when the institution of the synagogue developed; whatever the specific date, it arose during the Diaspora, when Jews could no longer worship at the temple in Jerusalem, and it serves Judaism to this day.

Along with the synagogue arose the figure of the **rabbi**. The rabbi is not a priest or a minister in the traditional sense. The word *rabbi* literally means "my master." With the establishment of the Torah as the voice of God, there also arose the need for someone to spend time studying the Scripture and teaching the community. Those persons who had the time, interest, and intelligence to study gradually began to be singled out and sought after by inquiring members of the Jewish community. They eventually became known as rabbis, and the sacrifice-based worship centered in the Jerusalem temple gave way necessarily to the scholarly, legal, and textual practices of what came to be known as rabbinic Judaism.

In addition to the synagogue and the rabbis, the Diaspora communities maintained other distinctive features that set them apart from the gentiles who surrounded them, and Jews maintained their separateness. Jews separated themselves from gentiles by refusing to work on the Sabbath. In the worlds of the Greeks and the Romans, where only religious holidays were days of rest from labor, the Jews were regarded as lazy because of their refusal to work one day out of seven. In addition, Jews refused to eat certain foods that gentiles ate. Kosher (clean, fit) food laws in the early Diaspora were not as broad or complex as they later became, but Jews of the Diaspora doubtless had to refuse many foods their neighbors ate.

The Mishnah and the Talmud

The greatest leader of Jews during the second century C.E. was Judah ha-Nasi (Judah the Prince). Judah's great contribution to Judaism was to bring together all the legal commentary that had been collected since the days of Ezra. The commentary, along with the disputes, was collected into a series of tractates arranged in six divisions. This collection by Judah was called the **Mishnah** (repetition), and it became one of the great literary milestones in Jewish history. Within the pages of the Mishnah, the reader finds the attempt of second-century Jews to live by the law of God. At this time, there was no Jewish nation; after 135 C.E., there was no hope of rebuilding the temple or re-establishing a priesthood. All that was left was the law—hence the growing importance of legal commentary like the Mishnah.

Following the compilation of the Mishnah, the center of Jewish life and learning gradually moved from the region of Palestine to Babylon, where Jews had lived since 586 B.C.E. Although there was occasional persecution of the Jews there, life for the Jews in Babylon was easier and more prosperous than it had become in Palestine.

In the Jewish community of Babylon, the discussion over the laws of God continued. Additional interpretative, illustrative, and sermonic material was brought together under the title of Gemara. Gemara was more than additional commentary on the Mishnah and Torah; this body of literature dealt with every area of Jewish life. Gemara developed in both the Palestinian and Babylonian communities. When Gemara was added to the Mishnah, the result was called the Talmud.

The Palestinian Talmud was completed about 425 C.E. The body of this Talmud is about one-third the size of its Babylonian counterpart. Both Talmuds are written mainly in Aramaic, with some Hebrew mixed in, whereas the Mishnah texts are entirely in Hebrew. The Babylonian Talmud is the larger (it runs to 2.5 million words) and more influential of the two; it was completed about 500 C.E. Both Talmuds are made up of two kinds of material: Halachah (the proper way), which consists of legal material, discussions, and decisions; and Haggadah (tale, narrative), which has sections concerning history, folklore, and sermons. About 30 percent of the Babylonian Talmud is Haggadah. As the repository of the oral law, the Talmuds became the most important non-biblical material in Judaism. Since their completion, they have been the object of many commentaries and endless study by all generations of Jews.

Medieval Judaism

10.5. Understand how Islam impacted Judaism during the medieval era.

Judaism and Islam

In the seventh century C.E., a new religion and a new culture sprang from the Arabian desert; the religion was Islam. Muhammad (570–632), the founder and prophet of Islam, had contact with Judaism through the Jewish tribes in Arabia. He learned stories from the Jewish Bible and knew of Judaism's worship of one eternal God and its condemnation of idolatry.

In the years following the death of Muhammad, the religion of Islam exploded out of Arabia into the entire Fertile Crescent and across North Africa. By the end of the seventh century and beginning of the eighth century, Jews living in Babylon, Palestine, Egypt, Turkey, North Africa, and Spain came under the control of Muslim rulers. Muslims treated Jews and Christians better than other non-Muslims under their control. Muslims considered Judaism and Christianity to be God-given faiths. Jews and Christians were not polytheists and had sacred books (Scripture), which Muslims accepted as revelations from God. However, the Muslim toleration of the Jews was sometimes uneven.

The Abbasid dynasty, which followed the Umayyads, was known for religious tolerance. Its capital at Baghdad became the center of science, philosophy, and medicine in the Middle Eastern world. Jews became part of a golden society. Arabic became their language, and the Bible was translated into it. Jewish and Muslim scholars worked side by side to translate into Arabic the works of Greek and Latin philosophers. Thus, these writings were saved from the neglect and destruction of classical materials that occurred in much of Europe during this period. Later, European scholars would rediscover Aristotle and other classical philosophers when their works were translated back from Arabic. It was in this tolerant Islamic world that the Jewish academies flourished, and Baghdad became the center of Jewish religious authority during this period.

The golden age did not last long, however. In 847 C.E. heavier taxes were levied against non-Muslims, and some Jewish synagogues were converted into mosques. Due to both this new persecution and internal divisions within the Jewish community, the leadership of Jewish life and thinking passed across the Mediterranean to Spain.

Judaism in Spain

Jews were in Spain as early as the first century C.E., and St. Paul mentions his hopes of visiting the Jewish community there.[15] When the Roman Empire converted to Christianity in the late fourth century, Jews in Spain were given the choice of conversion or expulsion. Apparently, however, this was not evenly enforced; Jews continued to survive in Spain as Jews. Judaism probably welcomed the conquest of Spain by the Muslims in 711. With the Muslim conquest began a golden age of freedom and tolerance for Jews. They freely entered the fields of government, science, medicine, philosophy, and literature. With the decline of the Babylonian community, Spanish Jews became the leaders of worldwide Judaism.

There were many outstanding Jews in Spain in the early Middle Ages. Samuel Ibn Nagdela was the grand vizier of Granada and wrote an introduction to the Talmud. Judah ha-Levi was a physician and a Hebrew poet. Moses Ibn Gikatella was a biblical scholar who advanced the theories of biblical criticism not espoused by Christian scholars for almost 1,000 years. Moses ben Nachman (Nachmanides, 1195–1270) was a Talmudic authority who was challenged to debate Judaism against Christian monks before the king of Aragon in 1263. He debated so rationally and refuted the Christian claims so clearly that he was rewarded by the king. Even so, he was banished in 1267 and spent his last years in Jerusalem.

Moses ben Maimon (Maimonides, 1135–1204), by far the greatest figure from Spanish Judaism, spent most of his life outside of Spain. Like others of his time, Maimonides was an expert in several fields. He was an outstanding philosopher, a Talmudist, and a physician. He and his family fled from religious persecution in Spain when he was thirteen. After traveling many lands, they eventually settled in Egypt, where Maimonides became the personal physician of Saladin, the Sultan of Egypt. Maimonides's two most famous works are his *Mishneh Torah* and *Guide to the Perplexed*. The *Mishneh Torah* contains fourteen volumes and is a summary of the laws of the Talmud. *Guide to the Perplexed*, completed in 1190, is an attempt to harmonize Judaism with the philosophy of Aristotle. This book caused a storm of controversy among the Jews of the time.

Muslim Spain began to decline at the beginning of the thirteenth century. The subsequent rise of Christian rulership meant hardship for the Jewish people. Persecutions and forced conversions increased. Thousands of Jews were massacred in 1391. Many accepted conversion rather than endure persecution, while others converted openly but secretly continued to practice Judaism. These persons were called *los conversos* (the converts). The pressure continued until 1492, when King Ferdinand and his queen, Isabella, not only sent Columbus on his historic mission but also expelled the Jews and Muslims from Spain. Thousands of Jews fled to Italy, Morocco, the Balkans, and Turkey from yet another area that had once been their home.

Judaism in Other European Nations

Although Jews resided in most of the European regions from the time of the Roman Empire onward, Babylon and Spain were the favored sites for Jewish life in the early medieval period. With the decline of these areas, Jews began to move throughout Europe in greater numbers. They were found in Italy, Germany, Portugal, and England. There were small but influential Jewish communities in India and China. In some cases, Jews were well treated and actually prospered. On the whole, however, the condition of Jews in Muslim lands was far better than it was in Christian Europe.

The Crusades

The Christian Crusades set off widespread attacks on Jews in Europe. The Crusades were instituted by Pope Urban II in 1095. He urged Christian rulers to attack the Muslims and win back the holy places in Palestine. Christian princes and their knights took up the challenge for a variety of religious, economic, and political reasons. However, it was easier to attack defenseless Jews who lived in Europe than it was to vanquish Muslim armies in Palestine. Jewish communities all over Europe, particularly those in the Rhineland, were ravaged by the Crusaders. Many were killed, others were forced to convert to Christianity, and still others committed suicide. A few were hidden by sympathetic Christian bishops. The wave of persecution set off by the Crusades was so severe by 1286 that many Jews fled to Poland or to Islamic countries, where authorities were more tolerant.

Judaism and the Modern World

10.6. Discuss Judaism after the fifteenth century and why many Jews became refugees.

By the end of the fifteenth century, Jews had been officially expelled or made to feel unwelcome in nearly every European nation. Most devastating was the expulsion of the Jews from Spain in 1492. Other nations had officially taken this step earlier: Edward I of England expelled them in 1290; Philip the Fair of France moved to drive all Jews from his country in 1306; they were driven from Germany in the fourteenth century. Portugal followed Spain's example: After 1498, there were no overt Jews in that country. Many fled the persecution of Christian governments and found homes in the Muslim states of the Ottoman Empire. In the Ottoman world, Jewish refugees from Spain and Portugal became known as Sephardim and developed their own *lingua franca*, which was similar to Spanish with some Hebrew loan words. The Sephardim also developed their own liturgy and a distinctive pronunciation of Hebrew.

Other refugees turned to Eastern Europe. Poland particularly attracted persecuted Jews because authorities allowed Jews to enter many vocations that were closed to them in other nations. Many became landlords and tax collectors for the absentee Polish nobility. By the end of the sixteenth century, it is estimated that there were more than a half million Jews in Poland, the largest concentration of Jews in the world. Jews in Eastern Europe became known as Ashkenazim. Their language was Yiddish, a combination of Middle High German and Hebrew, written in the Hebrew alphabet.

In the sixteenth century, Christianity was seized by a revolution that became known as the Protestant Reformation. The leader of this movement in Germany was Martin Luther. Luther was a biblical scholar who knew Hebrew and emphasized the study of both the Old and New Testaments as a true basis for faith. In his early writings, he denounced the Catholic Church for its treatment of Jews. However, when it became apparent that Jews were no more interested in converting to his interpretation of Christianity than they had been in converting to the Catholic faith, Luther turned against them and made fierce anti-Jewish statements in his later writings. The Counter-Reformation of the Catholic Church against the Protestant movement in the sixteenth century reinstituted the Inquisition, and the Jews again became its victims.

Another feature of the Counter-Reformation in Rome was the formation of the ghetto. Jews of that city were forced to move into a special section, known as the ghetto, where they were confined. Later, ghettos were found wherever Jews lived throughout Europe. At first, they probably entered these ghettos voluntarily for their own protection and because it was a place where they could maintain their culture, but later, they had no choice. The ghettos became crowded, sunless places in the very worst parts of the cities. They were walled, and their gates were locked after a certain hour each day, thus enforcing a curfew upon the inhabitants. To ensure that Jews could be distinguished from gentiles, the fourth Lateran Council in 1215 decreed that Jews should wear a yellow badge. In addition, many European communities demanded that Jews wear distinctive hats or caps.

In the seventeenth century, Jews living in Poland saw the end of their sheltered existence. In 1648, the Cossacks and the Ukrainian peasants rose in revolt against the Polish nobility. The Jews who had served the nobility became the objects of pogroms: outbreaks of cruel abuse, robbery, rape, and slaughter. Between 1648 and 1656, an estimated 300,000 to 500,000 Jews were slaughtered. Many of those who survived fled to Western Europe.

Responses to Modernity

10.7.   Analyze Jewish responses to modernity.

Shabbatai Zevi

Because of the misery of the Jews in the ghettos, there arose a strong messianic hope. The object of this hope in the seventeenth century was a charismatic figure named Shabbatai Zevi, who was born in Smyrna (now Izmir) in 1626. As a young man, he studied the mysticism of the Kabbalah and eventually gathered around him a band of disciples. Shabbatai Zevi and his followers wandered from place to place in the Middle East. In Egypt, he married a young woman named Sarah, who claimed that she was destined to be the bride of the Messiah; Shabbatai Zevi was eventually declared the Messiah by his disciples. These claims raised Jewish hopes all over the world. Jews danced for joy in the streets of many European cities; bets were taken in Lloyd's of London as to the exact day when Shabbatai Zevi would enter Jerusalem. In 1665, the Messiah and his party entered Constantinople with the purpose of dethroning the sultan of Turkey. The Turkish rulers imprisoned him and gave him the choice of conversion to Islam or death. Shabbatai Zevi converted and thus bitterly crushed the hopes of Jews everywhere.

Mendelssohn

Where Shabbatai Zevi had failed (after conversion to Islam), another figure arose in Germany; his life and influence would do much to deliver the Jews from their misery. In 1743, a frail, hunchbacked boy appeared at the only gate through which a Jew could enter Berlin. When asked his purpose in the city, he replied that he had come to learn. This was Moses, the son of Mendel of Dessau. He had been born in 1729, and learning was indeed his passion. The long hours spent studying under poor conditions had ruined his health and stooped his shoulders. After his arrival in Berlin, he spent his time learning and soon began to write essays in German that caused him to be widely accepted by the poets and philosophers of eighteenth-century Germany and the court of Frederick the Great. Moses germanized his name to Mendelssohn.

That a Jew could write in German prose and be accepted by the learned of that nation was phenomenal. Mendelssohn became the friend of German critic and dramatist Gotthold Ephraim Lessing and is believed to be the hero of his play *Nathan the Wise*. Mendelssohn encouraged the Jews to leave the ghettos and enter the modern world, to write and speak German rather than Yiddish.

Baal Shem Tov

At the same time, another movement that would influence modern Judaism was developing in Poland. About 1750, in Podolia, a simple, uneducated man named Israel ben Eliezer (1699–1760) began to preach to his Jewish brethren that God was not to be found in scholarly research in the Bible or the Talmud but in simple, heartfelt faith. Israel became known to his followers as Baal Shem Tov (master of the good name), and his followers became known as the Hasidim.

The Hasidic movement was widely accepted by the Jews of Eastern Europe, despite the strong disapproval of the Orthodox rabbis. One could not find more distant opposites than the two stellar figures of Judaism in the eighteenth century, Moses Mendelssohn and the Baal Shem Tov.

The end of the eighteenth century brought new winds of thought to Europe and North America, and these were to have an effect on Judaism. In North America, there was a revolution and a subsequent constitution, which stated that all people are to be treated equally under the law. For the first time in modern history, a gentile nation declared that Jews were to be granted the same rights as others. In France, the revolution of 1789 was followed by the Declaration of the Rights of Man, including the Jews. Wherever the armies of France went in the following years, ghettos were torn down and Jews were given civil rights. In that same year, Jews were first admitted to European universities. On the one hand, Mendelssohn encouraged the Jews of Western Europe to come out of the ghettos and join Christian societies in the adventure of modernity. On the other hand, the Baal Shem Tov and his followers in the Hasidic movement encouraged the Jews of Eastern Europe to search within their own traditions and find the resources to maintain Judaism as an independent entity in the midst of Christian societies.

Religion and Public Life

In 1790, George Washington, the new president of the United States, famously wrote to one of the oldest Jewish communities in North America. To the Jews of Newport, Rhode Island, Washington wrote:

> It is now no more that toleration is spoken of as if it were the indulgence of one class of people that another enjoyed the exercise of their inherent natural rights, for, happily, the Government of the United States, which gives to bigotry no sanction, to persecution no assistance, requires only that they who live under its protection should demean themselves as good citizens in giving it on all occasions their effectual support.

He continued:

> May the children of the stock of Abraham who dwell in this land continue to merit and enjoy the good will of the other inhabitants — while every one shall sit in safety under his own vine and fig tree and there shall be none to make him afraid.[16]

Since that time, the United States has become the country with the largest Jewish population in the world.

Reform Judaism

With Jews following the lead of Mendelssohn and entering European society on all levels, the demand for reforms in Judaism became apparent. If Jews were to be a part of Western civilization, many felt, some of the historical practices of Judaism were out of place. In 1843, a group of German Jewish leaders met and decided that it was time to distance modern Judaism from historical Judaism and accommodate themselves more to their surrounding societies.

This impulse became the basis for Reform Judaism. Reform Jews began to use more vernacular and less Hebrew in their worship; their synagogues were called temples; Kosher food laws were relaxed; choirs and organs were introduced. Indeed, Reform worship in the nineteenth century was in many respects like Protestant Christian worship. Many of the Jewish immigrants to the United States in the early nineteenth century were Reform.

Religion and Public Life

While Jews were enjoying new freedoms and rights in Western Europe in the nineteenth century, the lot of their kinspeople in Eastern Europe had scarcely changed in 200 years. Czarist Russia allowed fierce pogroms against its Jewish population. Harassment and second-class citizenship were their lot. In Russia, Jews were squeezed into certain areas called the Pale of Settlement and were forbidden to travel even into other parts of the empire. In 1881, after the assassination of Alexander II, the worst series of pogroms against the Jews broke out. As a result, a great exodus from Eastern Europe took place. Thousands of Jews fled to any country that would have them; the greatest number took refuge in the United States.

Zionism

In Western Europe, Jewish people may have believed that they had been accepted into the modern world as equals. Indeed, civil rights had been granted and Jews were making great contributions in every profession. But the anti-Jewish feeling of Christian Europe still lay beneath the surface. These feelings were brought into the open by the Dreyfus case. In 1894, Captain Alfred Dreyfus was accused of betraying French military secrets

Children behind a barbed wire fence at the Nazi concentration camp at Auschwitz, southwest Poland.

SOURCE: (Keystone/Hulton Archive/Getty Images)

during the Franco-Prussian War. On the basis of flimsy evidence, Dreyfus was convicted and condemned to life imprisonment on Devil's Island. During the trial, the hostility of the French toward the Jewish Dreyfus and all other Jewish people erupted. Captain Dreyfus was granted amnesty in 1899; seven years later, his court-martial was declared "erroneous."

The Dreyfus case was to have long-range effects on modern Judaism because of a young Austrian journalist named Theodor Herzl, who covered the trial for his newspaper. Herzl and others came to believe that regardless of the liberal facade of European countries, Jewish people would never be treated fairly until they had a land of their own. In a movement known as Zionism, Herzl and others pleaded the case for a Jewish state. Attempts were made to find land anywhere in the world where Jews might develop their own state, but in Jewish hearts, all locations took second place to the land they had left hundreds of years before, the land that had been called Palestine since the second century C.E.

In the early 1900s, Jews began buying land and developing settlements in Palestine. Herzl's work did not produce immediate results, but the seeds had been sown for what would eventually become the nation of Israel. In 1909, the Jewish city of Tel Aviv was founded; by 1920, approximately 50,000 Jews had migrated to Palestine. Many American Jews were suspicious of the Zionist program because they felt that it raised questions about their loyalty to their homeland.

The native populations of Palestine, which included both Arab Christians and Muslims, reacted strongly against the great number of Jewish immigrants and put pressure on the British to restrict immigration (Britain gained control of Palestine after World War I and the division of the Ottoman Empire). By 1928, there were 100,000 Jews in Palestine; by 1931, 175,000; by 1933, 220,000. The Arabs, fearing a new form of European colonialism and the loss of their land, reacted with riots and strikes. In 1939, the British government issued a white paper that set a quota, limiting Jewish immigration to 15,000 per year for the next five years. This quota came at a time when the Jews of Europe were desperately seeking refuge from the Nazis.

Anti-Semitism and the Holocaust

In 1933, Adolf Hitler became chancellor of Germany. Very quickly thereafter, that nation was changed into an anti-Semitic, Nazi dictatorship. Little by little, the rights of the Jews in Germany were taken away. The Nuremberg Laws of 1935 reduced Jews to second-class citizens who could not vote, hold office, work in most professions, or marry non-Jews. Jews who could see the handwriting on the wall fled to whatever refuge they could find. Immigration laws in the United States prevented large numbers of Jews from entering. Palestine was virtually closed as a result of the British white paper of 1939.

When Hitler's armies began to move across Europe in 1939 and throughout the rest of World War II, millions of Jews fell into their hands. In many cases, the non-Jewish citizens of these countries were only too happy to cooperate with the Nazis on the "Jewish question." The yellow badges and ghettos of the Middle Ages were restored for the Jews. How was the extermination of European Jews to be accomplished? Millions of Jews were trapped in Europe, and their numbers made a "solution" to the "Jewish problem" difficult. The first "solution" was the deportation of all Jews in Nazi-occupied countries to concentration camps in the east. Hundreds of thousands were jammed into cattle cars and sent to Eastern Europe, mainly Poland, where they were forced to work until they died.

By 1941, a "final solution" was reached by the Nazis: The Jews were to be annihilated in extermination camps set up for that purpose. Many extermination methods were attempted, but the one that was eventually accepted as the cheapest and most efficient was death by Zyklon B gas. Methodically, Jews in the death camps were driven into gas chambers and asphyxiated. Their bodies were shorn of all valuables, including hair and gold fillings. Skin, bones, and even body fat were put to use by the thorough Nazis. Bodies that were no longer of any use were then cremated in special ovens.

There are various estimates regarding the number of Jews killed during the Nazi years. The usual number given is six million. In Poland alone, the Jewish population was 3,500,000 prior to World War II. In 1945, only 500,000 Jews remained. Few Jews remain in Western Europe.

One might ask how such a thing could happen in the twentieth century, in one of the most civilized nations in the history of the world. Germany had given the world great musicians, philosophers, theologians, scientists, and leaders in nearly every profession, art, and craft. How could such a nation produce such evil? A number of explanations for the Nazi **Holocaust** have been suggested:

1. *German ethnocentrism and racism.* Adolf Hitler appealed to a very basic emotion in his people when he asserted that the so-called Aryans were the master race and that others, especially the Jews, were inferior. He also condemned, and subsequently executed, Roma (Gypsies) and mentally and physically handicapped people.
2. *German troubles following World War I.* Germany had been defeated in World War I and humiliated by the peace treaty that followed. German pride demanded that some reason be found for the defeat. The most common excuse was that Germany had been "stabbed in the back," and the traitor was supposedly the Jews. Germany also suffered from an economically disastrous inflation following the war, and this too was blamed on the Jews. The fraudulent *Protocols of the Elders of Zion*, written by officers of the Russian Secret Service, was believed to be the plan for an international Jewish conspiracy to destroy the economies of Christian nations. Many Americans, including Henry Ford, agreed with these views. Many Germans also believed that the Jews were behind an international Communist conspiracy. Therefore, Jews were accused of being the international bankers and financiers who would wreak havoc in the world economy—at the same time that they were accused of being the Marxist enemy of capitalist economies! Nothing could have been more absurd.

3. *Nazi madness.* It would seem that in some cases the destruction of the Jews was more important to the Nazis than anything else. There were occasions when trains that were needed to take German troops and supplies to the front were diverted to take Jews to extermination camps instead.

4. *Modern efficiency.* The very number of Jews murdered could not have been achieved at any other time in history. Neither the Romans nor the Cossacks could have killed so many persons in such a short period of time. Only modern technology made such a mass killing possible.

5. *The silence of the rest of the world.* At a time when Jews most needed a refuge, doors were shut to them all over the world. Many Christian leaders did very little to rescue the victims, and little protest was raised. No attempt was made by Allied bombers to wreck the machinery of the Holocaust. It was as though the rest of the world was willing to allow Hitler to have his way with the unfortunate Jews in his trap.

The Holocaust reduced the world population of Jews by as much as one-third. When the enormity of the crime was made public in the Nuremberg trials of 1946 and the Eichmann trial of 1960, it had a profound effect on Jewish thinking. It was one of the primary causes of the development of the nation of Israel in the years after World War II. The Holocaust may have had a lasting effect on Jewish theology also. At least one Jewish thinker, Richard Rubenstein, said in his book, *After Auschwitz*, that God died in the Holocaust for Judaism. Before the Nazi years, whenever there was a serious threat to the Jews, no matter how severe it was, God somehow answered the cries of his people. At Auschwitz and other death camps, there seemed to be no answer to their prayers as Jews were led to the gas chambers. The full story of the Holocaust and its effects on Judaism has not yet been told. **Anti-Semitism** has not vanished. It remains in Europe, Latin America, and the United States. In the 1960s, many Jews fled the American South in fear of the violent and anti-Semitic Ku Klux Klan. Neo-Nazis have also demonstrated in largely Jewish suburbs of Chicago.

The State of Israel

The birth of the state of Israel came quickly after World War II. By 1947, it was obvious that Britain could no longer control Palestine and its two warring factions. Zionists were determined to build a home for the thousands of displaced Jews, and the Palestinian Arabs were just as determined that it would not be established in Palestine, fearing that they might become the next group of displaced persons. In 1947, the United Nations voted to partition Palestine into a Jewish and an Arab state. The British left Palestine in May 1948, and Israel immediately proclaimed its statehood. Ironically, the United States and the Soviet Union vied to see who would be the first to recognize the new nation. Immediately, Israel was attacked by five neighboring Arab states. It

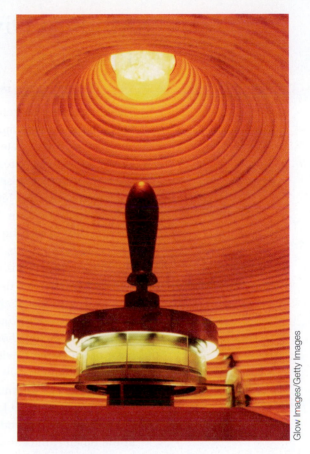

Shrine of the Dead Sea Scrolls, Israel. The Isaiah Scroll is pictured here.

SOURCE: (Ancient Art and Architecture/Danita Delimont.com)

Glow Images/Getty Images

survived these attacks and others and has answered, at least in part, the Zionists' dreams of a homeland for the Jews.

Unfortunately, with the development of the state of Israel, thousands of Palestinian Arabs were forced from or simply fled their homes in what became the new nation. Since 1948, many of them have eked out miserable existences in various refugee camps. During the Arab-Israeli war of 1967, more Arab territories were occupied by the Israelis, including the city of Old Jerusalem and one of the most sacred shrines of all to the Jews, the Wailing Wall, that portion of the temple remaining after the war of 70 C.E. The governance of the city of Jerusalem and the West Bank of the Jordan and an equitable solution to the displacement of the Palestinian refugees remain serious problems. The peace treaty between Israel and Jordan and the establishment of the Palestinian Authority on the West Bank of the Jordan River and the Gaza Strip were first steps toward resolving these problems, but much remains to be done before true peace is established in the region. The fact that Muslims as well as Jews regard Jerusalem as sacred territory makes the resolution of these problems even more difficult and even more important for the future of all of the people of the area.

Modern Divisions and Religious Practices

10.8. Recognize the modern divisions and religious practices in Judaism.

There are approximately fourteen million Jews in the world today. As already stated, the term *Jew* covers a multitude of religious practices and beliefs. The Jews of the world are widely divided in terms of these beliefs and practices.

Orthodox Jews are one group within Judaism. Orthodox Judaism strives to preserve traditional Jewish culture and religion and resist the secularizing elements of modernity. Orthodox Jews attempt to stay as close as possible to the nature of biblical and Talmudic Judaism. Kosher food laws are stressed, along with strict observance of the Sabbath. In worship, men and women are separated in the synagogue and both must cover their heads. Hebrew is the language of Orthodox worship.

Reform Judaism is popular mainly in the United States and Europe. The Reform tradition emphasizes the universality of traditional Jewish values, interfaith dialogue, and social activism. It attempts to be as modern as possible in its beliefs and practices. Its worship is usually on Friday evenings, and its synagogues are called temples. Men and women sit together with uncovered heads. The vernacular is used throughout most of the service, with Hebrew interspersed only occasionally. Organ music and choirs are common. Few members of Reform temples attempt to keep all of the Kosher food laws or the Talmudic restrictions on the Sabbath. One of the most important developments in Reform Judaism is the ordination of women as rabbis.

Between the Orthodox and the Reform is the Conservative movement, which arose in the nineteenth century, led by Sabato Morais, as a reaction against the perceived extremes of the Reform movement. Shocked at the excesses of the Reform leaders at the Pittsburgh Conference of American Rabbis in 1885, Morais and others organized the Jewish Theological Seminary of America in New York City. This seminary has been the voice of Conservative Judaism in the United States ever since. Conservative Judaism is firmly rooted in the rabbinical tradition but is somewhat more relaxed in matters of religious practice than is the Orthodox movement.

Conservative Judaism is distinguished from Orthodox Judaism by its greater concern with the historical and critical study of the Bible and rabbinical material. In its worship, the vernacular is used more than Hebrew. Unlike Reform Jews, Conservatives tend to worship on Saturday morning. Men cover their heads with the traditional skullcap (*yarmulke*) during worship. Many Conservatives attempt to abide by the biblical and Talmudic laws regulating food and Sabbath observance, especially during important religious observances in the Jewish calendar.

Growing out of the Conservative movement is Reconstructionist Judaism. Mordecai M. Kaplan, a professor of homiletics at the Jewish Theological Seminary in the 1930s, is regarded as the founder of Reconstructionism. He understood Judaism to be not only a religion but a culture, with its own history, laws, and arts. Therefore, it is not enough to practice Judaism as a religion only; the entire Jewish culture must be studied and experienced. The numerous Jewish community centers in American cities today are an organizational attempt to deal with Kaplan's ideals. Naturally, the Reconstructionists provide complete support to the state of Israel as the home of Jewish culture.

Yedidya Yos Mizrachi/PhotoStock-Israel/Alamy

Jewish men at the Wailing Wall in Jerusalem.

In both the United States and Israel there are now fundamentalist Jewish sects that demand complete acceptance of traditional Jewish law and are overtly hostile to non-Jews and to those Jews who do not accept their extreme views. Some of these groups have gone so far as to plan the destruction of Muslim shrines in Jerusalem and the reconstruction of the Temple of Solomon. Many of them are active in the settlement movement that establishes Jewish enclaves in Muslim areas on the West Bank of the Jordan River. Unlike most other Jewish communities, many of these groups have missionary agendas, directed almost exclusively at less observant Jews.

There also are large numbers of secular, or non-observant, Jews. Many value their Jewish culture and heritage but do not share the religious beliefs or practices of Jewish communities. Many celebrate traditional Jewish holy days in much the same way secular people of Christian heritage celebrate Christmas and Easter. They are celebrations of family, community, and tradition, but no longer of faith.

Jewish prayer book for morning services; ink, watercolor, gouache, and gold paint on parchment. Ashkenazi Europe, 1725.

Jewish Festivals and Holy Days

10.9. **Identify and explain the significance of Jewish festivals and holy days.**

Judaism has always been defined and understood by its adherents in terms of the actions of God. Therefore, commemorations of these acts of God tend to be extremely important. The holidays on which these great events are remembered are a unifying factor, bringing together Jews of all degrees of belief and practice. Judaism also depends on the community for its very existence. Therefore, although many portions of its annual festivals may be carried out in the Jewish home, most depend heavily on the community meeting in the synagogue. Because of this reliance upon the group, the events of Bar Mitzvah and Bat Mitzvah (when the young are officially recognized as adult members of the Jewish community) also comprise a significant festival.

Sabbath (Shabbat)

The most important and distinctive of all Jewish holidays is the Sabbath. Judaism gave the world the six-day work week, with the seventh day reserved for worship and rest. The Sabbath begins on Friday at sundown and continues until sundown on Saturday. On Friday night, the Sabbath is ushered in with the Kiddush, the benediction over wine or bread, and the lighting and blessing of Sabbath candles by the woman of the house. Traditionally, the best food of the week is served at the Friday evening meal. Conservative and Orthodox Jews attend synagogue on Saturday morning and also read the week's section of the Torah. Orthodox observance of the Sabbath forbids lighting or extinguishing fires or lights, riding in automobiles, smoking, carrying money, or performing any type of labor.

Passover (Pesach)

Another important festival in Judaism is the celebration of Passover. This holiday begins on the fifteenth of the Hebrew month of Nisan (March–April) and lasts for eight

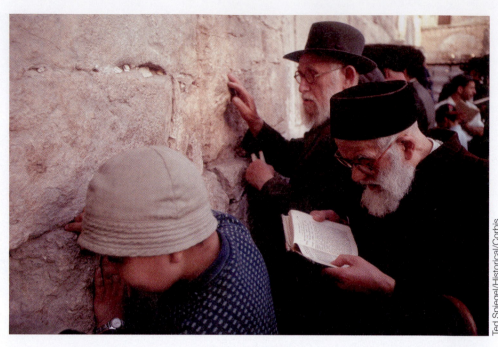

Ted Spiegel/Historical/Corbis

Jews praying at the Western Wall of the Temple in Jerusalem.

days.[17] It commemorates the deliverance of the Israelites from slavery in Egypt. On the first two nights of Passover, the Jewish family gathers for a ritual meal called Seder. The foods associated with the Exodus (lamb, unleavened bread, bitter herbs, and so on) are eaten as the family engages in rituals that recall the Exodus.

The Feast of Weeks (Shavuot)

Fifty days after Pesach—that is, on the sixth and seventh days of Sivan (May–June)—the Celebration of Weeks, or Shavuot, occurs. This holiday is called the Pentecost in the New Testament. Shavuot was originally a festival celebrating the first grain harvest, but later it was related to the Exodus event—when Moses received the Ten Commandments on Mt. Sinai. Jewish homes and synagogues are decorated with plants and flowers during the celebration of this holiday.

Rosh Hashanah

Rosh Hashanah is the Jewish New Year and is celebrated on the first and second days of the month of Tishre (September–October). Tradition says that the days of Rosh Hashanah were also the first days of creation. The season begins a period of penitence that culminates in the next holiday, the Day of Atonement (Yom Kippur). The New Year is celebrated by special prayers and by eating sweets in the hope of a good year to come.

Yom Kippur

The holiest of all Jewish holidays is the Day of Atonement, Yom Kippur. It is celebrated on the tenth of Tishre and at the end of the period of penitence begun at Rosh Hashanah. The day is traditionally observed by abstinence from work, food, and drink. The day is to be spent in the synagogue, where prayers are offered for forgiveness of sins and reconciliation. It is also an occasion for charity.

The Feast of Tabernacles (Sukkot)

Five days after Yom Kippur, on the fifteenth of Tishre, the Feast of Tabernacles is celebrated. Originally, this was a celebration of the autumn harvest. As did many of the

Mario Tama/Getty Images News/Getty Images

Purim celebration, Brooklyn, New York. Purim is a festive Jewish holiday, with prizes, noisemakers, costumes, and treats. This holiday commemorates a major victory over oppression and is recounted in the scroll of the story of Esther.

other holidays, Sukkot became attached to the Exodus experience and is now kept as a remembrance of the times when the Israelites wandered in the Sinai wilderness and lived in makeshift tabernacles (*sukkot*). For either reason, the festival is a joyous one.

Chanukah

On the twenty-fifth of the month of Kislev (November–December), Jews celebrate one of the few holidays not associated with the Exodus. In 165 B.C.E., Judas Maccabaeus retook the temple from the Syrian Greeks and rededicated it. Only one small container of oil was available to light the temple. It should have lasted only one day. Miraculously, however, the oil lasted eight days. In remembrance of that event, Jews light a candle each day for eight days. It is thus a festival of lights as well as a festival of dedication. Chanukah had been a minor holiday in Judaism until fairly recent times. It has become increasingly important for Jews in the United States because of its proximity to Christmas.

Purim

Another festival not associated with the Exodus is Purim, celebrated on the fourteenth of Adar (February–March) as a remembrance of Jewish victory over gentile foes. The Book of Esther says that Esther, who had become the Queen of Persia, learned of a plot to destroy her people. By boldly approaching the king and revealing this plot to him, Esther saved her people from a massacre and saw her enemies hanged upon the gibbet they had prepared for the Jews. Because lots were cast to determine the day when the Jews were to be destroyed, the festival is known as Purim (lots). On this day, the scroll of Esther is read, gifts are exchanged, and a special meal is eaten. Generally, it is a day of great joy and merrymaking.

Bar and Bat Mitzvah

Although the Bar and Bat Mitzvah is not an annual festival in the Jewish calendar, it is an important occasion in the life of the community. According to Judaism, a boy is technically a man when he reaches his thirteenth birthday. He can be one of the ten

When a Jewish child reaches the age of maturity (twelve for girls, thirteen for boys), that child becomes responsible for him- or herself under Jewish law. The event is commemorated with a Bat Mitzvah/Bar Mitzvah.

adults necessary for a minyan. Usually, the boy is prepared for the occasion by several years of instruction in his religion and in Hebrew. On the Sabbath after his thirteenth birthday, he reads from the Scripture at synagogue and may deliver a speech. This is a festive occasion for the boy and his parents, and the young man may receive many presents from his friends. The Bar Mitzvah may have been introduced as late as the fourteenth century, as a counter to Christian confirmation, although the age of thirteen has always been the age of majority in Judaism. A modern innovation is the Bat Mitzvah (daughter of the commandment), a similar ceremony for girls. The Bat Mitzvah is practiced by most non-Orthodox congregations.

Judaism Today

10.10.   **Understand the issues faced by modern Jews and Judaism as a whole.**

In the first decades of the twenty-first century, one of the primary tasks of Judaism continues to be interpreting the Holocaust. Throughout its history, Judaism has always sought to understand God through history. The biblical material seeks to understand the Exodus experience. The postexilic books try to make sense of the Babylonian exile. The Mishnah and Talmud seek to reinterpret Jewish life after the destruction of the temple. The single greatest tragedy for Judaism in the modern world was the murder of six million Jews by the Nazis. Does this event mean that God is dead for the Jews, or that he has turned his back on them, or that they were being punished for some sin? Does it mean that all Christians are hostile and murderous toward Jews? These and many other questions continue to be asked by the Jewish thinkers of today.

As has been the case many times in the past, Judaism today struggles with the issue of its place in a predominantly gentile society. There is a long-standing debate about whether Jews should compromise with the values of society at large, or whether they should find their values only in historical Judaism. One greatly feared compromise is intermarriage with gentiles and the consequent loss of Jewish offspring. This concern has created a revival of interest in forms of Orthodox Judaism such as Hasidism. Many of these movements are of great interest to modern young Jewish people.

Think About It

1. Why is the Exodus considered the most important event in Judaism? How did it affect the development of Judaism?

2. How did the religion of Israel change when David became king? What role did prophets play during this period of Hebrew monarchy?

3. What were some of the developments that arose during the period of the second temple?

4. What was the Diaspora, and what effect did it have on Jews' concept of God and their institutions of worship?

5. How did the development and spread of Islam during the medieval era affect Judaism?

6. By the end of the fifteenth century, Jews were made to feel unwelcome in nearly every European nation. As a result, where did they settle and what were living conditions like in these new lands?

7. One of the responses to modernity was the rise of Reform Judaism. What are the characteristics of Reform Judaism?

8. List four major divisions within modern Judaism. Explain how they differ from one another.

9. Describe three of the important Jewish holidays and their significance.

10. Explain the importance of the Nazi Holocaust to Jewish thinking. Discuss the state of Israel as a response to the Holocaust.

Suggested Reading

Baron, Salo W. *A Social and Religious History of the Jews*, 3 vols. New York: Columbia University Press, 1952.

Bokser, Ben Zion. *The Jewish Mystical Tradition*. Long Island City, N.Y.: Pilgrim Press, 1981.

Buber, Martin. *Tales of the Hasidim*, 2 vols. New York: Schocken Books, 1948.

Chabon, Michael. *The Yiddish Policemen's Union: A Novel*. San Francisco: Harper Collins, 2007.

Cohen, A., ed. *Everybody's Talmud*. New York: Schocken Books, 1975.

Hertzberg, Arthur, ed. *Judaism*. New York: George Braziller, 1961.

Küng, Hans. *Judaism: Between Yesterday and Tomorrow*. Translated by John Bowden. New York: Crossroads, 1992.

Lachs, Samuel T., and Saul P. Wachs. *Judaism*. Niles, Ill.: Argus Communications, 1979.

Neusner, Jacob. *The Way of the Torah. An Introduction to Judaism*. Belmont, Calif.: Wadsworth, 1988.

Plaskow, Judith. *Standing Again at Sinai. Judaism from a Feminist Perspective*. San Francisco: HarperCollins, 1990.

Trepp, Leo. *Judaism: Development and Life*. Encino, Calif.: Dickenson, 1966.

Source Material

Selections from Hebrew Scriptures

Jewish Scripture and commentary is so widely available and abundant that it is difficult to select a truly representative collection. However, the following materials tend to be illustrative of at least early Jewish thought. The Book of Deuteronomy, from the Torah, although it claims to be the words of Moses, is believed by many scholars to be the work of the disciples of the eighth-century B.C.E. prophets. It also is believed to have been the book found in the rubble of the temple in the sixth century B.C.E. (see II Kings 22). Deuteronomy 6 contains the Shema (the creedal assertion of Judaism that God is one). The Psalms make up a large part of the poetical material of early Israel.

Psalm 1, with its praise for the person who "delights in the law of the Lord," shows the growing concern for Scripture in Israel. Micah is representative of the prophetic movement in Israel, particularly with his strong emphasis on social justice.[18]

Deuteronomy 6:1–15

Now this is the commandment, the statutes, and the ordinances, which the LORD your God commanded to teach you, that you might do them in the land where you go over to possess it; that you might fear the LORD your God, to keep all his statutes and his commandments, which I command you; you, and your son, and your son's son, all the days of your life; and that your days may be prolonged. Hear therefore, Israel, and observe to do it; that it may be well with you, and that you may increase mightily, as the LORD, the God of your fathers, has promised to you, in a land flowing with milk and honey. Hear, Israel: The LORD is our God. The LORD is one. You shall love the LORD your God with all your heart, with all your soul, and with all your might. These words, which I command you today, shall be on your heart; and you shall teach them diligently to your children, and shall talk of them when you sit in your house, and when you walk by the way, and when you lie down, and when you rise up. You shall bind them for a sign on your hand, and they shall be for frontlets between your eyes. You shall write them on the door posts of your house, and on your gates. It shall be, when the LORD your God brings you into the land which he swore to your fathers, to Abraham, to Isaac, and to Jacob, to give you, great and goodly cities, which you didn't build, and houses full of all good things, which you didn't fill, and cisterns dug out, which you didn't dig, vineyards and olive trees, which you didn't plant, and you shall eat and be full; then beware lest you forget the LORD, who brought you out of the land of Egypt, out of the house of bondage. You shall fear the LORD your God; and you shall serve him, and shall swear by his name. You shall not go after other gods, of the gods of the peoples who are around you; for the LORD your God among you is a jealous God; lest the anger of the LORD your God be kindled against you, and he destroy you from off the face of the earth.

Psalms 1

Blessed is the man who doesn't walk in the counsel of the wicked,
nor stand on the path of sinners,
nor sit in the seat of scoffers;
but his delight is in the LORD's law.

On his law he meditates day and night.

He will be like a tree planted by the streams of water,
that produces its fruit in its season,
whose leaf also does not wither.

Whatever he does shall prosper.

The wicked are not so,
but are like the chaff which the wind drives away.

Therefore the wicked shall not stand in the judgment,
nor sinners in the congregation of the righteous.

For the LORD knows the way of the righteous,
but the way of the wicked shall perish.

Micah 6:1–9a

Listen now to what the LORD says:
"Arise, plead your case before the mountains,
and let the hills hear what you have to say.
Hear, you mountains, the LORD's controversy,
and you enduring foundations of the earth;
for the LORD has a controversy with his people,
and he will contend with Israel.
My people, what have I done to you?
How have I burdened you?
Answer me!
For I brought you up out of the land of Egypt,
and redeemed you out of the house of bondage.
I sent before you Moses, Aaron, and Miriam.
My people, remember now what Balak king of Moab devised,
and what Balaam the son of Beor answered him from Shittim to Gilgal,
that you may know the righteous acts of the LORD."
How shall I come before the LORD,
and bow myself before the exalted God?
Shall I come before him with burnt offerings,
with calves a year old?
Will the LORD be pleased with thousands of rams?
With tens of thousands of rivers of oil?
Shall I give my firstborn for my disobedience?
The fruit of my body for the sin of my soul?
He has shown you, O man, what is good.
What does the LORD require of you, but to act justly,
to love mercy, and to walk humbly with your God?

The Mishnah: Pesachim (The Feast of Passover)

The Mishnah is representative of rabbinic literature, which became so important to later Judaism. It is a collection of rabbinic opinions about how to keep the laws of God. It is believed that the Mishnah was collected and codified in the second century C.E. The following selection is taken from the section that deals with keeping the feast of Passover. Exodus 12:19 forbade the presence of any form of leaven or yeast in a Jewish household during the seven days of the feast of Passover. But what is yeast (*hametz*)? Where is it found? And to what lengths should one go to get rid of it? This section of the Mishnah attempts to answer these questions.[19]

1. The law concerning tire due observance of the Passover, will be transgressed by using the following articles: namely, Babylonian [porridge,] Median beer [made of wheat or barley], Edomite vinegar, Egyptian zeithum, the dough of bran used by dyers,

the dough used by cooks, and the paste used by writers; R. Eleazar says, also the paste used by women to adorn themselves with. This is the general rule: whatever is composed of any kind of grain, can cause a transgression of the paschal laws; and they that are guilty of this, incur the penalty attached to the transgression of an admonitory precept, but not that of being "utterly cut off."

2. If there be any dough in the holes or crevices of a kneading-trough: if there is as much as the size of an olive in any one place, it must be forthwith removed, but if less than that quantity is together in one place, it may be considered as non-existing, being so inconsiderable; and thus it is in respect to pollutions. But when the dough is cared for [when the owner wishes to use it], it forms a separation, [and the trough is unpolluted], but when it is desired to leave the dough in the trough, it must be considered as forming an integral part of the trough; a dull dough may not be used, if one of the same quality and size can become leavened in the same time.

3. How can the cake of the dough be separated on the Passover when it has become unclean? R. Eleazar says, "It is only to be named after it has been baked;" R. Jehudah, son of Beterah says, "This is not the leaven concerning which it is said, 'It shall not be seen nor found in thy house;'" it must, therefore, be separated, and left till the evening, without caring whether it becomes leaven or not.

4. Rabbon Gamaliel says, "Three women may knead dough on the Passover at one time, and bake it in the same oven, one after the other;" but the sages say, "Three women may occupy themselves with their dough, but in the following manner: one shall knead and another fashion the dough, whilst the third bakes;" R. Akivah says, "It is not the same with all women, wood, or ovens." This is the rule: as soon as dough becomes inflated, let the woman plunge her hand in cold water.

5. Dough which begins to become leavened must be burned; but the person who eats it has not incurred the penalty [of excision]. Dough which falls in holes or rents must be burned, and whoever eats it has incurred the penalty of excision. When is a dough to be considered as commencing to become leavened? When it exhibits small rents standing apart in different directions, like the antennae [horns or feelers] of locusts. A dough which falls in holes or rents is thus to be considered, when the rents cross each other: such is the dictum of R. Jehudah; but the sages say, "Whoever eats either incurs the penalty of excision." When is a dough to be considered as commencing to become leavened? When its surface has become pale, like [the face of] a person whose hair stands on end [through terror].

6. When the 14th of Nissan happens on the Sabbath, all [leaven] must be removed *before* the Sabbath commences: such is the dictum of R. Meir; but the sages say it is to be done at the proper time; R. Eleazar ben Zadok says, "The heave-offering must be removed before the Sabbath, and non-consecrated things at the proper time.

7. If a person went [on the 14th of Nissan] to slaughter his Passover-sacrifice, or to circumcise his son, or to eat the betrothing-meal at the house of his father-in-law, and remembers on the road that he has left leaven in his house: if he can return home and remove it, and then go back to execute any of the mentioned duties, he must do so, and remove it; but if not, he must mentally declare it as annulled. If his intention, on leaving home, was to aid persons to escape from armed foes, from inundation, robbers, or fire, or to save persons from under the ruins of fallen buildings, he may mentally annul the leaven; but if his intention was to obtain a sabbatical resting

8. Also, if a person on leaving Jerusalem, remembers having with him consecrated flesh: if he has gone beyond [the hill] Zophim, he may burn it where he is; but if not, he must return, and burn it before the sanctuary, with wood of the altar. What quantity [of flesh or leaven] makes it obligatory to return? R. Meir says, "When both are the size of an egg;" R. Jehudah says, "When of the size of an olive;" but the sages say, "Consecrated flesh when of the size of an olive, and leaven when of the size of an egg."

Chapter 11
Christianity

Learning Objectives

After reading this chapter, you should be able to:

11.1 Discuss the world of the first century and the characteristics of the Roman Empire.

11.2 Talk about the life of Jesus and the significance of the Gospels.

11.3 Analyze early Christianity and the rites that still exist in Christianity today.

11.4 Understand the growth of the Church of Rome and the ascendancy of the papacy.

11.5 Discuss the theological differences between the East and West during the Middle Ages.

11.6 Analyze the various people associated with the Protestant Reformation and the reforms they proposed.

11.7 Discuss the growth and global expansion of Christianity over time.

11.8 Name the holy days and holidays associated with the Christian calendar.

11.9 Analyze the challenges and issues facing Christianity today.

A Timeline of Christianity

6-4 B.C.E.	Birth of Jesus
29–33	Crucifixion of Jesus
50–60	Missionary travel of Saint Paul
150	Completion of New Testament writings
313	Edict of Toleration issued by Emperor Constantine legalizes Christianity following periodic persecution
325	Council of Nicaea issues creed affirming both humanity and divinity of Christ
379–395	Reign of Emperor Theodosius, who proclaims Christianity the official religion of the Roman Empire
1054	Split between Eastern Orthodox and Roman Catholic churches
1095–1300	The Crusades
1232	Start of the Inquisition
1517	Martin Luther begins Protestant Reformation

1520–present	Proliferation of Protestant denominations
1562–1648	European War of Religion pits Protestants against Catholics
1820s–present	Expansion of Protestant missionary activities around the globe
1830	Joseph Smith presents the Book of Mormon and founds the Church of Jesus Christ of Latter Day Saints (Mormons)
1895	Beginning of the rise of Protestant Fundamentalism
1945–present	The end of colonialism leads to the development of new local Christianities in Africa and Asia
1945–present	Rapid growth of secularism in Europe and North America
1962–1965	Second Vatican Council

Key Terms

Apostle	Gospels
baptism	missionary
denomination	Pentecostalism
epistle	Reformation
Eucharist	sacrament
evangelicalism	Vatican II

Christianity is the largest religion in the world. Today there are more than two billion Christians. The religion is growing rapidly in the so-called global South and is more diverse than ever before; a religion that encompasses so many people contains a great variety of beliefs and practices. In general, Christians share a common belief in the uniqueness of Jesus of Nazareth, that he in some way provided for the redemption of humankind by his death and was himself resurrected from the dead. Christians generally also believe in baptism as an initiation into the religion, and in the communion meal. They hold to the idea that believers have one life in which to determine their destiny for life after death. This destiny is usually thought to be either an eternity of bliss in heaven or an eternity of torment in hell. Around these basic themes are many variations within the body of Christianity.

The World of the First Century C.E.

11.1. Discuss the world of the first century and the characteristics of the Roman Empire.

Christianity began as a sect of Judaism in the first century C.E., when the Roman Empire was at its peak and Augustus Caesar (63 B.C.E. to 14 C.E.) ruled. Some knowledge of the condition of both Judaism and the Roman Empire of those days will help us understand the forces that created Christianity.

In the first century C.E., much of Europe, North Africa, and the Middle East were under Roman rule. The Mediterranean Sea was a "Roman lake." The various peoples of the Roman Empire shared a common language and a common intellectual culture that combined elements of Greek and Roman philosophy and religion. Under the rule of Augustus Caesar and his successors, the Roman legions had conquered almost everything that could be conquered. Wherever they went, they took with them Roman civilization, efficient administrators, and thorough engineers. They built cities and roads to link them. They swept the Mediterranean of pirates and made sea travel safe.

Communication and travel across the vast area had never been safer or more sure. When Christian missionaries, such as the Apostle Paul, began to spread the gospel of Christianity, the Roman Empire provided the path.

In addition to material benefits, as mentioned, the Roman Empire gave the world one language. Each captive nation continued to speak its own native tongue, of course, but wherever one went in the Roman world, the leaders of government and business would, in addition, be able to speak *Koine* Greek.[1] Although the language of the common people of Rome was Latin, many of the leaders had been educated by Greek slaves and tutors; they found Greek a more beautiful and expressive language. Furthermore, Alexander the Great had conquered much of the world that later became the Roman Empire, and he had sowed the seeds of Hellenistic culture and its Greek language wherever his armies had gone. Because ancient Greece had been the home of philosophy, the beautiful and accurate language of Greece is considered by many to be one of the best vehicles for expressing philosophical and theological thought. A Christian **missionary** (e.g., Paul) could go anywhere in the Roman Empire and be sure that he could converse with the populace in *Koine* Greek. He could also write letters, or **epistles**, to Christian communities in Greek and know that they would be read and understood.

The world of the first-century Roman Empire was one of political stability. The Romans governed with great cruelty, but they produced a world of relative peace. Augustus and his successors imposed their *pax romana* (the peace of Rome); although it was harsh, it was peace nonetheless. To be sure, there were local revolts against Roman government, such as the Jewish revolt of 66–70 C.E., but there were no major international wars during this period. Christianity developed in a time of stable government and international calm.

The Roman world of the first century had no major religious commitment. The Greeks and Romans had their pantheons, but belief in them had largely ceased, at least among the ruling elite. Sacrifices to the Roman gods were still carried on officially, but there was little popular support for them. The nations within the Empire had their own national religions, and many of these were alive and well. In Judaism, the rabbis were developing material that would eventually become the Mishnah and the Talmud. Indeed, Judaism was finding many converts from other religions. However, the Empire itself had no vital official religion during this era, and many people were seeking a new religion to take the place of the dead or dying faiths.

Many sought out astrology as a solution to the problems of life. Others turned to new religious cults that developed from various Eastern religions. Mithraism, which was a development from Persian thought, entered Roman life during the reign of Nero and quickly became a popular cult among Roman soldiers. The cult of Osiris spread from Egyptian religions into the Empire. In Greece, the worship of Dionysus was popular. These and other so-called mystery religions gained large followings among the citizens of the Roman Empire. Each offered the believer life after death in one form or another. Many had secret rituals to which only the initiated were invited. Many had sacred communion meals and baptisms that aided the participant in the search for eternal life. Most of the mystery religions accepted people into their groups without regard to race or social status. In the homogenized life of the Roman Empire, where a large portion of the population was made up of slaves, this was an important feature.

Another aspect of the first-century world (in Judaism and possibly other religions) that is becoming increasingly clear today is that some anticipated that the world was nearing its end or at least nearing a climactic moment. Among the political groups of Palestine was the hope that a messiah would emerge and lead the people in the overthrow of the Roman monster. This was therefore a time in which many would identify themselves, or at least would allow themselves to be identified, as Messiah. Among the people living at Wadi Qumran by the Dead Sea, who produced those documents popularly called the Dead Sea Scrolls, there was an anticipation of a swiftly approaching end of time. These people were so certain that the end was near that they had left their normal lives and come to this lonely wilderness to await the coming of the Lord. Into this religious and political situation came Jesus of Nazareth.

The Life and Teachings of Jesus

11.2.   **Talk about the life of Jesus and the significance of the Gospels.**

Jesus of Nazareth was not mentioned in non-Christian literature until the end of the first century C.E. Even then, references to him were vague and not very helpful in constructing the events in his life. Non-Christians sometimes assert that Jesus was not a historical figure, because up until the end of the first century there were only Christian stories about his life.[2] Whether or not this is true cannot be proved, but it is fact that there is limited first-century, non-Christian material about his life. The only truly objective facts we have about the life of Jesus are that a group of people called Christians began to be recognized in the Roman Empire around 60–65 C.E. and that they aroused hostility and persecution in an empire that was normally tolerant of religious variations. Christianity became the object of many official and unofficial persecutions, but it continued to grow until the fourth century, when it became the official religion of what remained of the Roman Empire. Although modern students of Christianity may not know exactly what the early church taught, the existence of this group cannot be questioned.

About forty years after the death of Jesus, members of this group began to write biographical statements about him, centered on his death and resurrection. These books, or **Gospels**, are not biographies in the true sense of the word but give most of their attention to the last few months in the life of Jesus. Only rarely are Jesus's childhood or early adult years mentioned, and none of the Gospels contains a physical description of Jesus. Even the exact details of Jesus's last few months differ among the four Gospels. If the earliest Gospel was written forty years after the death of Jesus, and if all of the Gospels were written by confessed Christians who had a biased point of view, then admittedly they may not be the most reliable sources of objective material. With all of their subjective biases, however, the Gospels still provide the best information we have about the life of Jesus.

Shrine of the Virgin Mary. National Cathedral, Jakarta, Indonesia.

Two Gospels, Mark and John, begin with the ministry of a mature Jesus. Only Matthew and Luke speak of his birth, and only Luke contains materials relating to Jesus's childhood. The reader must assume that for the early church, the years before Jesus's actual ministry were not terribly important. In those Gospels that do tell of his birth, there are problems in harmonizing details. They do agree, however, that Jesus was born in the ancestral home of David: Bethlehem. Matthew places the time of Jesus's birth in the years prior to the death of Herod the Great (4 B.C.E.).[3] Both Matthew and Luke assert that Jesus's birth was unique in that he was born of Mary, who was a virgin. They tie this event to the words of the eighth-century B.C.E. Hebrew prophet Isaiah: "Therefore the Lord himself will give you a sign. Behold, the virgin[4] [young woman] will conceive, and bear a son, and shall call his name Immanuel."[5]

All of the Gospels agree that Jesus was a resident of the village of Nazareth in the province of Galilee. About his childhood and young maturity,

we are told only of the event recorded in Luke, in which the twelve-year-old Jesus went to Jerusalem for a festival with his parents and became so involved in a discussion with the teachers of the law that he failed to find his way to the party returning to Nazareth. Except for this lone incident, the life of Jesus prior to his thirtieth year is not mentioned. Naturally, this blank has led to all sorts of speculation by Christians and non-Christians.

The Gospels all place Jesus within the background of first-century Judaism. He quotes the Hebrew Scriptures in his teaching. Each Gospel writer sees Jesus as a fulfillment of the promises of the Hebrew Bible. Jesus and his **Apostles** used the Jewish synagogue as the starting point of their ministry. The New Testament shows them celebrating the Jewish holidays and being concerned with the correct interpretation of Jewish laws. Jesus is often presented in variance with some forms of first-century Judaism, but the similarities are much more common.

The Gospel of Luke tells its readers that Jesus was about thirty years of age when he began his ministry, and all of the Gospels agree that his first public act was his baptism by John the Baptist in the Jordan River. The figure of John also is not clear in the Gospel accounts. Luke says that he was Jesus's second cousin. Whatever his relationship may have been, John was a powerful and charismatic figure in Judea. When he preached his message of repentance, large crowds came down to the Jordan River to hear him. A body of disciples followed him. Years later, the Apostle Paul encountered Jews in Ephesus who had heard of John but not of Jesus.[6]

After his baptism, Jesus went into the nearby Judean wilderness, where he fasted for forty days and pondered the nature of his ministry. According to the Gospels, Jesus was tempted by Satan to accept a wide variety of easy paths to glory during this time. After the period of temptations, Jesus returned to Galilee, where he began to preach. From the Galilean villages, he chose a band of followers who would be his disciples for the next few years. Some of them had originally been disciples of John the Baptist. The Gospels list twelve disciples, but this number must have varied. There were times in Jesus's ministry when only three or four disciples of this group were close to him. At other times, he seems to have been followed by thousands of disciples.

The exact length of Jesus's public ministry is not known. The events of this ministry given in the synoptic Gospels (Matthew, Mark, and Luke) could fit into one year, beginning and ending at Passover. However, the Gospel of John presents Jesus's ministry over several seasons that seem to fit into a three-year period. Traditionally, Christians accept John's outline and talk of a three-year ministry. The location of Jesus's ministry is also a matter of some dispute. The synoptic Gospels present Jesus working

A young man is baptized.

bst2012/fotolia

mainly in Galilee and appearing in Jerusalem only for special occasions. John's account has Jesus spending more time in the province of Judea, around Jerusalem.

All of the Gospels agree that during his public ministry, Jesus spent his time teaching and healing; whether to a small group of disciples or a large crowd in a public place, he was a teacher. In the truest sense of the word, he was called *rabbi* by his disciples. Occasionally, Jesus conveyed his message in direct, simple statements, such as the Beatitudes from the Sermon on the Mount:

From the Source

Blessed are the poor in spirit,
    for theirs is the Kingdom of Heaven.
Blessed are those who mourn,
    for they shall be comforted.
Blessed are the gentle,
    for they shall inherit the earth.
Blessed are those who hunger and thirst after righteousness,
    for they shall be filled.
Blessed are the merciful,
    for they shall obtain mercy.
Blessed are the pure in heart,
    for they shall see God.

Blessed are the peacemakers,
    for they shall be called children of God.
[1]Blessed are those who have been persecuted for righteousness' sake,
    for theirs is the Kingdom of Heaven.
Blessed are you when people reproach you, persecute you, and say all kinds of evil against you falsely, for my sake. Rejoice, and be exceedingly glad, for great is your reward in heaven. For that is how they persecuted the prophets who were before you.[7]

Jesus is most often remembered, however, for his use of a teaching device called the parable. The parable is a short, easily recognized story about very human characters and events. Because of the brevity and beauty of these stories, the parables of Jesus are among the best-remembered and most-quoted teachings of all of the religions of the world. The Gospel of Luke is particularly well stocked with Jesus's parables. Here the reader finds the stories of the prodigal son, the lost sheep, and (perhaps the best known of all) the parable of the good Samaritan.

From the Source

A certain man was going down from Jerusalem to Jericho, and he fell among robbers, who both stripped him and beat him, and departed, leaving him half dead. By chance a certain priest was going down that way. When he saw him, he passed by on the other side. In the same way a Levite also, when he came to the place, and saw him, passed by on the other side. But a certain Samaritan, as he traveled, came where he was. When he saw him, he was moved with compassion, came to him, and bound up his wounds, pouring on oil and wine. He set him on his own animal, and brought him to an inn, and took care of him. On the next day, when he departed, he took out two denarii, and gave them to the host, and said to him, 'Take care of him. Whatever you spend beyond that, I will repay you when I return.'[8]

Different Christian groups have focused on different aspects of Jesus's teaching to emphasize their own positions and interpretations. It is not unusual for those with a particular point of view to isolate those statements that seem to support their position and claim that this was indeed the main message of Christ.

An example of how Jesus's teachings can be read in various ways has to do with violence. Many of Jesus's teachings seem pacifistic. For example:

From the Source

You have heard that it was said, 'An eye for an eye, and a tooth for a tooth.' But I tell you, don't resist him who is evil; but whoever strikes you on your right cheek, turn to him the other also. If anyone sues you to take away your coat, let him have your cloak also. Whoever compels you to go one mile, go with him two.[9]

Yet it would be a mistake to say that pacifism was Jesus's total answer to the problems of his times. At one point, he urged his disciples to be armed (Luke 22:36), and at another, he stated that he had not come to bring peace but a sword (Matthew 10:34).

Other groups within Christianity contend that the central message of Jesus was people's superiority over the Jewish law. Indeed, many of Jesus's actions and teachings seem to suggest an attitude of indifference toward the laws of Judaism. He healed on the Sabbath, and he allowed his disciples to pluck grain on the Sabbath while they walked through the fields. He also stated,

From the Source

That which enters into the mouth doesn't defile the man; but that which proceeds out of the mouth, this defiles the man.[10]

This statement seems to put Jesus in conflict with the Kosher food laws. However, at times, Jesus had a very reverent attitude toward the laws of Judaism:

From the Source

Don't think that I came to destroy the law or the prophets. I didn't come to destroy, but to fulfill. For most certainly, I tell you, until heaven and earth pass away, not even one smallest letter or one tiny pen stroke shall in any way pass away from the law, until all things are accomplished. Whoever, therefore, shall break one of these least commandments, and teach others to do so, shall be called least in the Kingdom of Heaven; but whoever shall do and teach them shall be called great in the Kingdom of Heaven.[11]

Indeed, many of the teachings of Jesus are similar or parallel to those of the great rabbis of that era, whose words are remembered in the Mishnah.

Still others have chosen to see the central message of Jesus in terms of an overwhelming concern on his part for the coming end of the age. Those who agree see Jesus as a leader who believed that the world was very near the end of an old age and the beginning of a new one. Many associate this new age with the return of Jesus, the resurrection, and the judgment of the dead.

All of the Gospels record that Jesus was a worker of miracles. He healed the sick, the blind, and the lame; he fed the hungry; he raised the dead; he cast out demons; he walked on the waters and stilled the storms. Miracles were a very real part of the world of Jesus, and he performed them regularly.

After a time of public ministry, the opposition against Jesus began to grow. It became necessary for him to go away from the crowds of both friends and enemies and rest periodically. On one such occasion, he went to the north to Caesarea Philippi to be alone with his closest disciples. Here he asked his disciples:

From the Source

"Who do men say that I am?"
They told him, "John the Baptizer, and others say Elijah, but others: one of the prophets."

He said to them, "But who do you say that I am?"
Peter answered, "You are the Christ."[12]

This is the clearest statement of Jesus's identification as a messianic figure by his disciples and by himself. He followed this statement with the warning that he would soon go to Jerusalem and be put to death.

After these events, Jesus and his followers began their journey southward to Jerusalem. They arrived at the time of celebration of the Passover, when the city was crowded with pilgrims from the Diaspora communities all over the world. It was a season of great expectation because it commemorated God's greatest intervention in history on behalf of his people. On the Sunday before his death, Jesus entered the city and was widely accepted and acclaimed by the citizens. On this day and those that followed, Jesus spent much time in the temple teaching and engaging in debates with his opponents. Each afternoon, he left the city and went a few miles to the village of Bethany, where he stayed at the home of his friends Mary, Martha, and Lazarus.

On Thursday evening, Jesus entered Jerusalem and partook of a final meal with his disciples. It is not clear in all of the Gospels whether this was the Passover Seder or simply a common meal. He shared bread and wine with his disciples. The Gospel of Luke describes this final meal as follows:

From the Source

He received a cup, and when he had given thanks, he said, "Take this, and share it among yourselves, for I tell you, I will not drink at all again from the fruit of the vine, until God's Kingdom comes."

He took bread, and when he had given thanks, he broke, and gave it to them, saying, "This is my body which is given for you. Do this in memory of me." Likewise, he took the cup after supper, saying, "This cup is the new covenant in my blood, which is poured out for you.[13]

For Christians these verses are among the most important in the entire Bible. They have inspired the most common and universal of Christian rituals—the Lord's Supper—but are also the source of great controversy. Some Christians, particularly Catholics, have maintained that Jesus's statements support the doctrine that in the ritual bread and wine are transformed into the body and blood of Christ. Most Protestants believe that the bread and wine are symbolic of Christ and are a reminder of his sacrifice, but that they are not literally transformed into his body and blood. It is unlikely that this controversy will ever be resolved.

Following the meal, Jesus and his party went out of the city to the Garden of Gethsemane, where Jesus prayed for a few hours. Here he was betrayed by Judas, one of his closest disciples, and arrested by the temple guards. He was tried on charges of blasphemy by the Jewish high court, the *Sanhedrin*, early the next morning. This trial was followed by a hearing before Pontius Pilate, the Roman procurator of Judea, and a beating by his troops. Jesus was also interviewed by Herod Antipas, the governor of Galilee.

Finally, at about nine o'clock in the morning, he was sent out of the city and crucified with two felons. The Gospels record that a series of cataclysmic events occurred as Jesus was dying. By three o'clock in the afternoon, he was dead. He was taken from the cross and buried in a nearby borrowed tomb.

The Gospels state that the opposition to Jesus and the responsibility for his death came mainly from within the body of Jewish leadership, especially from the party of the Pharisees. The Pharisees were a group within Judaism made up mostly of the common people. They were fairly liberal and progressive in their theological outlook. They believed in the resurrection of the dead and accepted as canon books in the Bible beyond the first five books of Moses. The New Testament lists several of Jesus's disciples as Pharisees, including Paul, the great missionary of the early church. In truth, there were more similarities between Jesus and the Pharisees than there were differences. Some have suggested that Jesus himself was a Pharisee.

Other opposition came to Jesus from the Sadducees, an aristocratic group who controlled the temple in Jerusalem. Theologically, they were very conservative, accepting only the first five books of the Bible as the word of God. The Gospels present the Sadducean leaders as the ones who tried Jesus in Jerusalem and were ultimately responsible for his death.

Undoubtedly, Jesus was opposed by another party within Judaism, the Zealots. The Zealots, who had arisen in Galilee soon after the birth of Jesus, were fanatical anti-Roman patriots who stirred up revolution at every opportunity. Even though one of Jesus's closest disciples is listed as a Zealot, this party could not have been pleased with Jesus because he refused to be the leader of a political revolution against Rome.[14]

Although the Gospels fix the major share of the opposition to Jesus on these groups within Judaism, the ultimate and fatal opposition must surely have come from the Roman government. Because of the Zealots and other dissident groups, Roman rule of Judea was never easy. From the time of Pompey's entry into Jerusalem in 63 B.C.E., through the reign of Herod the Great in the first century B.C.E., and into the period of 130–135 C.E., Judea was not quiet for the Romans. The Gospels say that Jesus began the last week of his life by entering the city of Jerusalem during Passover week, riding a donkey and being received by the crowds as though he were a conquering hero. Because Jesus was from Galilee, the home of the Zealots, and because some of his close followers were known to be armed, it was only natural for the Roman authorities to assume that this was a potentially dangerous man.

The Gospel accounts place the responsibility for Jesus's death upon the Jewish leaders and the crowds in Jerusalem who were there for the Passover. These accounts lay the foundation for much of the anti-Jewish feeling and persecution that followed for more than 2,000 years.[15] Jesus surely would not have been executed had it not been the wish of the Roman authorities. He was crucified in Roman fashion, by a group of Roman soldiers, by order of the Roman procurator of Judea, Pontius Pilate.

Jesus was crucified on Friday and was placed in the tomb by Friday evening. When women came to tend to his body the following Sunday morning, they found the tomb empty. The four Gospels tell different tales about the events that followed: Mark records that the women found the tomb empty and conversed with a young man there who told them that Jesus had risen and gone into Galilee. The other Gospels present more elaborate statements. In them, Jesus appeared to different groups of disciples in Jerusalem and Galilee at various times over the next forty days. Eventually, he gathered his friends together at the Mount of Olives outside of Jerusalem and ascended into heaven. All of the Gospels agree, however, that the tomb was empty and that Jesus had conquered death. Most agree that he was seen after his resurrection by a number of reputable witnesses. Luke mentions that some of the Apostles doubted the resurrection of Jesus, and that he ate a piece of broiled fish to prove to them that he was not a ghost or spirit but a living man.[16] The resurrection event became central to the early Christian church and almost all subsequent Christian groups and denominations.

Early Christianity

11.3. **Analyze early Christianity and the rites that still exist in Christianity today.**

The Jerusalem Church

After Jesus's resurrection and ascension into heaven, his followers met in Jerusalem. They probably banded together out of fear that they might share Jesus's fate. At the festival of Pentecost (fifty days after Passover), however, the Christians were feeling more courageous because of the coming of the Holy Spirit and went out into the streets of Jerusalem to preach about their faith. Miraculously, they were able to preach in languages that they had not known before and as a result persuaded many people to join them.

It is important to note that this original group of Christians and others that sprang up throughout the world were considered by themselves and others to be a sect of Judaism. The members of this group were Jewish by background; their Bible was the

Hebrew Bible; and they continued to worship at the temple in Jerusalem. The only thing that distinguished them from other Jews was their belief that Jesus of Nazareth was somehow unique. The exact faith of these early Christians is difficult to define precisely. The systemization of Christian theology was not to come for several centuries, and after long years of debate.

Our knowledge of the Jerusalem church is drawn from the accounts of the New Testament book Acts of the Apostles. The leadership of the group seems to have resided in two men. The first was Simon Peter, who had been among the inner circle of Jesus's disciples. Although the organization was loose in the early days, Simon Peter was certainly a major spokesperson for the church. Others of Jesus's disciples are mentioned in Acts, but none seems to have had Simon Peter's authority. A second leader who came to have more and more influence in Jerusalem was James, the half-brother of Jesus. Tradition says that James was not a follower of Jesus during his ministry but came to believe in him after the resurrection. James assumed leadership of the Jerusalem church when Simon Peter moved out to other communities. Beyond these two, there seems to have been no official leadership.

The Acts record that seven men were chosen to serve the Hellenist Christians of Jerusalem in the distribution of charity. One of these was Stephen, who not only acted as a servant of the church but also preached in the streets. His preaching so enraged the authorities in Jerusalem that he was officially denounced and stoned to death. Thus Stephen became the first martyr of the Christian faith. His death was but one event in a series of persecutions against the Christians in Jerusalem as hostility against them increased. These persecutions caused many Christians to leave Jerusalem and carry their faith elsewhere in Judea and into other centers of the Roman Empire.

The Life of Paul

Because almost half of the Book of Acts is devoted to the missionary activities of Paul, and because he is traditionally considered the author of fourteen books of the New Testament, Paul is the best-known early Christian.[17] Undoubtedly, other missionary figures in the early church went as far and did as much as Paul, but they escaped the attention of the New Testament. Not only was Paul important as a missionary of the early faith, but he also made a great contribution as a theologian. He was among the first to attempt to state systematically the beliefs of Christianity. Indeed, Paul is sometimes called the "Second Founder of Christianity."

According to the biographical material presented in Acts and that which may be gathered from his epistles, Paul was reared in the Diaspora Jewish community of Tarsus in Asia Minor. He was educated in both Judaism and Hellenistic traditions. He studied with the great Rabbi Gamaliel and was a member of the Pharisee party. Paul was originally strongly anti-Christian, and when opposition to the Christian sect in Jerusalem became active persecution, Paul became a leader and observed the stoning of Stephen. On a mission to persecute the Christians in Damascus, he was struck down by a light from heaven and was converted from an enemy of the Christians to a spokesperson for them.

After a time of study, he began to preach on behalf of Christianity. With various companions, he traveled across the Roman Empire, preaching first in the Jewish synagogues and then to gentile audiences. It was Paul, perhaps more than anyone else, who led the movement to allow gentiles to become Christians without first becoming Jews and following the laws of Judaism. The fact that converts could come very easily into the church from almost any background, without a lengthy and arduous preparation for Judaism, made it possible for Christianity to become an independent universal religion rather than a sect of Judaism.

Paul and his companions carried out three missionary journeys, which took them to many of the cities of Asia Minor and Greece. Upon completion of his travels, Paul returned to Jerusalem, where he was arrested by the Roman authorities. He was imprisoned in Caesarea for several years and eventually sent to Rome, where he was to be tried by Caesar. Acts concludes with Paul's entering Rome somewhere around 60 C.E., and there is no biblical material about the remainder of his life. Tradition says he was imprisoned in Rome during the period of the Neronic persecution of the church (64 C.E.) and executed.

Tradition also states that Simon Peter, who had become bishop of the church at Rome, was executed there at approximately the same time. *The Annals* of Tacitus, a Roman historian who wrote approximately fifty years after Nero's persecution, claims that Nero set out to persecute the Christians to shift the blame from himself for having set a great fire in Rome. This was the first of the official persecutions of the Christians by the Roman government.

The Worship of the Early Church

Clearly the church modeled its worship after the forms used in the Jewish synagogue. The Jerusalem church, which continued to exist and exert authority until its destruction along with the city in 70 C.E., still used the temple as a place of worship. It may even have continued to practice the animal sacrifice that was a part of temple worship at that time. Wherever Paul went, he first sought out and preached at the local Jewish synagogue. Undoubtedly, the prayers, the Scripture reading, the hymns, and the simple sermons that were so much a part of synagogue worship were also a part of early Christian worship.

In addition to these modes of worship, Christians added others. **Baptism** was apparently a part of Christian worship from the earliest times. Baptism as an initiation into a new faith was practiced by the Pharisees when they took converts into Judaism. John the Baptist baptized people in the Jordan River as a symbol of repentance. Jesus's disciples baptized converts even during his ministry, and Paul baptized converts wherever he went.

Both the mode and the meaning of Christian baptism have been objects of debate throughout the history of the church. The word *baptize* comes from the Greek word *baptizein*, "to immerse." Presumably, John immersed his converts in the Jordan River. As Christians grew in number, the inconvenience of finding a body of water large enough to immerse the candidate may have ushered in a more moderate form of baptism. Pouring or sprinkling water on the head became accepted as the proper mode of baptism. Some Christian communities continue the practice of baptism by immersion.

It is not clear why Jesus's disciples baptized, nor does the New Testament tell the reader clearly why the early church continued the practice. It appears originally to have been an outward sign of the change in status from the pagan life to the Christian life. In later years, it took on deeper meanings. Eventually, baptism was understood to be the washing away of original sin. In the New Testament accounts, the converts who were baptized were adults, but baptism became more and more important to salvation; eventually infants were baptized to wash away the stain of original sin as quickly as possible. This is easy to understand when we recall that at the time the practice was initiated, infant mortality rates were extremely high. Whatever the original manner and meaning of baptism may have been, it has long been one of the most important rituals in Christianity.

The second addition of the early Christians was the **Eucharist**, or communion meal. This was probably modeled on the Seder meal of Judaism, in which community members recall divine history as they partake of sacred foods. Specifically, it was adopted by Christians from the model of Jesus's last supper with his disciples on the evening before his death. In the early years of the church, it became customary for Christians to gather together and eat a meal recalling the death of Jesus. Perhaps it was simply a meal of bread and wine, or it may have included other foods.[18] Again, both the manner and meaning of the communion meal have been debated within the church. Eventually, the Eucharist became a sacred meal in which the bread and wine actually became the flesh and blood of Jesus; individuals who received these elements were actually eating and drinking the body of Jesus and thus their souls were sanctified and aided in their journey toward eventual salvation. Like baptism, the Eucharist is considered a **sacrament** by most Christians. For Christians, a sacrament is an outward and material ritual act or behavior that communicates an inward working of God in their lives.

Leadership in the Early Church

The early church was not a highly organized structure. Both Acts and the Epistles of Paul indicate that many Christians were expecting Jesus to return to Earth at almost any time, and therefore the church had no need for a highly organized structure. As the years passed and it became apparent that Jesus was not returning immediately, as the number of Christians grew, and as the various interpretations of Christianity increased, it became necessary for the church to organize more fully. There had always been outstanding leaders, such as Simon Peter, Paul, and James; apparently, they held no titles and drew whatever authority they had from their relationship to Jesus and the force of their personalities. The Catholic Church claims that Simon Peter was intended by Jesus to be the cornerstone of the Church. This claim is based on the following biblical passage:

From the Source

Simon Peter answered, "You are the Christ, the Son of the living God."

Jesus answered him, "Blessed are you, Simon Bar Jonah, for flesh and blood has not revealed this to you, but my Father who is in heaven. I also tell you that you are Peter, and on this rock I will build my assembly, and the gates of Hades will not prevail against it. I will give to you the keys of the Kingdom of Heaven, and whatever you bind on earth will have been bound in heaven; and whatever you release on earth will have been released in heaven."[19]

Although it is not mentioned in the New Testament, a strong tradition says that Simon Peter went to Rome and became the leader of the church in that city. The bishops who were his successors became the popes of the Roman church.

The New Testament mentions several kinds of leaders in the early church, but their roles are never clearly delineated. One such leader was the bishop. The Greek word for bishop, *episkopos*, literally means "shepherd." Qualifications for this office were laid out by Paul in the epistles to Timothy and to Titus, and the bishop seems to have managed the church in a certain geographical area. Another officer was the deacon. The first seven servants chosen by the church of Jerusalem are frequently referred to as deacons, although the New Testament never calls them this. The office of deacon was, as the word *diakonos* (servant) implies, one of service.[20] The qualifications for deacon were as stringent as those for bishop.

Elders (*presbyteroi*) are also mentioned as leaders of the church. Acts makes a clear connection between the elders of Judaism and those of the church. Apparently, the latter were older persons who had been given authority to make decisions on religious matters by virtue of their age and wisdom. Paul's letters indicate that the elders also taught and preached. In addition to these offices, the New Testament mentions evangelists, prophets, apostles, pastors, and teachers. Never, however, is the reader given a complete list of the functions of these leaders.

The Christian church of the New Testament period (ca. 30–150 C.E.) seems to have been amorphous both in belief and structure. No strong organization imposed a creed on the Christian groups; therefore, they varied greatly in what they believed and practiced. Paul was constantly having to correct what he considered false doctrine among Christians in various parts of the Roman world. He disagreed with many of the Jerusalem leaders about the admittance of gentiles into the church. The churches of the various cities within the Roman Empire seem to have been loosely organized, meeting in the synagogues when they were welcome and in private homes when no other arrangements could be made. They soon changed their day of worship from the Jewish Sabbath of Saturday to Sunday, the day when Jesus rose from the dead. Their clergy apparently had little official status and usually were not paid for their preaching. Occasionally, offerings were taken for Christian preachers, but for the most part they lived by whatever trade or skills they had.

The Production of the New Testament and Early Creeds

The Bible of the early church was the Hebrew Bible. Christians read the prophets Isaiah, Micah, and Zechariah and saw in them predictions of the life of Jesus. As the years passed, specific Christian literature began to develop. Probably the earliest Christian writings were the letters (epistles) that Paul wrote to the Christian congregations he had established. They contain advice to the early church on doctrine, leadership, and worship. Additionally, they contain some biographical material about Paul and other early church leaders not found elsewhere. In his letters to the Romans and Galatians particularly, Paul sets forth the first systematic understanding of the importance of the life, death, and resurrection of Jesus.

In the years following Jesus's death, Christians undoubtedly wrote their remembrances of the events of his life as well as his sayings. We may speculate that collections of his teachings were compiled for use in the instruction of converts. However, Christians may not have made a careful attempt to write the story of Jesus because they were expecting his imminent return. As the years passed and as the people who personally knew of Jesus began to die (either from old age or persecution), fewer and fewer Christians were able to recount the events in Jesus's life with any certainty.

In 70 C.E., the Roman armies closed in on Jerusalem to finish off the Jewish rebellion that had begun four years earlier. By the end of the summer, Jerusalem and its temple were destroyed, along with the Jerusalem church and many witnesses to the life of Jesus. It may have been this event that caused a Christian to collect a brief statement of the events in the last few months of Jesus's life and to circulate it as the Gospel of Mark. In the next decade, two more elaborate Gospels, Matthew and Luke, were written using Mark as a base.

The Gospel that differs most from the others in terms of content, chronology, and message is the Gospel of John. This work supposedly was written between 90 and 100 C.E., although its date is by no means certain. The account of the early church in Jerusalem, Acts of the Apostles, was probably written by the author of Luke as a sequel to that Gospel.

Other epistles by anonymous authors were probably written between 90 and 150 C.E. and make up eight books in the current New Testament. In addition to these books, there were many other epistles, Gospels, and histories written in these early centuries that were circulated and read by Christians, but they were not popular or authoritative enough to have been maintained. The exact list and number of the books of the New Testament probably remained in flux for the first centuries of the life of the church. By the fourth century, Athanasius of Alexandria placed his authority behind the twenty-seven books that make up the New Testament. Despite official endorsement of the canon, questions remained about such books as Hebrews, James, and Revelation as late as the sixteenth century.

Because early Christianity was not a highly organized body with an established creed, and because it included a wide variety of members, early Christians had many different beliefs. In subsequent years, the church established creeds and an orthodox theology. Later Christians, looking back on the early believers who did not conform to the content of these creeds, referred to them as heretics. Many of the controversies concerned the nature of the Trinity, which is among the most complex Christian teachings.

To consolidate their views about the Trinity and the nature of Jesus, the winners of these early theological debates developed statements of faith, or creeds. They had to be simple enough to be memorized and used regularly; at the same time, they had to be thorough enough to combat heresies effectively. The result was the so-called Apostles' Creed. The critical mind cannot believe that this creed was developed by Simon Peter, James, and John, although it does have the ring of early authority. The following statement of this creed comes from about 340 C.E.:

From the Source

I believe in God almighty
And in Christ Jesus, his only son, our Lord
Who was born of the Holy Spirit and the Virgin Mary
Who was crucified under Pontius Pilate and was buried
And the third day rose from the dead
Who ascended into heaven
And sitteth on the right hand of the Father

Whence he cometh to judge the living and the dead.
And in the Holy Ghost
The holy church
The remission of sins
The resurrection of the flesh
The life everlasting.[21]

Growth of the Church of Rome

11.4.　Understand the growth of the Church of Rome and the ascendancy of the papacy.

In the early years of Christianity, Jerusalem exercised leadership over the church. After 70 C.E., other cities, such as Alexandria and Antioch, took over this leadership. These cities produced many of the outstanding thinkers, known as the church fathers, whose writings have influenced Christianity for all time. Each of the great cities of the Roman Empire had a bishop; the larger and more influential the city, the greater the authority of its bishop. The bishops of Alexandria, Antioch, Caesarea, and Rome were all considered to be leaders in the early church. Eventually, the bishop of the Church of Rome came to be recognized as the most important bishop of all and finally was designated as pope. There were several reasons for this ascendancy.

First, Simon Peter, whom Jesus had singled out as the rock upon which he would build his church, had become the first bishop of the Roman church and had passed on his authority to the bishops who succeeded him. Thus, the Roman church had a very strong tradition.

Second, Constantine, the first Roman emperor to support Christianity, moved his political capital from Rome to Byzantium in 330 C.E. This left Rome without a strong political leader. A series of strong bishops of the Roman church filled this void and were looked on by Western rulers as being extremely important.

Third, the churches of the East were split by various doctrinal controversies, and no one bishop could speak for all Eastern Christians. The West, however, was relatively free from these controversies; the bishop of Rome was the spokesperson for a widely accepted orthodoxy.

Thus, through a combination of fortuitous events and able leadership, the Church of Rome came to be the dominant church in Christendom, and its bishops became the Christian popes.

Emergence of Christianity as the Religion of the Roman Empire

During the period between 64 and 330 C.E., Christianity went through several periods of persecution and acceptance by the Roman Empire. Officially, the Empire was tolerant of all religions. However, the Christians occasionally found themselves in trouble because of their refusal to accept the official Roman gods and to worship them on state occasions. Jews also were in turmoil over this issue. In addition, the Christian sect was accused by the Romans of a variety of evils. Because Christians were often from the slave classes and often met in secret, they were accused of performing evil secret rituals that included eating human flesh and drinking human blood. They also were accused of sexual immorality.

As the number of Christians grew, as they refused to give first allegiance to the emperor, and as they occasionally refused to be members of the Roman army, opposition to them grew. Frequently, persecution was the result. Nero's persecution of Christians was local and brief. Emperor Domitian (who ruled from 81 to 96 C.E.) insisted that citizens of the Empire worship his person, and he instituted the first widespread persecution of Christians who refused to worship him. This persecution may have formed the background from which the Revelation of John was written. Early persecutions of Christians also led to the development of traditions concerning the sanctity of martyrdom that persist to this day.

Religion and Public Life

Persecution of Christians reached its peak in 303 C.E. under Diocletian (emperor from 284 to 305 C.E.) in an empirewide movement that lasted for more than ten years. This period was followed by the reign of Constantine. Constantine was not Christian but was strongly influenced by his wife and mother, who were. In 313 C.E., Constantine issued the Edict of Milan, which gave Christianity the same privileges as other religions. The official persecution of Christians was over. In 325 C.E., Constantine called the Church Council of Nicaea to stop the warring within Christian factions over the nature of Christ. Twelve years later, when he was dying, Constantine finally accepted baptism and officially became a Christian.

Several emperors who followed Constantine tried to reverse the tide and return to the old Roman religions. But with the reign of Theodosius (emperor from 379 to 395 C.E.), Christianity officially became the religion of the Roman Empire and all other religions were suppressed.

Augustine

Perhaps no other Christian after Paul and Constantine so deeply influenced the life and direction of Christianity as did Augustine (354–430 C.E.). Like many of the other leaders of the early church, he was born in North Africa. His mother was a devout Christian, but his father was pagan. Although he received Christian instruction as a child, he did not accept the faith until later in life. As a young man, he took a concubine and had a child by her. For a time, he was interested in Manichaeism, a religion that was a syncretism of Christian and Zoroastrian ideas. After a few years with Manichaeism, Augustine followed the teachings of Neoplatonism, but he was not completely satisfied with this either.

In Milan, Italy, Augustine came under the influence of the Christian bishop Ambrose. In a very dramatic conversion experience, Augustine became a Christian. He returned to North Africa, where he became a writer and eventually the bishop of Hippo. Two of his writings have become classics in Christian literature: his autobiographical *Confessions* and his *City of God*, an interpretation of history written in response to those who blamed the Christians for the fall of the city of Rome to the Goths.

Vittoriano Rastelli/Historical/Corbis

Christmas Mass at Saint Peter's Basilica in Vatican City.

The Monastic Movement

Introduced by the early medieval church, the monastic movement became a major part of Christianity. Of all the major religions of the Western world, Christianity is the only one to encourage monastic orders. Neither Judaism nor Islam has encouraged its members to live alone apart from the evils of normal life, although there have been minor movements in both religions in that direction.

The movement toward asceticism and monastic community life apparently began in Egypt in the middle of the third century C.E. Christians in Egypt may have been influenced by the asceticism of native Egyptian religions, or they may have been influenced by the basic distrust of the flesh taught by the Manichaeans, the Gnostics, and the Neoplatonists. Egypt itself, with its deserts and wild places, offered the ideal setting for men and women who wanted to leave the problems of normal life behind them and seek solitude in the wilderness. Some began to sell their possessions and go out into the desert regions to live simple lives dedicated to God. A number of them were widely known for their feats of asceticism. Simeon Stylites (d. 459 C.E.), for example, is said to have lived atop a pillar in the desert of Syria for thirty-six years. Others fasted for long periods, went without sleep, ate only the simplest of food, gave up bathing, and wore garments that were irritating to the skin. Still others gathered together and formed monastic communities.

The first Christian monastery is attributed to Pachomius, who was born in Egypt in the last decade of the third century. For a variety of reasons, the monastic movement soon became popular throughout Christendom. Benedict of Nursia (480?–543) is another important figure in the history of Christian monasticism and is especially remembered for his "Rule," a disciplinary guidebook that provided order for communities of monks and nuns.

Basically, monasteries were secluded places where people dedicated themselves to a simple life of hard manual labor, prayer, fasting, and sometimes study. What little learning and scholarship existed in the medieval period was kept alive in monasteries. Historically, some of the best minds of the church were produced by these communities. Jerome (345?–420 C.E.), who translated the Hebrew and Greek biblical material into the Latin Vulgate—the standard Bible for the Roman Catholic Church for over

1,500 years—was a product of the monastic movement. Some have suggested that the vitality and strength of the monasteries at any given time was an accurate gauge of the vitality of the entire church.

Medieval Christianity

11.5. **Discuss the theological differences between the East and West during the Middle Ages.**

The period between the fall of the Roman Empire and the rise of the modern European nations is usually called the medieval period or the Middle Ages. During this period, the Christian church was a major force in the total culture of Eastern and Western Europe.

Division between Eastern and Western Christianity

From the time of the establishment of the city of Constantinople as the new capital of the Roman Empire (330 C.E.), there developed a gradually widening division between the Christians of the East and those of Western Europe. This basic division was political and geographic as well as theological. When Constantine set up his capital in the East, he took an active role in the development and direction of the church and called the Council of Nicaea to settle theological differences. His successors followed his example and usually took an active part in directing religion. In the West, Rome had been left without an effective political leadership. The bishops of the Roman church stepped into this vacuum and even took some of the titles of the ancient caesars. When the barbarians massed at the walls of Rome, it was the popes who negotiated with them for the city.

The theological differences between East and West were basic. Most of the great thinkers and leaders of the early church were from North Africa and Asia Minor. Most of the early councils that established Christian doctrine were held in the East. Eastern Christians tended to be more interested in theological formulations and became bitterly divided over certain issues. Western Christians tended to be more practical and were concerned with survival in a hostile, decaying world. Eastern theologians tended to emphasize the divine nature of Christ, whereas those of the West emphasized his humanity.

The largest issue dividing Eastern and Western Christians was the papacy. The great cities of the East had outstanding bishops who became known as patriarchs. Although Constantinople was the capital, its patriarch could never gain authority over the patriarchs of the other major cities. In the West, there was only Rome, and the bishop of that city clearly led the Western church. Gradually, the bishop of Rome claimed to be the leader of all Christendom, but the Eastern patriarchs refused to accept his authority.

Numerous minor differences also developed between these churches, which came to be known as Eastern Orthodox and Roman Catholic. The Eastern church used icons—two-dimensional pictures of Jesus, Mary, and the disciples—in their worship, whereas the Western church long eschewed them. The East baptized infants by immersion, whereas the West allowed sprinkling. The East gave the people both bread and wine in the communion meal, whereas after the tenth

Eastern Orthodox Christian Easter celebration in Karpathos, Greece.

Gordon Mills/Alamy

Icons like this one are important devotional objects for Orthodox Christians.

century, the West gave them only bread. The East allowed its clergy the possibility of marriage before ordination, whereas the West came to insist on celibacy. The East used Greek as its language of worship, whereas the West used Latin until the mid-twentieth century.

The rift between the two branches of Christendom continued to grow during its first thousand years. Western Christians were busy repelling various barbarian invasions and building what has become Western Europe, while the East saw almost all of its empire fall into the hands of Muslim invaders in the seventh and eighth centuries. Antagonism reached a climax in 1054, when Leo IX sent delegates to Constantinople to excommunicate the Patriarch Cerularius. This event, often referred to as the "Great Schism," marks division of the Roman Catholic Church and Eastern Orthodox churches. Even this breach might have been healed, but Christian Crusaders from European nations stopped at Constantinople in 1204 on their way to the Holy Land and sacked the city. Even today, the modern ecumenical movement within Christendom is still seeking a reunion between these two branches of the church.

The Medieval Papacy

Because of its great missionary activities and basic attractiveness, Christianity had become virtually the only religion of Western Europe by the medieval period. The thrust of the Muslim movement into Western Europe was stopped by Charles Martel at the Battle of Tours in 732. Although Spain was Muslim for another seven centuries, the rest of Western Europe remained Christian. The implications of this for the papacy were immense. For Europeans, there was only one Holy Catholic Church, outside of which there was no salvation. This church had one head, Christ, who ruled through his vicar, Simon Peter, and his successors on the throne of the church in Rome. The line of succession from Simon Peter to the various popes was said to be an unbroken line of authority. This power and its potential were the occasion for both excellence and abuse by the medieval popes.

In the chaos that followed the decline of the Roman Empire, the papacy was often the only secure leadership in Europe, and the popes of the Christian church exercised much of the same power as did temporal rulers. Indeed, they were the makers of many temporal rulers, as it was the custom of those who would be emperors of the Holy Roman Empire to be crowned by the popes. Naturally, this power led to abuses. The

Mark R. Woodward

Three Kings bringing gifts.

papacy gathered lands, wealth, and art treasures and went to war in a manner similar to that of any other feudal state. Frequently, ecclesiastical offices were given to relatives (nepotism) or sold to the highest bidder (simony) because they carried so much potential power and wealth.

In terms of its moral leadership, the papacy reached its weakest point between 1309 and 1377, when the headquarters of the papacy moved from Rome to Avignon in what is now France. All of the popes and most of the cardinals of this era were French; at times, the papacy was virtually captive to the king of France, which weakened its power and prestige with nations that were not friendly to France. This was a period of papal wealth, luxury, moral laxity, and abuse.

In 1378, the Avignon cardinals elected a new pope, Urban VI, who then refused to return to Avignon with them and instead restored the papacy to Rome. The cardinals declared Urban's election void and elected another pope, who would rule from Avignon. Thereupon, Urban selected another college of cardinals. The European nations were divided in their support of the two men who claimed to be the successor to Saint (Simon) Peter. The Council of Pisa was called in 1409 to settle the issue but instead selected a third pope, who also claimed to be Christ's vicar on Earth. This division was finally healed by the Council of Constance, which met from 1414 to 1418, and the papacy was returned to one pope, with his capital in Rome.

Thomas Aquinas

The tenth through fourteenth centuries in Western Europe were a time of intense intellectual activity. During this period, many of the great universities were founded and their main intellectual pursuit was theology. The writings of Plato, Aristotle, and others had been preserved from destruction by the Muslim philosophers; by the late medieval period, there was enough peaceful contact between Muslim and Christian scholars to allow Christians to have access to these writings so that they could translate them into Latin. These translations gave impetus to the intellectual movement.

The issue that most concerned Christian thinkers was the relationship between faith and reason. Were Christian beliefs, which had been communicated through Scripture and the Church, consistent with what people perceived to be the truth by means of their ability to reason? The most outstanding Christian scholar to address this issue was Thomas Aquinas (d. 1274), a Dominican monk whose entire life was given over to scholarship. He was a student of Albertus Magnus at the University of Paris. Although Aquinas was a prolific writer of hymns, commentaries, and theological studies, he is best remembered for two works. The first was *Summa Contra Gentiles*, a series of arguments defending the Christian faith against infidels. The second and best known of his works was *Summa Theologiae*, a massive systemization of the Christian faith that became the standard theological formulation for the Roman Catholic Church.

Aquinas, more than anyone else, attempted to Christianize Aristotle. To prove part of the Christian scheme, Aquinas used Aristotle's arguments (based on reason) for the existence of God. However, Aquinas believed that reason could take the Christian only so far; beyond this point, there had to be divine revelation to complete the message. Therefore, both reason and revelation were necessary for Christian belief.

The Protestant Reformation

11.6.   **Analyze the various people associated with the Protestant Reformation and the reforms they proposed.**

In the sixteenth century, the Western church was torn asunder by a violent revolution. This revolution has been called the Reformation, but it went far beyond reforming Christianity; it upset it, destroyed its unified hold on Europe, challenged its authority, and disrupted it for centuries. The causes of this revolution are many, varied, and intricate. However, the major ones may be listed broadly as the beginning of European nationalism, the new learning of the Renaissance, and the decline of the papacy.

Early Reform Movements

The beginning of the Protestant **Reformation** is usually set at 1517, when Martin Luther posted his Ninety-five Theses on the door of the church in Wittenberg, in what is now Germany; however, there were reformers and reform movements more than a century before Luther. One of the earliest reformers was John Wycliffe of England (1320?–1384). Wycliffe was an Oxford scholar who eventually held many of the ideas that were later representative of the Protestant movement. His greatest contribution was the translation of the official Bible of the Church, the *Vulgate*, from Latin to English. To facilitate the reading of this Bible by the common people, Wycliffe organized a band of wandering preachers known as Lollards, who went about the country preaching and teaching.

Efforts to reform the Church met with fierce resistance. Wycliffe died peacefully in 1384 but was condemned by the Council of Constance in 1415. His remains were unearthed and burned in 1428 as an expression of this condemnation. Even though the Lollard movement was intermittently persecuted by the kings of England, it survived long after Wycliffe.

The early Reformation in Bohemia was led by John Hus (1374–1415). Rector of the University of Prague, Hus was influenced by the writings of Wycliffe. Hus denounced the evils of the current papacy and drew a large following from the citizens of Prague.

To raise money for various reasons, the medieval papacy had approved the sale of indulgences. For a price, a Christian could buy an indulgence that, drawing upon the treasury of good that the saints had developed, would pay for a sin committed by the living or by the dead who were in purgatory. Hus was particularly bold in denouncing this practice (that naturally led to all manner of corruption). Hus was condemned by the Council of Constance in 1415 and burned at the stake.

Martin Luther

The most outstanding figure of the Reformation was Martin Luther (1483–1546) of Saxony, in what is now Germany. An Augustinian monk, Luther's skills as a scholar were noted by his superiors, and he was sent as a teacher of theology to the University of Wittenberg. There he taught, preached, and obtained his Doctorate of Theology. While at Wittenberg, he lectured on Paul's letters to the Romans and Galatians. In both of these books, the phrase "the just shall live by faith" caught his eye and became a source of illumination to him. Luther was convinced that he, and all other humans, were unworthy of salvation, but that in return for unconditional faith, God would bestow his saving grace.

Like many others, Luther began to call for moral reform within the Church. He was particularly incensed by the sale of indulgences by a monk named Tetzel, who promised people that as soon as their

Martin Luther is traditionally regarded as the founder of the Protestant Reformation.

Famoso/Alamy

money fell into the coffer, a soul rose from purgatory. On the basis of his opposition to this sale of indulgences, Luther chose his Ninety-five Theses as grounds for debate and nailed them to the door of the castle church in Wittenberg on October 31, 1517. These theses were widely read all across Germany and created an immediate sensation. In the publications and debates that followed, Luther was led into more and more controversy with the papacy. He came to declare that every Christian was a priest who could interpret Scripture and that the popes and the church hierarchy were not superior to the believer. He also challenged the doctrine of transubstantiation, which taught that at the mass the bread and wine literally became the body and blood of Jesus. Luther's writings on these and many other controversial issues were widely distributed using a new technology: the printing press.

Because of the controversy Luther had caused, the emperor of the Holy Roman Empire, Charles V, convened an imperial diet (court) at the city of Worms in April 1521 to try Luther. When questioned, Luther admitted that the writings under scrutiny were his, but he refused to recant or retract any of their contents. He is reported to have said, "Here I stand. I cannot do otherwise." As a result of his actions before the diet, he was placed under an imperial edict that banned the printing and sale of his books and forbade anyone to provide hospitality or shelter for him or his friends. It had been expected that Luther would suffer the same fate as that of Hus 100 years before, but the emperor was too busy with other matters. Instead, Luther was kidnapped by friends and taken to the Wartburg Castle, where he lived in disguise for almost a year. During this time, he wrote nearly a dozen books and translated the New Testament into German. Later, he translated the Old Testament; his translations of Scripture became classics in the German language.

In 1522, Luther returned to Wittenberg, where he took charge of the rapidly developing Reformation. He repudiated the acts of radical reformers who wanted to destroy everything in the Christian church that was not specifically mentioned in Scripture. His own style was to remove only those things he felt were contrary to Scripture. In the following years, Luther was busy in many ways. He was, of course, organizing the Reformed Church in Germany. He was writing hymns, such as the Protestant classic, "A Mighty Fortress Is Our God." He was encouraging former priests and nuns to marry. He himself married a nun, Katherine von Bora, and became a father.

The Reformation sprang up in other nations during Luther's lifetime and immediately thereafter. In Germany, the decision to be reformed or to remain Catholic lay with the prince of any particular region. If the ruler were reformed, the region became reformed; if the ruler chose to remain Catholic, the region remained Catholic. Thus, the religious orientation of Germany became a kind of patchwork. The Scandinavian nations—Sweden, Denmark, and Norway—became Lutheran during the following decades.

Ulrich Zwingli

In Switzerland, the reform movement was led by Ulrich Zwingli (1484–1531). Zwingli was a contemporary of Luther and was much influenced by his writings. At first, the Reformed Church in Switzerland was very close to the Lutheran movement. However, Zwingli and Luther differed substantially over one central issue. Although Luther denied that the bread and wine of communion actually became the body and blood of Christ, he did believe that Christ was spiritually present in the elements. He believed that the words of Jesus at the Last Supper, "This is my body," were to be taken literally. Zwingli chose to emphasize the other words of Jesus at the Last Supper, "Do this in remembrance of me." Therefore, to the Swiss reformer, the communion meal was a memorial, a remembrance of Jesus's death. This issue prevented a union between the Swiss Protestants and the Lutherans.

John Calvin

Probably the greatest and most influential mind of the Reformation was John Calvin (1509–1564). Calvin was born in France and received a classical education at the University of Paris. By 1534, he had come under the influence of the Protestant movement and made his break with the Roman church. By the time he was twenty-six, he had turned his fine mind to theological matters and had written the massive book that became the classic of Protestant theology, *The Institutes of the Christian Religion*. This book, originally written in Latin and later translated into French, was revised four times in Calvin's lifetime. In it, he set forth his understanding of the nature of the true Christian faith before it was corrupted by Rome. He repeated many of the teachings of Augustine, stressing such ideas as the sovereignty of God, original sin, the total depravity of man, predestination, and election. Among the most important of his teachings was that God determined those who were destined for heaven and those doomed to hell prior to the time of creation.

Eventually, Calvin served as a minister in the Reformed Church of Geneva, Switzerland, and then in Strasbourg, on the French-German border. He was invited back to Geneva a second time and remained there from 1541 until his death in 1564. Although he was never more than a minister in Geneva, Calvin's influence over the life of the entire city was enormous. Despite opposition from theological and political foes, he was virtually the ruler of Geneva. He himself was given to hard work and simple living, and he impressed this upon the city. He discouraged frivolity of any kind. He encouraged commerce and industry as well as lending money at reasonable rates of interest.[22] He encouraged education and founded the University of Geneva. Under Calvin's leadership, Geneva became the home of oppressed Protestants from all over Europe. Calvin was very intolerant of interpretations of Christianity other than his own and condemned theologian Michael Servetus to be burned at the stake because he did not accept the doctrine of the Holy Trinity.

The importance of John Calvin to the Reformed Church cannot be stressed enough. His writings set the intellectual base for much of the later Protestant theology. His concern for the rightness of labor and thrift as proper expressions of Christianity continue to impact many Protestants today.

Other Reformation Leaders and Movements

Although the Reformation first centered on the writings and teachings of people like Luther and Calvin, and although it attracted large numbers of dissatisfied Christians throughout Europe, it soon became a fragmented movement. Within 100 years of the death of Luther, there were hundreds of **denominations** (and later, subdenominations) of Protestant churches. In the centuries that followed, the fragmentation continued. There were at least two major reasons for these divisions. First, Protestantism derived much of its force and early growth from nationalistic trends in sixteenth-century Western Europe. Whereas in medieval Europe one emperor was crowned by the pope and ruled much of Central Europe, postmedieval European states tried to limit the powers of both the emperor and Rome. Therefore, when the opportunity came for leaders of European nations to express their freedom from Rome through a new version of Christianity, many were willing to take it.

The best example of this expression of freedom was the establishment of the Church of England. Although England had been the home of Wycliffe and had theological differences with Rome, the major reason for the Reformation in that country was political. The strong king of England, Henry VIII, wanted a wife who would bear him a son. Because his wife Catherine did not bear him one, Henry asked the pope for an annulment so that he could remarry. When the pope refused, Henry married Anne Boleyn, established the Church of England, and appointed Thomas Cranmer Archbishop of Canterbury in 1533. Although the ostensible cause of the

Interior view of Knox Church, Otago, New Zealand. The elegance and simplicity of the design reflects the Protestant theological notion that there are no intermediaries between God and humankind.

Mark R. Woodward

breach between Rome and England was Henry's marital life, the drive toward political independence was perhaps the stronger force behind the establishment of the Church of England.

A second cause for the many divisions within Protestantism was the controversy about the "priesthood of all believers," which had been an important part of Luther's teachings. Many of the reformers thought that many priests, who heard confessions, administered the sacraments, and interpreted the Bible for the untrained parishioner—and indeed, the institution of the priesthood itself—were corrupt. Therefore, these reformers taught that in the spirit of the New Testament each believer was a priest who was qualified to perform many of these tasks. The reformers were strongly in favor of the translation of the Bible into vernacular languages so that it could be read by every Christian. Obviously, if all Christians could read the Bible and were free to interpret it for themselves, differences of interpretation were bound to occur, and these ultimately caused divisions within Protestantism.

One of the most radical dissenting groups was the Anabaptists. Luther and Calvin had rejected only those elements in the Catholic Church that they felt were expressly forbidden in the Bible. Anabaptists attempted to discard all of those elements not expressly found in the New Testament. Luther and Calvin advocated infant baptism because it was not condemned by the New Testament. Anabaptists rejected it because they could not find such a practice in the New Testament. They therefore baptized adults who had formerly been baptized as infants—thus the nickname *Anabaptists* (those who baptize a second time). Because this movement was inherently divisive, there were many Anabaptist subgroups with a great variety of beliefs. Anabaptists have ranged from pacifists to violent revolutionaries, although most today are committed pacifists. Many of the Anabaptist sects came to view the technological developments of the modern world as evil. Many of them do not use automobiles or other mechanized forms of transportation. Because they were different and their numbers were small, the Anabaptists were persecuted by both Catholics and other Protestants, to the point that they were almost eliminated from the European continent. They survived in southern Germany, Britain, and America as Mennonites and Amish. Most Amish live in rural communities and continue to farm with horses. Mennonites are more accepting of the modern world, and many are active in peace and human rights movements.

The Catholic Counter-Reformation

When it became apparent that large numbers of Christians were leaving the Catholic Church and following the reformers, the Catholic Church responded, in 1545, by convening the Council of Trent. Some who came to the Council wanted reforms that would bring reconciliation with the Protestants. Others wished to state the Catholic position so clearly that there could be no reconciliation. Generally, the decisions of Trent favored those who preferred the second path. To counter the Protestant emphasis on Scripture as the sole word of God, the Council declared that Catholic tradition was co-equal with Scripture as a source of truth for Christians. Therefore, when Protestants pointed to a Catholic practice that was contrary to Scripture, the Catholics replied that the Church had written Scripture and therefore its traditions were at least equal if not superior.

As a response to such Protestants as Wycliffe and Luther, who insisted on translating Scripture into the vernacular, the Council of Trent stated that the Latin Vulgate was to be the true sacred text of the Church. This also ran counter to the belief of reformers who had chosen to exclude certain Old Testament books not found in Jewish Scripture. The council also declared that only the Roman Catholic Church had the right to interpret Scripture. This flew in the face of the Protestant doctrine of the "priesthood of the believer."

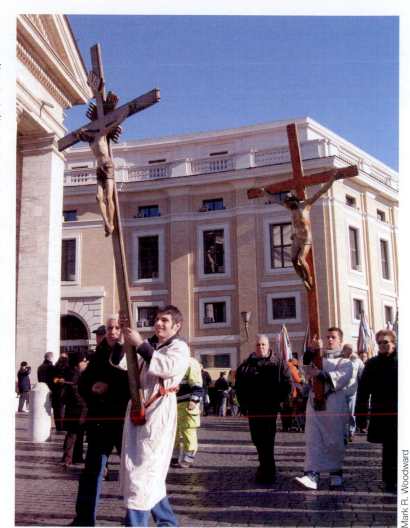

Eastern European Roman Catholic pilgrims, Saint Peter's Square, Rome.

Mark R. Woodward

Although most reformed churches had rejected all of the sacraments except baptism and communion, the Council of Trent reaffirmed the traditional seven:

1. **Baptism.**   Baptism of infants is necessary to wash away the taint of original sin. Any infant who dies without the benefit of baptism is technically destined for hell. Later, however, it became popular to say that the unbaptized infant was to spend eternity in a land called limbo.

2. **Confirmation.**   At some point before maturity, usually at about age thirteen, children must be confirmed as an extension of their baptism.

3. **Penance.**   Christians must confess their sins regularly in private to priests and receive absolution. Absolution, or forgiveness, may be conditioned upon acts of penance ordered by the priest, depending on the seriousness of the sin confessed.

4. **Eucharist.**   This sacrament is known throughout the Christian world as the Lord's Supper or communion. The Council of Trent not only reaffirmed this sacrament but also gave renewed support to the doctrine of transubstantiation. According to this doctrine, the bread and wine literally become the body and blood of Jesus during the mass. The council held that because the whole Christ was present in both the bread and the wine, it was not necessary to give the wine to the laity.[23]

5. **Extreme Unction.**   As a Catholic nears death, he or she is to be visited by a priest and anointed with healing oil. The priest then hears the last confession. In receiving these last rites, the Catholic is properly prepared to die.[24]

6. Marriage.   Perhaps as early as the eleventh century, the marriage of Christians had come to be regarded as a sacrament. This explains continued opposition to divorce by some Christian denominations.

7. Holy Orders.   For Christians who choose a religious vocation instead of marriage, taking the holy orders is considered a sacrament.

The Council of Trent also strongly supported the veneration of relics, saints, and sacred images—all contrary to most Protestant teaching. As a positive response to the challenge of Luther and others, the sale of indulgences was controlled and other abuses of the medieval church were corrected.

Growth and Global Expansion

11.7. Discuss the growth and global expansion of Christianity over time.

Like other religions, Christianity has had to deal with the challenges and opportunities of the modern world. Older forms of Christianity have worked to update themselves while remaining true to their history and traditions even as new forms of Christianity have spread throughout the world.

Modern Movements

John XXIII became pope in 1958 and was determined to revitalize the Church and bring it into line with the twentieth century. Therefore, he called the Second Vatican Council (often called **Vatican II**), which was to be the most revolutionary council since Trent.[25] Invited to the Council were representatives of Orthodox and Protestant Christian groups acting as observers to the proceedings. Meeting between 1962 and 1965, the Council effected some of the most sweeping changes ever made in the Catholic Church. Non-Catholics were recognized as true Christians, the vernacular was allowed in many parts of the mass, the Index of Prohibited Books was abolished, more congregational participation in worship was encouraged, and the Church officially declared that Jews were no longer to be held responsible for the death of Jesus. There also was an outreach toward dialogue with non-Christian religions. In general, Vatican II attempted to bring the Church up to date and took several steps toward reconciliation with Orthodox and Protestant groups.

The proliferation of Protestant denominations in the modern era is vast. There are so many Protestant denominations that not even the most exhaustive book on the history of Christianity could cover them all effectively. However, several modern Protestant movements merit our attention; these movements respond in creative ways to changing global circumstances. Methodism began in the eighteenth century as a response to the emotional coolness of the Church of England and the plight of urban dwellers during the early Industrial Revolution. The founder of Methodism was John Wesley (1703–1791). Wesley studied at Oxford and was ordained as an Anglican priest in 1728. While at Oxford, he and his brother Charles organized a small group for the purpose of religious support. The group was first called the Holy Club, but because of its disciplined ways it was nicknamed the Methodists.

In 1735, John and Charles were sent to Georgia in what is now the United States as missionaries. On the voyage to America, they encountered another Protestant group called the Moravians, who spoke to them of religious conversion. The Wesley brothers experienced this

Protestant Christian prayer service in Tulsa, Oklahoma, United States.

Annie Griffiths Belt/Encyclopedia/Corbis

conversion in 1738 in London. They began to preach about their experience, first in the churches and to religious societies and later in the fields and town squares. They were joined by an eloquent and fiery preacher, George Whitefield. Their emotional sermons appealed mainly to the lower and middle classes, and soon they had a large Methodist following. John organized the Methodists into societies formed into circuits and attended by preachers who traveled from society to society. Charles became the hymn writer and contributed hundreds of songs that are still treasured by many Protestants.

Although John Wesley had no desire to separate himself from the Church of England and form a new denomination, the break between the two groups was obvious by the time he died. At the end of the eighteenth century there were over 70,000 Methodists in England, but the denomination's greatest growth came among the colonists in America. The Methodist meeting and its circuit rider were a familiar part of the American frontier; Methodism became one of the largest Protestant denominations in the United States, second only to Baptist.

The most growth in Christianity in the United States in recent years has been among the ranks of **evangelical** Protestant groups. Evangelicals have mastered the techniques of modern mass communication. Evangelical "mega-churches" have thousands of members and offer a wide array of social services, from "job banks" to child care, counseling, and even dating services, in addition to preaching the Gospel. They appeal to urban and suburban Americans who live in increasingly complex and often alienating environments. Many of the more traditional and historic Protestant denominations are struggling to maintain their memberships, in part because they have not focused enough on the changing social and religious needs of modern Americans.

Pentecostalism blossomed in the United States in the early twentieth century. It can trace its roots to nineteenth-century evangelicalism and personal piety movements. Pentecostal churches embrace a charismatic worship style that frequently includes speaking in tongues. Pentecostals believe that the Holy Spirit gives them the ability to communicate in an ecstatic, spiritual language. With a great emphasis on personal emotional connection to God, divine healing, and pious behavior, Pentecostalism is one of the fastest growing movements in Christianity today.

Fundamentalism is also a powerful force in modern Christianity. Christian fundamentalism began at the end of the nineteenth century as an attempt to defend the teaching of biblical inerrancy against modern science and philosophy.[26] Fundamentalists believe that the Bible must be read as a historical and scientific account, as well as a moral and religious guide. Consequently, they have opposed the teaching of evolution and historical studies of the Old and New Testaments. In recent years they have turned their attention to combating liberalizing trends in American culture, including legalized abortion, feminism, and the push for legal protection for homosexuals, because they believe that these trends conflict with biblical morality.

Another modern movement in Christianity is the Church of Jesus Christ of Latter Day Saints, also known as the Mormons. Joseph Smith (1805–1844), a young man in upstate New York, experienced a series of visions in which he received spiritual instruction from God the Father; Jesus Christ; John the Baptist; the Apostles Peter, James, and John; and an angel known to church members as Moroni. The angel informed him of the location of a set of gold tablets and bestowed on him the ability to translate them. This is the *Book of Mormon*, which recounts the history and teaching of the Nephite prophets. The church teaches that the Nephites were a branch of the Israelites who migrated to the Americas. Its mission is to restore what is held to be the original Christianity. Smith continued to receive revelations concerning doctrinal and ritual matters. These were recorded in *Doctrines and Covenants*. A third Mormon scripture is *Pearl of Great Price*, an inspired translation of an Egyptian papyri.

Mormons are proud to call themselves Christians and at the same time their beliefs and teachings differ substantially from those of other Christian communities. Among the most important teachings of the church are these:

- Heavenly Father and Heavenly Mother are physical beings. They have spirit children who are subsequently born on Earth in human form.
- Marriage is eternal if "sealed" in a Mormon Temple ceremony.
- The afterlife is a transformative process through which humans can ultimately become divine.
- Between the time of his crucifixion and resurrection Jesus preached in the Americas.
- The Church is led by prophets who continue to receive revelations from God.

Because of these teachings and of the practice of polygamy, Mormons were severely persecuted. They were driven from Ohio, Missouri, and Illinois before settling in Utah in 1847.[27]

Despite persecution and the hostility of many other Christian denominations, the church has experienced phenomenal growth. Mormons are enthusiastic missionaries. Young men are expected to devote two years to mission activities. The result has been enormous growth of church members. In 1900 there were approximately 240,000 Mormons worldwide; today the number is more than 11,000,000. In the late 1990s conversion was responsible for more than 80 percent of annual growth in church membership.[28]

The Missionary Movement

Christians have been missionaries since the earliest days. The great theologian of the early church, Paul, was a far-traveling, zealous missionary. There is a strong tradition that Thomas, the doubting disciple of Jesus, spread the Christian Gospel in India. We have already spoken of Catholic missionaries, such as Francis Xavier who preached Christianity in Japan. Catholic missionaries accompanied Spanish explorers in the sixteenth century. The Wesleys served as Anglican missionaries in America. Protestant groups influenced by John Calvin were slower to enter the mission fields. They were probably impeded by Calvin's doctrine of predestination, which taught that God would save only the people he chose to save and it was therefore folly to send missionaries to "heathens." If God wished to save them, they would be saved without missionaries; if God did not wish to save them, it was a waste of time and money for anyone to try. By the nineteenth century, however, this attitude had changed except among the sternest Calvinists; most Protestant groups came to support some form of mission work.

Religion and Public Life

A complicated reality of much modern missionary activity is that it has taken place in tandem with European or U.S. colonial expansion into Africa, Latin America, and Asia. In the nineteenth century in the United States, Native Americans and enslaved Africans were missionized and converted to Christianity as part of the Euro-American domination of the North American continent. Most Latin American countries have large Catholic majorities today because of Catholic missions that accompanied Spanish and Portuguese conquistadors into the region in the sixteenth century. Likewise, many nations in Africa and Oceania claim large Christian populations because of former European colonial regimes.

The rise of nationalism among many peoples in these areas in recent years has sparked resistance to missionary activities, and not surprisingly, missionary efforts can lead to political controversy and conflict. There are, however, still many active missionary organizations working in Asia, Africa, and Latin America. The collapse of the Soviet Union created new opportunities for missionaries to work in areas in which Christianity and most other religions were suppressed during the period of Communist rule.

The Ecumenical Movement

One of the most important movements among Christians in the twentieth century was the ecumenical movement. As we have noted, Christianity has long been divided into two main branches, Eastern and Western; since the sixteenth century, the Western church has been divided into Protestant and Catholic. In the twentieth century, some Christians attempted to begin a hard journey toward reunion. The Catholic contribution to this journey was the Second Vatican Council. There were also attempts to reconcile theological differences dividing Protestant denominations.

The most visible attempt at reunion was the formation of the World Council of Churches in Amsterdam in 1948. This organization has been supported by many Protestant denominations and some representatives of Eastern Orthodoxy. Although the World Council is organized to promote church unity, little actual unification has been produced. In fact, there are few concrete examples of reunion within Christendom. One has been the uniting of a small number of Protestant denominations that had no great theological differences. Other more dramatic unions stemmed from the pressing needs of the mission fields in nations like India, where factions within Christianity had weakened the case for conversions.

Still, the reunification of Christianity is a long way off. Eastern Orthodoxy maintains aloofness toward the Western church. The post–Vatican II Catholic Church is more open to non-Catholic Christians than ever before, but the Protestant–Catholic dialogue, although progressing, still has many hurdles to clear. Protestants, as always, are vastly divided. Although some are eager for church union and willing to pay almost any price for it, the majority apparently still prefer to go it alone.

Mother Teresa, founder of the Missionaries of Charity, a Roman Catholic order devoted to aiding the poorest of the poor.

The Christian Calendar and Holy Days

11.8. Name the holy days and holidays associated with the Christian calendar.

At its beginning, the Christian church was a part of Judaism and followed its calendar of holy days and festivals. As the separation between the two religions grew, Christianity began to develop its own unique calendar. Some of Christianity's holidays, such as Easter and the Pentecost, were celebrated early in the life of the church. Others, such as Christmas, developed several centuries later.

As Christianity divided into Eastern and Western branches, these branches developed different sacred calendars. In the Western church, Christmas is celebrated on December 25, whereas many of the Orthodox churches keep this holiday in January. The calendars for Easter also vary within Christianity. At various times in history, some branches of Christianity, such as the English Puritans, have refused to celebrate Christmas or other major festivals at all because they considered the practice to be essentially pagan. In general, Christians today celebrate the following major holidays.

Sunday

The earliest Christians apparently continued to worship on Saturday, the Jewish Sabbath. By the late 50s C.E., however, references to offerings on the "first day of the week," Sunday, began to appear in the writings of Paul. It is believed that early Christians chose to worship on this day in memory of the resurrection of Jesus. With rare exceptions, Christians keep Sunday as a day of rest and worship. Some even refer to it as "Sabbath."

The Christian worship service has two primary foci. The first is the Christian Scripture, the Bible. Passages from the Bible are always read, and typically, the priest or minister preaches a sermon that relates the Scripture reading to the lives of people gathered for worship. The second focus is the celebration of sacraments like baptism or communion. In Catholic and Eastern Orthodox as well as in some Protestant churches, the Eucharist is observed at almost every gathering. Other Protestants have communion less frequently. Other common features of Christian worship include public prayers and hymn singing.

Advent, Christmas, and Epiphany

The Christian year begins with the season of Advent, the four weeks before Christmas. During this period, Christians read from the Old Testament, the prophets, and seek to prepare themselves for the coming of Christmas.

Christmas, which marks the birth of Jesus, is celebrated in Western Christianity on December 25 and in January by Eastern Orthodox Christians. Although Christmas was one of the last major holidays to be accepted, it has become the best known of all Christian celebrations. The season is kept by giving and receiving gifts and by participating in family gatherings, special worship services, and feasts.

Twelve days after Christmas (on January 6), Western Christians celebrate Epiphany to remember the wise men who came to Bethlehem to find the infant Jesus.

Easter

The oldest and most widely accepted holiday in the Christian calendar is Easter. The date for Easter is established each year according to a lunar calendar and may vary by a number of weeks from year to year.

Forty days before Easter, Christians observe Ash Wednesday. On this day, it is traditional to begin the season leading to Easter with a somber reminder of the burden of sin. Some Christians receive a mark of ashes on their foreheads at special Ash Wednesday services. For the next forty days, Christians observe the season of Lent. During this period, it has been customary for some to abstain from a certain food or habit or to fast on certain days to be more aware of the need for repentance.

The Lenten season closes with Holy Week. The first day of this week is known as Palm Sunday, when Christians commemorate Jesus's triumphal entry into Jerusalem. On Thursday of this week, Christians observe Maundy Thursday. This is traditionally the day of Jesus's last supper with his disciples. Some Christian communities partake of the communion meal, and some practice the ritual of foot washing on this night. The next day is known as Good Friday. On this day, Christians remember the trial, execution, and burial of Jesus. Special services are held to recount Jesus's last words from the cross.

The Sunday following Good Friday is designated as Easter. On this day, Christians remember the resurrection of Jesus. It is a time of joyous celebration. The early church used Easter as a time to receive its new members with baptism and new robes. The tradition of new clothing has continued in many modern Christian communities. It also is a time of family gatherings and special meals.

Forty days after Easter is Ascension Day, when Christians remember that Christ ascended into heaven after having spent time with his disciples following the resurrection.

Pentecost

Another of the most ancient of Christian holy days is the Pentecost. The word *Pentecost* was the Greek name for the Jewish festival of Shavuot. It was established fifty days after Passover and commemorated the giving of the law on Mt. Sinai after the Exodus. According to the Book of Acts, this day came fifty days after Jesus's resurrection: The Holy Spirit came upon the disciples gathered in Jerusalem and sent them into the streets to preach their new faith. Many modern Christians regard the Pentecost to be the birthday of the church and celebrate it with great joy.

Throughout the year, various Christian communities have other celebrations. Some observe the special days of certain saints. Many Christians recognize the first of November as All Saints' Day, in which all of the recently deceased are remembered and honored.

Christianity Today

11.9. **Analyze the challenges and issues facing Christianity today.**

Christianity is the world's largest religion and is spread over a wider area than any other. Branches of Orthodox Christianity, each associated with a particular national or language group, continue to predominate in parts of Eastern Europe, the Middle East, and Northeast Africa. In parts of Eastern Europe there is serious conflict between Orthodox Churches and Eastern Rite Catholics who use Orthodox-style liturgies but accept the authority of Rome. The Western Church is divided into Catholic and Protestant communities. Largely because of Luther's teaching of the priesthood of all believers and the translation of the Bible into many languages, the number of Protestant denominations continues to expand rapidly.

In the twenty-first century, the Christian community presents many faces. In Europe, even with its system of state churches, Christianity is in decline as the influence of secularism continues to grow. In some European countries church attendance is as low as 2 percent. In the United States, with its vast number of denominations, attendance remains remarkably high. The Catholic Church remains healthy, but has serious difficulty finding enough priests to serve the lay community. Some Catholic orders recruit priests and nuns abroad. Others encourage vocations with "popup" advertisements on the Internet.

Although Christianity may be declining in Europe and remaining stable in the United States, it is one of the most rapidly growing religions in other parts of the world. For the first time in history, the leader of the Catholic Church, Pope Francis, is a Latin American. In Africa, Christians are now more numerous than Muslims. In South Korea, which is traditionally Buddhist and Confucian, Christianity is also growing at the rate of 10 percent per year. Most of this growth cannot be attributed to the missions of Western Christians but is rather a grassroots movement. The last decade of the twentieth century may be remembered as being one of the great eras of the growth of Christianity. Particularly in Africa, the growth of Christianity has fostered the development of new denominations that use elements of local culture and symbolism to convey a Christian message. In the past, during the period of Western colonization, Christianity was strongly associated with Western cultures. Missionaries were frequently agents of cultural as well as religious change. The end of colonialism has meant that Africans and others formerly subject to colonial rule have come to control their religious destinies. Among the results are Christian theologies and modes of worship that differ sharply from those of Euro-American denominations.

Kim Jae-Hwan/AFP/Getty Images

Christianity is spreading rapidly in Asia and Africa. Here, Koreans participate in an emotional prayer and praise service.

Think About It

1. Discuss Christianity as a product of first-century Judaism and the Greco-Roman world.

2. In the production of the New Testament, which section was likely to have been written first? When were the Gospels written?

3. What form did worship take in the early church? What were some of the rites that originated at this time that are still present in Christianity today?

4. What were the reasons for the ascendancy of the papacy in the early years of Christianity?

5. What are the major differences between Eastern Orthodox and Western Christianity?

6. List several causes of the Reformation.

7. List three modern-day Christian movements or denominations and describe their main characteristics.

8. Easter is the oldest and most widely accepted holiday in the Christian calendar. What are the events that lead up to this holiday and why is it so significant to Christians?

9. What are the challenges faced by the Christian community in the twenty-first century?

Suggested Reading

Brown, Raymond E. *An Introduction to the New Testament*. New York: Doubleday, 1997.

Brown, Robert McAfee. *The Spirit of Protestantism*. New York: Oxford University Press, 1965.

Carmody, Denise Lardner, and John Tully Carmody. *Roman Catholicism: An Introduction*. New York: Macmillan, 1990.

Ehrman, Bart D. *Jesus, Apocalyptic Prophet of the New Millennium*. New York: Oxford University Press, 1999.

Hefner, Robert. *Conversion to Christianity. Historical and Anthropological Perspectives on a Great Transformation*. Berkeley: University of California Press, 1993.

Lawrence, Bruce. *Defenders of God, the Fundamentalist Revolt against the Modern World*. San Francisco: HarperCollins, 1989.

Linberg, Carter. *The European Reformations*. Oxford: Blackwell, 1999.

Norris, Kathleen. *The Cloister Walk*. New York: Riverhead Books, 1996.

Vermes, Geza. *Jesus the Jew*. London: Fontana, 1976.

Walker, Williston, et al. *A History of the Christian Church*, 4th ed. New York: Charles Scribner's Sons, 1985.

Ware, Timothy. *The Orthodox Church*, new ed. New York: Penguin, 1993.

SOURCE MATERIAL

Selections from the New Testament

The following selections from the New Testament illustrate some of the key issues and themes of early Christianity. Matthew 5, 6, and 7 contain Jesus's Sermon on the Mount. In this sermon, one finds many of the distinctive Christian materials, such as the Beatitudes (Matthew 5:3–12) and the Lord's Prayer (Matthew 6:9–13). I Corinthians 13 is perhaps the most beautiful passage from the New Testament, as it describes human and divine love. I Corinthians 15 is one of the best statements of early Christian understanding of the resurrection.[29]

Sermon on the Mount

MATTHEW 5–7 5 [1]Seeing the multitudes, he went up onto the mountain. When he had sat down, his disciples came to him. [2]He opened his mouth and taught them, saying,

[3]"Blessed are the poor in spirit, for theirs is the Kingdom of Heaven.

[4]Blessed are those who mourn, for they shall be comforted.

[5]Blessed are the gentle, for they shall inherit the earth.

⁶Blessed are those who hunger and thirst after righteousness, for they shall be filled.

⁷Blessed are the merciful, for they shall obtain mercy.

⁸Blessed are the pure in heart, for they shall see God.

⁹Blessed are the peacemakers, for they shall be called children of God.

¹⁰Blessed are those who have been persecuted for righteousness' sake, for theirs is the Kingdom of Heaven.

¹¹"Blessed are you when people reproach you, persecute you, and say all kinds of evil against you falsely, for my sake. ¹²Rejoice, and be exceedingly glad, for great is your reward in heaven. For that is how they persecuted the prophets who were before you.

¹³"You are the salt of the earth, but if the salt has lost its flavor, with what will it be salted? It is then good for nothing, but to be cast out and trodden under the feet of men. ¹⁴You are the light of the world. A city located on a hill can't be hidden. ¹⁵Neither do you light a lamp, and put it under a measuring basket, but on a stand; and it shines to all who are in the house. ¹⁶Even so, let your light shine before men; that they may see your good works, and glorify your Father who is in heaven.

¹⁷"Don't think that I came to destroy the law or the prophets. I didn't come to destroy, but to fulfill. ¹⁸For most certainly, I tell you, until heaven and earth pass away, not even one smallest letter or one tiny pen stroke shall in any way pass away from the law, until all things are accomplished. ¹⁹Whoever, therefore, shall break one of these least commandments, and teach others to do so, shall be called least in the Kingdom of Heaven; but whoever shall do and teach them shall be called great in the Kingdom of Heaven. ²⁰For I tell you that unless your righteousness exceeds that of the scribes and Pharisees, there is no way you will enter into the Kingdom of Heaven.

²¹"You have heard that it was said to the ancient ones, 'You shall not murder;'and 'Whoever murders will be in danger of the judgment.' ²²But I tell you, that everyone who is angry with his brother without a cause will be in danger of the judgment; and whoever says to his brother, 'Raca!' will be in danger of the council; and whoever says, 'You fool!' will be in danger of the fire of Gehenna.

²³"If therefore you are offering your gift at the altar, and there remember that your brother has anything against you, ²⁴leave your gift there before the altar, and go your way. First be reconciled to your brother, and then come and offer your gift. ²⁵Agree with your adversary quickly, while you are with him on the way; lest perhaps the prosecutor deliver you to the judge, and the judge deliver you to the officer, and you be cast into prison. ²⁶Most certainly I tell you, you shall by no means get out of there, until you have paid the last penny.

²⁷"You have heard that it was said, 'You shall not commit adultery;'²⁸but I tell you that everyone who gazes at a woman to lust after her has committed adultery with her already in his heart. ²⁹If your right eye causes you to stumble, pluck it out and throw it away from you. For it is more profitable for you that one of your members should perish, than for your whole body to be cast into Gehenna. ³⁰If your right hand causes you to stumble, cut it off, and throw it away from you. For it is more profitable for you that one of your members should perish, than for your whole body to be cast into Gehenna.

³¹"It was also said, 'Whoever shall put away his wife, let him give her a writing of divorce,' ³²but I tell you that whoever puts away his wife, except for the cause of sexual immorality, makes her an adulteress; and whoever marries her when she is put away commits adultery.

³³"Again you have heard that it was said to them of old time, 'You shall not make false vows, but shall perform to the Lord your vows,' ³⁴but I tell you, don't swear at all: neither by heaven, for it is the throne of God; ³⁵nor by the earth, for it is the footstool of his feet; nor by Jerusalem, for it is the city of the great King. ³⁶Neither shall you swear by your head, for you can't make one hair white or black. ³⁷But let your 'Yes' be 'Yes' and your 'No' be 'No.' Whatever is more than these is of the evil one.

³⁸"You have heard that it was said, 'An eye for an eye, and a tooth for a tooth.' ³⁹But I tell you, don't resist him who is evil; but whoever strikes you on your right cheek, turn to him the other also. ⁴⁰If anyone sues you to take away your coat, let him have your cloak also.

⁴¹"Whoever compels you to go one mile, go with him two. ⁴²Give to him who asks you, and don't turn away him who desires to borrow from you.

⁴³"You have heard that it was said, 'You shall love your neighbor and hate your enemy.' ⁴⁴But I tell you, love your enemies, bless those who curse you, do good to those who hate you, and pray for those who mistreat you and persecute you, ⁴⁵that you may be children of your Father who is in heaven. For he makes his sun to rise on the evil and the good, and sends rain on the just and the unjust. ⁴⁶For if you love those who love you, what reward do you have? Don't even the tax collectors do the same? ⁴⁷If you only greet your friends, what more do you do than others? Don't even the tax collectors do the

same? [48]Therefore you shall be perfect, just as your Father in heaven is perfect.

6 [1]"Be careful that you don't do your charitable giving before men, to be seen by them, or else you have no reward from your Father who is in heaven. [2]Therefore when you do merciful deeds, don't sound a trumpet before yourself, as the hypocrites do in the synagogues and in the streets, that they may get glory from men. Most certainly I tell you, they have received their reward. [3]But when you do merciful deeds, don't let your left hand know what your right hand does, [4]so that your merciful deeds may be in secret, then your Father who sees in secret will reward you openly.

[5]"When you pray, you shall not be as the hypocrites, for they love to stand and pray in the synagogues and in the corners of the streets, that they may be seen by men. Most certainly, I tell you, they have received their reward. [6]But you, when you pray, enter into your inner room, and having shut your door, pray to your Father who is in secret, and your Father who sees in secret will reward you openly. [7]In praying, don't use vain repetitions, as the Gentiles do; for they think that they will be heard for their much speaking. [8]Therefore don't be like them, for your Father knows what things you need, before you ask him. [9]Pray like this: 'Our Father in heaven, may your name be kept holy. [10]Let your Kingdom come. Let your will be done, as in heaven, so on earth. [11]Give us today our daily bread. [12]Forgive us our debts, as we also forgive our debtors. [13]Bring us not into temptation, but deliver us from the evil one. For yours is the Kingdom, the power, and the glory forever. Amen.'

[14]"For if you forgive men their trespasses, your heavenly Father will also forgive you. [15]But if you don't forgive men their trespasses, neither will your Father forgive your trespasses.

[16]"Moreover when you fast, don't be like the hypocrites, with sad faces. For they disfigure their faces, that they may be seen by men to be fasting. Most certainly I tell you, they have received their reward. [17]But you, when you fast, anoint your head, and wash your face; [18]so that you are not seen by men to be fasting, but by your Father who is in secret, and your Father, who sees in secret, will reward you.

[19]"Don't lay up treasures for yourselves on the earth, where moth and rust consume, and where thieves break through and steal; [20]but lay up for yourselves treasures in heaven, where neither moth nor rust consume, and where thieves don't break through and steal; [21]for where your treasure is, there your heart will be also.

[22]"The lamp of the body is the eye. If therefore your eye is sound, your whole body will be full of light. [23]But if your eye is evil, your whole body will be full of darkness. If therefore the light that is in you is darkness, how great is the darkness!

[24]"No one can serve two masters, for either he will hate the one and love the other; or else he will be devoted to one and despise the other. You can't serve both God and Mammon. [25]Therefore I tell you, don't be anxious for your life: what you will eat, or what you will drink; nor yet for your body, what you will wear. Isn't life more than food, and the body more than clothing? [26]See the birds of the sky, that they don't sow, neither do they reap, nor gather into barns. Your heavenly Father feeds them. Aren't you of much more value than they?

[27]"Which of you, by being anxious, can add one moment to his lifespan? [28]Why are you anxious about clothing? Consider the lilies of the field, how they grow. They don't toil, neither do they spin, [29]yet I tell you that even Solomon in all his glory was not dressed like one of these. [30]But if God so clothes the grass of the field, which today exists, and tomorrow is thrown into the oven, won't he much more clothe you, you of little faith?

[31]"Therefore don't be anxious, saying, 'What will we eat?', 'What will we drink?' or, 'With what will we be clothed?' [32]For the Gentiles seek after all these things; for your heavenly Father knows that you need all these things. [33]But seek first God's Kingdom, and his righteousness; and all these things will be given to you as well. [34]Therefore don't be anxious for tomorrow, for tomorrow will be anxious for itself. Each day's own evil is sufficient.

7 [1]"Don't judge, so that you won't be judged. [2]For with whatever judgment you judge, you will be judged; and with whatever measure you measure, it will be measured to you. [3]Why do you see the speck that is in your brother's eye, but don't consider the beam that is in your own eye? [4]Or how will you tell your brother, 'Let me remove the speck from your eye;' and behold, the beam is in your own eye? [5]You hypocrite! First remove the beam out of your own eye, and then you can see clearly to remove the speck out of your brother's eye.

[6]"Don't give that which is holy to the dogs, neither throw your pearls before the pigs, lest perhaps they trample them under their feet, and turn and tear you to pieces.

[7]"Ask, and it will be given you. Seek, and you will find. Knock, and it will be opened for you. [8]For everyone who asks receives. He who seeks finds. To him who knocks it will be opened. [9]Or who is there among you, who, if his son asks him for bread, will give him a stone? [10]Or if he asks for a fish, who will give him a serpent? [11]If you then, being evil, know how to give good

gifts to your children, how much more will your Father who is in heaven give good things to those who ask him! [12]Therefore whatever you desire for men to do to you, you shall also do to them; for this is the law and the prophets.

[13]"Enter in by the narrow gate; for wide is the gate and broad is the way that leads to destruction, and many are those who enter in by it. [14]How narrow is the gate, and restricted is the way that leads to life! Few are those who find it.

[15]"Beware of false prophets, who come to you in sheep's clothing, but inwardly are ravening wolves. [16]By their fruits you will know them. Do you gather grapes from thorns, or figs from thistles? [17]Even so, every good tree produces good fruit; but the corrupt tree produces evil fruit. [18]A good tree can't produce evil fruit, neither can a corrupt tree produce good fruit. [19]Every tree that doesn't grow good fruit is cut down, and thrown into the fire. [20]Therefore by their fruits you will know them. [21]Not everyone who says to me, 'Lord, Lord,' will enter into the Kingdom of Heaven; but he who does the will of my Father who is in heaven. [22]Many will tell me in that day, 'Lord, Lord, didn't we prophesy in your name, in your name cast out demons, and in your name do many mighty works?' [23]Then I will tell them, 'I never knew you. Depart from me, you who work iniquity.'

[24]"Everyone therefore who hears these words of mine, and does them, I will liken him to a wise man, who built his house on a rock. [25]The rain came down, the floods came, and the winds blew, and beat on that house; and it didn't fall, for it was founded on the rock. [26]Everyone who hears these words of mine, and doesn't do them will be like a foolish man, who built his house on the sand. [27]The rain came down, the floods came, and the winds blew, and beat on that house; and it fell—and great was its fall."

[28]When Jesus had finished saying these things, the multitudes were astonished at his teaching, [29]for he taught them with authority, and not like the scribes.

I Corinthians

13 [1]If I speak with the languages of men and of angels, but don't have love, I have become sounding brass, or a clanging cymbal. [2]If I have the gift of prophecy, and know all mysteries and all knowledge; and if I have all faith, so as to remove mountains, but don't have love, I am nothing. [3]If I give away all my goods to feed the poor, and if I give my body to be burned, but don't have love, it profits me nothing.

[4]Love is patient and is kind; love doesn't envy. Love doesn't brag, is not proud, [5]doesn't behave itself inappropriately, doesn't seek its own way, is not provoked, takes no account of evil; [6]doesn't rejoice in unrighteousness, but rejoices with the truth; [7]bears all things, believes all things, hopes all things, endures all things. [8]Love never fails. But where there are prophecies, they will be done away with. Where there are various languages, they will cease. Where there is knowledge, it will be done away with. [9]For we know in part, and we prophesy in part; [10]but when that which is complete has come, then that which is partial will be done away with. [11]When I was a child, I spoke as a child, I felt as a child, I thought as a child. Now that I have become a man, I have put away childish things. [12]For now we see in a mirror, dimly, but then face to face. Now I know in part, but then I will know fully, even as I was also fully known. [13]But now faith, hope, and love remain—these three. The greatest of these is love.

15 [1]Now I declare to you, brothers, the Good News which I preached to you, which also you received, in which you also stand, [2]by which also you are saved, if you hold firmly the word which I preached to you—unless you believed in vain. [3]For I delivered to you first of all that which I also received: that Christ died for our sins according to the Scriptures, [4]that he was buried, that he was raised on the third day according to the Scriptures, [5]and that he appeared to Cephas, then to the twelve. [6]Then he appeared to over five hundred brothers at once, most of whom remain until now, but some have also fallen asleep. [7]Then he appeared to James, then to all the apostles, [8]and last of all, as to the child born at the wrong time, he appeared to me also. [9]For I am the least of the apostles, who is not worthy to be called an apostle, because I persecuted the assembly of God. [10]But by the grace of God I am what I am. His grace which was given to me was not futile, but I worked more than all of them; yet not I, but the grace of God which was with me. [11]Whether then it is I or they, so we preach, and so you believed.

[12]Now if Christ is preached, that he has been raised from the dead, how do some among you say that there is no resurrection of the dead? [13]But if there is no resurrection of the dead, neither has Christ been raised. [14]If Christ has not been raised, then our preaching is in vain, and your faith also is in vain. [15]Yes, we are also found false witnesses of God, because we testified about God that he raised up Christ, whom he didn't raise up, if it is so that the dead are not raised. [16]For if the dead aren't raised, neither has Christ been raised. [17]If Christ has not been raised, your faith is vain; you are still in your sins. [18]Then they also who are fallen asleep in Christ have perished. [19]If we have only hoped in Christ in this life, we are of all men most pitiable.

[20]But now Christ has been raised from the dead. He became the first fruits of those who are asleep. [21]For since death came by man, the resurrection of the dead also came by man. [22]For as in Adam all die, so also in Christ all will be made alive. [23]But each in his own order: Christ the first fruits, then those who are Christ's, at his coming. [24]Then the end comes, when he will deliver up the Kingdom to God, even the Father; when he will have abolished all rule and all authority and power. [25]For he must reign until he has put all his enemies under his feet. [26]The last enemy that will be abolished is death. [27]For, "He put all things in subjection under his feet." But when he says, "All things are put in subjection", it is evident that he is excepted who subjected all things to him. [28]When all things have been subjected to him, then the Son will also himself be subjected to him who subjected all things to him, that God may be all in all.

[29]Or else what will they do who are baptized for the dead? If the dead aren't raised at all, why then are they baptized for the dead? [30]Why do we also stand in jeopardy every hour? [31]I affirm, by the boasting in you which I have in Christ Jesus our Lord, I die daily. [32]If I fought with animals at Ephesus for human purposes, what does it profit me? If the dead are not raised, then "let us eat and drink, for tomorrow we die." [33]Don't be deceived! "Evil companionships corrupt good morals." [34]Wake up righteously, and don't sin, for some have no knowledge of God. I say this to your shame.

[35]But someone will say, "How are the dead raised?" and, "With what kind of body do they come?" [36]You foolish one, that which you yourself sow is not made alive unless it dies. [37]That which you sow, you don't sow the body that will be, but a bare grain, maybe of wheat, or of some other kind. [38]But God gives it a body even as it pleased him, and to each seed a body of its own. [39]All flesh is not the same flesh, but there is one flesh of men, another flesh of animals, another of fish, and another of birds. [40]There are also celestial bodies, and terrestrial bodies; but the glory of the celestial differs from that of the terrestrial. [41]There is one glory of the sun, another glory of the moon, and another glory of the stars; for one star differs from another star in glory. [42]So also is the resurrection of the dead. The body is sown perishable; it is raised imperishable. [43]It is sown in dishonor; it is raised in glory. It is sown in weakness; it is raised in power. [44]It is sown a natural body; it is raised a spiritual body. There is a natural body and there is also a spiritual body.

[45]So also it is written, "The first man, Adam, became a living soul." The last Adam became a life-giving spirit. [46]However that which is spiritual isn't first, but that which is natural, then that which is spiritual. [47]The first man is of the earth, made of dust. The second man is the Lord from heaven. [48]As is the one made of dust, such are those who are also made of dust; and as is the heavenly, such are they also that are heavenly. [49]As we have borne the image of those made of dust, let's also bear the image of the heavenly. [50]Now I say this, brothers, that flesh and blood can't inherit God's Kingdom; neither does the perishable inherit imperishable.

[51]Behold, I tell you a mystery. We will not all sleep, but we will all be changed, [52]in a moment, in the twinkling of an eye, at the last trumpet. For the trumpet will sound, and the dead will be raised incorruptible, and we will be changed. [53]For this perishable body must become imperishable, and this mortal must put on immortality. [54]But when this perishable body will have become imperishable, and this mortal will have put on immortality, then what is written will happen: "Death is swallowed up in victory." [55]"Death, where is your sting? Hades, where is your victory?" [56]The sting of death is sin, and the power of sin is the law. [57]But thanks be to God, who gives us the victory through our Lord Jesus Christ.

[58]Therefore, my beloved brothers, be steadfast, immovable, always abounding in the Lord's work, because you know that your labor is not in vain in the Lord.

"O for a Thousand Tongues to Sing"

Christian hymns are one of the main ways in which Christians express their faith. The following hymn by Charles Wesley communicates the singer's understanding of Christian salvation.[30]

O for a thousand tongues to sing
My dear Redeemer's praise!
The glories of my God and King,
The triumphs of his grace!

My gracious Master, and my God,
Assist me to proclaim,
To spread through all the earth abroad
The honours of thy name.

Jesus, the name that charms our fears,
That bids our sorrows cease—
'Tis music in the sinner's ears,
'Tis life, and health, and peace.

He breaks the power of cancelled sin,
He sets the prisoner free;
His blood can make the foulest clean—
His blood availed for me.

Hear him, ye deaf; his praise, ye dumb,
Your loosened tongues employ;
Ye blind, behold your Saviour come,
And leap, ye lame, for joy!

Look unto him, ye nations, own
Your God, ye fallen race;
Look, and be saved through faith alone,
Be justified by grace!

See all your sins on Jesus laid:
The lamb of God was slain,
His soul was once an offering made
For every soul of man.

With me, your chief, ye then shall know,
Shall feel your sins forgiven;
Anticipate your heaven below,
And own that love is heaven.

Chapter 12
Islam

 Learning Objectives

After reading this chapter, you should be able to:

12.1 Understand the pre-Islamic Arab religions that existed around the seventh century.

12.2 Discuss the life of the Prophet Muhammad.

12.3 Summarize the basic teachings of the Qur'an.

12.4 Understand Islamic religious institutions and the Five Pillars of Islam.

12.5 Detail the spread of Islam through out the Middle East and beyond.

12.6 Recognize the significance of the caliphate.

12.7 Name the different divisions within Islam.

12.8 Discuss the place of Islam in the modern world.

12.9 Talk about the Muslim calendar and name the Islamic holy days.

12.10 Understand the challenges faced by Muslims in today's society.

A Timeline of Islam

570 C.E.	Birth of the Prophet Muhammad
610	Muhammad receives his initial revelation
622	Hijra (immigration) of the Muslim community from Mecca to Medina
630	Muhammad and the Muslim community return to Medina; rapid growth of Islam among Arabs
632	Death of the Prophet Muhammad
633–642	Wars of Conquest; spread of Islam across the Middle East and North Africa; large-scale conversion of non-Arabs
661–750	Ummayad Caliphate expands east toward Indian subcontinent and west across North Africa and into the Iberian peninsula
680	Death of Husayn, grandson of the Prophet Muhammad, leads to split between Sunni and Shi'ite Islam
691	Construction of the Dome of the Rock in Jerusalem
700–900	Emergence of Sufism
711	Conquest of Spain

732	Battle of Tours; halt of Muslim advance in Western Europe
750–1258	Abbasid Dynasty; Baghdad becomes the intellectual center of Western civilization
1095–1270	The Crusades
1258	Conquest of Baghdad by the Mongols; severe persecution of Muslims
1281–1324	Life of Osman, founder of the Ottoman Empire
13th century	Transmission of Islam to Southeast Asia
1453	Constantinople renamed Istanbul following Ottoman conquest
1492	Reconquest of Spain by Christians; Muslim population expelled
16th century	Expansion of the Ottoman Empire in Arabia, North Africa, and Europe
1501	Shi'ite Islam becomes official religion of Persia (Iran)
1556	Founding of India Mughal Empire
1744	Founding of Wahhabi Islam in Arabia
19th century	Decline of Ottoman Empire
Early 20th century	Emergence of nationalist movements in the Muslim world
1918	End of Ottoman Empire; British and French occupation of much of the Middle East
1945–present	Growth of Islam in Europe and North America
1945–1960	Muslims in colonial territories regain independence
1979	Iranian Revolution and establishment of the Islamic Republic

Key Terms

hadith	Qur'an
hajj	Ramadan
Hijra	Shi'ite
imam	Sufism
jihad	Sunni
Kaaba	ummah
masjid	Wahhabism
Mecca	

Islam is one of the largest religions in the world, with more than one billion adherents. Islam is the dominant religion in many of the nations in the Middle East, Africa, and Asia. These factors make Islam one of the most interesting and important religions.

The most basic belief of Islam is that there is only one God, who is called Allah, the same God worshiped by Jews and Christians. He is the sole and sovereign ruler of the universe. Although Allah has made himself known through other prophets at other times, his final revelation was to the Prophet Muhammad in the seventh century C.E. Islam teaches that a person has just one life to live.

How believers live this life determines how they will spend their eternal existence. During this one life, believers must submit to the will of Allah. Thus adherents of this religion are called Muslims, meaning "those who submit to God."

Pre-Islamic Arab Religion

12.1. **Understand the pre-Islamic Arab religions that existed around the seventh century.**

Islam began among the Arabian desert people in the seventh century C.E. It did not spring out of a religious vacuum. The people of this area had developed religious forms of their own and had been exposed to various other religions for centuries. Although the influence was not strong, Byzantine Christianity had been a factor in the lives of these people. Judea, the home of Christianity, was not very far from Arabia. Such cities as Damascus, Caesarea, Antioch, and Alexandria were neighbors to Mecca and Yathrib (Medina). Christian princes ruled from these cities, and many of the early church fathers wrote and taught there.

The people of Arabia were also familiar with Judaism. Several of the desert tribes were Jewish. Although the origins of these tribes are unclear, many historians believe they were the descendants of Jews forced out of Judea when the Romans squelched rebellion in the land in 70 C.E. and again in 135. When Muhammad, the Prophet of Islam, entered Medina in 622 C.E., some of the residents of that city were Jewish.

Perhaps the major religious force from which Islam grew—and reacted against—was the native religion of the Arab people. We know very little about the basic religion of these people because the only material we have about them comes from Muslim sources, including the **Qur'an**, which naturally are critical of the earlier religion.[1] Apparently, the pre-Islamic people worshiped a variety of gods. They recognized one supreme High God, who was separate and unapproachable by human beings, whom they called Allah (literally, "the God"). The deities that received the most worship and attention were the local and tribal gods. Images of these gods were carved and cared for, and blood sacrifices were made to them. In addition to a great pantheon of the gods of heaven and Earth, there were lesser divine creatures. There were angels and other kind and helpful spirits, and there were demonic creatures, who often tried to harm humans.

The courtyard of the great mosque of Surakarta, Indonesia.

(Mark R. Woodward)

Perhaps the most obvious characteristic of basic pre-Islamic religion is its relation to the natural environment. Gods and spirits were found in stones, trees, wells, and animals; these spirits had to be placated and asked for help. The city of **Mecca** became a holy place because of associations to these spirits.[2] Mecca is in west-central Arabia and was located on the major north-south caravan route. Its fame was rooted in a meteoric stone known simply as the "black stone." The stone became an object of veneration to the animistic population; by the time of Muhammad, pilgrims had built an enclosure around it called the **Kaaba**.

The Kaaba gradually filled with images, relics, and paintings. One report claims that it even contained a painting of Jesus and Mary. Islamic legend says that the black stone fell from heaven during the time of Adam and Eve and that Abraham and his son Ishmael built the Kaaba. A period of several months each year was set aside as a time of truce between warring tribes so pilgrims could travel safely to Mecca to worship at this shrine. Naturally, the black stone was an object of both pride and profit to Meccans, and there was a constant struggle among the various clans of Mecca over who would control the Kaaba.

The Life of Muhammad

12.2.   **Discuss the life of the Prophet Muhammad.**

Because Islam is one of the youngest of the world's religions, the details of the life of its founder are more readily available than are those of other founders. No one seriously questions that Muhammad was a historical figure and lived in the seventh century C.E. He was born about 570 C.E. into the clan of Hashim of the tribe of Quraysh, the group that controlled the Kaaba in Mecca. His father, Abd-Allah, died before Muhammad was born, and his mother died before he was six years old. After that, Muhammad was raised by his uncle, abu-Talib, chief of the Quraysh tribe. Life for an orphan in those times was very difficult. There was no chance for any kind of formal education, and Muslim tradition makes much of the fact that Muhammad was illiterate. Thus the revelation of the Qur'an to him was even more miraculous because of this.

In the sixth century C.E., the merchants of Mecca controlled the trading caravans that moved between the Indian Ocean and the Mediterranean Sea. This, along with the Kaaba, brought great wealth to the city of Mecca and allowed the young Muhammad an opportunity to work and travel with the caravans. It is likely that during these travels Muhammad had contact with representatives of the religions and cultures of the Middle East. Covering the Arabian peninsula and traveling to Byzantine cities such as Damascus, he no doubt met Christians and Jews. Each of these religions had several things in common and must have influenced Muhammad. They all believed in one God; they all had a Scripture believed to be the word of God. Their eschatology taught that the world would one day end and that the righteous would be rewarded, while the evil would be tormented in hell. Muhammad seems to have been especially affected by eschatology, and he became concerned about the future of his people, who worshiped a multitude of gods and idols. He was equally concerned with social justice.

These years as a caravan worker also gave Muhammad the opportunity to meet the woman who would become his wife: Khadija, the owner of a caravan. Khadija was a wealthy widow who was about forty years old when she married the twenty-five-year-old Muhammad. Although it was permissible to have more than one wife, Muhammad was married only to Khadija as long as she lived. During their marriage of twenty-five years, she bore him two sons and four daughters. The sons died in infancy; only one daughter, Fatima, survived her father. Khadija provided the wealth and love that the orphaned Muhammad had never had as a child. She became his strongest supporter, and her wealth also gave him the freedom to consider theological questions.

In the years following his marriage to Khadija, Muhammad began to go into the hills surrounding Mecca to ponder the fate of his people. He was especially concerned about their idolatry and the fate they would have on judgment day, when the world ended. During these periods of meditation, he received a visit from an angel, whom he later identified as Gabriel (who is mentioned in both the Hebrew and Christian Bibles). Tradition says that during the month of Ramadan, in a cave on Mount Hira, Gabriel brought the following command from God:

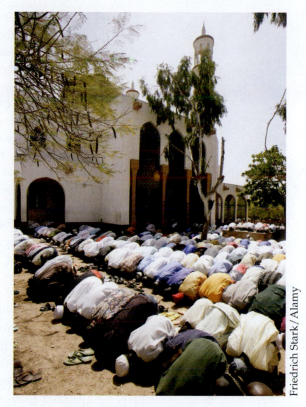

Muslims at Friday prayer in front of the mosque of Wase in Nigeria.

Friedrich Stark / Alamy

From the Source

Read! In the name of your Lord who created: He created man from a clinging form. Read! Your Lord is the Most Bountiful One who taught by [means of] the pen, who taught man what he did not know.[3]

At frequent intervals during the rest of his life, Muhammad received revelations from God in this fashion. Islamic tradition teaches that inspiration came like the painful sounding of a bell and Muhammad's forehead became covered with sweat. At times, visions came to him in his sleep. Muhammad memorized the contents of these divine messages and taught them to his companions; eventually, they were committed to writing, to become the scripture of Islam, called the Qur'an.

After a series of revelations, Muhammad became convinced that there was only one God, whom his people had called Allah and whom other religions called by other names. He also became convinced that he was the last of a series of God's prophets, who included Abraham, Moses, and Jesus, among others, and that these former prophets had had only an incomplete revelation of Allah, but that he had the complete and final revelation. Thus Islam, at its very inception, did not deny the validity of other religions but rather looked upon itself as the completion of what others had begun. The idea of religious tolerance is one of Islam's great contributions to humankind. It is also noteworthy that Muhammad never considered himself to be anything more than a prophet. He was not divine; he died like any other person. His mission was much like that of the classical Hebrew prophet: to present the word of God to his people.

As the Prophet of Allah, Muhammad began to preach his new understanding of religion to the people of Mecca. He received little encouragement from his neighbors; indeed, there was much discouragement and open hostility. He was preaching that there was only one God, who was not to be worshiped with idols. This of course worked against the livelihood of many Meccans, who depended on pilgrims' coming to Mecca to worship the various deities housed in the Kaaba.

Muhammad's first convert was his wife Khadija. There is debate in the traditions regarding the first male convert. It was either Ali, a cousin, or Zayd, a slave boy who had been freed by Muhammad. The third convert was a friend, abu-Bakr. In the following years, other converts joined the Muslim movement. They came mainly from the young and the poorer classes in Mecca. As opposition grew from the older, richer, established clan leaders of the city, Muhammad received protection from his uncle abu-Talib and other members of his clan, even those who were not Muslims. As the opposition and persecution became more severe, however, Muhammad finally had to urge some of his followers to leave the country.

In 615 C.E., about fifteen Muslim families fled Mecca and took refuge in the Christian kingdom of Abyssinia (Ethiopia today). The Prophet and the remainder of the Muslims stayed behind in Mecca to continue to preach and face persecution. This persecution took the form of a boycott against Muhammad and his entire clan by the rest of the Meccans, but it proved ineffective.

In 619 C.E. Muhammad suffered the loss of his two greatest benefactors, his uncle abu-Talib and his beloved Khadija. After the death of his wife, the Prophet married the first of a number of wives whom he was to have during the remainder of his life. The death of abu-Talib left him without the protection of his clan, and life became very difficult for Muslims. Muhammad tried to move out of Mecca to a nearby town but was rejected there and had to return.

One of the most significant events in the history of Islam occurred in the year 620 C.E., when a group of six men journeyed from the city of Yathrib (later renamed Medina in honor of the Prophet), located 250 miles to the north, to Mecca to confer with Muhammad. They were impressed with his honesty, his sense of justice, and the power of his personality. Yathrib was a city torn by clan warfare and internal strife. It needed an impartial judge to settle its disputes, and the delegation believed Muhammad could be that judge. The following year, twelve delegates came from Yathrib to meet the Prophet. Ten of the twelve were from Jewish tribes, some of whom believed that Muhammad might possibly be the Messiah. An invitation was extended to him to become the ruler of the city.

It was 622 C.E. before Muhammad could leave Mecca because a group of assassins had pledged to kill him, and he had to avoid them with great care. His followers slipped out a few at a time, and finally the Prophet made the journey. On 24 September 622 C.E. Muhammad arrived to be the judge of the city of Yathrib. The journey from Mecca to Yathrib is called **Hijra** (migration), and it is the time from which Muslims have since dated their calendars. Dates are listed as A.H. (*anno hijra*).

In Yathrib, the Muslims were established as a clan among other clans, and although Muhammad had been brought to the city as an arbitrator, many people did not accept Islam at the beginning. An agreement that became known as the "Medina Charter" granted political authority to Muhammad but gave freedom of religious belief and practice to members of other communities. Three of the tribes in Yathrib were Jewish. There also was a Christian community. Up to this point, Muhammad had only had to deal with the polytheists of Mecca, but in Yathrib, he met with resistance from Jewish monotheists. Eventually a division developed between the Prophet and the Jews. At first, Muhammad commanded the Muslims to pray toward Jerusalem, but with the passing of time he commanded his disciples to pray toward Mecca instead. Jerusalem remains, however, the third holiest city in Islam, following Mecca and Medina.

In 623, Muhammad married Aishah, the daughter of his friend abu-Bakr. This also was the year of the first conflict between the Medinans, under the leadership of Muhammad, and the Meccans. The natural rivalry between these two cities was of course intensified by the Hijra. At first, the conflicts were merely scattered raids against the Meccan caravans, but they later developed into full military campaigns.

Conflict between the Muslims and the Jewish tribes in the area also intensified during this period. At times, they supported the Meccans against the Prophet. As a result, the Jewish tribes were offered the choice of conversion or exile from the city. According to Muslim tradition, the final break occurred when Zainab, a matron from the Jewish community, invited the Prophet and his friends to dinner and fed them poisoned lamb. Although Muhammad ate only a small amount of the meat, he suffered the effects the rest of his life.

In 627, a force of 10,000 Meccans attacked Medina but withdrew after failing to take the city. Islamic historians consider this to have been a great victory for Muhammad and a major turning point in the history of the Muslim community. The following year Muhammad attempted to travel to Mecca for a pilgrimage with his followers, but the Meccans barred the way. A peace treaty was arranged, and the Muslims were allowed to make the pilgrimage the following year. By 629, Islam had grown so strong that when the Muslims entered Mecca on their pilgrimage, no one dared stop them. In 630, Muhammad conquered Mecca with a force of 10,000 men. He went to the Kaaba and, although he respected the black stone and its enclosure, he destroyed the idols and images. With this symbolic act, the Prophet virtually became the sole leader of the Arabian people.

During the next few years, Islam grew stronger. Qur'an reciters were sent to convert the Bedouin tribes of the Arabian desert. Muhammad sent messages to surrounding nations inviting them to join the community of Islam. His followers returned from Abyssinia to join him. He married new wives, many of whom were the widows of Muslims who had died in battle. Other marriages strengthened political ties.

In 632, Muhammad led the Muslims in another pilgrimage to Mecca. By this time, he was sixty-two years old and in poor health, having never fully recovered from the effects of the poison he had eaten a few years earlier. Upon his return to Medina, he delivered a farewell message to the Muslims and then died in the arms of his wife Aishah. Because he had made no arrangements regarding his successor, there was, for a time, confusion among Muslims regarding leadership. It was finally agreed that abu-Bakr should be the *caliph*, or successor.[4] At Muhammad's funeral, the following words, attributed to abu-Bakr, summed up the Muslim understanding of the Prophet: "O ye people, if anyone worships Muhammad, Muhammad is dead, but if anyone worships God, He is alive and dies not."[5]

The Qur'an

12.3.   Summarize the basic teachings of the Qur'an.

The scripture of Islam is called the Qur'an. The word *Qur'an* literally means "reading" or "recitation"; thus the title indicates the basic belief that Muslims hold about this book, that it is a recitation of an eternal scripture, written in heaven and revealed, chapter by chapter, to Muhammad. The title may also reflect the words of the first *sura*, or chapter, to be revealed, "Read! In the name of your Lord who created. . . ."[6]

Perhaps no scripture has ever been as influential to its people as the Qur'an. Surely no scripture is read as much or committed to memory as often. Although Christians and Jews take their Bibles seriously, human, although inspired, authorship is acknowledged. Such is not the case in Islam; the Qur'an is the word of God: It is eternal, absolute, and irrevocable. The Qur'an is believed to be God's last word to humanity. Islam respects the scriptures of the Jews and Christians, but the Qur'an is understood to be God's final message. It was literally revealed to Muhammad, who acted only as a stenographer or loudspeaker for Allah, and has been transmitted virtually unchanged since the days of the Prophet. Recitation of the Qur'an is an important ritual act and a source of Allah's blessing because it reproduces his divine speech. While the meaning of the Qur'an can be rendered into other languages, it cannot be translated. Reading or hearing it recited in a language other than Arabic does not convey the divine blessing that the Arabic original does.

The first things many Muslims hear when they are born are selections from the Qur'an. Verses from it are inscribed on the walls of Muslim homes for decoration; its words are often the last a person hears before death. Among Muslims, it is considered a supreme act of piety to commit the entire Qur'an to memory. Any person who does this is given the honorific title *hafiz*.

The Qur'an is said to contain the exact words of Allah to the Prophet, from the time of the first revelation to the end of Muhammad's life. Because Muhammad was illiterate, the messages were memorized by him and passed on to Zayd, his secretary, who wrote them on leaves, stones, bones, or parchment. After Muhammad's death, these materials were collected. Tradition says that the third caliph, Uthman, worked with Zayd and others to develop an authorized version of the Qur'an that replaced several variations of the text.

The revelations that make up the Qur'an are organized into 114 chapters called *suras*. The suras contain approximately 6,000 verses called *ayas*. The entire text is somewhat smaller than the Christian New Testament. With the exception of a brief introductory statement, the text is arranged according to the length of the suras, in descending order. Therefore, the non-Muslim reader is sometimes confused because there is no topical or chronological arrangement of the material. The revelations are a great deal like the materials one finds in the prophetic books of the Hebrew Bible, an anthology of prophetic material without regard to arrangement. The longest sura contains 287 verses, the shortest only 3.

The Nature of God

Because the Qur'an is the word of God, its messages are the authority for all Muslims on God, how God expects people to live, and the eternal destiny of humankind. Allah is revealed as the one sovereign God over the entire universe. The religion of Islam demands strict monotheism and requires its followers to say each day, "There is no God but God, and Muhammad is his messenger." In contrast to the polytheists of Mecca and the Byzantine Christians who were in dispute over what part Jesus played in the Godhead, Muslims state that there is only the one God, complete, eternal, and undivided.

From the Source

Exalted is He who has sent the Differentiator down to His servant so that it may be a warning to all people. It is He who has control over the heavens and the earth and has no offspring—no one shares control with Him—and who created all things and made them to an exact measure.[7]

Say, "He is God the One, God the eternal. He begot no one nor was He begotten. No one is comparable to Him."[8]

Allah's role as an omnipresent, omniscient, and omnipotent creator of the universe is heavily emphasized in the Qur'an.

From the Source

Your Lord is God, who created the heavens and earth in six Days, then established Himself on the throne; He makes the night cover the day in swift pursuit; He created the sun, moon, and stars to be subservient to His command; all creation and command belong to Him. Exalted be God, Lord of all the worlds![9]

According to Muslim tradition, Allah has ninety-nine names, such as the Holy One, the Merciful, the Compassionate, the Guardian, and the Creator. Devout Muslims repeat these names in a manner as an act of devotion and prayer.

Although Allah possesses the characteristics of power, sovereignty, and majesty, he also is characterized by justice and mercy. He will repay the evil with justice and the righteous with mercy.

From the Source

Everything in the heavens and earth belongs to God. He will repay those who do evil according to their deeds, and reward, with what is best, those who do good. As for those who avoid grave sins and foul acts, though they may commit small sins, your Lord is ample in forgiveness. He has been aware of you from the time He produced you from the earth and from your hiding places in your mothers' wombs, so do not assert your own goodness: He knows best who is mindful of him.[10]

The mercy of Allah is often emphasized in Muslim worship and practice. It is traditional for a Muslim who is giving a speech or writing to begin with the words, "In the name of God, the Merciful and Compassionate."

Although Allah is alone as the God figure in Islam, he is surrounded and aided by certain other heavenly figures. His angels act as his messengers, as did Gabriel when he revealed the Qur'an to Muhammad, and his warriors fight at the side of believers against infidels. Another creation halfway between humans and angels is called the *jinn*. The jinn are created of fire. Some are beneficial creatures who act as guardian angels for humankind; others are demons. The good jinn are believed to be Muslims, the evil ones unbelievers. The leader of the evil jinn is a fallen angel called Iblis.[11] Iblis acts very much like Satan in the biblical Book of Job. He is not a secondary god of evil, but he acts as a tempter and a prosecuting attorney against humankind. According to Muslim tradition, Iblis was responsible for the fall of Adam.

Predestination

In the Qur'an it is revealed that humans were created by God and must obey him. Righteous persons who would win the favor of God must submit to his will. Because of this emphasis on God's power and sovereignty, the words *fatalism* and *predestination* have been used to describe Islam. Carried to its ultimate extreme as it is in some Islamic sects, Calvinist Christianity, and early Greek philosophy, the belief in an all-powerful force that rules the universe and knows all things, leads one to believe that people have no choice in life. Whether one does good or evil or enjoys success or suffers failure is entirely in the hands of the God who rules the world and who has planned each event in advance. When the idea is carried to this extreme, people do not possess freedom of choice; therefore they are not responsible for their acts. God is all, and people are but his puppets.

However, it is inaccurate to call Islam a fatalistic religion. Perhaps the most common theological position is that humans have the ability to choose from among a set of divinely created acts. Some Muslim theologians maintain that God has endowed humans with reason, through which they are able to distinguish good from evil and choose between them. Allah in his wisdom and mercy allows human beings to make choices in the areas in which they will be judged. A related view is that while God ultimately decides our fates, humans have a religious obligation to vigorously exert themselves in the quest for the common good.

Eschatology

The judgment of humanity by Allah at the conclusion of time is one of the basic beliefs of Islam. The Qur'an says that when a person dies, the body returns to the Earth but the soul remains conscious in the grave. There is a preliminary judgment, after which the wicked suffer and the good enjoy a pretaste of paradise. On resurrection day, the angel of Allah will sound his trumpet, the Earth will split, and the bodies will rejoin their souls.[12] The resurrected are then judged by Allah. Those who have been faithful and virtuous will be rewarded; those who have been evil will be punished. All people are judged on the basis of the record of deeds in a book kept for the purpose.

From the Source

The record of their deeds will be laid open and you will see the guilty, dismayed at what they contain, saying, "Woe to us! What a record this is! It does not leave any deed, small or large, unaccounted for!" They will find everything they ever did laid out in front of them: your Lord will not be unjust to anyone.[13]

Muslim beliefs concerning heaven and hell are similar to those of Jewish and Christian eschatological schemes. The only differences are features that would be particularly appealing or distasteful to a desert dweller. Heaven is located in a beautiful garden with flowing water and shade. The righteous are fed wine—normally forbidden to Muslims—that does not disturb the senses and does not leave the drinker with a hangover. Hell is a horrid place filled with fire, scalding winds, black smoke, and brackish water.

Religious Institutions

12.4. **Understand Islamic religious institutions and the five pillars of Islam.**

From the Qur'an and the early years of Islamic life, certain religious institutions developed that are almost universally recognized by Muslims.

The Masjid

Islam is not a temple-oriented religion. Although certain places are venerated by Muslims, it would not have suited the nomadic life of the Arab people to require them to worship in any sort of temple. The nature of their lives demanded that they

(Reed Kaestner/Corbis)

The Dome of the Rock, the third most sacred place in Islam, located in Jerusalem.

be free to worship Allah every day, wherever they might be. Generally, Muslim worship is carried out in a variety of places. Muhammad decreed Friday to be a special day of Muslim worship, as Saturday was the Sabbath for Jews and Sunday was for Christians. Unlike the Jewish and Christian Sabbaths, however, Friday is not a day of rest; rather, it is the only day of the week when the Muslim is required to pray at a **masjid**, or mosque, with fellow Muslims. The word *masjid* is Arabic for "mosque" and, in English-speaking contexts, it is becoming common to use the Arabic term. There believers are led in prayer by an **imam**. The imam is not a priest but a community member who has been chosen to lead the prayers because of his reputation as a knowledgeable and pious man. The Friday service also includes a sermon, which may be delivered in Arabic or the language of the congregation. The remainder of the religious duties of a Muslim can be performed away from the masjid and its leadership.

Masjids have also served as schools and libraries. For much of the history of Islam the mosques of Mecca and Medina were among the most important centers of Islamic learning. In time educational institutions known as *madrassas* developed alongside large urban masjids. These schools offer instruction in Qur'an recitation and interpretation, hadith scholarship, theology, law, and in many cases mystical knowledge and practice. In major centers of Islamic learning there are many madrassas. Some of these have developed into great Islamic universities that attract students from around the world. Perhaps the most famous of these is al Azhar in Cairo. Al Azhar is one of the world's oldest universities and has long been considered to be the most important theological school in the Sunni Muslim world. The madrassas of the Iranian city of Qom are comparable centers of Shi'ite learning.

The Five Pillars

Those things that one must do to be a good Muslim are usually referred to as "the five pillars of Islam." These five pillars, or obligations, are repetition of the creed, daily prayer, almsgiving, the fast during the month of **Ramadan**, and the pilgrimage to Mecca.

1. *Repetition of the Creed (shahada).* The most common religious act of the Muslim is the frequent repetition of the creed of Islam: *La ilaha illa Allah; Muhammad rasul Allah.* (There is no God but God, and Muhammad is his messenger.) This statement

Islamic Cultural Center and Mosque in Tempe, Arizona, United States. The architecture is based on that of the Dome of the Rock.

is known as *Shahada* (confession of faith). These are the first words a Muslim child hears, and they are likely to be the last words uttered by the dying Muslim. The devout utter this statement as often as possible every day, and the mere utterance of it with conviction makes the reciter a Muslim.

2. *Daily Prayer (salat).* In addition to the recitation of the creed, the Muslim is expected to pray five times daily. The five accepted times for prayer are dawn, midday, midafternoon, sunset, and nightfall. In many Muslim communities, strong-voiced men called *muezzins* climb to the tops of graceful towers known as minarets five times a day and cry out that it is time for prayer. In other communities the call to prayer is spoken at the entrance to the masjid. Wherever Muslims are, they pause for a prescribed prayer. Before they pray, however, they must wash themselves and be cleansed of any impurities. Mosques are almost always built with facilities for washing the hands, feet, and face before prayer. If water is not available, Muslims may cleanse themselves with sand. Properly cleansed, the worshipers prostrate themselves, facing Mecca, and offer their prayers. Traditionally, men and women have not prayed together because of the possibility of inappropriate physical contact. Prayer in the masjid is limited to men in many Middle Eastern countries. In much of Asia, mosques are divided into male and female sections.

3. *Almsgiving (zakat).* Muslims are expected to share their possessions with the poor, widows, and orphans. Alms may also be used to support religious institutions, scholars, and students. Almsgiving is obligatory according to Islamic law and is assessed as a tax amounting to approximately 2.5 percent of one's wealth. Muslims teach that zakat payments are not charity but rather are parts of one's wealth that already belong to the poor; to keep them is tantamount to stealing from the poor. Receiving as well as giving zakat is considered a source of God's blessing.

4. *Fasting (sawm).* Many religions require fasting in one form or another during the year, but usually it is for a very brief period. Jews, for example, fast on the Day of Atonement. Other religions restrict certain foods at special times; for example, Roman Catholic Christians are expected to keep certain fast days and to avoid meat on Fridays during the season of Lent. Islam, however, requires the longest and most stringent fast of all. Every year during the lunar month of Ramadan, Muslims are expected

to abstain from eating, drinking, smoking, and engaging in sexual relations during the daylight hours. The fast is kept in remembrance of the month when the Prophet first received his revelation. Because of the Muslim lunar calendar, the month of Ramadan varies from year to year. Some years it may fall in the summer months, when abstaining from water during daylight hours is very difficult. The only Muslims excused from this fast are the sick, travelers, mothers nursing infants, and small children. When the month of Ramadan concludes, Muslims celebrate with a feast that lasts three days. It is believed that Allah will pardon the sins of all of those believers who complete the fast.

5. *Pilgrimage (hajj).* Pilgrimage to Mecca was part of pre-Islamic Arab religion. It played an important role in the early history of Islam, and it is mentioned in the Qur'an as a ritual duty. The Prophet Muhammad purged the Kaaba of its idols and, according to Muslim tradition, re-established it as a shrine dedicated to the one God. Every Muslim who can afford the trip should make the pilgrimage to Mecca once in his or her lifetime. The pilgrimage takes place during a special month in the Muslim calendar called the Dhu al-Hijjah. During this month, pilgrims from all over the world arrive at Mecca. The poor sometimes use their life's savings to make the trip. Before the advent of air travel, the elderly and the ill began the long journey with little hope of returning home, but no devout Muslim could ask for a more blessed way to die than on the hajj to Mecca. Outside of Mecca the pilgrims must leave whatever mode of transportation they used for the journey and walk the rest of the way. They must be clad in simple pilgrims' garments with no head covering and only the briefest of sandals, so that rich and poor cannot be distinguished by their apparel. During most of the hajj, pilgrims must abstain from food and drink during the daylight hours, they must abstain from sexual intercourse, and they must not cut their hair and nails.

During the days of the pilgrimage, visitors to Mecca visit the Zamzam well, which is believed to have been established by Hagar and Ishmael.[14] They make seven trips around the Kaaba and kiss the sacred black stone. They offer a sacrifice of a sheep or goat on the tenth day of the hajj to commemorate Abraham's willingness to sacrifice even his own son to obey God's command. After these duties, they may visit Medina to pay respect to the grave of the Prophet Muhammad and to visit his mosque. When the pilgrims return home, they may have the title *hajji* attached to their names so all the world will know they have fulfilled this religious obligation.

Islam and Women

The position of women in pre-Islamic Arabia was very low. Apparently female infanticide was common. A woman was considered property, owned by her father, husband, or elder brother. If she displeased her husband, he could divorce her without any recourse on her part. Women like Khadija (the first wife of the Prophet) who could control their own wealth and destinies were extremely rare. Although Muhammad did not raise the status of women to that of men, he did raise it significantly.

The practice of female infanticide was forbidden by Islam. Whereas Muhammad allowed polygamy to continue and was married to many women himself, he limited the number of wives a Muslim could have to four, provided a man could afford them and treat them equally. In a society whose males were frequently killed in battle and in which marriage was the only acceptable state for a woman, the polygamy rules probably worked to the benefit of women. Many of the wives of the Prophet were the widows of Muslims killed in battle.

If a Muslim wished to divorce his wife, it was an easy process compared to modern Western methods. When the husband said, "I divorce you, I divorce you, I divorce you," the divorce was final. However, the Muslim woman was not left destitute. She had as her possession the dowry that the husband paid the wife when the marriage was initially arranged. If there was a divorce, the property of the dowry remained the

Muslim girls at a school in Wonosobo, Indonesia, that teaches both religious and secular subjects.

wife's.[15] In most contemporary Muslim societies women have a legal right to demand a divorce if their husbands treat them unjustly or cruelly.

The status of women in Muslim societies varies considerably, as status is as much the product of culture as it is of religious conviction. In Saudi Arabia, Iran, and Afghanistan, for example, women are required to conform to very strict regulations concerning dress and public behavior. They generally are not allowed to work or study with men. In Saudi Arabia, women are not permitted to drive. Prior to the fall of the Taliban government in Afghanistan, women could be stoned if they did not conform with dress restrictions. Progressive Muslim scholars denounce these restrictions and argue that those who impose them are guilty of the sin of prohibiting that which is not prohibited by Allah. In many Asian and African Muslim societies, women have much more visible public roles. Although modest dress is expected, face veiling is the exception, not the rule. In Indonesia and Malaysia, women who choose to wear head coverings as visible signs of Islamic piety participate in almost all aspects of public life. In Indonesia and Pakistan, women have held the offices of president and prime minister. Many Muslim women consider Western criticisms of modest Muslim dress to be insulting and ethnocentric. Many Muslim feminists also think that polygamy is outdated and that it should no longer be allowed.

Islamic Dietary Restrictions

The Qur'an and Muslim tradition have established a series of dietary restrictions that in many ways are similar to those described in the Hebrew Bible. Many of these rules concern foods that are allowed (*halal*) and those that are forbidden (*haram*). Like Jews, Muslims are required to slaughter animals by cutting their throats and must invoke the name of Allah over the beasts. Muslims are not allowed to eat pork, which is considered the most unclean of all meats. Dogs also are considered unclean. They cannot be eaten and can be kept only for the purpose of guarding herds and other property. Eating birds and beast of prey, donkeys, and mules is also prohibited. These restrictions became increasingly important as Islam spread to urban areas and as Muslims came into contact with Christians. Muslims also are forbidden to drink alcohol in any form or to gamble.

Religion and Public Life

Jihad

One of the most controversial aspects of Islam is **jihad**, all too often translated as "holy war." In fact, jihad is something very different. Today the word *jihad* often evokes images of terrorists and suicide bombers. The real meaning of the term *jihad* is "struggle in the path of God." It can mean struggle in the physical sense, which can include building mosques or leaving home to work for the spread of Islam or to avoid religious persecution, as well as armed struggle. It can also mean struggle against the human passions and instincts that can prevent people from acting in accordance with the commandments of the faith. Muslim tradition teaches that Allah rewards both types of struggle. Indeed, some modern Muslim theologians even think of the struggle for economic justice and development as a type of jihad.

Historically, Muslim nations waged war to spread Muslim rule, as well as for more clearly political and economic reasons. Muslim scholars teach that only defensive wars are truly jihad. Muslim leaders have, however, often used the concept of "holy war" to justify their actions, usually with mixed results. Because Muslim resistance to the Christian Crusades was considered a war to defend Islam, it was rightly called jihad. In World War I, a leader of Muslims in Turkey called for jihad against the Allied forces. His call was not widely heeded by world Islam. In fact, some Muslims joined the Allies against Turkey. In Algeria, Egypt, Indonesia, and other Muslim societies, post–World War II struggles for national independence were often thought of as jihad, but only within the borders of those countries. Many Muslims have called the struggle against the modern nation of Israel jihad. Others, including some Christian Palestinians, consider it to be a legitimate political struggle for land, water, and Arab self-determination. Saddam Hussein's attempt to justify Iraq's invasion of Kuwait as a "holy war" was almost completely ignored. Prior to the September 11, 2001, attacks on the World Trade Center in the United States, Osama bin Laden called for a global jihad against both Western and Muslim governments. The vast majority of Muslims believe that attacking non-combatants, especially women and children, violates Islamic notions of just war. Most Muslim scholars conclude that this use of the Qur'an to justify the attacks of September 11, 2001, is a perversion of Islamic teachings.

The Spread of Islam

12.5. **Detail the spread of Islam through out the Middle East and beyond.**

Islam appeared and developed at exactly the right time in history for expansion. It came at a time when the Arab people were ready for a unifying force, when the Byzantine Empire in the Middle East was on the verge of collapse from internal corruption and misrule, and when the Persian Empire also was vulnerable. In the early seventh century c.e., the Persians had invaded Palestine and had taken Jerusalem and Caesarea. The Byzantine rulers fought back and recaptured the territory, but the battles had left both empires exhausted.

Within a century of the death of the Prophet, the religion of Islam had become the unifying force for Arabs. Muslim armies conquered Palestine, Syria, Persia, and Egypt and swept across North Africa into Spain. In the centuries that followed, Islam spread throughout the Middle East and moved into India, China, and Central and Southeast Asia. There were several reasons for this rapid and massive expansion:

1. *Islam is a universal religion.* Although it arose in the Arab world, Islam recognizes no national barriers and knows no distinctions among races. All people were created by Allah and all are accepted as Muslims.

2. *Islam is a religion with wide appeal.* Unlike religions that require learning, meditation, or great sacrifice, Islam at its most basic level is a simple, easily practiced faith. A person who repeats the creed is a Muslim. A person who keeps the five pillars of Islam is a good Muslim.

3. *The world that surrounded the early Muslims was confused and corrupt.* Byzantine Christian rulers had mistreated and abused Jews and Arab Christians; therefore the Muslim conquerors were frequently received not as an invading army but as deliverers.

(Mark R. Woodward)

Qur'an school in Pattani, South Thailand. Approximately 90 percent of the people in this part of Thailand are Muslim.

Before the death of Muhammad, Islam had begun to conquer and unite the Arabian peninsula. With every conquest and every addition to Islam, others were encouraged to join and share in the benefits of the worldwide Muslim community, called the **ummah**. After the death of the Prophet, the movement gathered momentum and moved outside of Arabia. Damascus was taken in 635; Persia fell by 636; Jerusalem became Muslim in 638; Caesarea was conquered, after stubborn resistance, in 640; and Egypt was also taken in 640. In the following decades, Islam consolidated its victories. Most of North Africa became Muslim by the end of the seventh century.

In 711, the Muslims entered Spain, where they were dominant for the next seven centuries. In 732, they were turned back from further conquest in Europe by Charles Martel, at the Battle of Tours. On the eastern side of the Mediterranean, the expansion of the ummah also began to slow down. Constantinople, the capital of the Byzantine Empire, resisted Muslim attacks until 1453. The island of Sicily fell to the Muslims in the ninth century and for a period was a base for raids against Italy.

In the eleventh century, the caliphs of Baghdad extended their conquests into India and China. Today, the South Asian nations of Pakistan and Bangladesh are almost completely Muslim. There also are large Muslim populations in India and China. In the fifteenth century, most of what now constitutes Indonesia and Malaysia was converted to Islam. The Muslim world remained within these boundaries until the end of the nineteenth century, when missionary activity began to make renewed and rapid strides in Africa. Today, Islam is expanding rapidly in Europe and North America. The huge majority of Muslims are not Arabs. The world's most populous Muslim country today is Indonesia. India has the second largest Muslim population.

The Caliphate

12.6. **Recognize the significance of the caliphate.**

Islam is not highly structured or centralized. One reason is that Islam can be practiced privately. Most duties of a good Muslim can be done at home, without a priest. Another

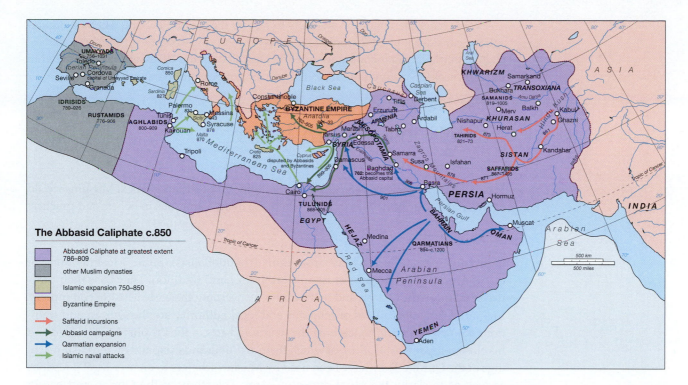

The Abbasid Caliphate c.850

- Abbasid Caliphate at greatest extent 786–809
- other Muslim dynasties
- Islamic expansion 750–850
- Byzantine Empire
- → Saffarid incursions
- → Abbasid campaigns
- → Qarmatian expansion
- → Islamic naval attacks

reason for its lack of structure is that Muhammad never clearly left a successor or a plan for the succession of his leadership. Only one of his children, Fatima, lived longer than the Prophet, and Muhammad never clearly designated her as the leader who was to follow him. The only hint of succession the Prophet made was to appoint his friend abu-Bakr to lead the community in prayers. After the death of Muhammad, there was great confusion among Muslims, but after a time it was agreed that abu-Bakr should be the caliph (from *khalifa*, "deputy" or "representative") who would rule the Muslims in temporal matters. It was presumed that spiritual rule would be left to the Qur'an.

The caliphate is the one central unifying office in the history of Islam. At first, the caliphs were friends of the Prophet and acted as pious leaders of the faithful. They were chosen by election or common consent. In later years, the caliphate became hereditary and the office was more like that of king. The first four caliphs are often called the orthodox caliphs because they were selected from the circle of friends of the Prophet and ruled from Arabia. They include abu-Bakr (632–634), Umar (634–644), Uthman (644–656), and Ali (656–661), the husband of the Prophet's daughter Fatima. Life was not easy for these caliphs: abu-Bakr had to suppress rebellion and also try to unify the nation the Prophet had built; Uthman was murdered; and Ali had the caliphate wrested from his hands in 661 by those who formed the first dynasty of Islam—the Umayyads.

Between 661 and 750, Islam was ruled by the Umayyad caliphs, who made their headquarters in Damascus, Syria. The Umayyads were more interested in ruling as kings, in conquering territory, and in sharing booty than in being leaders of a religious community. They were succeeded by the Abbasid dynasty, which ruled from Baghdad between 750 and 1258. The Abbasids outdid the Umayyads, ruling with great pomp and splendor. It was in this period that Jews, Christians, and Muslims worked together in studying and preserving the texts of the Greek philosophers and scientists. These efforts contributed directly to the resurgence of learning in Europe at the time of the Italian Renaissance.

After the tenth century, however, the golden age of Muslim civilization began to decline and the caliphate began to lose its power. The Abbasids were replaced by the Mamelukan Turks, who ruled the Muslim Empire from Egypt. The Mamelukes were replaced in the sixteenth century by the Ottoman Turks, who made the title *caliph* synonymous with that of "sultan" of Turkey. When the Ottoman Empire was dissolved after World War I, the caliphate ceased to exist. By that time, however, it was only a title and carried with it none of the glory and power it had once held in the days of the Abbasid caliphs.

There have been periodic attempts to restore the caliphate. Some Islamist organizations consider it to be the only legitimate form of government in Muslim societies. Hizbul Tahrir, an organization founded in Jerusalem in the 1950s and now centered in London, seeks to restore the caliphate by means of peaceful persuasion.

Variations Within Islam

12.7.   Name the different divisions within Islam.

Like most large religions, Islam is not a monolithic body. Although most Muslims would agree on the basic principles of Islam, there are many variations in beliefs and practice.

The Sunnis

Eighty-five percent of Muslims are **Sunnis** (traditionalists). Sunni Muslims think of themselves as the guardians of Islamic orthodoxy and tradition. They base their practice of Islam on the Qur'an and on traditions concerning the early Muslim community. In Sunni Islam, the sources of religious and legal authority are the Qur'an and traditions, known as *hadith*, concerning the words and acts of the Prophet Muhammad and his close companions. Hadith, of which there are thousands, expand on the basic teachings of the Qur'an. They have been used by Muslim scholars to answer legal questions as well as to clarify the ritual duties of Islam. The study of the Qur'an and hadith continues to form the basics of religious education in Sunni Muslim societies. Analogy and consensus are used to arrive at solutions to problems that are not mentioned in the Qur'an and hadith. They are particularly important for Muslim scholars striving to find Islamic solutions to the problems of the modern world.

As Islam grew and adopted the character of the many nations into which it spread, schools of interpretation arose that varied in the amount of weight they gave to the Qur'an, the hadith, and human reason in interpreting the life of Islam. There are four of these schools of thought, and every Sunni Muslim is a member of one of them. Generally the four schools represent different geographic regions. The first is the Hanifites, who follow the teachings of Abu-Hanifah (d. 767 C.E.). The Hanifites are found today in western Asia, India, and lower Egypt. The second is the Malikites, who follow the teachings of Malik ibn-Anas (d. 795 C.E.) and are found in North and West Africa and upper Egypt. The third is the Shafi'ites, who follow the patterns established by al-Shafi'i (d. 820 C.E.) and are found in lower Egypt, East Africa, Syria, India, Malaysia, and Indonesia. The last is the Hanbalites, who follow Ahmad ibn-Hanbal (d. 855 C.E.) and are today found in Saudi Arabia and communities in other countries influenced by them. Generally, the Hanbalites are the most conservative of the four groups. The Shafi'ites are generally the most liberal and the most willing to strike a balance between the demands of Islamic Scripture and local cultures.

The Shi'ites

The **Shi'ite** element within Islam represents a basic rupture in the body of the religion. It began as a political dispute over the leadership of Islam but later took on theological overtones. Because Muhammad had left no clear message regarding who was to succeed him, he was followed by three of his close associates. However, some Muslims believed that Muhammad had actually named Ali, his cousin and son-in-law, as his successor. Ali was finally named caliph in 656 but gradually lost control of the Muslim world. He was murdered in 661, and the Umayyad dynasty took the caliphate. Ali's youngest son, Husayn, challenged the Umayyad caliphs in 680 but was defeated at the Battle of Karbala in Iraq. Husayn and most of his family were killed in the battle. They are considered martyrs by the Shi'ites.

Throughout the history of Islam, certain elements have always believed that the descendants of Ali should be the leaders of the faith. In earlier times, these people were called Alids, but they gradually became known as Shia Ali (the party of Ali) and finally as Shi'ites. The Shi'ites differ from Sunni Muslims in the following ways:

1. The Shi'ites believe that while revelation ended with Muhammad and the Qur'an, in later generations there were divinely inspired figures called imams. To Sunnis, an imam is one who leads community prayers, but the word carries far more importance for Shi'ites. For them, an imam speaks with the authority of God.

2. Shi'ites believe that after the disastrous events of 680, the next imam was Zain, another son of Ali. Some believe that Zain was followed by a series of six other imams. These Shi'ites are called Seveners because they believe that there was a total of seven imams in history. Others believe that Zain was followed by eleven other imams, who are called Twelvers. Both the Seveners and the Twelvers believe that some of these imams did not die but went into hiding and are now waiting to return to Earth.

3. Shi'ites have also traditionally believed in the existence of a *Mahdi* (guided one), a messiah figure who will one day appear on Earth and lead the world into an era of justice.

4. Because of the importance of the martyrdom of Husayn, Shi'ites tend to prize martyrdom. Each year, on the tenth of the month of Muharran, the passion of Husayn is re-enacted. The site of his martyrdom in Iraq and other locations that were important in his life are places of special pilgrimages for Shi'ite Muslims.

5. The traditional Sunni reading and interpretation of the Qur'an is mistrusted by Shi'ites. It is reasoned that because the current version of the Qur'an does not mention Ali as Muhammad's successor it must have been tampered with by his enemies. The Qur'an must have hidden meanings that can be known only through allegorical interpretations.

In 1502, Shia Islam became the established religion of Persia and has maintained its hold on present-day Iran. The neighboring country of Iraq is approximately 60 percent Shi'ite. There are Shi'ite minorities in Saudi Arabia, India, Pakistan, Yemen, and some areas in East Africa. Today there are large Shi'ite populations in the United States and Europe because of emigration following the Iranian revolution of 1979. It is estimated that between 10 and 15 percent of all Muslims are Shi'ites.

Religion and Public Life

Relations between Sunnis and Shi'ites are often strained. In some Sunni countries there have been efforts to declare them to be legally non-Muslims. Sunnis have also often accused Shi'ites of not being true monotheists because of Shi'ite reverence for their imams, the Mahdi, and other saints in their history. The war in Iraq and especially the destruction of major Shi'te shrines by Sunni insurgents has contributed to deepening the rift between the two communities.

The Mystical Element

Islam, like Judaism, has always been a religion that emphasizes obedience to the will of God in the here and now. Therefore, it has never encouraged the ascetic life so characteristic of Indian religions and some forms of Christianity. Nevertheless, in every religion there is a hunger for the mystical experience. Furthermore, Islam arose in a land dominated by Byzantine Christianity, which highly prized the ascetic life; in later years it developed in India, where there is also a strong concern for communion with God through asceticism.

In Islam, the concern for a mystical connection with God was expressed by a group called the Sufis. The word *sufi* means "woolen" and refers to the coarse wool garments worn by early Muslim mystics as a symbol of poverty and the rejection of worldly pleasures. Sufis claim they have always been a part of Islam and trace their origins back to the Prophet and the Qur'an. They teach that in Islam's earlier days Muslims were more pious and more concerned with true spiritual matters than they were later. It is probably true that the expansion of Islam into a world empire caused Muslims to become more materialistic than they had been at the time of the Prophet Muhammad. With the development of the Abbasid dynasty and its grandeur in Baghdad, a cry arose among some for a simpler, more

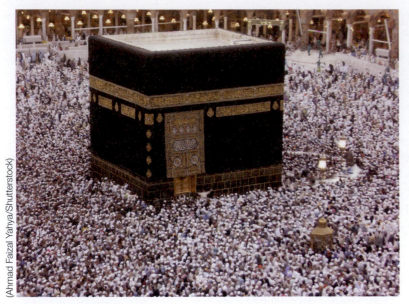

Over 500,000 Muslims before the Kaaba, the most sacred site in Islam, within the precincts of the Great Mosque at Mecca.

(Ahmad Faizal Yahya/Shutterstock)

austere life. Therefore, the ninth century probably was the era when the Sufi movement began.

One of the most famous Sufis of the early period was Mansur al-Hallaj. His quest for mystical oneness with God finally brought him to proclaim, "I am the truth." For this offense and for ignoring the ritual duties of orthodox Islam, he was executed in 922. He went to his death asking forgiveness for his persecutors. The martyrdom of one of their number and similar persecutions in the following years forced the more extreme elements of the Sufi movement to go underground. As the orthodox Muslim teachers increasingly emphasized the formal and legalistic aspects of Islam, however, the Sufis emphasized the emotional and mystical aspects and thus came to appeal to the common people as well as to members of the elite with mystical orientations.

Abu-Hamid al-Ghazali (1058–1111 C.E.), a professor of theology at the Nizamiyah School in Baghdad, attempted to unite the legalistic and mystical dimensions of Islam. Al-Ghazali was a brilliant theologian and legal scholar. However, as he grew older, he found less and less personal satisfaction in orthodox Muslim theology. He abandoned his position and his family and, like the Christian Saint Francis of Assisi, set out to find God by experiencing poverty and having mystical experiences. He found his satisfaction among the Sufis. His books, *The Revivification of the Religious Sciences*, *The Folly of the Philosophers*, and the *Niche of the Lights,* had a great impact on Islam and served to make orthodox doctrine more mystical. He prescribed **Sufism** as a remedy for spiritual ills, but he taught that even the most advanced mystics were bound by the ritual duties of the orthodox faith.

Also in the twelfth century the Sufis began to organize themselves into spiritual fraternities, which were usually centered on a Sufi saint. When a convert came to join the order, he was known as a *fakir* or a *dervish*.[16] Traditionally, novices stayed in the order and studied with the master until they became masters themselves. Sufi practices vary but generally emphasize discipline, poverty, and abstinence from worldly pleasures. Sometimes the extremes of asceticism and emotionalism, which Westerners have come to associate with the titles of *fakir* and *dervish*, were experienced. There are recorded reports of Sufis walking on coals, swallowing snakes, and so on; of course, there are various Turkish dervishes who seek oneness with God by whirling in one spot for hours at a time. These are only the extremes of the Sufi movement, however, and are not representative of the totality in any sense. The real contribution of the Sufis to Islamic thought is their insistence on the possibility of knowledge of God through mystical experience.

Islam in the Modern World

12.8. **Discuss the place of Islam in the modern world.**

In the years following the glories of the caliphate of Baghdad, Islam settled down to a relatively routine existence. There were the battles with the Christian Crusaders over the holy sites in Palestine in the twelfth and thirteenth centuries, which produced one of the most outstanding Muslim leaders of all time, Saladin; there was the eastward spread of Islam into India, China, and Central and Southeast Asia; and there was the development of the Ottoman Empire in the sixteenth century. But on the whole, Islam never regained the wealth, power, and political unity it had enjoyed during the golden age of the Abbasid caliphs.

When the European countries were moving out of the medieval twilight into the industrial age, many Islamic nations continued to live in preindustrial societies. Several reasons are suggested for this era of quiet in the Islamic world. One reason for the lack of change among Muslims may have been their sense of self-satisfaction relative to European countries. The Muslims had decidedly defeated the Christian Crusaders who had invaded their lands. Later, they had taken the supposedly invincible city of Constantinople from its Christian defenders. The Islamic world therefore had a sense of military and cultural superiority toward Christian countries. Advancements in naval and military technology, along with the newfound wealth of the Americas, shifted the world balance of power in favor of Europeans in the sixteenth century. Particularly in the Middle East, Muslims were slow to understand or appreciate the nature of these developments. Some scholars have suggested that it was not until the conquest of Egypt by Napoleon in the early nineteenth century that Islamic nations became aware that Europeans might present a significant challenge or threat.

(Mark R. Woodward)

Muslim boys in Jombong, Indonesia, reading the Qur'an at the grave of Hashim Ashari, a late-nineteenth-century Sufi saint.

Another reason for the slowness with which Muslim nations moved into the modern era was the development of extremely conservative groups within Islam; these groups took an active leadership in the struggle against any change. The most outstanding force against change occurred with the Wahhabi movement, founded in 1744 by Muhammad ibn-Abd al-Wahhab. The **Wahhabis** were traditionalists who opposed all forms of change. Naturally they opposed internal innovations, such as those proposed by the Sufis. The Wahhabi movement came to be attached to the house of the Sa'ud family, and when the Sa'ud family came to control Arabia, this puritanical religious movement came with them. In the nineteenth century, the Wahhabis suppressed and persecuted the Sufis and others whom they considered to have departed from what they understood as the Islam of the Prophet Muhammad and his close companions. Today, the Wahhabi movement is strongest in Saudi Arabia. The enormous wealth of the Saudis has enabled them to send missionaries throughout the Muslim world. There are few Muslim societies in which there are not Wahhabi-inspired puritanical movements.

The isolation of the Muslim world from the modern world came to an end in the early part of the twentieth century. By that time, transportation and communication had advanced to the point that the Muslim world came within easy reach of the Europeans. World War I brought the Ottoman Empire into the struggle on the side of Germany and Austria. At the end of the war, the victorious Allies (Britain, France, and the United States) broke up the Ottoman Empire. European powers took control of most of the Middle East. During the post–World War I years, the Muslim territories that had been part of the Ottoman Empire developed into independent nations. The boundaries of most of the nations of the modern Middle East are based on these post–World War I developments. They reflect the political divisions of colonial power and are not natural geographic or cultural entities.

The Middle Eastern Arab nations were found to have the world's largest supply of crude oil. As world demand for oil increased and domestic production in the United States and Europe could no longer meet the demand, the wealth and political power of the Arab states increased dramatically. These factors have caused a resurgence of interest in Islam, both internally and externally. The Muslim states of the Middle East can never again be overlooked; they are extremely important to the industrialized world. The same can be said of Indonesia, which has a population of over 200 million and an enormous petroleum reserve and is destined to play a much larger role in the Asian and Islamic worlds in the twenty-first century.

The internal resurgence of interest in Islam has manifested itself in several ways. First are the reform movements from within. Some Muslims have suggested, and practiced, textual criticism of the Qur'an in a manner similar to that practiced by Christians and Jews with their Bibles. Their purpose is to find what the Pakistani scholar Fazlur Rahman (1919–1988) called the "major themes of the Qur'an" and to use them to formulate solutions to the political and economic problems of the modern world.[17] Others have shifted the focus of traditional Islamic scholarship to questions such as the formulation of a philosophy of science based on Islamic ethical concepts and the search for what the Indonesian reformer Nurcholish Madjid called the "Islamic roots of modern pluralism."[18] Islamic feminists have used portions of the Qur'an and hadith concerning the just treatment of women as the basis for expanding the religious, social, and economic roles of women in the modern Islamic world. Many now strongly oppose polygamy.[19]

One of the most obvious results of the resurgence of Islam in the twentieth century was its extremely active missionary movement in Africa. The move south of the Sahara by Muslim missionaries began in the late nineteenth century, when the slave trade had ended and conversion of Africans was possible. Yet Islam has existed in portions of Africa since the seventh century. North Africa was among the first lands to be conquered and converted to Islam. Portions of the interior, particularly the cities, have also known Muslim influence for a long time. Muslim merchants and traders worked in many parts of the Continent. However, European colonial forces in the eighteenth and nineteenth centuries made Muslim missionary activity possible in the interior. The colonial powers opened Africa to both Christian and Muslim missions, with maps, modern transportation, and communications.

The abuses of the Africans by the colonial powers also opened doors for Islam. As African nations struggled for and gained their independence, hostility toward white Europeans and their religion could be expressed by conversion to Islam. Because Islam knows no bias of color or ethnic origin, it has often been thought of as an alternative to the Christianity of European colonialists. For many people in Africa, Asia, and the Middle East, Islam has come to be associated with the struggle for social justice and self-determination. Likewise, many African Americans have converted to Islam in response to the fraught history of Christianity and slavery in the United States.

(Mark R. Woodward)

Sultan Mosque, Singapore.

Muslim Calendar and Holy Days

12.9.   Talk about the Muslim calendar and name the Islamic holy days.

Islam has its own distinctive calendar, made up of twelve lunar months of twenty-nine or thirty days for a total of 354 days each year. To make up some of the difference between the lunar and solar year, one day is added to the last month of the year eleven times each thirty years. Even with this correction, however, 103 Muslim years are the equivalent of 100 solar years. Muslims date their calendars from the Hijra, so the date of the Prophet's death is not known as 632 C.E. but 10 A.H.

Among the five pillars of Islam, Muslims are commanded to pray each day, to fast during the holy month of Ramadan, and to try to make the pilgrimage to Mecca at least once in their lives. Thus these holy times are established for Muslims as being basic to their religion. In addition to these holy times, Muslims are required to participate in two annual feasts.

Feast of Fast-Breaking (Eid al-Fitr)

This feast is kept on the first day of Shawwal, the month after Ramadan, and celebrates a return to normal life after the prolonged fast. It is a time of feasting and may last for three days. In many Muslim societies, it is a time for exchanging gifts, visiting friends and relatives, and paying respect to the dead. Today it is common for Muslims to send Eid al-Fitr cards in much the same way Christians send Christmas cards.

Feast of Sacrifice (Eid al-Adha)

This feast comes on the tenth of dhul-Hijjah, the month of the pilgrimage. It is one of the requirements of the hajj, but it is also observed throughout the Muslim world. It commemorates the time when Abraham was commanded by God to sacrifice his son Ishmael.[20] When Abraham's faithfulness was revealed, God provided a ram as a substitute sacrifice. On this date in the Muslim year, the head of each household is to kill an animal and provide a feast. Some of the food is given to the needy in the community.

New Year

The month of Muharram is the beginning of the Muslim year. It also is celebrated because it is believed to have been the month of the Hijra. In Sunni communities, the tenth of Muharram is kept as a day of fasting, called *Ashura*. Among the Shi'ites, the tenth of Muharram commemorates the Battle of Karbala.

Birthday of the Prophet Muhammad (Mawlid an-Nabi)

The traditional celebration for the birth of Muhammad is established on the twelfth day of the third month. The recitation of the Prophet's biography and prayers for him are among the most common elements of this feast. In many places there are also processions, feasts, and special community prayers. The ultraconservative Wahhabis of Arabia do not celebrate the birthday because they consider it a modern invention. Muslim saints, particularly the founders of the Sufi orders, are remembered on their birthdays by many Muslim communities.

Islam Today

12.10.   Understand the challenges faced by Muslims in today's society.

In recent decades, Islam has become an increasingly important force in world politics. Many of the newly emerging nations of the so-called Third World are Muslim. Some of these nations are very important to the world's economy because they control vital natural resources such as oil, natural gas, and minerals.

Islam again is a growing religion. Mention has already been made of Muslim missionary activity in Africa. Islam is growing in other parts of the world as well. The Muslim population of Western Europe has been increasing because of the immigration of workers from Muslim nations and fertility rates higher than those of non-Muslim Europeans. Immigration has also been a factor in the growth of the Muslim population in the United States. There also have been many converts to Islam in the United States, particularly among African Americans. Islam is now the second most popular religion in many European countries.

Religion and Public Life

European Muslims confront problems integrating into largely secular European populations and the unwillingness of some Europeans to accept Muslims as fellow citizens rather than as temporary "guest workers." This is particularly true in France, where young women have not been allowed to cover their hair in public schools and where there have been violent confrontations between young Muslim men and security forces in impoverished communities. Fear of and discrimination against Muslims in Western countries has increased substantially because of the terrorist attacks of the last decade. There is an unfortunate tendency to blame an enormous religious community for the actions of a very tiny minority. Blaming the Muslim community for the attacks of September 11, 2001, is similar to blaming the Christian community for the terrorist bombing in Oklahoma City carried out by Timothy McVeigh on April 19, 1995.

The most dramatic change occurring in Islam today is the emergence of Islamic fundamentalism. In the 1960s and 1970s, Iran, Saudi Arabia, and several other Muslim nations became enriched by oil profits. In many cases, factions within these nations turned to Western society for a model. In time, the introduction of Western universities and customs (such as the increased participation of women in public life) was perceived as a threat by some conservative Muslims. Devout Muslims were shocked by what they perceived as the sexual vices and loose morality of Western Christian nations. They believed that the perceived moral decay of these nations had been caused by secularization of their societies.

This sense of threat produced a call for a return to the old ways and to nations controlled by historic Islamic culture. One sees this movement particularly in Iran, but it can be found, to some extent, throughout Islam. Iran represents the "left wing" of Islamic fundamentalism and has produced a revolution. In 1979, the Shi'ite Muslims of Iran deposed the shah and accepted the Ayatollah Ruhollah Khomeini as their leader. The new government called itself an Islamic Republic and is based on a strict interpretation of Shi'ite Islamic law. Since that time, Iran has supported anti-Western fundamentalist movements in many Islamic countries. Saudi Arabia represents the more conservative or "right wing" of Islamic fundamentalism. The Saudi government has attempted to isolate its people from foreign influences and enforces Wahhabi social and religious norms at home, while maintaining close economic and diplomatic relationships with the United States and other Western powers. Saudi dissidents advocate the abolition of the monarchy and the establishment of an even stricter Islamic order. They provide financial support and manpower for the Taliban in Afghanistan and have declared a global jihad against Muslim rulers and their Western allies.

It remains to be seen if Iran or any other Muslim nation can exist for long in the modern world with a political system based on ancient religious customs. The dreams of Islamic fundamentalism are particularly difficult for Muslims living in the non-Muslim world. This has not, however, prevented the emergence of militant groups in the United States and in many European countries. In most of the Islamic nations of the Middle East, Africa, and Asia, the majority of Muslims and their governments are strongly opposed to fundamentalism. In most Muslim societies, religious scholars are engaged in a struggle to define a vision of modernity that is based on Islamic values and yet is compatible with contemporary concepts of human rights and democracy. In 1999, twenty years after the Iranian revolution, Abdurrahman Wahid, one of the most articulate proponents of this understanding of Islam, was elected president of Indonesia, the world's most populous Muslim nation. In 2011, after many successful elections at local, provincial, and national levels, Indonesia was considered to be a consolidated democracy. Pakistan, Malaysia, and Indonesia all have strong pro-democracy movements. It seems likely that the struggle between forces of modernization and those of fundamentalism will continue for many decades to come. It is important to remember that very similar debates are taking place in Hindu, Jewish, and Christian communities.

Think About It

1. What were some characteristics of basic pre-Islamic religion?

2. After a series of revelations, Muhammad began to lay the foundation for Islam. How did the religion take shape under Muhammad? Was Islam universally accepted from the beginning? Why or why not?

3. Briefly summarize the basic teachings of the Qur'an.

4. List the five pillars or duties of a good Muslim.

5. What were the reasons for the rapid expansion of Islam throughout the Middle East, India, China, and Central and Southeast Asia in the century after the death of the Prophet?

6. What is the significance of the caliphate in the history of Islam? What roles have caliphs played throughout the years?

7. Summarize the different divisions within Islam. How are they different?

8. What were some of the reasons for the slowness with which Muslims entered the modern era, as the world moved out of the Middle Ages and into an industrial age?

9. What are the holy days in Islam and what is their significance?

10. What are some challenges facing Muslims and Islam today?

Suggested Reading

Ahmed, Leila. *Women and Gender in Islam: Historical Roots of a Modern Debate*. New Haven, Conn.: Yale University Press, 1992.

Bodansky, Yossef. *Bin Laden: The Man Who Declared War on America*. New York: Random House, 2001.

Denny, F. M. *An Introduction to Islam*. New York: Macmillan, 1985.

Esposito, John L. *Islam the Straight Path*. New York: Oxford University Press, 1991.

Madjid, Nurcholish, "In Search of Islamic Roots for Modern Pluralism: The Indonesian Experiences." In *Toward a New Paradigm. Recent Developments in Indonesian Islamic Thought*, edited by Mark Woodward. Tempe: Arizona State University, 1996.

Martin, Richard. *Islamic Studies. A History of Religions Approach*. Englewood Cliffs, N.J.: Prentice Hall, 1995.

Martin, Richard, Mark Woodward, and Dwi Atmaja. *Defenders of Reason in Islam. Mu'tazilism from Medieval School to Modern Symbol*. Oxford: One World, 1997.

Mottaheden, Roy. *The Mantle of the Prophet. Religion and Politics in Iran*. New York: Pantheon Books, 1985.

Rahman, Fazlur. *Islam*, 2nd ed. Chicago: University of Chicago Press, 1979.

———. *Major Themes of the Qur'an*. Minneapolis: Bibliotheca Islam, 1989.

Watt, W. Montgomery. *Muhammad, Prophet and Statesman*. New York: Oxford University Galaxy Press, 1974.

Source Material

The Muslim Vision of God

In the following selections from the Qur'an, the qualities of Allah as absolute creator and ruler, the only God, are presented.[21]

II 255–57

God: there is no god but Him, the Ever Living, the Ever Watchful. Neither slumber nor sleep overtakes Him. All that is in the heavens and in the earth belongs to Him. Who is there that can intercede with Him except by His leave? He knows what is before them and what is behind them, but they do not comprehend any of His knowledge except what He wills. His throne extends over the heavens and the earth; it does not weary Him to preserve them both. He is the Most High, the Tremendous.

There is no compulsion in religion: true guidance has become distinct from error, so whoever rejects false gods and believes in God has grasped the firmest hand-hold, one that will never break. God is all hearing and all knowing. God is the ally of those who believe: He brings them out of the depths of darkness and into the light. As for the disbelievers, their allies are false gods who take them from the light into the depths of darkness, they are the inhabitants of the Fire, and there they will remain.

VI *102, 103*

This is God, your Lord, there is no God but Him, the Creator of all things, so worship Him; He is in charge of everything. No vision can take Him in, but He takes in all vision. He is the all Subtle, the All Aware.

XXVII *60–63*

Who is it that made the earth a stable place to live? Who made rivers flow through it? Who set immovable mountains on it and created a barrier between the fresh and salt water? Is it another god beside God? No! But most of them do not know. Who is it that answers the distressed when they call upon Him? Who removes their suffering? Who makes you successors in the earth? Is it another god beside God? Little notice you take! Who is it that guides you through the darkness on land and sea? Who sends the winds as heralds of good news before His mercy? Is it another god beside God? God is far above the partners the put beside Him!

XXX *48–54*

It is God who sends out the winds; they stir up the clouds; He spreads them over the skies as He pleases; He makes them break up and you see the rain falling from them. See how they rejoice when He makes it fall upon whichever of His servants He wishes, though before it is sent they may have lost all hope. Look, then, at the imprints of God's mercy, how He restores the earth life after death: this same God is the one who will return people to life after death—He has power over all things. Yet they will continue in their disbelief, even if We send a [scorching] wind and they see their crops turn yellow. You [Prophet] cannot make the dead hear and you cannot make the deaf hear your call when they turn their backs and leave; you cannot lead the blind out of their error: the only ones you can make hear you are those who believe in Our revelations and devote themselves [to Us]. It is God who creates you weak, then gives you strength, then weakness after strength, together with your grey hair: He creates what He will; He is the All Knowing, the All Powerful.

XXXV *38–41*

God knows all that is hidden in the heavens and earth; he knows the thoughts contained in the heart; it is He who made you [people] successors to the land. Those who deny the truth will bear the consequences: their denial will only make them more odious to their Lord, and add only to their loss. Say, "Consider those 'partners' of yours that you call upon beside God. Show me! What part of the earth did they create? What share of the heavens do they possess? Have We given them a book that contains clear evidence? No indeed! The idolaters promise each other only delusion.

God keeps the heavens and earth from vanishing; if they did vanish no one else could stop them. God is most forbearing, most forgiving.

LVII *1–6*

In the name of God, the Lord of Mercy, the Giver of Mercy

Everything in the heavens and earth glorifies God—He is the Almighty, the Wise. Control of the heavens and earth belongs to Him; He gives life and death; He has power over all things. He is the First and the Last; the Outer and the Inner; He has knowledge of all things. It was He who created the heavens and earth in six Days and then established himself upon the throne. He knows what enters the earth and what comes out of it; what descends from the sky and what ascends to it. He is with you wherever you are; He sees all that you do; control of the heavens and earth belongs to Him. Everything is brought back to God. He makes night merge into day and day into night. He knows what is in every heart.

LVIII *7*

Do you not see [Prophet] that God knows everything in heavens and earth? There is no secret conversation between three people where His is not the fourth, nor between five where He is not the sixth, nor between less or more than that without Him being with them, wherever they may be. On the Day of Resurrection, He will show them what they have done: God truly has full knowledge of everything.

LIX *23–25*

He is God: there is no god other than Him, the Controller, the Holy One, Source of Peace, Granter of Security, Guardian over all, the Almighty, the Compeller, the Truly Great; God is far above anything they consider to be His partner. He is God: the Creator, the Originator, the Shaper. The best names belong to Him. Everything in the heavens and earth glorifies Him: He is the almighty, the Wise.

The Prescriptions of Islam

In the following sections from the Qur'an, many of the duties of a faithful Muslim are detailed.

II *172–79, 183–185*

You who believe, eat the good things We have provided for you and be grateful to God, if it is Him that you worship.

He has only forbidden you carrion, blood pig's meat, and animals over which any name other than God's has been invoked. But if anyone is forced to eat such things by hunger, rather than desire or excess, he commits no sin: God is most merciful and forgiving.

As for those who conceal the Scripture that God sent down and sell it for a small price, they only fill their bellies with Fire. God will not speak to them on the Day of Resurrection, nor will He purify them: an agonizing torment awaits them. These are the ones who exchange guidance for error, and forgiveness for torment. What can make them patient in the face of the Fire? This is because God has sent the Scripture with the Truth; those who pursue differences in the Scripture are deeply entrenched in the opposition.

Goodness does not consist in turning your face towards East or West. The truly good are those who believe in God and the Last Day, in the angels, the Scripture, and the prophets; who give away some of their wealth, however much they cherish it, to their relatives, to orphans, the needy, the travelers and beggars, and to liberate those in bondage; those who keep up the prayer and pay the prescribed alms; who keep pledges whenever they make them; who are steadfast in misfortune, adversity, and times of danger. These are the ones who are true, and it is they who are aware of God.

You who believe, fair retribution is prescribed for you in cases of murder: the free man for the free man, the slave for the slave, the female for the female. But if the culprit is pardoned by his aggrieved brother, this shall be adhered to fairly, and the culprit shall pay what is due in a good way. This is an alleviation from your Lord and act of mercy. If anyone then exceeds these limits, grievous suffering awaits him. Fair retribution saves life for you, people of understanding, so that you may guard yourselves against what is wrong.

You who believe, fasting is prescribed for you, as it was prescribed for those before you, so that you may be mindful of God. Fast for a specific number of days, but if one of you is ill, or on a journey, on other days later. For those who can fast only with extreme difficulty, there is a way to compensate—feed a needy person. But if anyone does good of his own accord, it is better for him, and fasting is better for you, if only you knew. It was in the month of Ramadan that the Qur'an was revealed as guidance for mankind, clear messages giving guidance and distinguishing between right and wrong. So any one of you who is present that month should fast, and anyone who is ill or on a journey should make up for the lost days by fasting on other days later. God wants ease for you, not hardship. He wants you to complete the prescribed period and to glorify Him for having guided you, so that you may be thankful.

On the Day of Judgment

The following passage describes the Islamic understanding of God's ultimate justice on the day of judgment.

LVI, 1–25

In the name of God, the Lord of Mercy, the Giver of Mercy

When that which is coming arrives, no one will be able to deny it has come, bringing low and raising high. When the earth is shaken violently and the mountains are ground to powder and turn to scattered dust, then you will be sorted into three classes. Those on the Right—what people they are! Those on the Left—what people they are! And those in front—ahead indeed! For these will be the ones brought nearest to God in Gardens of Bliss: many from the past and a few from later generations. On couches of well-woven cloth they will sit facing each other; everlasting youths will go round among them with glasses, flagons, and cups of a pure drink that causes no headache or intoxication; [there will be] any fruit they choose; the meat of any bird they like; and beautiful companions like hidden pearls: a reward for what they used to do. They will hear no idle or sinful talk there, only clean and wholesome speech.

Chapter 13
Baha'i

 ## Learning Objectives

After reading this chapter, you should be able to:

13.1 Discuss the origins, growth, and development of the Baha'i faith.

13.2 Understand the teachings of Baha'i.

13.3 Analyze and discuss Baha'i practices.

13.4 Name the important Baha'i holy days.

13.5 Understand the challenges faced by Baha'i today.

A Timeline of Baha'i

1844	Ali Muhammad, also known as the Bab, declares himself to be twelfth Imam
1858	The Bab executed, and his followers persecuted
1863	Husayn Ali, known as Baha'u'llah, founds Baha'i faith
1892	Death of Baha'u'llah; Abbas Effendi assumes leadership
1863–1908	Repression of Baha'is in the Middle East
1908–present	Global missionary efforts undertaken
1963	Universal House of Justice established
1979–present	Severe repression of Baha'i in Iran

Key Terms

the Bab   **Ridvan**

Baha'u'llah   **Universal House of Justice**

Baha'i began as a sect of Shi'ite Islam but has moved so far away from that religion that it now is considered a separate religion altogether. Several themes are central to Baha'i. Baha'i assumes that all of the religions of the world spring from one source, that there is a basic unity of all religious truth, and that all the prophets have had a partial message from the one God. Baha'i further maintains that religion must work in harmony with science and education to provide a peaceful world order; Baha'i also believes in equal opportunity among races and between sexes. By emphasizing these themes, Baha'i has attracted followers in many nations.

Origin and Development of Baha'i

13.1. **Discuss the origins, growth, and development of the Baha'i faith.**

The Shi'ite branch of Islam, particularly in Persia, has always taught that Ali, Muhammad's son-in-law and legitimate successor, was succeeded by a series of twelve descendants. These twelve imams were often referred to as gates, whereby the believers gained access to the true faith. The twelfth of these successors disappeared in the ninth century C.E., and the Shi'ites have always believed that one day he would reappear as a messiah.

In 1844, a Shi'ite Muslim named Ali Muhammad declared that he was the promised twelfth imam and called himself Bab-ud-Din (the gate of faith), or, in its shortened form, **the Bab**. He advocated sweeping religious and social reforms, such as raising the status of women; thus, the Bab gathered around him a group of disciples who called themselves Babis. The movement was short-lived, as the religious and political forces of Persia moved to crush it. The Bab was publicly executed in 1850, and many of his disciples were imprisoned or executed. Before he died, however, the Bab predicted that he had prepared the way for one who was yet to come, one who would found a universal religion. The body of the Bab was rescued by some of his followers and preserved for several years. Ultimately, it was transported to the city of Haifa, in Palestine, where it was finally buried.

One of the Bab's imprisoned disciples, Husayn Ali, was the son of one of the most distinguished families in Persia. Because of his family, Husayn Ali was not executed with the Bab but was imprisoned in Tehran. In 1852, another of the Bab's followers attempted to assassinate the shah of Iran, which brought further persecution upon the group. Husayn Ali was exiled to Baghdad, where he spent the next ten years of his life. During his imprisonment and exile, it was revealed to Husayn Ali that he was the one whom the Bab had foretold. In 1863, Husayn Ali and the remaining Babis were exiled from Baghdad to Constantinople; on the eve of their departure, Husayn Ali revealed to the Babis that he was the one promised by the Bab. This revelation was made in **Ridvan**, near Baghdad, and today is commemorated annually by the Baha'is with a feast. Husayn Ali assumed the name **Baha'u'llah** (the glory of God), and those Babis who accepted him and followed his teachings became known as Baha'is.

In the following years, Baha'u'llah and the Baha'is were forced from one capital city in the Middle East to another. From Constantinople, they went to Edirne (formerly Adrianople). Finally, they were banished to the Acre, which was the Turkish prison city of Akko but is now in the state of Israel. At first, Baha'u'llah and about eighty of his followers were incarcerated for two years in an army barracks, where they suffered from hunger and disease. After this period, the group was transferred to other quarters, which were somewhat more comfortable. Eventually, more freedom was given to Baha'u'llah, but he spent the remainder of his life as a prisoner of the Turkish government in Acre.

Although he was imprisoned during these years in Acre, Baha'u'llah was able to send out missionaries and receive guests, and he thus spread his teachings of unity and world peace. During this period, he wrote many letters and books. One series of letters was sent to the pope and to various heads of state, announcing his mission and calling for their help in furthering world peace. He wrote books such as the *Kitab-i-Aqdas* (The Most Holy Book), the *Kitab-i-Iqan* (The Book of Certitudes), and *The Hidden Words*. He died in Acre in 1892 at the age of seventy-five.

Leadership of the movement passed to the son of Baha'u'llah, Abbas Effendi, who became known as Abdul Baha (the servant of Baha). Abdul Baha carried on his father's program of writing, and in 1908, the Turks freed him. For the remaining years of his life, he traveled widely in Europe and North America, preaching the doctrines of Baha'i and establishing Baha'i assemblies in many nations. In 1920, the British conferred the Order of the British Empire on Abdul Baha because of his work for world peace.

Upon Abdul Baha's death in 1921, leadership of the movement was passed to his grandson Shoghi Effendi, who continued the work of establishing local and national

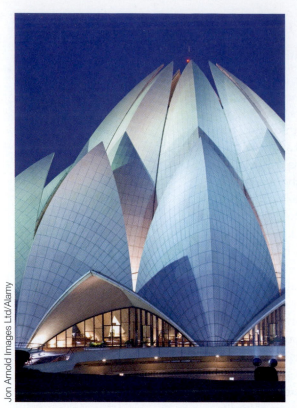

Opened in 1986, the Baha'i House of Worship in New Delhi is designed as a half-open lotus flower.

assemblies in many nations until his death in 1957. At this point, Baha'i came to be governed not by one of the descendants of Baha'u'llah but by a body elected from Baha'is all over the world.

The Teachings of Baha'i

13.2.   Understand the teachings of Baha'i.

Although Baha'i originated within the Shi'ite branch of Islam, it quickly developed to differ radically from it. Baha'i does not revere the Qur'an to the same degree Islam does. Much of the Qur'an is considered by Baha'i to be allegorical or symbolic. Belief in angels and evil spirits has been discarded by Baha'i, and heaven and hell are considered symbolic. The Qur'an takes its place, along with the Christian and Hebrew Bibles and the sacred writings of other religions, as holy scripture and as a source for Baha'i worship.

The basic belief of Baha'i is that all religions come from the same source. Baha'u'llah taught that divine revelation is a continuous and progressive process and that the missions of the Messengers of God (including Moses, Jesus, Muhammad, Buddha, the Bab, and Baha'u'llah) represent successive stages in the spiritual growth of humanity. Baha'is believe that Baha'u'llah is the most recent messenger of God, with God's message for humankind today. Baha'u'llah taught that other messengers of God would appear in the future. Baha'is believe that Baha'u'llah fulfills prophecies of the past manifestations of God and that his coming ushers in the age of fulfillment in religion.[1] Baha'u'llah's greatest message was the oneness of the human race. All of humankind, all races, both sexes, and all religious truths are the work of the one God. In the words of Baha'u'llah,

From the Source

There can be no doubt whatever that the peoples of the world, of whatever race or religion, derive their inspiration from one heavenly source and are the subjects of one God.[2]

On the basis of these religious truths found in the writings of Baha'u'llah, Abdul Baha left Acre to preach the following Baha'i doctrines to the world.

From the Source

1. There is oneness of the entire human race. This is the pivotal principle and fundamental doctrine of the faith and is essential to Baha'i. It is the basis for most of its teachings and practices.
2. There must be an independent search after truth, unfettered by superstition or tradition. Anyone who wishes to be a Baha'i must be willing to search out the truth of God without relying on the prophets and traditions of the past. "The freedom of man from superstition and imitation, so that he may discern the manifestations of God with the eye of Oneness, and consider all affairs with keen sight . . ." is one of the basic teachings of Baha'i.[3]

3. There is a basic unity of all religions. Baha'i teaches that all religions essentially preach the same message. This is not to say that differences do not exist among the religions of the world, but Baha'i doctrine states that the basic message of every religion is the same and that all minor differences should be ignored. In a conversation with a visitor, Baha'u'llah said,

   That all nations should become one in faith and all men as brothers; that the bonds of affections and unity between the sons of men should be strengthened; that diversity of religion should cease, and differences of race be annulled . . . these strifes and this bloodshed and discord must cease, and all men be as one kindred and one family.[4]

4. All forms of prejudice, whether religious, racial, class related, or national, are condemned. In one of his speeches in Paris, Abdul Baha said,

> Religion should unite all hearts and cause wars and disputes to vanish from the face of the earth; it should give birth to spirituality, and bring light and life to every soul. If religion becomes a cause of dislike, hatred and division, it would be better to be without it. . . . Any religion which is not a cause of love and unity is no religion.[5]

5. Harmony must exist between religion and science. Baha'i arose in the nineteenth century, when great battles were fought between the established religions and the newly emerging sciences. These two forces must be harmonized. According to Baha'i teachings, Ali, the son-in-law of Muhammad, said,

> That which is in conformity with science is also in conformity with religion. Whatever the intelligence of man cannot understand, religion ought not to accept. Religion and science walk hand in hand, and any religion contrary to science is not the truth.[6]

6. There is equality of men and women. Baha'i may be the only religion in the world that has asserted from the beginning that women are equal to men.

> Humanity is like a bird with its two wings—the one is male, the other female. Unless both wings are strong and impelled by some common force, the bird cannot fly heavenwards. According to the spirit of this age, women must advance and fulfill their mission in all departments of life, becoming equal to men.[7]

7. Compulsory education must prevail. Although neither Baha'u'llah nor Abdul Baha had the opportunity to receive a formal education, both preached that universal education was a necessary condition for world peace and stability.

8. There should be a universal language. Baha'u'llah said,

> We commanded the Trustees of the House of Justice, either to choose one of the existing tongues, or to originate a new one, and in like manner to adopt a common script, teaching these to the children in all the schools of the world, that the world may become even as one land and one home.[8]

9. Extremes of wealth and poverty should be abolished. Coming from a family of high rank and then spending much of his life in prison, Baha'u'llah was acutely aware of the extremes of wealth and poverty in the world. Believing that both extremes were unhealthy and abnormal, he urged their abolition. He did not offer an elaborate plan to bring about this change; rather, he suggested to the rich of the world that they open their hearts and contribute to the poor. He also advocated that the governments of the world pass laws to prevent the two extremes.

10. A world tribunal for the adjudication of disputes among nations should be instituted. Forty years before the establishment of the League of Nations, Baha'u'llah was urging such an organization from his prison cell in Acre. When the League of Nations was formed after World War I, however, Abdul Baha considered it too weak to be effective.

11. Work performed in the spirit of service should be exalted to the rank of worship. According to Baha'i, a good society is one in which everyone works at some task. There are no loafers or idlers.

> It is enjoined on every one of you to engage in some occupation—some art, trade, or the like. We have made this—your occupation—identical with the worship of God, the true One.[9]

12. Justice should be glorified as the ruling principle in human society and religion for the protection of all peoples and nations.

13. The establishment of a permanent and universal peace should be the supreme goal of humankind.[10] This is a capstone to all of the teachings of Baha'i. Unlike most followers of Islam and Christianity, Baha'i maintains that heaven and hell are not places but conditions of the soul. The soul, which is the reality of humankind, is eternal and in continuous progress. When the soul is close to God and God's purposes, that is heaven; when the soul is distant from God, that is hell. Thus, the descriptions of heaven and hell found in other religions are regarded as symbolic rather than actual.

When Baha'is speak of the unity of humankind, they mean not only the unity of humanity in this life but the unity of the living and the dead as well. Thus it is possible that the living and the dead may commune with each other. Abdul Baha believed that this connection was the reason for the peculiar powers of the prophets and saints to see into the other world and commune with it.

According to the Baha'i belief in the total unity of God, there can be no such thing as positive evil. If God is one and all, there can be no Satan figure in the universe. Just as darkness is only the absence of light, that which appears evil is only the absence of good. According to Abdul Baha,

From the Source

In creation there is no evil; all is good. Certain qualities and natures innate in some men and apparently blameworthy are not so in reality.[11]

Baha'i Practices

13.3. **Analyze and discuss Baha'i practices.**

The daily life of Baha'is is governed by many regulations. The Baha'i is required to pray every day. In fact, the entire life of a Baha'i is supposed to be prayer. One's work, thoughts, and deeds are all to be done in the spirit of prayer. This is one of the most important aspects of Baha'i life. Baha'u'llah stressed this in the Kitab-i-Aqdas.

From the Source

Chant (or recite) the Words of God every morning and evening. The one who neglects this has not been faithful to the Covenant of God and His agreement, and he who turns away from it today is of those who have turned away from God.[12]

Although a Baha'i may recite many formal prayers in daily devotions, Baha'u'llah established three obligatory prayers. Baha'is are free to choose any one of these as a part of their meditations.

For Baha'is, monogamy is the rule of marriage. Baha'is may marry only after they have the consent of both sets of parents. Baha'u'llah taught,

From the Source

Verily in the Book of Bayan (the Bab's Revelation) the matter is restricted to the consent of both (bride and bridegroom). As We desired to bring about love and friendship and the unity of the people, therefore We made it conditional upon the consent of the parents also, that enmity and ill-feeling might be avoided.[13]

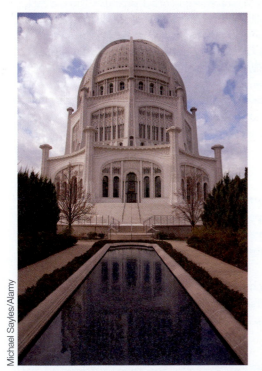

Michael Sayles/Alamy

Like all of the seven Baha'i Houses of Worship around the world, the temple in Wilmette, Illinois, features nine sides and a domed roof that symbolizes oneness in the diversity of the world's religions.

Divorce is permitted for Baha'is but only in extreme cases of incompatibility. At such a point, the couple must wait one year and seek to reestablish their relationship. If this does not happen, then a divorce may be granted. If a Baha'i couple have children, they are obligated to provide them with the best possible education. Alcohol and narcotics are forbidden to Baha'is.

Baha'i differs from many other religions in its manner of worship. Services of worship are held in the homes of members or in other buildings designated for that purpose, but there are often no special houses of worship. Neither is there a special clergy to conduct the worship. Worship for Baha'is tends to be simple, with a minimum of form and no ritual. There are readings from the writings of Baha'u'llah and from the scriptures of other world religions. Readings and prayers are led by several members of the community. No one person is designated as leader. Baha'i community worship is so simple in form that it rejects two elements that Christians and others often find essential: the sermon and the offering. Although Baha'is are expected to contribute to the support of their religion, they refuse to take offerings from non-Baha'is.

Baha'is are organized on three levels. The most basic is the local spiritual assembly already mentioned. In every community where there are nine or more adult Baha'is, a nine-member administrative body is elected each April 21 to govern their affairs. The second level of administration is the national spiritual assembly. This too is a nine-member body elected annually by delegates to the national conventions. The top level is the **Universal House of Justice**, a nine-member body elected by members of the national spiritual assemblies throughout the world. These representatives serve a five-year term, and gather at the Seat of the Universal House of Justice located in Haifa, Israel.

Baha'is have constructed several magnificent Houses of Worship at key locations around the world. These houses of worship are found in Frankfurt am Mein, Germany; Sydney, Australia; Kampala, Uganda; Wilmette, Illinois; Panama City, Panama; New Delhi, India; and Apia, Western Samoa. Each of these buildings reflects a somewhat different style of architecture, but all must be nine-sided and covered with a dome. The number nine is symbolic for Baha'i because it is the largest unit number and thus represents the worldwide unity that Baha'i seeks to develop. In addition to these temples, the world center of Baha'i is on Mount Carmel in Haifa, Israel—near Acre (where Baha'u'llah spent his last days). In the midst of splendid gardens stands the gold-domed shrine of the Bab and the archive building.

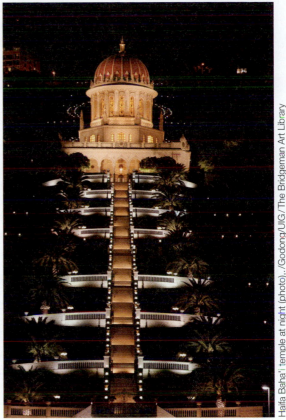

The Shrine of the Bab in Haifa, Israel, sits amidst lushly maintained gardens. The religion's world headquarters are located nearby.

Baha'i Calendar and Holy Days

13.4. **Name the important Baha'i holy days.**

Like other religions, Baha'i has established its own calendar and holy days. Its solar calendar is made up of nineteen months, each containing nineteen days. To achieve 365 days, four days are added after the last month of the year (five days are added in leap years). The new year begins on March 21, at the birth of spring. As is the case with the Hebrew calendar, the day begins at sunset.

Baha'is are encouraged to fast for one of the nineteen months in their calendar. During the month of Ala (loftiness), which begins near the first of March, Baha'is are expected to fast for nineteen days. A full fast, with complete abstinence from food, is not required; Baha'is must not eat during the daylight hours only. Because the fast occurs during the early spring each year, no food or drink is taken between about 6 A.M. and 6 P.M. According to Abdul Baha,

From the Source

Fasting is a symbol. Fasting signifies abstinence from lust. Physical fasting is a symbol of that abstinence, and is a reminder; that is, just as a person abstains from physical appetites, he is to abstain from self-appetites and self-desires. But mere abstention from food has no effect on the spirit. It is only a symbol, a reminder. Otherwise it is of no importance.[14]

At other times during the Baha'i year, followers engage in certain feasts that celebrate various events in the history of Baha'i. These include the feast of the New Year (celebrated on March 21) and the feast of Ridvan (celebrated between April 21 and May 2). Ridvan commemorates Baha'u'llah's declaration that he was the promised one. The birth of Baha'u'llah is celebrated on November 12.

Baha'i Today

13.5. **Understand the challenges faced by Baha'i today.**

From its beginning, the Baha'i faith has been subjected to persecution. In Iran, the land of its birth, Baha'is are considered heretics. This rejection by many Muslims is based on the Baha'i belief in a divine revelation coming after Muhammad.

Persecution against Baha'is in Iran became especially harsh after the Islamic revolution of 1979, when the Baha'i religion was officially outlawed. Many Baha'is were imprisoned; business and personal property was seized. The Baha'is are now forbidden to organize in Iran, and all church property, including cemeteries and holy places, is under government control. World attention became focused on this problem when it was revealed that Iran had in place a plan that called for legal persecution of Baha'is. The objective of this plan seems to be the elimination of the Baha'i faith from Iran.[15]

Religion in Public Life

Part of Baha'is' public witness of their religion is to work for world peace, the advancement of women, and economic development. They have also been active participants in global interfaith dialogue. Baha'is support the United Nations, an institution that they believe has an important role to play in establishing and maintaining Baha'i values in the world. Baha'is yearn for a future where nations are unified, education is universally available, and global networks of communication facilitate peace and understanding. Due to the persecution of Baha'is in Iran, they also greatly support human rights efforts.[16]

Although exact statistics are not available, there are over five million Baha'is spread around the globe. Although still relatively small in terms of members, this religion appears to be growing. Like Christianity and Islam, the Baha'i faith is a missionary religion. It has established communities in 218 independent countries, territories, and islands, with the largest number of adherents in Asia and Africa. In Central and South America Baha'i missionaries are especially active among indigenous peoples.

Think About It

1. How did Baha'i originate? How is it governed today?

2. How is Baha'i different form the Shi'ite branch of Islam? What is the basic belief system of Baha'i?

3. What are some of the regulations that govern the daily life of someone who practices Baha'i? How is Baha'i worship different from other religions?

4. What are the two major Baha'i holy days or feasts? What role does fasting play in the practice of Baha'i?

5. What are some of the challenges faced by Baha'i practitioners today?

Suggested Reading

Baha'u'llah. *The Kitab-i-Iqan* (The Book of Certitudes). Translated by Shoghi Effendi. Wilmette, Ill.: Baha'i Publishing Trust, 1931.

———. *Gleanings from the Writings of Baha'u'llah.* Translated by Shoghi Effendi. Wilmette, Ill.: Baha'i Publishing Trust, 1952.

Effendi, Shoghi. *God Passes By.* Wilmette, Ill.: Baha'i Publishing Trust, 1970.

Esslemont, J. E. *Baha'u'llah and the New Era.* Wilmette, Ill.: Baha'i Books, 1976.

Hatcher, William S., and J. Douglas Martin. *The Baha'i Faith: The Emerging Global Religion.* New York: Harper & Row, 1984.

Lee, Anthony A., Ed. *Circle of Unity: Baha'i Approaches to Current Social Issues.* Los Angeles: Kalimat Press, 1984.

Source Material

Selections from the Writings of Baha'u'llah

Although the Baha'i religion maintains that all of the scriptures of the world contain God's revelation and are sacred, it still holds a special place of reverence for the writings of its founder, Baha'u'llah.

It is incumbent upon ye every man, in this Day, to hold fast unto whatsoever will promote the interests, and exalt the station, of all nations and just governments. Through each and every one of the verses which the pen of the most high hath revealed, the doors of love and unity have been unlocked and flung open to the face of men. We have erewhile declared—and Our Word is the truth—"Consort with the followers of all religions in a spirit of friendliness and fellowship." Whatsoever hath led the children of men to shun one another, and hath caused dissensions and divisions amongst them, hath, through the revelation of these words, been nullified and abolished. From the haven of God's Will, and for the purpose of ennobling the world of being and of elevating the minds and souls of men, hath been sent down that which is the most effective instrument for the education of the whole human race. The highest essence and most perfect expression of whatsoever the peoples of old have either said or written hath, through this most potent Revelation, been sent down from the heaven of the Will of the All-possessing, the Ever-Abiding God. Of old it hath been revealed: "Love of one's country is an element of the Faith of God." The Tongue of Grandeur hath, however, in the day of His manifestation proclaimed: "It is not his to boast who loveth his country, but it is his who loveth the world." Through the power released by these exalted words He hath lent a fresh impulse, and set a new direction, to the birds of men's hearts, and hath obliterated every trace of restriction and limitation from God's holy Book.[17]

Lay not aside the fear of God, O kings of the earth, and beware that ye transgress not the bounds which the Almighty hath fixed. Observe the injunctions laid upon you in His book, and take good heed not to overstep their limits. Be vigilant, that ye may not do injustice to anyone, be it to the extent of a grain of mustard seed. Tread ye the path of justice, for this, verily, is the straight path.

Compose your differences, and reduce your armaments, that the burden of your expenditures may be lightened, and that your minds and hearts may be tranquilized. Heal the dissensions that divide you, and ye will not longer be in need of any armaments except what the protection of your cities and territories demandeth. Fear ye God, and take heed not to outstrip the bounds of moderation, and be numbered among the extravagant.

We have learned that you are increasing your outlay every year, and are laying the burden thereof on your subjects. This verily, is more than they can bear, and is a grievous injustice. Decide justly between men, and be ye the emblems of justice amongst them. This, if ye judge fairly, is the thing that behooveth you, and beseemeth your station.

Beware not to deal unjustly with any one that appealeth to you, and entereth beneath your shadow. Walk ye in the fear of God, and be ye of them that lead a godly life. Rest not on your own power, your armies and treasures. Put your whole trust and confidence in God, Who created you, and seek ye His help in all your affairs. Succor cometh from Him alone. He succoreth whom He will with the hosts of the heavens and of the earth.

Know ye that the poor are the trust of God in your midst. Watch that ye betray not His trust, that ye deal not unjustly with them and ye walk not in the ways of the treacherous. Ye will most certainly be called upon to answer for His trust on the day when the Balance of justice shall he set, the day when unto every one shall be rendered his due, when the doings of all men, be they rich or poor, shall be weighed.[18]

Notes

Introduction

1. For more on the academic study of religion, see http://www.studyreligion.org/.

2. For a history of how certain religions have come to be featured as "world religions" over others, see Tomoko Masuzawa, *The Invention of World Religions: Or, How European Universalism Was Preserved in the Language of Pluralism* (Chicago: University of Chicago Press, 2005).

3. The word *Manism* was taken from the Latin word *manes*, meaning "spirit" or "ghost."

4. Karl Marx, "Contribution to the Critique of Hegel's Philosophy of the Right," in Karl Marx and Friedrich Engels, *On Religion* (Atlanta: Scholars Press, 1964 [1844]).

5. Sigmund Freud, *Totem and Taboo* (Mineola, N.Y.: Dover, 1998 [1918]), 113–114.

6. Ibid., 123–125.

7. Sigmund Freud, *The Future of an Illusion*, trans. James Strachey (New York: Norton, 1961 [1927]), 38.

8. James Calvin Davis, *In Defense of Civility: How Religion Can Unite America on Seven Moral Issues That Divide Us* (Louisville, Ky.: Westminster John Knox, 2010), 19.

Chapter 1

1. Ludwig Wittgenstein, *Philosophical Investigations*, trans. G. E. M. Anscombe (Oxford: Basil Blackwell, 1958), 32.

2. See pages 4–5 in the Introduction for a discussion of Tylor's contributions.

3. Recent archaeological investigation at the ancient city of Carthage reveals that this rather advanced culture burned hundreds of its children as sacrifices throughout the history of the city. The Aztec of central Mexico regularly sacrificed prisoners and even fought wars for the sole purpose of obtaining victims to sacrifice to the gods. Human sacrifice is mentioned in the Hebrew Bible, for example. It is regarded as a supreme sacrifice, which is usually prompted by extremely rare circumstances. See Genesis 22, Judges 11, II Kings 3:27, and Micah 6:7.

4. Linda Greenhouse, "Animal Sacrifice; Court, Citing Religious Freedom, Voids a Ban on Animal Sacrifice," *New York Times*, June 12, 1993.

5. A sign in front of a Jain temple in Bombay is as follows: "Do not enter with shoes on. Women in menstrual cycle not allowed." Madeleine L'Engle, *A Stone for a Pillow* (Wheaton, IL: Harold Shaw, 1985), 148.

6. For examples of these rites, see the chapters on Native American and African religions.

Chapter 2

1. Although this is the most commonly accepted theory, some Native American religious leaders maintain that their people are literally "native," that they originated in the Americas and never migrated from any other continent.

2. Some estimate that prior to the arrival of the Europeans, there may have been as many as 2,000 different Native American cultures in North America.

3. Ruth M. Underhill, *Red Man's Religion* (Chicago: University of Chicago Press, 1965), 116.

4. T. C. McLuhan, *Touch the Earth* (New York: Outerbridge & Dienstfrey, 1971), p. 15.

5. Human sacrifice and similar practices, including collecting and saving portions of the bodies of slain enemies, were most common among warlike communities, including the Aztec of the Valley of Mexico, the Inca of Peru, and some communities in the Southwest of what is now the United States. They were practiced for one of two reasons: Some of the warrior spirits demanded human victims in return for providing aid in battle. In other cases, the bodies of slain enemies were believed to contain spiritual power. Until very recently, similar practices were found in many other parts of the world.

6. Underhill, *Red Man's Religion*, 116.

7. For an analysis of the Sun Dance among contemporary Native Americans, see Joseph G. Jorgensen, *The Sun Dance Religion* (Chicago: University of Chicago Press, 1972). Also Arthur Amiotte, "The Lakota Sun Dance: Historical and Contemporary Perspectives," in *Sioux Indian Religion*, ed. Raymond J. DeMallie and Douglas R. Parks (Norman: University of Oklahoma Press, 1987), 75–89.

8. During colonial times, if individuals had a choice between white and native healing, they would have been well advised to go to the native healer. The medicine man might perform rituals and give the patient herbs, some of which, including aspirin, are now known to be of real medicinal value. The spiritual aspects of Native American medicine may or may not have been effective, but they were certainly harmless. The white healer, on the other hand, often resorted to bleeding the patient or prescribing medicines containing mercury and other substances now known to be poisonous. Such practices frequently weakened the sick person and hastened death.

9. Weston La Barre, *The Peyote Cult* (New York: Schocken Books, 1969), 7.

10. See Hultkrantz, *Belief and Worship in Native North America*, 283.

11. The use of peyote and other hallucinogenic substances in Native American religious ceremonies is not a social problem in the same sense that drug use is in other contemporary American communities. These substances are used only for religious purposes, in part because their use is accompanied by extended periods of nausea and physical discomfort before a vision is achieved. In Native American communities, the most serious problems with chemical dependency are caused by alcohol abuse. These problems are particularly serious in areas with high rates of unemployment and among some groups that appear to have a genetic predisposition

for diabetes, which, when coupled with alcohol abuse, often leads to serious health problems and premature death.

12. Similar practices can be found in ancient Chinese religion and in the religions of many tribal peoples of southern China and Southeast Asia.

13. Most of the Native American rugs, paintings, and Kachina dolls made for tourists and non-native art collectors are secular in this sense. Objects used in religious ceremonies are carefully guarded and generally are not sold to non-native people.

14. Frances Densmore, *Teton Sioux Music* (Bureau of American Ethnology, Bulletin 61, 1918), 65–66.

15. Reprinted from *Lakota Myth* by James R. Walker, edited by Elaine A. Jahner, by permission of the University of Nebraska Press. Copyright 1983 by the University of Nebraska Press.

Chapter 3

1. From the sixteenth to the nineteenth century many Yoruba were brought to the new world as slaves. Yoruba religion continues to flourish in Brazil, the Caribbean, and areas of the United States with large Latino/a immigrant populations.

2. Susan Feldman, ed., *African Myths and Tales* (New York: Dell, 1963), 36–37.

3. Geoffery Parrinder, *African Traditional Religion* (Chicago: Hutchinson House, 1954), 48.

4. Diedre Badejo, *Osun Seegesi. The Elegant Deity of Wealth, Power and Femininity* (Trenton, N.J.: Africa World Press, 1996), 103–122.

5. Benjamin C. Ray, *African Religions* (Englewood Cliffs, N.J.: Prentice Hall, 1976), 149.

6. Ibid., 80.

7. Feldman, *African Myths and Tales*, pp. 278–280.

8. Parrinder, *African Traditional Religion*, 94. In many African cultures, and in others throughout the world, a clear distinction is made between the mother's brothers and sisters and those of the father, who often play very different roles in the life of a child. Often the mother's brothers and sisters are authority figures, while the father's are regarded in a less formal, often familiar way.

9. Female circumcision is also practiced by some Muslim peoples in North Africa even where it is prohibited by the government. Male circumcision is a universal practice in Muslim and Jewish societies and is very widely practiced by Christians and secular people in the United States. It is less common in European and other Christian communities.

10. Ray, *African Religions*, 80.

11. Noel Q. King, *Religions of Africa* (New York: Harper & Row, 1970), 30.

12. Ray, *African Religions*, 106–108.

13. Pew Forum on Religion and Public Life, *Tolerance and Tension: Islam and Christianity in Sub-Saharan Africa* (Washington, DC: Pew Research Center, 2010), 33–34.

14. Monica Wilson, *Communal Rituals of the Nyakyusa* (International African Institute, 1959), pp. 40–46.

15. Maria Leach, *The Beginning: Creation Myths around the World* (New York: Krishna Press, 1956), 145–147.

Chapter 4

1. For more on the debates about early Indian history, see Bryant Edwin F. and Laurie L. Patton, eds., *The Indo-Aryan Controversy: Evidence and Inference in Indian History* (New York: Routledge, 2005).

2. The word *Veda* is used in two ways. Generally, it refers to only the ancient collection of hymns to the Aryan gods. In another sense, it refers to an entire collection of sacred literature that includes the hymns and the later additions: the Brahmanas, the Aranyakas, and the Upanishads. In this text, we use the word in the latter sense.

3. Ralph T. H. Griffith, trans., *The Hymns of the Rig-Veda*, vol. I (Banaras: E. J. Lazarus and Co., 1920), 133, 134.

4. Ibid., 294.

5. Ibid., 398.

6. Satapatha Brahmana, 1:8.

7. The basic meaning of the word *Upanishad* seems to be "near sitting," indicating that these are materials developed in the discussions between teachers (gurus) and their students as they sat together and spoke of the philosophical implications of the Vedas.

8. Maitrâyana Brâhmana Upanishad, VI, 17. *The Upanishads*, trans. F. Max Müller (Oxford: Clarendon Press, 1884).

9. Svetasvatara Upanishad, IV, 9–10. *The Upanishads*, trans. F. Max Müller (Oxford: Clarendon Press, 1884).

10. Vâgaseneyi Samhitâ Upanishad, 9; Maitrâyana Brâhmana Upanishad, VI, 17. *The Upanishads*, trans. F. Max Müller (Oxford: Clarendon Press, 1884).

11. Svetasvatara Upanishad, IV, 6. *The Upanishads*, trans. F. Max Müller (Oxford: Clarendon Press, 1884).

12. Katha Upanishad, I, 3, 14. *The Upanishads*, trans. F. Max Müller (Oxford: Clarendon Press, 1884).

13. Khândogya Upanishad, VI, 13. *The Upanishads*, trans. F. Max Müller (Oxford: Clarendon Press, 1884).

14. Griffith, trans., *The Hymns of the Rig-Veda*.

15. G. Buhler, trans., *The Law of Manu*, 1:31, in *Sacred Books of the East* (Oxford: Oxford University Press, 1886).

16. In Hinduism, the word *dharma* is used in many ways. It comes from the root word *dhri*, which means "to support." It can mean duty or teaching or truth. Here, *dharma* came to refer to rules that support or maintain a proper society.

17. Buhler, trans., *The Law of Manu*, 1:88–91.

18. Ibid., 12:9.

19. Ibid., 6:92 and 9:26.

20. The *Mahabharata* contains 110,000 couplets, or 220,000 lines. The English translation of the *Mahabharata* fills thirteen volumes.

21. *Bhagavad Gita* I:26–32. R. C. Zaehner, trans., *The Bhagavad Gita* (Oxford: Oxford University Press, 1969).

22. *Bhagavad Gita* III:4, 5. Edwin Arnold, trans., *The Bhagavad Gita* (Boston: Roberts Brothers, 1885).

23. *Bhagavad Gita* IV:7. Edwin Arnold, trans., *The Bhagavad Gita* (Boston: Roberts Brothers, 1885).

24. *Bhagavad Gita* IV:7. Edwin Arnold, trans., *The Bhagavad Gita* (Boston: Roberts Brothers, 1885).

25. The god Brahma is to be distinguished from the all-pervading god-force of the Upanishads, Brahman. The word *Brahman*

is neuter. The word *Brahma* is masculine and refers to a distinct entity.

26. Geoffrey Moorhouse, *Calcutta* (San Diego: Harcourt Brace Jovanovich, 1971), 6.

27. On the goddesses of postclassical Hinduism, see C. Dimmitt and J. A. van Buitenen, *Classical Hindu Mythology. A Reader in the Sanskrit Puranas* (Philadelphia: Temple University Press, 1978), 219–41.

28. The most common posture used in meditation is the so-called lotus position, in which one sits with the right foot upon the left thigh, the left foot upon the right thigh, and the back is erect. In this extremely balanced position, concentration is easier than in most other seated positions.

29. R. C. Zaehner, *Hinduism* (New York: Oxford University Press, 1962), 4.

30. The Sanskrit word that Indians have traditionally applied to the caste system is *jati*, or "birth."

31. Adrian C. Mayer, *Caste and Kinship in Central India. A Village and Its Region* (Berkeley: University of California Press, 1960).

32. Griffith, trans., *The Hymns of the Rig-Veda*, vol. I

33. Ibid., vol. II, pp. 566, 567.

34. Brihadâranyaka Upanishad IV, 4, 1–2 and V, 10. *The Upanishads*, trans. F. Max Müller (Oxford: Clarendon Press, 1884).

35. G. Buhler, trans., *Law of Manu*, in *Sacred Books of the East*, vol. XXV (New York: Charles Scribner's Sons, 1882–1902), 204–210.

36. Selections from *Bhagavad Gita* II:16–27, XI:15–21, 24, 25, 31–34. Edwin Arnold, trans., *The Bhagavad Gita* (Boston: Roberts Brothers, 1885).

Chapter 5

1. According to some Jain legends, the parents of Mahavira died of self-imposed starvation. Because Jainism places such high value on asceticism, this form of death becomes the ideal.

2. Herman Jacobi, trans., "Sutrakrtanga," *Gaina Sutras*, in *Sacred Books of the East*, vol. XL (Oxford: Clarendon Press, 1895), 1–3, 18.

3. *Tattvartha Sutra*, 10, 2. George Thibaut, trans., *Shankara, Commentary on Vedanta Sutra*, vol. 1, in *Sacred Books of the East*, vol. XXXIV (Oxford: Clarendon Press, 1890), passim.

4. *Ayaranya Sutra*, 1, 1, 6, 6. George Thibaut, trans. *Shankara, Commentary on Vedanta Sutra*, vol. 1, in *Sacred Books of the East*, vol. XXXIV (Oxford: Clarendon Press, 1890), passim.

5. The well-known story of the blind men and the elephant is said to have been of Jain origin and illustrates the relativity of truth. In this tale, several blind men are asked to describe an elephant. Each touches a different part of the elephant's body, and thus each describes the animal in a different way. To one man, the elephant is like a stone wall because he has touched the side; to another, the elephant is like a rope because he has touched the tail; and to another, the elephant is like a fan because he has touched the ear. Each man truthfully described the animal, but because each had contacted it from a different point, the descriptions varied tremendously.

6. In the fourth century B.C.E., when Alexander the Great entered India, he encountered the naked Jain philosophers

and was fascinated by them. The Jains only stamped their feet in Alexander's presence. When he inquired about this strange behavior, he was told, "King Alexander, every man can possess only so much of the earth's surface as this we are standing on. You are but human like the rest of us, save that you are always busy and up to no good, travelling so many miles from your home, a nuisance to yourself and to others. Ah well! You will soon be dead, and then you will own just as much of the earth as will suffice to bury you" (Arrian 7:1.4–7:2.1).

7. For example, when rats were a problem in Mumbai, Jains established hospices for them. Captured rats were given a home, were separated by sex so they could not reproduce, and were fed and cared for until they died of natural causes.

8. From *Sources of Indian Tradition* by de Bary, Wm. Theodore. Copyright © 1964. Columbia University Press. Reprinted with permission of the publisher.

9. From *Sources of Indian Tradition* by de Bary, Wm. Theodore. Copyright © 1964. Columbia University Press. Reprinted with permission of the publisher.

Chapter 6

1. Some chronologies place the Buddha's death as late as 368 B.C.E. Nevertheless, the older and probably more reliable Sri Lankan sources place his life in the sixth century B.C.E.

2. Rahula is an unusual name. It means "fetter," thus indicating that at the time of the child's birth, Gautama was at the point of considering that all things, even a beautiful child, could bind one to life like a fetter. The choice of this name indicates that even at the time of the birth of his first child, Gautama had come to see family life as an impediment to the quest for spiritual liberation.

3. This tradition continues to influence lay Buddhist practice. In many Buddhist societies, women take the leading role in supporting Buddhist monks and supplying them with food and other necessities of life.

4. Because he found enlightenment (*bodhi*) under this tree, it has become known as the *bo* or *bodhi* tree.

5. Although the Buddha spent little time preaching against the abuses of the caste system, he effectively struck at its heart by admitting persons of any caste into his order. Only in Sri Lanka has Buddhism retained the caste system. There are monastic orders for each of the major caste groups.

6. E. J. Thomas, trans., "Pali Sermons, Morality (1)," in *Samannaphala-sutta*, Digha I, 47 (London: Kegan Paul International, 1935), 54–69.

7. "Tathagata" was the Buddha's term for himself. It means "truth gatherer."

8. E. J. Thomas, trans., "Pali Sermons, the First Sermon," in *Samyutta*, V, 420 (London: Kegan Paul International, 1935), 29–33.

9. Whether these missionaries actually visited the Western nations or whether they succeeded in influencing people for Buddhism is not known. There is evidence of cultural interchange between India and the Hellenized world. See A. D. Nock, *Conversion* (Lanham, MD: University Press of America, 1985), 44–47.

10. *Dhammapada*, 90–94, 98. *The Dhammapada*, translated from the Pâli by F. Max Müller (Oxford: Clarendon Press, 1881).

11. On the Jataka tradition, see Peter Khoroche, *Once the Buddha Was a Monkey: Arya Sura's "Jatakamala"* (Chicago: University of Chicago Press, 1989).

12. Seth Mydans, "Monks' Protest Is Challenging Burmese Junta," *New York Times*, September 24, 2007. For more information about the All Burmese Monks Alliance, see http://allburmamonksalliance.org/.

13. *Wat* is a Thai word. In Burma, similar clusters are called *phongyi-chaung*, which means "buildings for monks."

14. Theravada Buddhists also believe in the existence of many Buddhas, but they maintain that like other humans they are mortal, and that there can be only one at a time. According to Theravada teachings, long periods of time exist during which there is no Buddha in the world.

15. In China, this Buddha is known as O-mi-tuo, and, in Japan, as Amida.

16. Edward Conze, trans., "The Pure Land, 15, 16," in *Sukhavativyuha. Buddhist Texts through the Ages* (Oxford: Bruno Cassirer, Ltd. 1954), 202.

17. Similar, although lesser-known, texts can be found in other Buddhist and Hindu traditions. A Theravada text from Thailand, *Phra Malai Kham Luang* (The Legend of the Monk Malai) tells the story of a monk who visits the Buddhist heavens and hells and asks their residents what good or evil deeds caused their rebirths. Bonnie Brereton, *Thai Tellings of Phra Malai. Text and Rituals Concerning a Popular Buddhist Saint* (Tempe: Arizona State University, Program for Southeast Asian Studies, 1995). The Balinese text *Bhima Swarga* (Bhima Goes to the Land of the Gods), trans. Idanna Pucci, *Bhima Swarga. The Balinese Journey of the Soul* (Boston: Little, Brown and Company, 1992), tells a similar story from a Hindu perspective.

18. The word *dalai* literally means "ocean" and indicates the vastness and depth of the person.

19. See Chapters 8 and 9 for more detailed information about this and other festivals in China and Japan.

20. On Buddhism in the West, see Rick Fields, *How the Swans Came to the Lake. A Narrative History of Buddhism in America* (Boston: Shambala Publications, 1992).

21. Lord Chalmers, trans., *Further Dialogues of the Buddha*, vol. 1 (New York: Krishna Press, 1926), 53–57.

22. E. J. Thomas, *Buddhist Scriptures* (E. P. Dutton, 1913).

23. Edward Conze, trans., *Buddhist Texts through the Ages* (Oxford: Bruno Cassirer, Ltd., 1954), 131–32.

24. From *Sources of Japanese Tradition* by de Bary, Wm. Theodore. Copyright © 1958. Columbia University Press. Reprinted with permission of the publisher.

Chapter 7

1. Asa Ki War, Slok VI, *The Sacred Writings of the World's Great Religions*, ed. S. E. Frost (New York: McGraw-Hill, 1943), 362.

2. Rick Romell, "7 Dead, Including Shooter, at Sikh Temple in Oak Creek," *Milwaukee Journal Sentinal*, August 6, 2012.

3. From *Siri Guru Granth Sahib*, translation copyright © 2013 Dr. Sant Singh Khalsa.

Chapter 8

1. Arthur Waley, *The Way and Its Power* (London: George Allen & Unwin, 1956), 86.

2. Lao-Tzu, *Tao Te Ching*, translated by J. H. McDonald for the public domain, 1996.

3. Ibid.

4. Herbert A. Giles, *Religions of Ancient China* (Salem, NH: Books for Libraries Press, 1969), 47.

5. Lao-Tzu, *Tao Te Ching*.

6. D. Howard Smith, *Chinese Religions* (New York: Holt, Rinehart, and Winston, 1968), 71.

7. James Legge, trans., "How pure and still the *Tao* is. I do not know whose song it is. It might appear to have been before God." In *Sacred Books of the East*, vol. XXXIX (Oxford: Clarendon Press, 1891), 50.

8. Ibid., 73.

9. The principal form of divination taught by Confucius was probably the Chinese classic, the *Yijing*. Current versions of the *Yijing* are believed to have been edited by Confucius.

10. Arthur Waley, trans., *The Analects of Confucius* (London: George Allen & Unwin, Ltd., 1938), 6:20.

11. James Legge, trans., *Li Chi: Book of Rights*, vol. II (1885).

12. James Legge, trans., *The Chinese Classics, Volume I: Confucian Analects* (1891).

13. Ibid.

14. Ibid.

15. His name was *Mengzi*, but his Chinese name has been Latinized by Western scholars as *Mencius*.

16. S. E. Frost, ed., *The Sacred Writings of the World's Great Religions* (New York: McGraw-Hill, 1943), 114.

17. Smith, *Chinese Religions*, p. 54.

18. Xunzi, *Xunzi*, vol. II, trans. John Knoblock (Hunan: Hunan People's Publishing House, Foreign Language Press, 1999), 601.

19. Dexter Roberts, "Confucius Makes a Comeback in China," *Businessweek*, November 1, 2012.

20. Self-government, self-support, and self-propagation.

21. Zhuangzi, *Zhuangzi: The Essential Writings*, trans. Brook Ziporyn (Indianapolis: Hackett, 2009), 20–21.

22. Waley, *The Analects of Confucius*, 94–106.

23. From *Sources of Chinese Tradition* by de Bary, Wm. Theodore. Copyright © 1958. Columbia University Press. Reprinted with permission of the publisher.

Chapter 9

1. *Sources of the Japanese Tradition* by de Bary, Wm. Theodore. Copyright © 1958. Columbia University Press. Reprinted by permission of the publisher.

2. Basil Hall Chamberlain, trans. *The Kojiki: Records of Ancient Matters* (Transactions of the Asiatic Society, 1919), 19–21.

3. For a further discussion of these forms, see Chapter 6 of this text.

4. Floyd Ross, *Shinto: The Way of Japan* (Boston: Beacon Press, 1965), 138, 139.

5. Most Japanese found this statement to be highly peculiar because they had never thought of the emperor as a god, but rather as a human descendent of the sun goddess.

6. Chamberlain, trans., *The Kojiki*, 15–18, 28.

7. William T. de Bary, ed., *Sources of Japanese Tradition* (New York: Columbia University Press, 1958), pp. 29–31.

Chapter 10

1. The use of the plural here is a mystery. It is possible that at one point the patriarchs may have been polytheists, in the sense that they recognized a number of gods but chose to worship only one. It is clear that nothing in the narrative points to the worship of any but the one God.

2. The events of the Exodus are mentioned only in biblical literature. Known Egyptian records do not speak of the escape of a nation of slaves. Therefore, the actual date of the Exodus is subject to debate. The most widely accepted date is the early thirteenth century B.C.E., during the reign of Ramses II.

3. The usual reading of this body of water as "Red Sea" is based on an ancient mistranslation.

4. This is one way to divide the material in Exodus 20:1–17. Differing religious traditions in Judaism and Christianity sometimes divide the commandments differently. From World English Bible, http://eBible.org.

5. I Samuel 19:24. From World English Bible, http://eBible.org.

6. The prophet about whom there is the most information in the Bible, and who fits this pattern, is Elisha. See II Kings 2:1–13; 13:21.

7. Amos 2:6, 7a. From World English Bible, http://eBible.org.

8. Amos 5:14, 15. From World English Bible, http://eBible.org.

9. Psalm 137:1–4. From World English Bible, http://eBible.org.

10. The visions of Ezekiel 1 emphasize the mobility of God.

11. Chapters 40–66 of the biblical book of Isaiah are usually attributed to a sixth-century B.C.E. author.

12. Isaiah 49:6b. From World English Bible, http://eBible.org.

13. The Septuagint. At this time Greek was the language of learning and scholarship throughout the Middle East.

14. Hans Kung, *Judaism: Between Yesterday and Tomorrow*, trans. John Bowden (New York: Crossroad, 1992), 141.

15. Romans 15:24, 28.

16. *George Washington: A Collection*, ed. W. B. Allen (Liberty Fund: Indianapolis, 1988), 548.

17. For its religious festivals, Judaism relies on an ancient lunar calendar that is synchronized with the solar calendar by adding an extra month each leap year. This calendar is dated from the supposed date of creation, which would make the year beginning in the fall of 2000 C.E. the Jewish year 5760.

18. The source material that follows is taken from World English Bible, http://eBible.org.

19. D. A. De Sola and M. J. Raphall, trans., *Eighteen Treatises from the Mishna* (London: Sherwood, Gilbert, and Piper, 1843), 101–104.

Chapter 11

1. *Koine*, or common, Greek was that version of the Greek language used throughout the Hellenized world. It differs somewhat from classical Greek.

2. The absence of non-Christian accounts of the life of Jesus of Nazareth cannot be understood as definitive evidence that there was never such a man, but rather that the historical Jesus did not attract serious attention from Roman authors during his lifetime. This is not surprising, particularly in light of the fact that there were so many apocalyptic religious movements during this period of Roman history.

3. If Matthew is correct, Jesus was born between 6 and 4 B.C. This is possible because those who established the Christian calendar, marking time into B.C. (before Christ) and A.D. (Anno Domini, in the year of our Lord), lived several hundred years after the time of Jesus and simply miscalculated the date by a few years. This calendar corresponds with what is called the Common Era (abbreviated C.E.). There is no year 0 in either system.

4. The translation of the Hebrew word *almah* has been a source of contention between Christians and Jews for years. In other contexts, the word nearly always means "young woman." Matthew translates it with the Greek word *parthenos*, which always means "virgin."

5. Isaiah 7:14.

6. Acts 19:1–7. This quotation is taken from *The New Revised Standard Version Bible* (New York: National Council of the Churches of Christ in the U.S.A., 1989).

7. Matthew 5:3–12.

8. Luke 10:30–35.

9. Matthew 5:38–41.

10. Matthew 15:11.

11. Matthew 5:17–19.

12. Mark 8:27–29.

13. Luke 22:17–20.

14. One of the lesser-known disciples was Simon the Zealot. See Luke 6:15.

15. The Second Vatican Council (1962–1964) issued a statement that said that although Jewish authorities had pressed for the death of Jesus, his execution cannot be charged against all Jews.

16. Luke 24:43. This quotation is taken from *The New Revised Standard Version Bible* (New York: National Council of the Churches of Christ in the U.S.A., 1989).

17. Although fourteen of the New Testament books are traditionally attributed to Paul, most scholars agree that only seven of these were actually written by him. The others were likely written by others who used Paul's name as their pseudonym, a not uncommon practice at the time.

18. The admonitions of Paul to the church at Corinth indicate that the supper eaten by early Christians was not always sober or simple. See I Corinthians 11.

19. Matthew 16:16–19.

20. On several occasions, the New Testament lists women who served as deacons (see Romans 16:1). This may indicate that at least in the earliest days of the Church, congregations were led by either women or men.

21. Martin E. Marty, *A Short History of Christianity* (New York: World Publishing Company, 1958), p. 75.

22. Indeed, some scholars, including sociologist Max Weber, have suggested that Calvin's teachings of worldly asceticism contributed to the development of the spirit of modern capitalism.

23. Although this was the traditional practice of the Roman Catholic Church during much of its history, the Vatican II encouraged the use of both bread and wine for the laity at the Eucharist.

24. In the modern Catholic Church, this sacrament is known as "Anointing of the Sick." It is administered only to the seriously ill and dying.

25. After the Council of Trent closed in 1563, the Roman Catholic Church called no general council until the Vatican Council of 1869. This council dealt with the sensitive issue of papal infallibility. After much debate and controversy, the council declared as dogma that the pope was infallible when he spoke *ex cathedra*—that is, as the pastor of all Christians on the issues of faith and morals. Naturally, this dogma widened the gap between Catholics, on the one hand, and Orthodox and Protestant groups, on the other hand.

26. See Bruce Lawrence, *Defenders of God, The Fundamentalist Revolt against the Modern World* (San Francisco: Harper Collins, 1989), 153–188.

27. The Church banned polygamy in 1890.

28. *Deseret News 1999–2000 Church Almanac*, Salt Lake City; Deseret News 1988, 111.

29. The source material that follows is taken from *The New Revised Standard Version Bible* (New York: National Council of the Churches of Christ in the U.S.A., 1989)

30. Franz Hildebrandt, ed., *The Works of John Wesley*, vol. 7, *A Collection of Hymns for the Use of the People Called Methodists* (Nashville, Tenn.: Abingdon, 1983), 79–81.

Chapter 12

1. The word *Qur'an* is sometimes transliterated as "Koran" in English texts.

2. The name *Mecca* is probably derived from an old Arabic word meaning "sanctuary."

3. Qur'an 96:1–5. M. A. S. Abdel Haleem, trans., *The Qur'an* (New York: Oxford University Press, 2004), 428.

4. The Shia do not accept this interpretation of Islamic history. Their view is that Muhammad designated his cousin and son-in-law Ali as his successor.

5. W. Montgomery Watt, *Muhammad: Prophet and Statesman* (New York: Oxford University Galaxy Press, 1961), 228.

6. Qur'an 96:1, M. A. S. Abdel Haleem, trans., *The Qur'an* (New York: Oxford University Press, 2004), 428. Unlike the Hebrew and Christian scriptures, the Qur'an is not ordered chronologically. The order of chapters is, with the exception of the opening verses, determined by their length—from longest to shortest.

7. Qur'an 25:1–2. M. A. S. Abdel Haleem, trans., *The Qur'an* (New York: Oxford University Press, 2004), 227.

8. Qur'an 112. M. A. S. Abdel Haleem, trans., *The Qur'an* (New York: Oxford University Press, 2004), 444.

9. Qur'an 7:54. M. A. S. Abdel Haleem, trans., *The Qur'an* (New York: Oxford University Press, 2004), 98.

10. Qur'an 53:31–32. M. A. S. Abdel Haleem, trans., *The Qur'an* (New York: Oxford University Press, 2004), 348.

11. It is believed that this word is Arabic for the Greek word "devil," *diabolos*.

12. Qur'an 82. M. A. S. Abdel Haleem, trans., *The Qur'an* (New York: Oxford University Press, 2004).

13. Qur'an 18:49. M. A. S. Abdel Haleem, trans., *The Qur'an* (New York: Oxford University Press, 2004), 186.

14. According to both Jewish and Muslim tradition, Ishmael was the son Abraham and Hagar. Genesis 21 says that Hagar and Ishmael were driven from the home of Abraham by the jealousy of Abraham's first wife, Sarah. It also is believed that Ishmael became the forebear of all of the Arab people.

15. Although these regulations may appear restrictive to modern people, the fact that Islam allows divorce at all can also be understood as a liberal teaching that recognizes the imperfection of humans and their choices. In many modern Muslim nations, the state has taken jurisdiction over divorce and the rights of women are protected. The practice of polygamy is forbidden in Turkey and Tunisia and is allowed only with permission of the first wife in Indonesia and some other Muslim majority countries. Universities in some Muslim nations contain a higher percentage of women faculty than those of Europe and Asia.

16. The word *faqir* (*fakir*) literally means "a poor man," and the word *darwish* (*dervish*) connotes "one who comes to the door" (i.e., a beggar). Thus, both words indicated the universal ascetic practices of poverty and begging.

17. Rahman Fazlur, *Major Themes of the Qur'an* (Minneapolis: Bibliotheca Islam, 1989).

18. Nurcholish Madjid, "In Search of Islamic Roots for Modern Pluralism: The Indonesian Experiences," in *Toward a New Paradigm. Recent Developments in Indonesian Islamic Thought*, ed. Mark R. Woodward (Tempe: Arizona State University, 1996).

19. Leila Ahmed, *Women and Gender in Islam: Historical Roots of a Modern Debate* (New Haven: Yale University Press, 1992).

20. In the Hebrew Bible and in Jewish and Christian tradition, Abraham was commanded to sacrifice his son Isaac. In Muslim tradition, Ishmael was the son to be sacrificed. Muslim tradition also says that Abraham took Ishmael to the black stone in Mecca for the sacrifice.

21. M. A. S. Abdel Haleem, trans., *The Qur'an* (New York: Oxford University Press, 2004), 19–20, 29, 88, 242, 260, 279, 356, 359, 362, 365–366.

Chapter 13

1. Anonymous, *Baha'u'llah: God's Messenger to Humanity* (Wilmette, IL: The National Spiritual Assembly of the Baha'is of the United States, 1994), 4.

2. Baha'u'llah, *Gleanings from the Writings of Bahaullah*, trans. Shoghi Effendi (Wilmette, IL: Baha'i Publishing Trust, 1952), p. 217. Copyright 1952 © 1976 National Spiritual Assembly of the Baha'is of the United States.

3. J. E. Esslemont, *Baha'u'llah and the New Era* (Wilmette, IL: Baha'i Books, 1976), 6.

4. Ibid., 126.

5. Ibid,. 165

6. Ibid., 202.

7. Ibid., 154.

8. Ibid., 170. Abdul Baha advocated the adoption of Esperanto as the universal language.

9. Ibid., 286.

10. These thirteen principles are taken from information supplied by the Public Information Department, National Baha'i Headquarters, 112 Linden Avenue, Wilmette, IL 60091.

11. Abdul Baha, *Some Answered Questions* (Wilmette, IL: Baha'i Publishing Trust, 1964), 250.

12. Esslemont, *Baha'u'llah and the New Era*, 103.

13. Baha'u'llah, *Kitab-i-Aqdas*, trans. Shoghi Effendi (Wilmette, IL: Baha'i Publishing Trust, 1931), 182.

14. Abdul Baha, cited by Esslemont, *Baha'u'llah and the New Era*, 189.

15. "Iran's Nuremberg Laws" (editorial). *New York Times*, 27 February 1993, sect. 1, p. 18, col. 1.

16. "Baha'is and the United Nations," *Baha'i Topics*, http://info.bahai.org/bahais-united-nations.html.

17. Baha'u'llah, *Gleanings from the Writings of Bahaullah*, trans. Shoghi Effendi (Wilmette, IL: Baha'i Publishing Trust, 1952), p. 94–96. Copyright 1952 © 1976 National Spiritual Assembly of the Baha'is of the United States.

18. Ibid., 250, 251.

Glossary

Adi Granth   Scriptures of Sikhism.

African-initiated churches   Christian churches in Africa that originate not with foreign missions but with local leaders and movements. These churches often incorporate local African customs and religious practices in their expressions of Christianity.

Agamas   The scriptures of Jainism; some believe that the Agamas contain the actual sermons given by Mahavira to his disciples.

Agni   Early Vedic god of fire.

ahimsa   Noninjury of living beings. This concept, found in many Indian religions, is especially important for Jains. Adherents of ahimsa make every effort to care for all forms of life and seek to avoid injuring or killing any creature.

ajiva   See "jiva."

ajwaka   African religious functionary whose primary purpose is to heal by driving out evil spirits believed to cause sickness.

Allah   Literally, "the God"; Arabic name for the deity, used by Muslims and Christian Arabs.

Amaterasu   Sun goddess (kami) in Japanese mythology.

Amitabha   A Buddha who presides over the paradise called "the Pure Land of the West."

Analects   The collected sayings and philosophy of Confucius.

anatman (anatta)   The state of nonsoulness that, according to the Buddha, was the natural state of humanity.

ancestor veneration   Veneration of deceased members of the family. It frequently involves upkeep and care of graves, memorization of the names from past generations, and prayers and sacrifices in honor of the dead.

anti-Semitism   Prejudice against Jews for religious or ethnic reasons.

apocalypse   Literally, "that which is revealed"; describes certain forms of literature popular in Christianity, Judaism, and Zoroastrianism in the second century B.C.E. to the second century C.E. Apocalyptic books were often written in secret or coded language and spoke about a dramatic end of the world.

Apostles   The original twelve followers of Jesus.

arhat (arahat)   Individuals, other than Buddhas, who have attained Nirvana.

asceticism   The practice of self-denial through various means, for the attainment of spiritual goals.

Ashkenazim   Jews who lived in Europe, especially Eastern Europe.

atman   In Hinduism, atman is the self, or soul, that, due to karma, is reborn in the cycle of rebirth.

avatar   Incarnation of a deity. In Hinduism, the god Vishnu is believed to have taken human or other forms on several occasions.

Babis   Religious group, immediate forerunner of the Baha'i religion.

the Bab   Founder of the Babi movement.

Baha'u'llah   Founder of the Baha'i faith.

baptism   Christian initiatory ritual that includes symbolic cleansing with water.

Bar Mitzvah, Bat Mitzvah   Literally, "son or daughter of the covenant." Jewish rituals in which young men and young women, respectively, are officially recognized as adult members of the community.

Bhagavad Gita   "The Song of the Blessed Lord." Epic poem of Indian culture and religion.

bhakti   Devotion to the gods of Hinduism.

Bible   The scriptures of Jews and Christians. The Jewish Bible includes the Torah, prophetic books, historical writings, and poetry, collectively referred to as the Tanakh, or the Hebrew Bible. Christians include this material, which they call the Old Testament, as well as the New Testament, which includes the Gospels, epistles, and other writing.

bodhisattva   A being destined to become a Buddha who, out of compassion, aids others in their journey to enlightenment.

Brahma   One of the three important gods in Hindu worship, generally regarded as the creator of the world.

Brahman   Impersonal god seen as total reality in the Upanishads.

Brahmin   Priestly caste of Indian society.

Brahmo Samaj   A monotheistic form of Hinduism founded by Ram Mohan Roy that was involved in creating the modern Indian state.

Buddha   One who obtains Nirvana on the basis of his own efforts. Also the title commonly ascribed to Siddharta Gautama.

Bushido   Code of the Samurai.

Butsu-dan   Japanese Buddhist household altar.

caliph   From *khalifa* (literally, "deputy," "representative"); successors of Muhammad in leading Islam. At first, the caliphate was limited to the companions of the Prophet Muhammad, but as Islam grew, the caliphate took on the role of a dynastic political leadership.

caste   From Portuguese, *casta,* "race." The multiple classes into which traditional Indian society has been divided.

Chanukah (Hanukkah)   Jewish festival that celebrates the rededicating of the temple by Judas Maccabeus in 165 B.C.E.

Council of Trent   Convened in 1545 by the Roman Catholic Church to reform the church and oppose the actions of Protestants.

Dalai Lama   Leader of the Yellow Hat group of Tibetan Buddhists and, until 1950, the spiritual and political ruler of Tibet.

Dao   Literally, "The Way," or "The Way of Nature."

Daodejing   Literally, "The Classic of the Way and Its Power or Virtue"; the book that became the basis for the philosophy of Daoism.

denomination   Different branches of Protestant Christianity are referred to as denominations.

dharma   Duties incumbent on a person in traditional Hindu life, based on caste and station in life. In Buddhism, the teachings of the Buddha.

Diaspora   Scattering of the Israelites from their homeland, which began with the Assyrian destruction of Israel in 721 B.C.E.

Digambara   Literally, "the sky clad"; the more conservative sect of Jainism, which holds nudity as an ideal for its monks.

Divali   Hindu festival of lights that welcomes the new year; also celebrated by Jains.

divination   Prediction of the future through various ritual means (e.g., tarot cards, I Ching, reading of tea leaves).

Durga (Kali)   Consort of Shiva. Also known as Parvati.

Earth Mother   The female earth spirit and personification of nature in Native American religions.

Ecumenical Movement   Action among modern Christian denominations to attempt to minimize differences among various Christian groups and achieve some form of unity.

Eid al-Adha   Muslim feast of sacrifice.

Eid al-Fitr   Muslim feast of fast breaking. Celebrates a return to normal life after the prolonged fast of Ramadan.

epistles   Letters written by Paul and others to the early Christian churches.

Eucharist   Literally, "thanksgiving"; Christian memorial meal of bread and wine that celebrates the sacrifice of Jesus.

evangelicalism   Protestant Christian movement that emphasizes conversion, a personal relationship with Jesus, biblical literacy, and recruiting new members.

Exodus   The flight of the ancient Israelite people from bondage in Egypt.

Four Noble Truths   In Buddhism, these are the central teachings of the Buddha concerning enlightenment.

Gandhi, Mohandas K   Indian leader who helped India achieve independence from Great Britain. Well known for his nonviolent methods of protest.

Ganesha   A popular Hindu deity, depicted with the head of an elephant. Ganesha is known as the remover of obstacles.

ghetto   Section of certain European cities where Jews were forced to live.

Ghost Dance   A ritual and resistance movement of the Plains Indians that combined Native American and Christian ideas. Led by a prophetic figure named Wovoka.

Golden Temple   Also called the "harimandir," the Golden Temple is an important Sikh gurdwara in Amritsar, India. It was built in the sixteenth century to house the Sikh scriptures, the *Adi Granth*.

Gospels   Literally, "good news"; the message concerning Christ, the kingdom of God, and salvation; the first four books of the New Testament (Matthew, Mark, Luke, and John) tell the story of Jesus's ministry and are called the Gospels.

Great Spirit   Also known as the "High God" in some Native American traditions; a divine or spritual power that is revealed in humans, nature, and the spirit world.

gurdwara   Sikh temple and meeting place.

guru   In Hinduism, the word connotes "teacher"; in Sikhism, it refers to the leaders of the religion.

hadith   Collections of traditions concerning the life and words of the Prophet Muhammad.

Haggadah   Literally, "narrative"; history, folklore, and sermons in the Talmud.

hajj   Pilgrimage each Muslim is supposed to make once in a lifetime to religious sites in and around Mecca.

Halakhah   Legal material, discussions, and rabbinic decisions in the Talmud.

High God   Certain religions maintain that one Supreme God created the world and then withdrew from active participation. Although this god is often recognized and given token worship, the bulk of active worship is given to lesser deities, who participate more fully in the activities of the world.

Hijra   Literally, "flight"; the migration of Muhammad and his community from Mecca to Medina in 622 B.C.E.

Holi   Hindu festival dedicated to the god Krishna.

Holocaust   The murder of six million Jews by the Nazis during World War II.

I Ching   Ancient Chinese book of divination.

imam   To Sunni Muslims, the imam leads the community in prayers; to Shi'ite Muslims, imams were the legitimate successors of Ali.

Indra   Vedic god of thunder, rain, and the ruler of heaven.

Izanagi and Izanami   Mythological male and female who participated in the creation of the Japanese islands.

jihad   Arabic term meaning "struggle in the cause of God." Examples range from mission work to armed conflict.

jinn   Spiritual creatures recognized in pre-Islamic Arabia. Some could be friendly; others were hostile and demonic.

jiva and ajiva   Soul and matter, respectively, in Jain philosophy.

Kaaba   Black cube-shaped structure at the center of Mecca. Pilgrims on the hajj circumambulate the Kaaba.

Kali   Important Hindu goddess and wife of Shiva; also known as Durga.

kami   Japanese for "spirits," the revered beings in Shinto.

kami-dana   Literally, "kami shelf"; the center of domestic Shinto in a Japanese home. A shelf where sacred objects are kept and daily prayers are said.

karma   In Indian thought, that which binds one to the endless cycles of life, death, and rebirth.

Khalsa   A Sikh order formed to protect the Sikh community. Initiates of the Khalsa can be both men and women and maintain a special position in Sikhism.

koan   Literally, "case study"; a riddle, tale, or short statement used by Zen masters to bring students to sudden insight.

Kojiki   Literally, "chronicles of ancient events"; the source book of Japanese mythology.

Kosher   Literally, "fit," "proper"; that which is ritually clean or acceptable in Judaism; usually applied to food or food preparation.

Krishna   Avatar of the Hindu god Vishnu, who appears as a main character in the *Bhagavad Gita*.

Kshatriya   Warrior caste of Indian society.

Kwoth Nhial   The high god of the Nuer. Associated with the sky.

Lakshmi   The Hindu goddess of prosperity and wealth. She is the wife of Vishnu.

lama   A leader of the Tibetan Buddhist monastic communities.

langar   The dining areas where Sikhs offer meals to the community.

lesser spirits   Religions that have a distant high god often focus worship and ritual life around lesser spirits or deities. This is a common feature in many African religions.

li   Confucian term translated as "propriety," "rites," "ceremonies," or "courtesy."

lingam and yoni   Together, these Shaivite symbols represent the balance of male and female forces and indicate life and rebirth.

Lotus Sutra   A central sacred text for Mahayana Buddhists that discusses the eternal cosmic nature of Buddhahood. The text itself is revered by many Buddhists.

Mahavira   The last tirthankara and founder of Jainism.

Mahayana   Literally, "the great vehicle"; the larger branch of Buddhism.

mantra   Ritual sound, word, or phrase used to evoke a certain religious effect.

Manu, Code of   Classical Hindu literature that describes life in India between 300 B.C.E. and 300 C.E.

masjid   Muslim house of prayer. Also called a "mosque."

maya   False knowledge; in the Upanishads, all that is not Brahman—all perceptions, all individuality.

Mecca   The city in the Arabian peninsula where the Prophet Mohammad was born. Muslims make a pilgrimage to Mecca (the hajj) and face Mecca when they pray.

Mishnah   Collection of oral laws gathered by Judah ha Nasi (born c. 135 C.E.); the Mishnah contained the bulk of extrabiblical Jewish law up to the second century C.E.

missionary   In Christianity, someone who goes to another region or country and preaches the Christian religion.

moksha   Release from the cycle of death and rebirth in Indian religions.

muezzin   One who calls the Muslim community to prayer five times a day.

murti   In Hinduism, the image or statue that represents a deity.

Nanak   The first guru and founder of Sikhism.

Native American Church   Religious movement combining elements of Christianity and Native American religions.

Nichiren   Literally, "sun lotus"; sociopolitical school of Mahayana Buddhism found primarily in Japan.

Nirvana   Literally, "blowing out"; cessation of consciousness and achievement of Enlightenment in Buddhism.

Nuer   East African ethnic group with a particularly strong belief in the High God.

Om mani padmi hum   Mantra in Tibetan Buddhism that means "Om, the jewel of the lotus, hum."

orishas   In the Yoruba religion of West Africa, lesser deities who participated in the creation of the world. Because of the slave trade, the *orishas* are worshiped in many parts of the Americas.

Parvati   The Hindu goddess of power. She is Ganesha's mother and Shiva's wife.

Passover (Pesach)   Jewish holiday celebrated in the spring, commemorating the deliverance of the Israelites from Egyptian slavery.

Pentecost   Christian festival that comes fifty days after the Passover and celebrates the coming of the Holy Spirit to the church.

Pentecostalism   A modern Christian movement that is characterized by enthusiastic worship and a commitment to receiving gifts from the Holy Spirit, such as divine healing and speaking in tongues.

peyote   Cactus plant that bears small button growths. These buttons contain mescaline, a hallucinogenic sometimes used in the religious rites of the Native American Church.

prasad   Food and other items that are blessed and offered in worship to the gods in Hinduism.

puja   The ritual act of worship in Hinduism. Puja occurs both in temples and in homes.

puranas   Hindu sacred texts of the gods' exploits.

Pure Land Buddhism   Popular version of Mahayana Buddhism; it teaches that its devotees can be reborn in a paradise, called the "Pure Land of the West," where they can reach enlightenment.

Purim   Jewish holiday that celebrates the deliverance of the Jews from destruction at the hands of the Persians.

Qur'an   Literally, "reading," "recitation"; Muslim Scripture.

rabbi   Literally, "my master"; teacher associated with the Jewish synagogue.

Ramadan   Month during which devout Muslims do not eat or drink between sunrise and sunset. The fast celebrates the month in which the Prophet received the Qu'ran.

Reformation   The movement to reform and renovate the medieval Catholic Church led by Martin Luther, John Calvin, and others. The Reformation led to a major division in Christianity.

ren   Confucian principle translated as "love," "goodness," and "humaneness."

Ridvan   A twelve-day festival of the Baha'i faith.

Rosh Hashanah   The Jewish New Year.

Sabbath (Shabbat)   The seventh day, set aside as a day of rest and worship in Judaism.

sacraments   In Christianity, rituals that commemorate important moments or doctrines. Almost all Christians recognize baptism and the Eucharist as sacraments. Others also include confirmation, penance, anointing of the sick, marriage, and Holy Orders.

samsara   In the Upanishads and in Buddhism, the endless cycle of birth, life, death, and rebirth experienced by all humans.

samurai   Medieval Japanese knights.

Sangha   Buddhist monastic order.

Satori   State of enlightenment that one can achieve in Zen Buddhism.

Sephardim   Jews who fled from Spain and Portugal and took refuge in the Ottoman Empire and elsewhere.

Shahada   Creedal statement of Islam, "There is no God but God, and Muhammad is the messenger of God."

Shangdi   Supreme God recognized by the Chou dynasty of ancient China.

Shavuot   "Feast of Weeks"; Jewish holiday in remembrance of the giving of the Ten Commandments.

Shi'ite   Literally, "the party of." This Muslim group, which accounts for approximately 10 to 15 percent of all Muslims, began as "the Party of Ali." Shi'ites believe the legitimate successor to Muhammad was his cousin and son-in-law, Ali.

Shiva   One of the most popular gods in postclassical Hinduism, regarded as the god of death and destruction but also of rebirth and reproduction.

Shivaite (also Shaivite)   Devotee of the god Shiva.

shu   Confucian law of reciprocity.

Siddhantas   With the agamas, some of the sacred texts of Jainism.

Sikh   Literally, "disciple"; an adherent of Sikhism.

Sufism   Literally, "woolen"; Muslim mystical brotherhoods that seek a direct experience and knowledge of God.

Sukkot   Jewish autumn festival of thanksgiving.

Sun Dance   Summer celebration performed by Native Americans of the Great Plains.

Sunni   Most Muslims are Sunnis (traditionalists), who accept orthodox Muslim theology and the traditional line of caliphs.

Svetambara   Literally, "the white clad"; the more liberal sect of Jainism.

synagogue   Literally, "assembly"; the meeting of Jews of the Diaspora for study and prayer.

Talmud   Encyclopedic collection of Mishnah and Gemara, the literary source of postbiblical Judaism. There are two Talmudim: Palestinian and Babylonian.

temple   In Judaism, the temple in Jerusalem was the center place of worship and sacrifice. The First Temple was destroyed in 586 B.C.E. by the Babylonians. The Second Temple was destroyed in 70 C.E. by the Romans and has never been rebuilt.

Tenrikyo   Literally, "Teaching of Heavenly Reason"; a sect of Shinto that emphasizes faith healing.

Theravada   Literally, "the tradition of the elders"; the smaller branch of Buddhism common in Southeast Asia and Sri Lanka.

Tirthankaras   Literally, "bridge-builders"; the twenty-four founders of Jainism; they forged the bridge between life and Nirvana. The last of the Tirthankaras was Mahavira.

Torah   Usually translated as "law"; general term in the Hebrew scriptures referring to divine law and instruction but can also refer to the first five books of the Bible or to revelation in general.

torii   The symbolic gates that demarcate sacred space in Shinto.

The True Name   The name of God for Sikhs.

Trimurti   The three most important Hindu gods: Shiva, Vishnu, and Brahma.

ummah   The global Muslim community.

Universal House of Justice   The administrative headquarters of Baha'i, located in Haifa, Israel.

Upanishads   Philosophical materials in the Vedic literature.

Vaisakhi   New Year's Day throughout northern India. Of special importance for Sikhs, who celebrate the formation of the Khalsa on this day.

Vaishya   Merchant caste of Indian society.

Vajrayana   Literally, "the diamond vehicle." Another word for Tibetan Buddhism.

varnas   The four major divisions of the Indian caste system.

Vatican II   Council called by the Catholic Church in 1962; it took broad steps to modernize the Church and mend relationships with Jews, members of the Orthodox Church, and Protestants.

Vedanta   Literally, "the end of the Vedas"; this Hindu philosophical system takes its major materials from the Upanishads and assumes that there is only one true reality in the world, Brahman.

Vedas   Basically, a collection of hymns to the early Indian gods. The term also applies to the entire collection of Indian sacred literature, including the Vedas, the Brahamanas, the Aranyakas, and the Upanishads.

Vishnu   One of the three most popular gods of postclassical Hinduism, known as the god of love.

vision quest   Exercises undertaken by Native Americans seeking contact with the spirit world.

Vivekenanda   A Hindu guru who was largely responsible for introducing Vedanta and other Hindu thought to the Western world.

Wahhabism   Ultraconservative Muslim movement founded in the eighteenth century and opposed to all forms of change within religion and culture.

Wakan Tanka   The name of the great and powerful force or spirit of the Lakota people.

wu wei   Daoist principle of effortlessness and no action.

yinyang   The balance of positive and negative forces in nature recognized in early Chinese religions.

Yom Kippur   Jewish Day of Atonement.

yoni   See "lingam."

Yoruba   West African ethnic group whose religion strongly influenced the development of African American religions.

Zen, Ch'an Buddhism   Form of Mahayana Buddhism that teaches that the real truth about life comes from intuitive flashes of insight.

Zionism   Movement founded in the late nineteenth century by Theodore Herzl; Zionism sought to find a national home for the Jews scattered throughout the world.

Credits

Cover   Thinley Namgyel

Intro   Page 6: Karl Marx, "Contribution to the Critique of Hegel's Philosophy of the Right" in Karl Marx and Friedrich Engels, *On Religion* (Atlanta: Scholars Press, 1964 [1844]); 8: James Calvin Davis, *In Defense of Civility: How Religion Can Unite America on Seven Moral Issues That Divide Us* (Louisville, Ky.: Westminster John Knox, 2010), 19

Chapter 1   Page 14: DC Premiumstock/Alamy; 15: Statue of Confucius in the Great Hall of Ceremonies in a Taoist temple (photo)/Hanoi, Vietnam/Luca Tettoni/The Bridgeman Art Library; 18: Jake Lyell/Alamy

Chapter 2   Page 26: Source: T. C. McLuhan, *Touch the Earth* (New York: Outerbridge & Dienstfrey, 1971), p. 15; 26: Source: Ruth M. Underhill, *Red Man's Religion* (Chicago: University of Chicago Press, 1965) p. 116; 28: Michael Matthews/Alamy; 28&29: Source: Ruth M. Underhill, *Red Man's Religion* (Chicago: University of Chicago Press, 1965) p. 116; 30: Denver Post/Getty Images; 31: Mark R. Woodward; 31: Mike Greenlar/The Image Works; 35: Source: Frances Densmore, *Teton Sioux Music* (Bureau of American Ethnology, Bulletin 61, 1918), pp. 65–66; 36: Source: Reprinted from *Lakota Myth* by James R. Walker, edited by Elaine A. Jahner, by permission of the University of Nebraska Press. Copyright 1083 by the University of Nebraska Press

Chapter 3   Page 41: Source: Geoffery Parrinder, *African Traditional Religion* (Hutchinson House, 1954), p. 48; 42: Marsha van der Heyden/Pearson Education/PH College; 43: Source: Benjamin C. Ray, *African Religions* (Englewood cliffs, NJ: Prentice Hall, 1976), p. 80; 44: Irene Abdou/Alamy; 46: Christoph Henning/Das Fotoarchiv/Black Star/Alamy; 46: Source: Benjamin C. Ray, *African Religions* (Englewood cliffs, NJ: Prentice Hall, 1976), p. 80; 47: John Elk III/Alamy; 50–52: Monica Wilson, *Communal Rituals of the Nyakyusa* (International African Institute, 1959), pp. 40–46

Chapter 4   Page 61: Mark R. Woodward; 61: (c) Pearson Education, Inc; 62: John Henry Claude Wilson/Alamy; 64: Source: Ralph T. H. Griffith, trans., *The Hymns of the Rig-Veda*, vol. I (Banaras: E.J. Lazarus and Co., 1920), pp. 133, 134; 64: Source: Ralph T. H. Griffith, trans., *The Hymns of the Rig-Veda*, vol. I (Banaras: E.J. Lazarus and Co., 1920), pp. 294; 65: Source: Ralph T. H. Griffith, trans., *The Hymns of the Rig-Veda*, vol. I (Banaras: E.J. Lazarus and Co., 1920), pp. 398; 65: Source: Satapatha Brahmana, 1:8; 66: Mark R. Woodward; 66: Vâgasaneyi Samhitâ Upanishad 9 Maitrâyana Brâhmana Upanishad VI, 17, *The Upanishads*, trans. F. Max Müller (Oxford: Clarendon Press, 1884); 67: Maitrâyana Brâhmana Upanishad VI, 17, *The Upanishads*, trans. F. Max Müller (Oxford: Clarendon Press, 1884); 67: Katha Upanishad I, 3, 14, *The Upanishads*, trans. F. Max Müller (Oxford: Clarendon Press, 1884); 67: Svetâsvatara Upanishad IV, 17, *The Upanishads*, trans. F. Max Müller (Oxford: Clarendon Press, 1884); 67: Svetasvatara Upanishad IV, 9, *The Upanishads*, trans. F. Max Müller (Oxford: Clarendon Press, 1884); 68: Khândogya Upanishad VI, 13, *The Upanishads*, trans.

F. Max Müller (Oxford: Clarendon Press, 1884); 68: Source: G. Buhler, trans., *Law of Manu*, 1:31; 68: Source: Ralph T. H. Griffith, trans., *The Hymns of the Rig-Veda*, vol. 1 (E. J. Lazarus and Co., 1920); 68: G. Buhler, trans., *Law of Manu*, 1:88–91; 69: G. Buhler, trans., *Law of Manu*, 12:9; 69: Mark R. Woodward; 70: OlegD/Shutterstock; 71: imagebroker/Alamy; 74: Mark R. Woodward; 76: Mark R. Woodward; 77: Mark R. Woodward; 79: Mark R. Woodward; 80: Source: R. C. Zaehner, *Hinduism* (New York: Oxford University Press, 1962), p. 4; 82: John Henry Claude Wilson/Alamy; 82: Mark R. Woodward; 86&87: Source: Ralph T. H. Griffith, trans., *The Hymns of the Rig-Veda*, vol. I (Banaras: E.J. Lazarus, 1920), pp. 448, 449; 87: Brihadâranyaka Upanishad IV, 4, 1–2 and Brihadâranyaka Upanishad V, 10, *The Upanishads*, trans. F. Max Müller (Oxford: Clarendon Press, 1884); 87: Source: Ralph T. H. Griffith, trans., *The Hymns of the Rig-Veda*, vol. I (Banaras: E.J. Lazarus, 1920), pp. 448, 449; 87–88: Source: G. Buhler, trans., *Law of Manu*, *Sacred Books of the East*, vol. XXV (New York: Charles Scribner's Sons, 1882–1902), pp. 204–10; 88: *The Bhagavad Gita*, translated by Edwin Arnold (1885); 88&89: *The Bhagavad Gita*, translated by Edwin Arnold (1885)

Chapter 5   Page 92: Private Collection/Ann & Bury Peerless Picture Library/The Bridgeman Art Library; 92: Source: Herman Jacobi, trans., "Sutrakrtanga," *Gaina Sutras*, in *Sacred Books of the East*, vol. XL (Oxford: Clarendon Press, 1895), pp. 1–3, 18; 92: Source: Tattvartha Sutra, 10,2. Gerorge Thibaut, trans., *Shankara, Commentary on Vendanta Sutra*, vol. 1, in *Sacred Books of the East*, vol. XXXIV (Oxford: Clarendon Press, 1890), passim; 93: Source: Gerorge Thibaut, trans., *Shankara, Commentary on Vendanta Sutra*, vol. 1, in *Sacred Books of the East*, vol. XXXIV (Oxford: Clarendon Press, 1890), passim. Ayaranya Sutra, 1, 1, 6, 6; 94: Chinch Gryniewicz/The Bridgeman Art Library; 95: Michael Busselle/Digital Vision/Getty Images; 95: Robert Harding Picture Library Ltd/Alamy; 97–98: Source: From *Sources of Indian Tradition* by de Bary, Wm. Theodore. Copyright © 1964. Columbia University Press. Reprinted with permission of the publisher; 98–99: Source: From *Sources of Indian Tradition* by de Bary, Wm. Theodore. Copyright © 1964. Columbia University Press. Reprinted with permission of the publisher

Chapter 6   Page 102: Mark R. Woodward; 103: Mark R. Woodward; 103&104: *The Fruit of the Homeless Life: The Samannaphala Sutta by Silacara (Bhikkhu)* (The Buddhist Society of Great Britain and Ireland, 1917); 106: Source: Dhammapada, 90–94, 98. *The Dhammapada*, translated from the Pâli by F. Max Müller (Oxford, the Clarendon Press, 1881); 109: Photodisc/Getty Images; 110: Source: Edward Conze, trans., "The Pure Land 15,16," Sukhavativyuha, in *Buddhist Texts through the Ages* (Oxford: Bruno Cassierer, Ltd. 1954), p. 202; 112: Alison Wright/Corbis; 113: Mark R. Woodward; 114: Mark R. Woodward; 115: Mark R. Woodward; 118–121: Source: Lord Chalmers, trans., *Further Dialogues of the Buddha*, vol. 1 (New York: Krishna Press, 1926), pp. 53–57; 120: E. J. Thomas, *Buddhist Scriptures* (E.P. Dutton, 1913); 120: Source: Edward Conze, trans., *Buddhist Texts through the Ages*

(Oxford: Bruno Cassierer, Ltd. 1954), pp. 131–132; 120&121: Source: From *Sources of Japanese Tradition* by de Bary, Wm. Theodore. Copyright © 1958. Columbia University Press. Reprinted with permission of the publisher

Chapter 7 Page 125: Archenova/Alamy; 125: Source: Asa Ki War, Slok VI, in *The Sacred Writings of the World's Great Religions*, ed. S. E. Frost (New York: McGraw-Hill, 1943), p. 362; 126: Sylvain Leser/Haytham Pictures/Alamy; 127: ArkReligion. com/Alamy; 127: From Siri Guru Granth Sahib, translation copyright (c) 2013 Dr. Sant Singh Khalsa

Chapter 8 Page 134: D. Howard Smith, *Chinese Religions* (New York: Holt, Rinehart, and Winston, 1968), p. 71; 135: (c) Pearson Education, Inc; 137: Mark R. Woodward; 138: xPACIFICA/ Alamy; 139: Mark R. Woodward; 139: Top Photo/Asia Photo Connection/Henry Westheim Photography/Alamy; 140: Lao-Tzu, *Tao Te Ching*, translated by J. H. McDonald for the public domain, 1996; 141: Source: Herbert A. Giles, *Religions of Ancient China* (Salem, NH: Books for Libraries Press, 1969), p. 47; 142: Lao-Tzu, *Tao Te Ching*, translated by J. H. McDonald for the public domain, 1996; 142: Lao-Tzu, *Tao Te Ching*, translated by J. H. McDonald for the public domain, 1996; 143: Source: James Legge, trans., "How pure and still the Tao is. I do not know whose song it is. It might appear to have been before God." In *Sacred Books of the East*, vol. XXXIX (Oxford: Clarendon Press, 1891), p. 73; 147: Chinese School, (17th century)/The Art Gallery Collection/Alamy; 148: James Legge, translator, *The Chinese Classics, Volume 1: Confucian Analects* (1891); 148: James Legge (trans) *Li Chi: Book of Rights*, vol. II (1885); 151: Source: Dexter Roberts, "Confucius Makes a Comeback in China," *Businessweek*, November 1, 2012; 152: Henry Westheim Photography/Alamy; 156: Source: *Zhuangzi, Zhuangzi: The Essential Writings*, trans. Brook Ziporyn (Indianapolis: Hackett, 2009), pp. 20–21; 156–158: James Legge, translator, *The Chinese Classics, Volume 1: Confucian Analects* (1891); 156–158: James Legge, translator, *The Chinese Classics, Volume 1: Confucian Analects* (1891); 159: Source: From *Sources of Chinese Tradition* by de Bary, Wm. Theodore. Copyright © 1964. Columbia University Press. Reprinted with permission of the publisher

Chapter 9 Page 161: Source: From *Sources of Japanese Tradition* by de Bary, Wm. Theodore. Copyright © 1958. Columbia University Press. Reprinted with permission of the publisher; 161: Source: Basil Hall Chamberlain, trans., *The Kojiki: Records of Ancient Matters* (Transactions of the Asiatic Society, 1919), pp. 19–21; 163: Pearson Education; 165: chuong/Shutterstock; 166: Source: Floyd Ross, *Shinto: The Way of Japan* (Boston: Beacon Press, 1965), pp. 138, 139; 166: Danita Delimont/ Alamy; 168: Paul Fusco/Magnum Photos; 170: *The Kojiki*, translated by B.H. Chamberlain (1882); 171: Source: From *Sources of Japanese Tradition* by de Bary, Wm. Theodore. Copyright © 1958. Columbia University Press. Reprinted with permission of the publisher

Chapter 10 Page 180: Fabian von Poser/imagebroker/ Alamy; 182: Rafael Ben-Ari/Alamy; 182: Source: From *World English Bible*, eBible.org.; 183: Source: From *World English Bible*, eBible.org.; 184: Source: From *World English Bible*, eBible.org.; 184: Source: From *World English Bible*, eBible.org.; 185: Bill Aron/PhotoEdit; 191: Keystone/Hulton Archive/ Getty Images; 191: Source: *George Washington: A Collection*, ed. W. B. Allen (Liberty Fund: Indianapolis, 1988), 548; 191: (c) Pearson Education, Inc.; 193: Glow Images/Getty Images; 194: Yedidya Yos Mizrachi/PhotoStock-Israel/Alamy;

10–181: (c) Pearson Education, Inc; 195: The Jewish Museum, New York/Art Resource, NY; 196: Ted Spiegel/Historical/ Corbis; 197: Mario Tama/Getty Images News/Getty Images; 198: Jules Selmes. Pearson Education Ltd. Courtesy of Middlesex New (Reform) Synagogue (Harrow); 199–200: Source: From *World English Bible*, eBible.org.; 200–201: Source: D. A. De Sola and M. J. Raphall, trans., *Eighteen Treatises from the Mishna* (London: Sherwood, Gilbert, and Piper, 1843), pp. 101–104

Chapter 11 Page 205: Mark R. Woodward; 205: Source: Isaiah 7:14. This quotation is taken from *The New Revised Standard Version Bible* (New York: National Council of the Churches of Christ in the U.S.A., 1989); 206: bst2012/fotolia; 207: Source: Matthew 5:3–12. This quotation is taken from *The New Revised Standard Version Bible* (New York: National Council of the Churches of Christ in the U.S.A., 1989); 207: Source: Luke 10:30–35. This quotation is taken from *The New Revised Standard Version Bible* (New York: National Council of the Churches of Christ in the U.S.A., 1989); 207: Source: Matthew 5:38–41. This quotation is taken from *The New Revised Standard Version Bible* (New York: National Council of the Churches of Christ in the U.S.A., 1989); 208: Source: Matthew 15:11. This quotation is taken from *The New Revised Standard Version Bible* (New York: National Council of the Churches of Christ in the U.S.A., 1989); 208: Source: Matthew 5:17–19. This quotation is taken from *The New Revised Standard Version Bible* (New York: National Council of the Churches of Christ in the U.S.A., 1989); 208: Source: Mark 8:27–29. This quotation is taken from *The New Revised Standard Version Bible* (New York: National Council of the Churches of Christ in the U.S.A., 1989); 209: Source: Luke 22:17–20. This quotation is taken from *The New Revised Standard Version Bible* (New York: National Council of the Churches of Christ in the U.S.A., 1989); 213: Source: Matthew 16:16–19. This quotation is taken from *The New Revised Standard Version Bible* (New York: National Council of the Churches of Christ in the U.S.A., 1989); 215: Source: Martin E. Marty, *A Short History of Christianity* (New York: World Publishing Company, 1958), p. 75; 217: Vittoriano Rastelli/Historical/Corbis; 218: IML/SuperStock; 219: Gordon Mills/Alamy; 220: Mark R. Woodward; 221: Famoso/Alamy; 224: Mark R. Woodward; 225: Mark R. Woodward; 226: Annie Griffiths Belt/Encyclopedia/Corbis; 229: Tim Graham/Alamy; 231: Kim Jae-Hwan/AFP/Getty Images; 232–236: Source: The *New Revised Standard Version Bible* (New York: National Council of the Churches of Christ in the U.S.A., 1989) 237: Source: Franz Hildebrandt, ed. *The Works of John Wesley, vol. 7, A Collection of Hymns for the Use of the People Called Methodists* (Nashville, TN: Abingdon, 1983), 79-81;

Chapter 12 Page 240: Mark R. Woodward; 241: Friedrich Stark/Alamy; 241: Source: THE QUR'AN translated by Haleem (2004) 1727w from pp. 19–20, 29, 88, 242, 260, 279, 356, 359, 362, 365–366. By permission of Oxford University Press; 243: Source: W. Montgomery Watt, Muhammad: Prophet and Statesman (New York: Oxford University Galaxy Press, 1961), p. 228; 245: Source: THE QUR'AN translated by Haleem (2004) 1727w from pp. 19–20, 29, 88, 242, 260, 279, 356, 359, 362, 365–366. By permission of Oxford University Press; 245: Source: THE QUR'AN translated by Haleem (2004) 1727w from pp. 19–20, 29, 88, 242, 260, 279, 356, 359, 362, 365–366. By permission of Oxford University Press; 245: Source: THE QUR'AN translated by Haleem (2004) 1727w from pp. 19–20, 29, 88, 242, 260, 279, 356, 359, 362, 365–366. By permission of Oxford University Press; 245: Source: THE QUR'AN translated by Haleem (2004)

Index